BOND'S Top 100 FRANCHISES

2006 (2ND) EDITION

Robert E. Bond, *Publisher*
Christine Kimmel, *Editor*
Joan Lee, *Editor*
Stephanie Woo, *Editor*
Angie Hinh, *Editorial Assistant*

Source Book Publications
Serving the Franchising Industry
1814 Franklin Street, Suite 815
Oakland, CA 94612
510.839.5471

ISBN 978-1-887137-51-5

DISCLAIMER

BOND'S TOP 100 FRANCHISES is based on data submitted by the franchisors themselves. Every effort has been made to obtain up-to-date and reliable information. As the information returned has not been independently verified, we assume no responsibility for errors or omissions and reserve the right to include or eliminate listings and otherwise edit and present the data based on our discretion and judgment as to what is useful to the readers of this directory. Inclusion in the publication does not imply endorsement by the editors or the publisher. Errors brought to the attention of the publisher and verified to the satisfaction of the publisher will be corrected in future editions. The publisher specifically disclaims all warranties, including the implied warranties of merchantability and fitness for a specific purpose.

This publication is designed to provide its readers with accurate and authoritative information with regard to the subject matter covered. It is sold with the understanding that neither the author nor the publisher is engaged in rendering legal, accounting or other professional services. If legal advice or other expert assistance is required, the services of a competent professional person should be sought.

From a Declaration of Principles jointly adopted by a Committee of the American Bar Association and a Committee of Publishers.

Cover Design by Joyce Coffland, Artistic Concepts, Oakland, CA.

ISBN 978-1-887137-51-5
Printed in the United States of America.

10 9 8 7 6 5 4 3 2 1

BOND'S TOP 100 FRANCHISES is available at special discounts for bulk purchase. Special editions or book excerpts can also be created to specifications. For details, contact Source Book Publications, 1814 Franklin Street, Suite 815, Oakland, CA 94612. Phone: (510) 839-5471; Fax: (510) 839-2104.

Preface

At its best, purchasing a franchise is a time-tested, paint-by-the-numbers method of starting a new business. It avoids many of the myriad pitfalls normally encountered by someone starting anew and vastly improves the odds of success. It represents an exceptional blend of operating independence with a proven system that includes a detailed blueprint for starting and managing the business, as well as the critical on-going support. But purchasing a franchise is clearly not a fool-proof investment that somehow guarantees the investor financial independence.

At its worst, if the evaluation and investment decision is sloppy or haphazard, franchising can be a nightmare. If things don't work out, for whatever reason, you can't simply walk away. You are still responsible for the long-term lease on your retail space, the large bank loan that underwrote your entry into the business and/or the binding, long-term financial obligation to the franchisor. While it is easy to sell a profitable business, an unprofitable business will most likely result in a significant financial loss. If that loss is all equity, that might be an acceptable risk. If, however, you still have obligations to the bank, landlord and others, your hardship is greatly compounded. This says nothing about the inevitable stress on a marriage and one's own self-esteem.

Your ultimate success as a franchisee will be determined by two factors:

> 1. The homework you do at the front-end to ensure that you are selecting the optimal franchise for your particular needs, experience and financial resources.

> 2. Your commitment to work hard and play by the rules once you have signed a binding, long-term franchise agreement. For most new franchisees in the retail industry, this involves working 60+

hours per week until you can justify delegating some of the day-to-day responsibilities. It also requires being a team player — not acting as an entrepreneur who does his or her own thing without regard for the system as a whole. A franchise system is only as good as the franchisees make it. This means following the script.

Another harsh reality, unfortunately, is that there is no such thing as the Top 100 franchises. Similarly, there isn't a list of the Top 10 colleges, the Top 5 professional basketball players or the Top 3 sports cars. Like everything else in life, the beauty is in the eye of the beholder. Picking the optimal retail franchise is a good example. What appeals to me, even after exhaustive and, hopefully, well-thought-out research, may not appeal to you or be appropriate for you. Whereas I might be prepared to work 70-hour weeks for the first year my new business is open, you might not. Whereas I might be willing to invest $500,000 in a specific franchise concept, you might feel that the projected rewards do not outweigh the inherent risks. Whereas you might be exceptional at working with minimum wage personnel, I might be unable to communicate effectively with younger, less-educated personnel. These are just a few of the literally hundreds of weighty considerations that you will have to evaluate before deciding to invest in a specific franchise system.

In short, one prospective franchisee will clearly not have the same life experiences, talents, God-given abilities and financial wherewithal as the next. It is therefore critical that you take what we say only as a best effort on our part to go through literally hundreds of concepts before arriving at those which, we feel, best answer our collective needs and experiences as professionals within the franchising industry.

My strong suggestion is that you take the time to read the first two chapters of the book to better understand the industry and the variables that you will have to consider in making a long-term investment decision. Even though you may already have a sense as to what type of franchise you want to purchase, maybe even a specific franchise, keep an open mind to the other options available to you. Request marketing information on all of the competing systems and rigorously evaluate each. Look at the various websites. You may be pleasantly surprised to learn that one system offers a range of benefits that better complements your experience and capabilities. Also keep in mind that, in the final analysis, it is up to you — not the franchisor — as to how successful you will be.

Remember, this is not a game: I cannot overemphasize the fact that, in most cases, you will be making a once-in-a-lifetime investment decision. It is incumbent on you to do it right at the outset. This can only be done by taking your time, properly researching all the options, realistically addressing both the "best case" and "worst case" scenarios, seeking the advice of friends and professionals and, in general, doing the due diligence required. You want to invest in a system that will take advantage of your unique talents and experiences and not take advantage of you in the process! Don't take short-cuts. Listen carefully to what the franchisor and your advisors tell you. Don't think you are so clever or independent that you can't benefit from the advice of outside professionals. Don't assume that the franchisor's required guidelines regarding the amount of investment, experience, temperament, etc., somehow don't apply to you. Don't accept any promises or "understandings" from the franchisor that are not committed in writing to the franchise agreement. Invest the additional time to talk to and/or meet with as many franchisees in the system as you can. The additional front-end investment you make, both in time and money, will pay off handsomely if it saves you from making a marginal, or poor, investment decision. This is one of the few times in business when second chances are rare. Make the extra effort to do it right the first time.

Good luck and Godspeed.

Robert Bond

Table of Contents

Introduction

Determining which franchises should be in the Top 100 (and, equally importantly, which ones should not) was a daunting task. It was difficult to choose only 100. Since franchises are so diverse, it was our intention to include at least one franchise from each industry category. Based on our comprehensive research, the 100 in this book are, in our opinion, among the best in the franchising industry.

The franchising industry is a large and sometimes confusing one. There are several industry categories, each with its own characteristics and subcategories. While we will try to provide you with as meaningful an overview as we can, it is your responsibility to aggressively research every aspect of any company you're interested in. Buy a franchise much like you would a house. Whereas you can always sell a house for roughly what you bought it for, you may not be so lucky liquidating a poorly-researched franchise investment. It's a big investment and takes time.

Methodology

How did we arrive at our choices? There were several criteria that were taken into consideration. Primary among these were name recognition, product quality, litigation, total investment, on-going expenses, the company's training program, on-going support and the exclusive territory awarded to new franchisees. Many are personal choices. Is the franchise something you're interested in? Will you have the time and passion to manage it like you want to? These are questions that you'll have to answer for yourself. The information in this book will help you once you've decided what you want to do.

We chose both companies that have already established a strong brand name identity and those that are in the process of establishing a recognizable identity.

ServiceMaster Clean, for example, is known the world over by millions of people. Conversely, companies like Spring-Green Lawn Care and Furniture Medic are less well-known now, but as their concepts become more and more popular, they will undoubtedly increase their name recognition in the near future.

Litigation was a silent factor in determining the Top 100 franchises. We don't have a litigation section in each profile, but while reviewing each franchisor's UFOC (Uniform Franchise Offering Circular — a required document containing 23 categories of information that must be provided by the franchisor to the prospective franchisee at least ten days prior to the execution of the franchise agreement), we most definitely took into account Item Three. This lists any relevant court cases, past and present, involving the company and tells us volumes about franchisor-franchisee relations. If a franchisor had no legal problems or a few court cases inconsequential to the reputation and operation of the company, then it was certainly a viable candidate for the Top 100.

The total investment is usually the determining factor in choosing a franchise. After all, money talks. Initially, investing in a franchise takes considerable patience. You are faced with numerous questions such as "Which items do I finance and which do I purchase?", "Are real estate costs included?", "Will the company help me with financing?", etc. We don't attempt to explore these questions in depth, but we do give you a brief overview of what you will be expected to invest. A Top 100 company may have a low total investment cost, financing assistance and a detailed account of what each item costs. We looked at all the franchisors and chose the ones which exemplified the best combination of these factors.

Before you open a franchise, one of the most critical steps is the initial training program, during which you will learn the basics about the franchise you choose. Training is usually held at the franchisor's headquarters and can last anywhere from five days to 12 weeks. The companies in this book all have strong, comprehensive training courses that include hours of both classroom and on-site training.

On-going expenses are made up of two fees: a royalty fee and an advertising fee. The royalty fee is a portion of your sales (usually four to eight percent) that you give to the franchisor in exchange for its expertise, on-going support and brand name. The advertising payment (three to five percent of sales) is also paid to the franchisor, and in return you receive advertising, marketing and promotional assistance. If these fees were within an acceptable range, then a company was a good candidate for the Top 100.

Most companies listed give exceptional on-going support to their franchisees: continual managerial aid, advertising assistance, access to the operations manual, etc. The basic tenet of franchising is, as Ray Kroc, the founder of McDonald's, said, "to be in business for yourself, not by yourself." Make sure the franchisor is going to support you over the long-term.

Another very important aspect of franchising that often gets overlooked is the franchisor's exclusive territory policy. An exclusive territory awarded by the franchisor describes the specific area or market in which you can operate your business. Why is this so important? By giving you an exclusive territory of, say, a three-mile radius surrounding your location, the franchisor is agreeing that it will not establish another location within that three-mile radius. So, logically, your business will have less competition. Most of the companies in the Top 100 have some sort of exclusive area policy.

All of these factors are important by themselves. Many companies exhibit some of them. But it's the rare few that combine the majority of these characteristics into one fluid franchising system. From those companies, we chose the Top 100.

Additional Factors to Consider

Three additional areas that clearly require serious examination before investing are 1) outstanding legal/litigation issues; 2) the current financial status of the franchisor; and 3) issues regarding renewal, termination, transfer and dispute resolution. Because the first two areas can change on a daily basis, coupled with the fact that we lack the necessary expertise to comment authoritatively on either, we have intentionally left these important responsibilities to the investor.

If there is any reason to think that an outstanding legal issue may impact the company's ability to prosper or support the franchise system, you will most likely require the interpretation of a qualified and experienced franchise attorney. Prior to signing a franchise agreement, be confident that no new or potential litigation has come up since the publication of the UFOC. The franchisor is obligated to give you an accurate status report.

Similarly, the franchisor's financial health is critical to your own success. How to determine that health? Each franchisor is required to include detailed financial statements in its UFOC. Depending upon the date of the UFOC, the information may be very current. Most likely, however, it may be outdated by 6–12 months. If this is the case, request current financials from the franchisor. If the company is publicly traded, there are numerous sources of detailed information. Go to the firm's website. If you don't have the expertise to judge the financial information, ask the advice of an accountant or financial consultant. As all of the companies included in the Top 100 have in excess of 40 operating units, they most likely are enjoying a positive cash flow from operations and, therefore, are in a much stronger financial position than smaller franchisors. This is not an excuse to avoid an investigation, however.

Item 17 of the UFOC covers "Renewal, Termination, Transfer and Dispute Resolution." These are critical areas that should be fully understood before you find out that, after you have developed a profitable business, the franchisor has the unilateral right to terminate your franchise or capriciously deny a sale to a qualified buyer. Don't get blind-sided because you were too lazy or frugal to get a legal interpretation. Again, this is the province of a qualified attorney.

The Food-Service Industry

The franchising industry contains over 2,800 different concepts. Food-service constitutes roughly one-third of the entire industry -- by far the largest. Within the food-service industry, there are several different themes: bakery/coffee, fast-food or quick-service, ice cream, sit-down, subs and sandwiches and other miscellaneous categories. Frequently, concepts are further subdivided. For example, in the fast-food industry, there are various different segments such as pizza, hamburger, chicken, Asian, seafood and Mexican, to name a few. What does all of this mean? Simply that food-service is a large, dominant and sometimes confusing industry that has to be fully researched before settling in on a specific franchise concept.

The following table lists the 30 food-service franchises featured in Chapter 4.

Company Name	Franchise Fee	Total Investment	Royalty	Total Units
Auntie Anne's Hand-Rolled Soft Pretzels	$30K	$192,550-382,500	7.0%	861
Baskin-Robbins	$30K	$142.2–511.1K	5.0–5.9%	4,704
Big Apple Bagels	$25K	$228.3–377.5K	5.0%	122
Blimpie	$10–18K	$131.2–287.8K	6.0%	1,220

Burger King Corporation	$50K	$1.172–2.141MM	4.5%	11,141
Carl's Jr.	$10-35K	$920.5–1,366.7K	4.0%.	1,006
Carvel Corporation	$30K	$246,674–387,924	1.82/Gal	538
Dunkin' Donuts	$40-80K	$354.9–1,714.9K	5.9%	6,590
El Pollo Loco	$30-35K	$498,500-1,954,250	4.0%	333
Friendly's Restaurants	$30–35K	$630K–1.9MM	4.0%	520
Great Wraps	$19.5K	$215.2–319.8K	5.5%	87
KFC	$25K	$1,142.3–1,732.3K	4.0%	5,525
The Krystal Company	$32.5K	$560.5K-1.055MM	4.5%	436
La Salsa	$30K	$451–632K	5.0%	102
Long John Silver's	$20K	$786–1,695K	6.0%	1,200
Maui Wowi Hawaiian Coffees and Smoothies	$27.5-59.5K	$116,000–417,315	0%	350
The Melting Pot	$35K	$598,800–1,011,303	4.5%	101
Mrs. Fields	$30K	$179–251K	6.0%	431
Pretzel Time	$25K	$119.5-317.5K	7.0%	232
Rita's Italian Ice	$30K	$164.4–340K	6.5%	342
Shake's Frozen Custard	$30K	$162–295K	5.0%	45
Uno Chicago Grill	$35K	$1,103.5-2,673K	5.0%	211
Wienerschnitzel	$2.5-32K	$136.1–10,518K	5.0%	350
Wing Zone	$20-25K	$176–249K	5.0%	113

The Retail Industry

Of the 2,800 different franchise concepts, roughly 350 are retail franchises. There are several different types of retail companies: Specialty retailers, clothing, athletic wear, art supplies, convenience stores, home improvement, pet products, photographic products and electronics/computer products. Like the food-service and service-based franchises, the retail industry is large and needs to be fully researched before settling in on a specific franchise concept.

The following table lists the 16 retail franchises featured in Chapter 5.

Company Name	Franchise Fee	Total Investment	Royalty	Total Units
7-Eleven	$0-371.1K	$187,546-1,032,312	N/A	27,516
Aaron's Sales & Lease	$50K	$268.67-573.98K	6.0%	1,149
The Athlete's Foot	$39.9K	$199.4–449.4K	3.5–5.0%	594
Aussie Pet Mobile	$35K	$76,550-229,350	8.0%	350
Baby USA	$23.4-60.2K	$370.9–688.7K	3.0%	70
Cartridge World	$30K	$104.1-172.1K	6.0%	1,143
EmbroidMe	$19.5-37.5K	$163-222K	5.0%	300
FASTFRAME	$25K	$105.7–150K	7.5%	316
Foot Solutions	$27.5K	$186.3-236.8K	5.0%	183
KaBloom	$30K	$176,050-302,400	5.5%	105
Merkinstock	$25.5-45K	$186.3-403.1K	6.0%	59
Merle Norman Cosmetics	$10,774-23,662	$44,854-155,862	0.0%	1,940
More Space Place	$18-29.5K	$113–188K	4.5%	38
MotoPhoto	$0	$14-219K	6.0%	144
Party America	$25K	$250.8-460.5K	4.0%	288
Wild Bird Center	$18K	$86,150-124,300	3.4%	92
Wild Birds Unlimited	$18K	$90,570–152,619	4.0%	315

The Service-Based Industry

Service-based franchises make up the remaining chunk of the franchising industry. There are several different types of service-based companies: automotive services, child development, real estate, travel, etc. The industry is large and needs to be fully researched before settling in on a specific franchise concept.

The following table lists the 54 service-based franchises featured in Chapter 6.

Company Name	Franchise Fee	Total Investment	Royalty	Total Units
Action International	$30-50K	$62–92K	5.0%	601
Allegra Print & Imaging	$30K	$199,956–291,373	3.6-6.0%	450
AlphaGraphics	$25.9K	$273,119–366,719	1.5-8.0%	266
The Alternative Board	$25-55K	$42,225-103,450	3.5%	162
American Leak Detection	$57.5-100K	$71,255–155,050	6.0-10.0%	313
AmeriSpec Home Inspection Service	$17–29.9K	$26.56–64.8K	7.0%	362
Century 21 Real Estate	$0–25K	$11,713–522,511	6.0%/$500	7,680
Children's Orchard	$25K	$115.6-197K	5.0%	86
Choice Hotels International	$25-60K	$41,337–80,700	2.75-5.1%.	5,003
Coldwell Banker Real Estate	$13–25K	$23,470–70,050	6.0%	3,500
Comfort Keepers	$23,225	$44,525-66,700	4%	530
Cottman Transmission	$31.5K	$161-208.7K	7.5%	411
Coverall Cleaning Concepts	$6-32.2K	$6,291-35,920	5.0%	7,085
Crestcom International, LTD.	$12.5–61.5K	$26,545–89,755	1.5%	149
The Entrepreneur's Source	$49K	$87.5–95.5K	0.0%	300
ERA Franchise Systems	$20K	$42.7–205.9K	6.0%	2,841
Express Personnel Services	$25K	$114,350–161,800	8.0-9.0%	512
Fantastic Sams	$25-30K	$138-193.5K	$227/Wk	1,377
FasTracKids International, LTD.	$22K	$42,300–181,050	Varies	200
FASTSIGNS	$25K	$209,694–302,256	6.0%	503
Fish Window Cleaning Services	$29.9K	$80–94.1K	6.0-8.0%	186

Furniture Medic	$4.9-24.5K	$17,105–81,894	7.0%.	595
Geeks on Call	$25K	$55,850-87,150	11.0%	345
Glass Doctor	$22K	$109,681-261,681	4.0-7.0%	143
Great Clips	$20K	$96.55-182.05K	6.0%	2,500
Gymboree Play & Music	$45K	$141,400–286,765	6.0%	543
Hilton	$85K	$33-57MM	5.0%	236
House Doctors Handyman Service	$15.9–35.9K	$31,450–60,550	6.0%	235
HouseMaster Home Inspections	$18-30K	$31,000-66,950	6.75%	365
Huntington Learning Center	$40K	$158,270-273,400	8.0%	300
InterContinental Hotels Group	$50K	$5,366,870-8,891,454	5.0-6.0%	3,597
Interiors by Decorating Den	$29.9K	$40,119–46,296	7.0-9.0%	468
Jani-King	$8,600-16,250	$11,300–34,050	10.0%	11,027
Kampgrounds of America	$30K	$986,745-2,070,643	8.0%	430
Kinderdance International	$12–28K	$14–34.1K	6.0-15.0%	113
Kitchen Solvers	$27.5K	$49,450-64,970	6.0%	132
Kumon North America	$1K	$10,038–30,353	$30-33K	1,574
Liberty Tax Service	$30K	$43.8-54.9K	Varies	2,022
The Little Gym	$64.5K	$155.7-238K	8.0%	230
Martinizing Dry Cleaning	$35K	$252.5-411K	4.0%	625
Meineke Car Care Centers	$30K	$212,762.54–352,497	3.0-7.0%	875
Merry Maids	$3.8–27K	$23,350–54,450	5.0-7.0%	1,447
Midas	$15-20K	$243.15–329,7K	10.0%	2,673
Motel 6	$25K	$1,901,500–2,284,650	4.0%	843

Mr. Electric Corp.	$19.5K	$65.55–158.5K	3.0-6.0%	183
Mr. Rooter Corp.	$22.5K	$50.95-142K	4.0-7.0%	300
Navis Pack & Ship Centers	$34.5K	$93.75-180.45K	5.0%	66
New Horizons Computer Learning Center	$20K–75K	$354,931–547,925	6.0%	298
PostNet	$29.9K	$174,325–195,800	5.0%	900
RE/MAX International	$12.5-25K	$22.5–129K	Varies	6,150
Red Roof Inn	$30K	$2,636,100-2,985,450	4.5%	346
Renaissance Executive Forums	$24.5K	$55,345-73,264	20%	44
ServiceMaster Clean	$16.9–45K	$44,903–117,765	4.0-10.0%	4,488
Sign-A-Rama	$19.5K	$149,129-204,559	6.0%	758
Spherion	$10K	$57.5–133.2K	3.0-6.0%	595
Spring-Green Lawn Care	$30-36K	$96,911–118,397	6.0-9.0%	121
Supercuts	$22.5K	$106,860-170,080	4.0-6.0%	2,003
Sylvan Learning Centers	$40–48K	$195,948–249,400	8.0-9.0%	1,050
The UPS Store	$19,950-29,950	$145,531–245,494	5.0%	5,554
Window Genie	$29.5K	$61.7–73.4K	6.0%	39

In closing, I'd like to emphasize that the 100 companies included in this book are here as the result of many months of intensive research and independent evaluation. We did not draw names out of a hat. We did not necessarily choose the industry "heavyweights." We did, however, pore over countless UFOCs, confer with many franchise directors and staff members, visit actual operating units and view numerous websites. In addition to studying each company's UFOC and marketing materials, we took full advantage of recent articles about each company we evaluated. We sought the opinion of friends, industry experts and existing franchisees. As we do not allow advertising in any of our publications, we do not have a built-in bias toward any of the companies selected. Nor do we have any financial or other "hidden agendas."

It is our hope that, as a potential franchisee, you will benefit from these efforts. In designing the format, we decided the best way to present the information would be to ask the same questions you would: "How much?", "Why are they better than their competitors?", "What do I get out of it?" Those questions and more are answered as we present what we feel are the 100 best franchises.

30 Minute Overview 1

In presenting this data, we have made some unilateral assumptions about our readers. The first is that you purchased the book because of the depth and accuracy of the data provided — not as a how-to manual. Chapter Three, Recommended Reading, lists several resources for anyone requiring additional background information on the franchising industry and on the process of evaluating a company. Clearly, dedication to hard work, adequate financing, commitment, good business sense and access to trusted professional counsel will determine your ultimate success as a franchisee. A strong working knowledge of the industry, however, will help ensure that you have made the best choice of franchise opportunities. I advise you to acquaint yourself with the dynamics of the industry before you initiate the evaluation and negotiation phases of selecting a franchise.

The second assumption is that you have already devoted the time necessary to conduct a detailed personal inventory. This self-assessment should result in a clear understanding of your skills, aptitudes, weaknesses, long-term personal goals, commitment to succeed and financial capabilities. Most of the books in the Recommended Reading Chapter provide worksheets to accomplish this important step.

ଛ

There are three primary stages to the franchise selection process: 1) the investigation stage, 2) the evaluation stage and 3) and the negotiation stage. This book is intended primarily to assist the reader in the investigation stage by providing a thorough list of the options available. Chapters One and Two include various observations based on our 15 or so years of involvement with the franchising industry. Hopefully, they will provide some insights that you will find of value.

Understand at the outset that the entire process will take many months and involve a great deal of frustration. I suggest that you set up a realistic time-line for signing a franchise agreement and that you stick with that schedule. There will be a lot of pressure on you to prematurely complete the selection and negotiation phases. Resist the temptation. The penalties are too severe for a seat-of-the-pants attitude. A decision of this magnitude clearly deserves your full attention. Do your homework!

Before starting the selection process, you would be well advised to briefly review the areas that follow.

Franchise Industry Structure

The franchising industry is made up of two distinct types of franchises. The first, and by far the larger, encompasses product and trade name franchising. Automotive and truck dealers, soft drink bottlers and gasoline service stations are included in this group. For the most part, these are essentially distributorships.

The second group encompasses business format franchisors. This book only includes information on this latter category.

Layman's Definition of Franchising

Business format franchising is a method of market expansion by which one business entity expands the distribution of its products and/or services through independent, third-party operators. Franchising occurs when the operator of a concept or system (the **franchisor**) grants an independent businessperson (the **franchisee**) the right to duplicate its entire business format

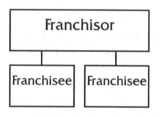

Classic Business Format Model

at a particular location and for a specified period, under terms and conditions set forth in the contract (**franchise agreement**). The franchisee has full access to all of the trademarks, logos, marketing techniques, controls and systems that have made the franchisor successful. In effect, the franchisee acts as a surrogate for a company-owned store in the distribution of the franchisor's goods and/or services. It is important to keep in mind that the franchisor and the franchisee are separate legal entities.

In return for a front-end **franchise fee** — which usually ranges from $15,000–35,000 — the franchisor is obligated to "set up" the franchisee in business. This generally includes assistance in selecting a location, negotiating a lease, obtaining financing, building and equipping a site and providing the necessary training, operating manuals, etc. Once the training is completed and the store is open, the new franchisee should have a carbon copy of other units in the system and enjoy the same benefits they do, whether they are company-owned or not.

Business format franchising is unique because it is a long-term relationship characterized by an on-going, mutually beneficial partnership. On-going services include research and development, marketing strategies, advertising campaigns, group buying, periodic field visits, training updates, and whatever else is required to make the franchisee competitive and profitable. In effect, the franchisor acts as the franchisee's "back office" support organization. To reimburse the franchisor for this support, the franchisee pays the franchisor an on-going **royalty fee**, generally four to eight percent of gross sales or income. In many cases, franchisees also contribute an **advertising fee** to reimburse the franchisor for expenses incurred in maintaining a national or regional advertising campaign.

For the maximum advantage, both the franchisor and the franchisees should share common objectives and goals. Both parties must accept the premise that their fortunes are mutually intertwined and that they are each better off working in a co-operative effort, rather than toward any self-serving goals. Unlike the parent/child relationship that has dominated franchising over the past 30 years, franchising is now becoming a true and productive relationship of partners.

Legal Definition of Franchising

The Federal Trade Commission (FTC) has its own definition of franchising. So do each of the 16 states that have separate franchise registration statutes. The State of California's definition, which is the model for the FTC's definition, follows:

> *Franchise means a contract or agreement, express or implied, whether oral or written, between two or more persons by which:*
>
> *A franchisee is granted the right to engage in the business of offering, selling, or*

distributing goods or services under a marketing plan or system prescribed in substantial part by a franchisor;

The operation of the franchisee's business pursuant to that plan or system as substantially associated with the franchisor's trademark, service mark, trade name, logotype, advertising, or other commercial symbol designating the franchisor or its affiliates; and

The franchisee is required to pay, directly or indirectly, a franchise fee.

Multi-Level Franchising

With franchisors continually exploring new ways to expand their distribution, the classic business format model shown above has evolved over the years. Modifications have allowed franchisors to grow more rapidly and at less cost than might have otherwise been possible.

If a franchisor wishes to expand at a faster rate than its financial resources or staff levels allow, it might choose to sell development rights in an area (state, national or international) and let the new entity do the development work. No matter which development method is chosen, the franchisee should still receive the same benefits and support provided under the standard model. The major difference is that the entity providing the training and on-going support and receiving the franchise and royalty fees changes.

Three variations of the master franchising model include: 1) master (or regional) franchising, 2) sub-franchising and 3) area development franchising.

In **master (or regional) franchising,** the franchisor sells the development rights in a particular market to a master franchisee who, in turn, sells individual franchises within the territory. In return for a front-end master franchise fee, the master franchisee has sole responsibility for developing that area under a mutually agreed upon schedule. This includes attracting, screening, signing and training

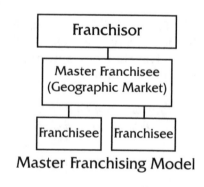

Master Franchising Model

all new franchisees within the territory. Once established, on-going support is generally provided by the parent franchisor.

The master franchisee is rewarded by sharing in the franchise fees and the on-going royalties paid to the parent franchisor by the franchisees within the territory.

Sub-franchising is similar to master franchising in that the franchisor grants development rights in a specified territory to a sub-franchisor. After the agreement is signed, however, the parent franchisor has no on-going involvement with the individual franchisees in the territory. Instead, the sub-franchisor becomes the focal point. All fees and royalties are paid directly to the sub-franchisor. It is solely responsible for all recruiting, training and on-going support, and passes on an agreed upon percentage of all incoming fees and royalties to the parent franchisor.

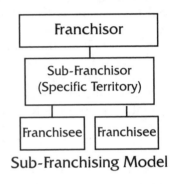

Sub-Franchising Model

In a sub-franchising relationship, the potential franchisee has to be doubly careful in his or her investigation. He or she must first make sure that the sub-franchisor has the necessary financial, managerial and marketing skills to make the program work. Secondarily, the potential franchisee has to feel comfortable that the parent franchisor can be relied upon to come to his or her rescue if the sub-franchisor should fail.

The third variation is an **area development agreement**. Here again, the franchisor grants exclusive development rights for a particular geographic area to an area development investment group. Within its territory, the area developer may either develop individual franchise units for its own account or find independent franchisees to develop units. In

Area Development Model

21

the latter case, the area developer has a residual equity position in the profits of its "area franchisees."

In return for the rights to an exclusive territory, the area developer pays the franchisor a front-end development fee and commits to develop a certain number of units within a specified time period. (The front-end fee is generally significantly less than the sum of the individual unit fees.) Individual franchisees within the territory pay all contractual franchise, royalty and advertising fees directly to the parent franchisor. The area developer shares in neither the franchise fee nor in on-going royalty or advertising fees. Instead, the area developer shares only in the profitability of the individual franchises that it "owns." In essence, the area developer is buying multiple locations over time at a discount, since the franchise fee and (frequently) the royalty fee are less than the per unit rate.

Franchise Industry Statistics

The International Franchise Association (IFA) estimated that product and trade name franchising accounted for $554 billion in sales in 1992. This represents roughly 28% of all retail sales.

Business format franchising produced total sales of $249 billion in 1992, roughly 13% of all retail sales. In layman's language, this means that for every $1.00 spent at the retail level, more than $0.13 went to franchised establishments. There is no question that franchising has had a profound impact on the way business is conducted in the U.S. Most analysts anticipate that the overall numbers and market share of retail business will continue to grow well into the foreseeable future and at a faster rate than the economy in general.

According to the IFA's 1997 "Profile of Franchising (Statistical Profile of the 1997 Uniform Franchise Offering Circular Data)," 18% of the industry was concentrated in fast-food and 11% in retail, while only one percent of the concentration was in travel or printing. In terms of system size, about half of the systems analyzed had more than 50 units, with 27% (the largest concentration) having between 11 and 50 franchised units and 75% having ten or fewer company-owned units. Sixty percent of the companies had been in business 12 or more years, but only 44% had been franchising for more than eight years. Only 4% of the franchisors had an initial franchise fee of over $50,000; fast-food, which was the largest category, had an average fee of $19,999. The average total investment for most companies was under $250,000, and most had renewable franchise contracts. Although

BOND'S FRANCHISE GUIDE
ANNUAL FRANCHISING INDUSTRY OVERVIEW
(As of 12/31/2005)

Exhibit 1

CATEGORY	# of Fran- chisors	Fran- chised Units	Company- Owned Units	Total Operating Units	See Chapter
Automotive Products & Services	161	26,627	2,319	28,946	4
Auto / Truck / Trailer Rental	27	3,976	610	4,586	5
Building & Remodeling / Furniture / Appliance Repair	131	8,512	218	8,730	6
Business: Financial Services	58	13,750	7,890	21,640	7
Business: Advertising & Promotion	30	1,480	91	1,571	8
Business: Internet / Telecommunications / Misc.	75	8,880	870	9,750	9
Child Development / Education / Products	99	7,518	954	8,472	10
Education / Personal Development / Training	60	4,957	1,427	6,384	11
Employment & Personnel	68	5,284	2,945	8,229	12
Food: Donuts / Cookies / Bagels	65	14,065	1,529	15,594	13
Food: Coffee	41	1,593	509	2,102	14
Food: Ice Cream / Yogurt	58	15,250	1,175	16,425	15
Food: Quick Service / Take-out	419	146,547	25,176	171,723	16
Food: Restaurant / Family-Style	188	19,791	10,008	29,799	17
Food: Specialty Foods	118	7,869	962	8,831	18
Hairstyling Salons	40	7,701	3,447	11,148	19
Health / Fitness / Beauty	130	20,022	2,089	22,111	20
Laundry & Dry Cleaning	22	2,467	40	2,507	21
Lawn and Garden	26	3,566	102	3,668	22
Lodging	68	28,396	2,891	31,287	23
Maid Service & Home Cleaning	23	4,392	184	4,576	24
Maintenance / Cleaning / Sanitation	135	47,181	637	47,818	25
Medical / Optical / Dental Products & Services	20	1,513	289	1,802	26
Packaging & Mailing	23	16,175	38	16,213	27
Printing & Graphics	17	3,299	61	3,360	28
Publications	29	1,261	62	1,323	29
Real Estate Inspection Services	24	3,106	421	3,527	30
Real Estate Services	62	26,092	1,483	27,575	31
Recreation & Entertainment	40	2,242	143	2,385	32
Rental Services	9	2,253	3,523	5,776	33
Retail: Art, Art Supplies & Framing	13	777	34	811	34
Retail: Athletic Wear / Sporting Goods	17	1,755	44	1,799	35
Retail: Clothing / Shoes / Accessories	15	154	115	269	36
Retail: Convenience Stores / Supermarkets / Drugs	23	29,914	4,805	34,719	37
Retail: Home Furnishings	45	3,511	230	3,741	38
Retail: Home Improvement & Hardware	14	15,576	176	15,752	39
Retail: Pet Products & Services	34	1,573	380	1,953	40

CATEGORY	# of Fran- chisors	Fran- chised Units	Company- Owned Units	Total Operating Units	See Chapter
Retail: Photographic Products & Services	20	744	42	786	41
Retail: Specialty	110	9,001	4,643	13,644	42
Retail: Video / Audio / Electronics	30	4,396	9,720	14,116	43
Retail: Miscellaneous	18	1,921	68	1,989	44
Security & Safety Systems	21	997	97	1,094	45
Signs	13	2,188	6	2,194	46
Travel	20	4,185	133	4,318	47
Miscellaneous	141	7,671	581	8,252	48
Industry Total	**2,800**	**540,128**	**93,167**	**633,295**	
% of Total		**85.3%**	**14.7%**	**100.0%**	

Exhibit 2

Relative Size - By Number of Total Operating Units:	#	%	Cum. %
> 5,000 Total Operating Units	24	0.9%	0.9%
1,000 - 4,999 Total Operating Units	80	2.9%	3.7%
500 - 999 Total Operating Units	91	3.3%	7.1%
250 - 499 Total Operating Units	191	6.8%	13.9%
100 - 249 Total Operating Units	377	13.5%	27.4%
50 - 99 Total Operating Units	356	12.7%	40.7%
25 - 49 Total Operating Units	351	12.5%	53.2%
15 - 24 Total Operating Units	228	8.1%	61.4%
Less Than 15 Total Operating Units	1,102	39.4%	100.7%
Total	**2,800**	**100.0%**	

Exhibit 3

Country of Origin:	#	%
United States	2,512	89.7%
Canada	288	10.3%
Total	**2,800**	**100.0%**

royalties varied greatly from franchise to franchise, most based it on sales/ revenue and ranged from three to six percent monthly. Forty-eight percent of franchisors had an advertising fee based on percentage, usually ranging between 0.01–2%. Franchisor-sponsored financing was offered by 37% of the companies.

Exhibits 1–5, noted on the previous pages, are the result of querying our proprietary franchisor database (which has some 30 fields of information on 2,500 franchisors) and the database of some 1,200 detailed questionnaires that were returned as a result of our 2001 industry survey. You should spend some time reviewing the various Exhibits to get a better idea of the relative size, fees and investment levels required in various industry categories. If the size of the franchise fee, total investment or royalty fee fall far outside the averages noted, the franchisor should have a ready explanation as to why.

The Players

Franchisors

After extensive research, we have selected 100 of what we think are the best franchises the industry has to offer.

Selecting the most appropriate franchisor for your needs is crucial to becoming a successful franchisee. By providing general information, in addition to a detailed analysis of each company's identity, financial requirements, training, support and territory offering, we hope to aid the prospective franchisee in making the right choice.

The Regulatory Agencies

The offer and sale of franchises are regulated at both the federal and state levels. Federal requirements cover all 50 states. In addition, certain states have adopted their own requirements.

In 1979, after many years of debate, the Federal Trade Commission (FTC) implemented Rule 436. This Rule requires that franchisors provide prospective franchisees with a disclosure statement (called an offering circular) containing specific information about a company's franchise offering. The Rule has two objectives: to ensure that the potential franchisee has sufficient background information to make an educated investment decision and to provide him or her with adequate time to do so.

Certain "registration states" require additional safeguards to protect potential franchisees. Their requirements are generally more stringent than the FTC's requirements. These states include California, Florida, Hawaii, Illinois, Indiana, Maryland, Michigan, Minnesota, New York, North Dakota, Oregon, Rhode Island, South Dakota, Virginia, Washington and Wisconsin. Separate registration is also required in the province of Alberta, Canada.

For the most part, registration states require a disclosure format know as the Uniform Franchise Offering Circular (UFOC). As a matter of convenience, and because the state requirements are more demanding, most franchisors have adopted the UFOC format. This format requires that the franchisor provides a prospective franchisee with the required information at their first face-to-face meeting or at least ten business days prior to the signing of the franchise agreement, whichever is earlier. Required information includes:

1. The Franchisor and Any Predecessors.
2. Identity and Business Experience of Persons Affiliated with Franchisor.
3. Litigation.
4. Bankruptcy.
5. Franchisee's Initial Fee/Other Initial Payments.
6. Other Fees.
7. Franchisee's Initial Investment.
8. Obligations of Franchisee to Purchase or Lease from Designated Sources.
9. Obligations of Franchisee to Purchase or Lease in Accordance with Specifications or from Approved Suppliers.
10. Financing Arrangements.
11. Obligations of the Franchisor; Other Supervision, Assistance or Services.
12. Exclusive Area of Territory.
13. Trademarks, Service Marks, Trade Names, Logotypes and Commercial Symbols.
14. Patents and Copyrights.
15. Obligations of the Franchisee to Participate in the Actual Operation of the Franchise Business.
16. Restrictions on Goods and Services Offered by Franchisee.
17. Renewal, Termination, Repurchase, Modification and Assignment of the Franchise Agreement and Related Information.
18. Arrangements with Public Figures.
19. Actual, Average, Projected or Forecasted Franchise Sales, Profits

or Earnings.
20.   Information Regarding Franchises of the Franchisor.
21.   Financial Statements.
22.   Contracts.
23.   Acknowledgment of Receipt by Respective Franchisee.

If you live in a registration state, make sure that the franchisor you are evaluating is, in fact, registered to sell franchises there. If not, and the franchisor has no near-term plans to register in your state, you should consider other options.

Keep in mind that neither the FTC nor any of the states has reviewed the offering circular to determine whether the information submitted is true or not. They merely require that the franchisor make representations based upon a prescribed format. If the information provided is false, franchisors are subject to civil penalties. That may not help a franchisee, however, who cannot undo a very expensive mistake.

It is up to you to read and thoroughly understand all elements of the offering circular. There is no question that it is tedious reading. Know exactly what you can expect from the franchisor and what your own obligations are. Under what circumstances can the relationship be unilaterally terminated by the franchisor? What is your protected territory? Specifically, what front-end assistance will the franchisor provide? You should have a professional review the UFOC. It would be a shame not to take full advantage of the documentation that is available to you.

The Trade Associations

The **International Franchise Association** (IFA) was established as a non-profit trade association to promote franchising as a responsible method of doing business. The IFA currently represents over 650 franchisors in the U.S. and around the world. It is recognized as the leading spokesperson for responsible franchising. For most of its 30+ years, the IFA has represented the interests of franchisors only. In recent years, however, it has initiated an aggressive campaign to recruit franchisees into its membership and represent their interests as well. The IFA's address is 1350 New York Avenue, NW, Suite 900, Washington, DC 20005. (202) 628-8000; FAX (202) 628-0812, 501 K Street, www.franchise.org.

The **Canadian Franchise Association** (CFA), which has some 250+ members, is the Canadian equivalent of the IFA. Information on the CFA can be obtained from its offices at 2585 Skymark Avenue, Suite 300, Mississauga, ON L4W 4L5 Canada. (905) 625-2896; FAX (905) 625-9076, www. CFA.CA.

The **American Association of Franchisees and Dealers** (AAFD) represents the rights and interests of franchisees and independent dealers. Formed in 1992 with the mission of "Bringing Fairness to Franchising," the AAFD represents thousands of franchised businesses, representing over 250 different franchise systems. It provides a broad range of services designed to help franchisees build market power, create legislative support, provide legal and financial support and provide a wide range of general member benefits. P.O. Box 81887, San Diego, CA 92138. (800) 733-9858, (619) 209-3775; FAX: (619) 209-3777.

Franchise Survival/Failure Rate

In order to promote the industry's attractiveness, most literature on the subject of franchising includes the same often-quoted, but very misleading, statistics that leave the impression that franchising is a near risk-free investment.

In the 1970s, the Small Business Administration produced a poorly documented report that 38% of all small businesses fail within their first year of operation and 77% fail within their first five years. With franchising, however, comparative failure rates miraculously drop to only three percent after the first year and eight percent after five years. No effort was made to define failure. Instead, "success" was defined as an operating unit still in business under the same name at the same location.

While most people would agree that the failure rates for franchised businesses are substantially lower than the failure rates for independent businesses, that assumption is not substantiated by reliable statistics. Part of the problem is definitional. Part is the fact that the industry has a vested interest in perpetuating the myth rather than debunking it.

FRANDATA, a Washington, DC-based franchise research firm, recently conducted a review of franchise terminations and renewals. It found that 4.4% of all franchisees left their franchise system each year for a variety of reasons, excluding sales to third parties (to be fully meaningful, the data should include sales to third parties and the reasons behind a sale).

The critical issue is to properly define failure and success, and then require franchisors to report changes in ownership based on these universally accepted definitions. A logical starting point in defining success should be whether the franchisee can "make an honest living" as a franchisee. A "success" would occur when the franchisee prefers to continue as a franchisee rather than sell the business. A "failure" would occur when the franchisee is forced to sell his or her business at a loss.

A reasonable measure of franchise success would be to ask franchisees "would you do it again?" If a legitimate survey were conducted of all franchisees of all systems, my guess is that the answer to this question would indicate a "success rate" well under 70% after a five-year period. Alternatively, one could ask the question "has the franchise investment met your expectations?" I estimate that fewer than 50% would say "yes" after a five-year period. These are just educated guesses.

The failure rate is unquestionably lower for larger, more mature companies in the industry that have proven their systems and carefully chosen their franchisees. It is substantially higher for smaller, newer companies that have unproven products and are less demanding in whom they accept as a franchisee.

As it now stands, the Uniform Franchise Offering Circular (UFOC) only requires the franchisor to provide the potential franchisee with the names of owners who have left the system within the past 12 months. In my opinion, this is a severe shortcoming of the regulatory process. Unless required, franchisors will not willingly provide information about failures to prospective franchisees. There is no question in my mind, however, that franchisors are fully aware of when and why past failures have occurred.

It is patently unfair that a potential investor should not have access to this critical information. To ensure its availability, I propose that the UFOC be amended to require that franchisors provide franchisee turn-over information for the most recent five-year period. Underlying reasons for a change in ownership would be provided by a departing franchisee on a universal, industry-approved questionnaire filled out during an "exit" interview. The questionnaire would then be returned to some central clearing house.

The only way to make up for this lack of information is to aggressively seek out as many previous and current franchisees as possible. Request past UFOC's to get the names of previous owners, and then contact them. Whether successful or not, these owners are an invaluable resource. Try to determine the reason for their failure and/or disenchantment. Most failures are the result of poor management or inadequate finances on the part of the departing franchisee. But people give up franchises for other reasons.

Current franchisees are even better sources of meaningful information. For systems with under 25 units, I strongly encourage you to talk to all franchisees. For those having between 25 and 100 units, I recommend talking to at least half. And for all others, interview a minimum of 50.

What Makes a Winning Franchise

Virtually every writer on the subject of franchising has his or her own idea of what determines a winning franchise. I maintain that there are five primary factors.

1. A product or service with a clear advantage over the competition. The advantage may be in brand recognition, a unique, proprietary product or 30 years of proven experience.

2. A standardized franchise system that has been time-tested. Look for a company in which most of the bugs in the system have been worked out through the cumulative experience of both company-owned and franchised units. By the time a system has 30 or more operating units, it should be thoroughly tested.

3. Exceptional franchisor support. This includes not only the initial training program, but the on-going support (research and development, refresher training, [800] help-lines, field representatives and on-site training, annual meetings, advertising and promotion, central purchasing, etc.).

4. The financial wherewithal and management experience to carry out any announced growth plans without short-changing its franchisees. Sufficient depth of management is often lacking in high-growth franchises.

5. A strong mutuality of interest between franchisor and franchisees. Unless both parties realize that their relationship is one of long-term partners, it is unlikely that the system will ever achieve its full potential. Whether they have the necessary rapport is easily determined by a few telephone calls to existing franchisees.

Financial Projections

The single most important factor in buying a franchise — or any business for that matter — is having a realistic projection of sales, expenses and profits. Specifically, how much can you expect to make after working 65 hours a week for 52 weeks a year? No one is in a better position to supply accurate information (subject to caveats) about a franchise opportunity than the franchisor itself. A potential franchisee often does not have the experience to sit down and project what his or her sales and profits will be over the next five years. This is especially true if he or she has no applied experience in that particular business.

Earnings claim statements (Item 19 of the Uniform Franchise Offering Circular) present franchisor-supplied sales, expense and/or profit summaries based on actual operating results for company-owned and/or franchised units. Since no format is prescribed, however, the data may be cursory or detailed. The only constraint is that the franchisor must be able to substantiate the data presented. Further complicating the process is the fact that providing an earnings claim statement is strictly optional. Accordingly, less than 15% of franchisors provide one.

Virtually everyone agrees that the information included in an earnings claim statement can be exceedingly helpful to a potential franchisee. Unfortunately, there are many reasons why franchisors might not willingly choose to make their actual results available to the public. Many franchisors feel that a prospective investor would be turned off if he or she had access to actual operating results. Others may not want to go to the trouble and expense of collecting the data.

Other franchisors are legitimately afraid of being sued for "misrepresentation." There is considerable risk to a franchisor if a published earnings claim statement is interpreted in any way as a "guarantee" of sales or income for new units. Given today's highly litigious society, and the propensity of courts to award large settlements to the "little guy," it's not surprising that so few franchisors provide the information.

As an assist to prospective franchisees, Source Book Publications has recently published the fifth edition of *"How Much Can I Make?"* It includes 116 earnings claim statements covering a diverse group of industries. It is the only publication that contains current earnings claim statements submitted by the franchisors. Given the scarcity of industry projections, this is an invaluable resource for potential franchisees or investors in determining what he or she might make by investing in a franchise or similar business. The book is $29.95, plus $7.00 shipping. See the inside rear cover of the book for additional details on the book and the companies that have submitted earnings claim statements. The book can be obtained from Source Book Publications, 1814 Franklin Street, Suite 815, Oakland, CA 94612, by calling (510) 839-5471, faxing a request to (510) 839-2401, or visiting our online bookstore at www.sourcebookpublications.com.

New vs. Used

As a potential franchisee, you have the option of becoming a franchisee in a new facility at a new location or purchasing an existing franchise. It is not an easy decision. Your success in making that choice will depend upon your business acumen and your insight into people.

Purchasing a new franchise unit will mean that everything is current, clean and under warranty. Purchasing an existing franchise will probably involve a smaller investment and allow greater financial leverage. However, you will have to assess the seller's reason for selling. Is the business not performing to expectations because of poor management, poor location, poor support from the franchisor, an indifferent staff, obsolete equipment and/or facilities, etc.? The decision is further clouded because you may be working through a business broker who may or may not be giving you good information. Regardless of the obstacles, considering a "used" franchise merits your consideration. Apply the same analytical tools you would to a new franchise. Do your homework. Be thorough. Be unrelenting.

The Negotiation Process

Once you have narrowed your options down to your top two or three choices, you must negotiate the best deal you can with the franchisor. In most cases, the franchisor will tell you that the franchise agreement cannot be changed. Do not accept this explanation. Notwithstanding the legal requirement that all of a franchisor's agreements be substantially the same at any point in time, there are usually a number of variables in the equation. If the franchisor truly wants you as a franchisee, it may be willing to make concessions not available to the next applicant.

Will the franchisor take a short-term note for all or part of the franchise fee? Can you expand from your initial unit after you have proven yourself? If so, can the franchise fee be eliminated or reduced on a second unit?

Can you get a right of first refusal on adjacent territories? Can the term of the agreement be extended from ten to fifteen years? Can you include a franchise cancellation right if the training and/or initial support don't meet your expectations or the franchisor's promises? The list goes on ad infinitum.

To successfully negotiate, you must have a thorough knowledge of the industry, the franchise agreement you are negotiating (and agreements of competitive franchise opportunities) and access to experienced professional advice. This can be a lawyer, an accountant or a franchise consultant. Above all else, they should have proven experience in negotiating franchise agreements. Franchising is a unique method of doing business. Don't pay someone $100+ per hour to learn the industry. Make them demonstrate that they have been through the process several times before. Negotiating a long-term agreement of this type is extremely tricky and fraught with pitfalls. The risks are extremely high. Don't be so smug as to think that you can handle the negotiations yourself. Don't be so frugal as to think you can't afford outside counsel. In point of fact, you can't afford not to employ an experienced professional advisor.

The Four Rs of Franchising

We are told as children that the three Rs of reading, 'riting, and 'rithmetic are critical to our scholastic success. Success in franchising depends on four Rs — realism, research, reserves and resolve.

Realism

At the outset of your investigation, it is important that you be realistic about your strengths and weaknesses, your goals and your capabilities. I strongly recommend that you take the time necessary to do a personal audit — possibly with the help of outside professionals — before investing your life's savings in a franchise.

Franchising is not a money machine. It involves hard work, dedication, set-backs and long hours. Be realistic about the nature of the business you are buying. What traits will ultimately determine your success? Do you have them? If it is a service-oriented business, will you be able to keep smiling when you know the client is a fool? If it is a fast-food business, will you be able to properly manage a minimum-wage staff? How well will you handle the uncertainties that will invariably arise? Can you make day-to-day decisions based on imperfect information? Can you count on your spouse's support after you have gone through all of your working capital reserves, and the future looks cloudy and uncertain?

Be equally realistic about your franchise selection process. Have you thoroughly evaluated all of the alternatives? Have you talked with everyone you can to ensure that you have left no stone unturned? Have you carefully and realistically assessed the advantages and disadvantages of the system offered, the unique demographics of your territory, near-term market trends, the financial projections, etc.? The selection process is tiring. It is easy to convince yourself that the franchise opportunity in your hand is really the best one for you. The penalties for doing so, however, are extreme.

Research

There is no substitute for exhaustive research!

It is up to you to spend the time required to come up with an optimal selection. At a minimum, you will probably be in that business for five years. More likely, you will be in it ten years or more. Given the long-term commitment, allow yourself the necessary time to ensure you don't regret having made a hasty decision. Research is a tedious, boring process. But doing it carefully and thoroughly can greatly reduce your risk and exposure. The benefits are measurable.

Based on personal experience, you may feel you already know the best franchise. Step back. Assume there is a competing franchise out there with a comparable product or service, comparable management, etc., that charges a royalty fee two percent of sales less than your intuitive choice. Over a ten-year period, that could add up to a great deal of money. It certainly justifies your requesting initial information.

A thorough analysis of the literature you receive should allow you to reduce the list of prime candidates down to six to eight companies. Aggressively evaluate each firm. Talking with current and former franchisees is the single best source of information you can get. Where possible, site visits are invaluable. My experience is that franchisees tend to be candid in their level of satisfaction with the franchisor. However, since they don't know you, they may be less candid about their sales, expenses and income. Go to the library and get studies that forecast industry growth, market saturation, industry problems, technical break-throughs, etc. Don't find out a year after becoming a franchisee of a coffee company that earlier reports suggested that the coffee market was over-saturated or that coffee was linked to some form of colon cancer.

Reserves

As a new business, franchising is replete with uncertainty, uneven cash flows and unforeseen problems. It is an imperfect world that might not bear any relation to the clean pro formas you prepared to justify getting into the business. Any one of these unforeseen contingencies could cause a severe drain on your cash reserves. At the same time, you will have fixed and/or contractual payments that must be met on a current basis regardless of sales: rent, employee salaries, insurance, etc. Adequate back-up reserves may be in the form of savings, commitments from relatives, bank loans, etc. Just make certain that the funds are available when, and if, you need them. To be absolutely safe, I suggest you double the level of reserves recommended by the franchisor.

Keep in mind that the most common cause of business failure is inadequate working capital. Plan properly so you don't become a statistic.

Resolve

Let's assume for the time being that you have demonstrated exceptional levels of realism, research and reserves. You have picked an optimal franchise that takes full advantage of your strengths. You are in business and bringing in enough money to achieve a positive cash flow. The future looks bright. Now the fourth R — resolve — comes into play. Remember why you chose franchising in the first place: to take full advantage of a system that has been time-tested in the marketplace. Remember also what makes franchising work so well: the franchisor and franchisees maximize their respective success by working within the system for the common good. Invariably, two obstacles arise.

The first is the physical pain associated with writing that monthly royalty check. Annual sales of $250,000 and a six percent royalty fee result in a monthly royalty check of $1,250 that must be sent to the franchisor. Every month. As a franchisee, you may look for any justification to reduce this sizable monthly outflow. Resist the temptation. Accept the fact that royalty fees are simply another cost of doing business. They are also a legal obligation that you willingly agreed to pay when you signed the franchise agreement. They are the dues you agreed to pay when you joined the club.

Although there may be an incentive, don't look for loopholes in the contract that might allow you to sue the franchisor or get out of the relationship. Don't report lower sales than actual in an effort to reduce royalties. If you have received the support that you were promised, continue to play by the rules. Honor your commitment. Let the franchisor enjoy the rewards it has earned from your success.

The second obstacle is the desire to change the system. You need to honor your commitment to be a "franchisee" and to live within the franchise system. What makes franchising successful as far as your customers are concerned is uniformity and consistency of appearance, product/service quality and corporate image. The most damaging thing an individual franchisee can do is to suddenly and unilaterally introduce changes to the proven system. While these modifications may work in one market, they only serve to diminish the value of the system as a whole. Imagine what would happen to the national perception of your franchise if every franchisee had the latitude to make unilateral changes in his or her operations. Accordingly, any ideas you have on improving the system should be submitted directly to the franchisor for its evaluation. Accept the franchisor's decision on whether or not to pursue an idea.

If you suspect that you may be a closet entrepreneur, for unrestrained experimenting and tinkering, you are probably not cut out to be a franchisee. Seriously consider this question before you get into a relationship, instead of waiting until you are locked into an untenable situation.

Summary

I hope that I have been clear in suggesting that the selection of an optimal franchise is both time- and energy-consuming. Done properly, the process may take six to nine months and involve the expenditure of several thousand dollars. The difference between a hasty, gut-feel investigation and an exhaustive, well-thought out investigation may mean the difference between finding a poorly-conceived, or even fraudulent, franchise and an exceptional one.

My sense is that there is a strong correlation between the efforts you put into the investigative process and the ultimate degree of success you enjoy as a franchisee. The process is to investigate, evaluate and negotiate. Don't try to bypass any one of these critical elements.

How to Use the Data 2

The data at the beginning of each company profile is the result of a 42-point questionnaire that we send out annually to the franchising community. This information is intended as a brief overview of the company; the text that follows provides a more in-depth analysis of the company's requirements and advantages.

In some cases, an answer has been abbreviated to conserve room and to make the profiles more directly comparable. All of the data is displayed with the objective of providing as much background data as possible. In those cases where no answer was provided to a particular question within the questionnaire, an "NR" is used to signify "No Response."

Please take 20 minutes to acquaint yourself with the composition of the sample questionnaire data. Supplementary comments have been added where some interpretation of the franchisor's response is required.

ॐ

Blimpie Subs and Salads has been selected to illustrate how this book uses the collected data.

BLIMPIE
7730 East Greenway Road, #104
Scottsdale, AZ 85260
Tel: (800) 447-6256 (770) 984-2707 + 123

Fax: (770) 933-6109
E-Mail: jwcampbell@kahalacorp.com
Web Site: www.blimpie.com
Ms. J. Archer, VP Franchise Development

International submarine sandwich chain, serving fresh-sliced, high-quality meats and cheeses on fresh-baked

37

bread. Also offering an assortment of fresh-made salads and other quality products.

BACKGROUND: IFA MEMBER
Established: 1964; 1st Franchised: 1977
Franchised Units: 1,210
Company-Owned Units   10
Total Units: 1,220
Dist.:   US-1,210; CAN-0; O'seas-10
  North America: 50 States, 4 Provinces
  Density: 209 in FL, 193 in GA
Projected New Units (12 Months):
                NR
Qualifications: 4, 3, 2, 2, 2, 5
Registered: CA,FL,HI,IL,IN,MI,M
        N,NY,ND,OR,RI,SD,WA,WI

FINANCIAL/TERMS:
Cash Investment: $25-100K
Total Investment: $75-250K
Minimum Net Worth: $100K
Fees: Franchise — $10-18K
        Royalty — 6%; Ad. — 4%
Earnings Claim Statement: No

Term of Contract (Years):   20/5
Avg. # Of Employees: 4 FT, 8 PT
Passive Ownership: Discouraged
Encourage Conversions: Yes
Area Develop. Agreements: Yes
Sub-Franchising Contracts: Yes
Expand In Territory: Yes
Space Needs: 1,200 SF; FS, SF, SC, RM

SUPPORT & TRAINING:
Financial Assistance Provided: Yes(I)
Site Selection Assistance: Yes
Lease Negotiation Assistance: Yes
Co-Operative Advertising: Yes
Franchisee Assoc./Member: Yes/Yes
Size Of Corporate Staff: 100+
On-Going Support: B,C,D,E,F,G,H,I
Training: 80 Hours in Atlanta,
        GA; 120 Hours in Local Franchise.

SPECIFIC EXPANSION PLANS:
US: All United States
Canada: All Canada
Overseas: All except Anti-American
        Countries

Address/Contact

1. **Company name, address, telephone and fax numbers.**

Comment: All of the data published in this book were current at the time the completed questionnaire was received or upon subsequent verification by phone. Over a 12-month period between annual publications, 10–15% of the addresses and/or telephone numbers become obsolete for various reasons. If you are unable to contact a franchisor at the address/telephone number listed, please call Source Book Publications at (510) 839-5471 or fax us at (510) 839-2104 and we will provide you with the current address and telephone number.

2. **(800) 447-6256; (770) 984-2707 + 123.** In many cases, you may find that you cannot access the (800) number from your area. Do not conclude that the company has gone out of business. Simply call the local number.

Comment: An (800) number serves two important functions. The first is to provide an efficient, no-cost way for potential franchisees to contact the franchisor. Making the prospective franchisee foot the bill artificially limits the number of people who might otherwise make the initial contact. The second function is to demonstrate to existing franchisees that the franchisor is doing everything it can to efficiently respond to problems in the field as they occur. Many companies have a restricted (800) line for their franchisees that the general public cannot access. Since you will undoubtedly be talking with the franchisor's staff on a periodic basis, determine whether an (800) line is available to franchisees.

3. **Contact.** You should honor the wishes of the franchisor and address all initial correspondence to the contact listed. It would be counter-productive to try to reach the president directly if the designated contact is the director of franchising.

Comment: The president is the designated contact in approximately half of the company profiles in this book. The reason for this varies among franchisors. The president is the best spokesperson for his or her operation, and no doubt it flatters the franchisee to talk directly with the president, or perhaps there is no one else around. Regardless of the justification, it is important to determine if the operation is a one-man show in which the president does everything or if the president merely feels that having an open line to potential franchisees is the best way for him or her to sense the "pulse" of the company and the market. Convinced that the president can only do so many things well, I would want assurances that, by taking all incoming calls, he or she is not neglecting the day-to-day responsibilities of managing the business.

Description of Business

4. **Description of Business:** The questionnaire provides franchisors with adequate room to differentiate their franchise from the competition. In a minor number of cases, some editing was required.

Comment: In instances where franchisors show no initiative or imagination in describing their operations, you must decide whether this is symptomatic of the company or simply a reflection on the individual who responded to the questionnaire.

Background

5. **IFA.** There are two primary affinity groups associated with the franchising industry — the International Franchise Association (IFA) and the Canadian Franchise Association (CFA). Both the IFA and the CFA are described in Chapter One.

6. **Established: 1964.** Blimpie was founded in 1964, and, accordingly, has 40 years of experience in its primary business. It should be intuitively obvious that a firm that has been in existence for over 40 years has a greater likelihood of being around five years from now than a firm that was founded only last year.

7. **1st Franchised: 1977.** 1977 was the year that Blimpie's first franchised unit(s) were established.

Comment: Over ten years of continuous operation, both as an operator and as a franchisor, is compelling evidence that a firm has staying power. The number of years a franchisor has been in business is one of the key variables to consider in choosing a franchise. This is not to say that a new franchise should not receive your full attention. Every company has to start from scratch. Ultimately, a prospective franchisee has to be convinced that the franchise has 1) been in operation long enough, or 2) its key management personnel have adequate industry experience to have worked out the bugs normally associated with a new business. In most cases, this experience can only be gained through on-the-job training. Don't be the guinea pig that provides the franchisor with the experience it needs to develop a smoothly running operation.

8. **Franchised Units: 1,210.** As of 3/16/06, Blimpies had 1,210 franchisee-owned and operated units.

9. **Company-Owned Units: 10.** As of 3/16/06, Blimpie had 10 company-owned or operated unit.

Comment: A younger franchise should prove that its concept has worked successfully in several company-owned units before it markets its "system" to an inexperienced franchisee. Without company-owned prototype stores, the new franchisee may well end up being the "testing kitchen" for the franchise concept itself.

If a franchise concept is truly exceptional, why doesn't the franchisor commit some of its resources to take advantage of the investment opportunity? Clearly, a financial decision on the part of the franchisor, the absence of company-owned units should not be a negative in and of itself. This is especially true of proven franchises, which may have previously sold their company-owned operations to franchisees.

Try to determine if there is a noticeable trend in the percentage of company-owned units. If the franchisor is buying back units from franchisees, it may be doing so to preclude litigation. Some firms also "churn" their operating units with some regularity. If the sales pitch is compelling, but the follow-through is not competitive, a franchisor may sell a unit to a new franchisee, wait for him or her to fail, buy it back for $0.60 cents on the dollar, and then sell that same unit to the next unsuspecting franchisee. Each time the unit is resold, the franchisor collects a franchise fee, plus the negotiated discount from the previous franchisee.

Alternatively, an increasing or high percentage of company-owned units may well mean the company is convinced of the long-term profitability of such an approach. The key is to determine whether a franchisor is building new units from scratch or buying them from failing and/or unhappy franchisees.

10. **Total Units: 1,220.** As of 3/16/06, Blimpie had a total of 1,220 operating units.

Comment: Like a franchisor's longevity, its experience in operating multiple units offers considerable comfort. Those franchisors with over 15–25 operating units have proven that their system works and have probably encountered and overcome most of the problems that plague a new operation. Alternatively, the management of franchises with less than 15 operating units may have gained considerable industry experience before joining the current franchise. It is up to the franchisor to convince you that it is providing you with as risk-free an operation as possible. You don't want to be providing a company with its basic experience in the business.

11. **Distribution: US-1,210; CAN-0; O'seas-10.** As of 3/16/06, Blimpie had 1,210 operating units in the U.S., 0 in Canada and 10 Overseas.

12. **Distribution: North America: 50 States.** As of 3/16/06, Blimpie had operations in 50 states.

Comment: It should go without saying that the wider the geographic distribution, the greater the franchisor's level of success. For the most part, such distribution can only come from a large number of operating units.

If, however, the franchisor has operations in 15 states, but only 18 total operating units, it is unlikely that it can efficiently service these accounts because of geographic constraints. Other things being equal, a prospective franchisee would vastly prefer a franchisor with 15 units in New York to one with 15 units scattered throughout the U.S., Canada and overseas.

13. **Distribution: Density: FL, GA.** The franchisor was asked "what three states/provinces have the largest number of operating units." As of 3/16/06, Blimpie had the largest number of units in Florida and Georgia.

Comment: For smaller, regional franchises, geographic distribution could be a key variable in deciding whether to buy. If the franchisor has a concentration of units in your immediate geographic area, it is likely you will be well-served.

For those far removed geographically from the franchisor's current areas of operation, however, there can be problems. It is both time consuming and expensive to support a franchisee 2,000 miles away from company headquarters. To the extent that a franchisor can visit four franchisees in one area on one trip, there is no problem. If, however, your operation is the only one west of the Mississippi, you may not receive the on-site assistance you would like. Don't be a missionary who has to rely on his or her own devices to survive. Don't accept a franchisor's idle promises of support. If on-site assistance is important to your ultimate success, get assurances in writing that the necessary support will be forthcoming. Remember, you are buying into a system, and the availability of day-to-day support is one of the key ingredients of any successful franchise system.

14. **Projected New Units (12 Months): NR.** Blimpie did not provide a projected number of new units for the next 12 months.

Comment: In business, growth has become a highly visible symbol of success. Rapid growth is generally perceived as preferable to slower, more controlled growth. I maintain, however, that the opposite is frequently the case. For a company of Blimpie's size, adding 30 new units over a 12-month period is both reasonable and achievable. It is highly unlikely, however, that a new franchise with only five operating units can successfully attract, screen, train and bring multiple new units on-stream in a 12-month period. If it suggests that it can, or even wants to, be properly wary. You must be confident a company has the financial and management resources necessary to pull off such a Herculean feat. If management is already thin, concentrating on attracting new units will clearly diminish the time it can and should spend supporting you. It takes many months, if not years, to develop and train a second level of management. You don't want to depend upon new hires teaching you systems and procedures they themselves know little or nothing about.

15. **Qualifications: 4,3,2,2,2,5.** This question was posed to determine which specific evaluation criteria were important to the franchisor. The franchisor was asked the following: "In qualifying a potential franchisee, please rank the following criteria from Unimportant (1) to Very Important (5)." The responses should be self-explanatory:

Financial Net Worth (Rank from 1–5)
General Business Experience (Rank from 1–5)
Specific Industry Experience (Rank from 1–5)
Formal Education (Rank from 1–5)
Psychological Profile (Rank from 1–5)
Personal Interview(s) (Rank from 1–5)

16. **Registered** refers to the 16 states that require specific formal registration at the state level before the franchisor may offer franchises in that state. State registration and disclosure to the Federal Trade Commission are separate issues that are discussed in Chapter 1.

Capital Requirements/Rights

17. **Cash Investment: $25-100K.** On average, a Blimpie franchisee will have made a cash investment of $25,000–100,000 by the time he or she finally opens the initial operating unit.

Comment: It is important that you be realistic about the amount of cash you can comfortably invest in a business. Stretching beyond your means can have grave and far-reaching consequences. Assume that you will encounter periodic set-backs and that you will have to draw on your reserves. The demands of starting a new business are harsh enough without adding the uncertainties associated with inadequate working capital. Trust the franchisor's recommendations regarding the suggested minimum cash investment. If anything, there is an incentive for setting the recommended level of investment too low, rather than too high. The franchisor will want to qualify you to the extent that you have adequate financing. No legitimate franchisor wants you to invest if there is a chance that you might fail because of a shortage of funds.

Keep in mind that you will probably not achieve a positive cash flow before you've been in business more than six months. In your discussions with the franchisor, be absolutely certain that its calculations include an adequate working capital reserve.

18. **Total Investment: $75-250K.** On average, Blimpie franchisees will invest a total of $75,000-250,000, including both cash and debt, by the time the franchise opens its doors.

Comment: The total investment should be the cash investment noted above plus any debt that you will incur in starting up the new business. Debt could be a note to the franchisor for all or part of the franchise fee, an equipment lease, building and facilities leases, etc. Make sure that the total includes all of the obligations that you assume, especially any long-term lease obligations.

Be conservative in assessing what your real exposure is. If you are leasing highly specialized equipment or if you are leasing a single-purpose building, it is naive to think that you will recoup your investment if you have to sell or sub-lease those assets in a buyer's market. If there is any specialized equipment that may have been manufactured to the franchisor's specifications, determine if the franchisor has any form of buy-back provision.

19. **Minimum Net Worth: $100K.** In this case, Blimpie feels that a potential franchisee should have a minimum net worth of $100,000. Although net worth can be defined in vastly different ways, the franchisor's response should suggest a minimum level of equity that the prospective franchisee should possess. Net worth is the combination of both liquid and illiquid assets. Again, don't think that franchisor-determined guidelines somehow don't apply to you.

20. **Fees (Franchise): $10-18K.** Blimpie requires a front-end, one-time-only payment of $10,000–18,000 to grant a franchise for a single location. As noted in Chapter One, the franchise fee is a payment to reimburse the franchisor for the incurred costs of setting the franchisee up in business — from recruiting through training and manuals. The fee usually ranges from $15,000–30,000. It is a function of competitive franchise fees and the actual out-of-pocket costs incurred by the franchisor.

Depending upon the franchisee's particular circumstances and how well the franchisor thinks he or she might fit into the system, the franchisor may finance all or part of the franchise fee. (See Section 32 below to see if a franchisor provides any direct or indirect financial assistance.)

The franchise fee is one area in which the franchisor frequently provides either direct or indirect financial support.

Comment: Ideally, the franchisor should do no more than recover its costs on the initial franchise fee. Profits come later in the form of royalty fees, which are a function of the franchisee's sales. Whether the franchise fee is $5,000 or $35,000, the total should be carefully evaluated. What are competitive fees and are they financed? How much training will you actually receive? Are the fees reflective of the franchisor's expenses? If the fees appear to be non-competitive, address your concerns with the franchisor.

Realize that a $5,000 differential in the one-time franchise fee is a secondary consideration in the overall scheme of things. You are in the relationship for the long-term.

By the same token, don't get suckered in by an extremely low fee if there is any doubt about the franchisor's ability to follow through. Franchisors need to collect reasonable fees to cover their actual costs. If they don't recoup these costs, they cannot recruit and train new franchisees on whom your own future success partially depends.

21. **Fees (Royalty): 6%** means that six percent of gross sales (or other measure, as defined in the franchise agreement) must be periodically paid directly to the franchisor in the form of royalties. This on-going expense is your cost for being part of the larger franchise system and for all of the "back-office" support you receive. In a few cases, the amount of the royalty fee is fixed rather than variable. In others, the fee decreases as the volume of sales (or other measure) increases (i.e., 6% on the first $200,000 of sales, 5% on the next $100,000 and so on). In others, the fee is held at artificially low levels during the start-up phase of the franchisee's business, then increases once the franchisee is better able to afford it.

Comment: Royalty fees represent the mechanism by which the franchisor finally recoups the costs it has incurred in developing its business. It may take many years and many operating units before the franchisor is able to make a true operating profit.

Consider a typical franchisor who might have been in business for three years. With a staff of five, rent, travel, operating expenses, etc., assume it has annual operating costs of $300,000 (including reasonable owner's salaries). Assume also that there are 25 franchised units with average annual sales of $250,000. Each franchise is required to pay a 6% royalty fee. Total annual royalties under this scenario would total only $375,000. The franchisor is making a $75,000 profit. Then consider the personal risk the franchisor took in developing a new business and the initial years of negative cash flows. Alternatively, evaluate what it would cost you, as a sole proprietor, to provide the myriad services included in the royalty payment.

In assessing various alternative investments, the amount of the royalty percentage is a major on-going expense. Assuming average annual sales of $250,000 per annum over a 15 year period, the total royalties at 5% would be $187,500. At 6%, the cumulative fees would be $225,000. You have to be fully convinced that the $37,500 differential is justified. While this is clearly a meaningful number, what you are really evaluating is the quality of management and the competitive advantages of the goods and/or services offered by the franchisor.

22. **Fees (Advertising): 4%.** Most national or regional franchisors require their franchisees to contribute a certain percentage of their sales (or other measure, as determined in the franchise agreement) into a corporate advertising fund. These individual advertising fees are pooled to develop a corporate advertising/marketing effort that produces great economies of scale. The end result is a national or regional advertising program that promotes the franchisor's products and services. Depending upon the nature of the business, this percentage usually ranges from 2–6% and is in addition to the royalty fee.

Comment: One of the greatest advantages of a franchised system is its ability to promote, on a national or regional basis, its products and services. The promotions may be through television, radio, print medias or direct mail. The objective is name recognition and, over time, the assumption that the product and/or service has been "time-tested." An individual business owner could never justify the expense of mounting a major advertising program at the local level. For a smaller franchise that may not yet have an advertising program or fee, it is important to know when an advertising program will start, how it will be monitored and its expected cost.

23. **Earnings Claims Statement: No** means Blimpie does not provide an earnings claims statement to potential franchisees. Unfortunately, only 12–15% of franchisors provide an earnings claims statement in their Uniform Franchise Offering Circular (UFOC). The franchising industry's failure to require earnings claims statements does a serious disservice to the poten-

tial franchisee. See Chapter Two for comments on the earnings claims statement.

24. **Term of Contract (Years): 20/5.** Blimpie's initial franchise period runs for 20 years. The first renewal period runs for an additional five years. Assuming that the franchisee operates within the terms of the franchise agreement, he or she has 25 years within which to develop and, ultimately, sell the business.

Comment: The potential (discounted) value of any business (or investment) is the sum of the operating income that is generated each year plus its value upon liquidation. Given this truth, the length of the franchise agreement and any renewals are extremely important to the franchisee. It is essential that he or she has adequate time to develop the business to its full potential. At that time, he or she will have maximized the value of the business as an on-going concern. The value of the business to a potential buyer, however, is largely a function of how long the franchise agreement runs. If there are only two years remaining before the agreement expires, or if the terms of an extension(s) are vague, the business will be worth only a fraction of the value assigned to a business with 15 years to go. For the most part, the longer the agreement and the subsequent extension, the better. (The same logic applies to a lease. If your sales are largely a function of your location and traffic count, then it is important that you have options to extend the lease under known terms. Your lease should never be longer than the remaining term of your franchise agreement, however.)

Assuming the length of the agreement is acceptable, be clear under what circumstances renewals might not be granted. Similarly, know the circumstances under which a franchise agreement might be prematurely and unilaterally canceled by the franchisor. I strongly recommend you have an experienced lawyer review this section of the franchise agreement. It would be devastating if, after spending years developing your business, there were a loophole in the contract that allowed the franchisor to arbitrarily cancel the relationship.

25. **Avg. # of Employees: 4 FT, 8 PT.** The question was asked "Including the owner/operator, how many employees are recommended to properly staff the average franchised unit?" In Blimpie's case, four full-time employees and eight part-time employees are required.

Comment: Most entrepreneurs start a new business based on their intuitive feel that it will be "fun" and that their talents and experience will be put to good use. They will be doing what they enjoy and what they are good at. Times change. Your business prospers. The number of employees increases. You are spending an increasing percentage of your time taking care of personnel problems and less and less on the fun parts of the business. In Chapter One, the importance of conducting a realistic self-appraisal was stressed. If you found that you really are not good at managing people, or you don't have the patience to manage a large minimum wage staff, cut your losses before you are locked into doing just that.

26. **Passive Ownership: Discouraged.** Depending on the nature of the business, many franchisors are indifferent as to whether you manage the business directly or hire a full-time manager. Others are insistent that, at least for the initial franchise, the franchisee be a full-time owner/operator. Blimpie discourages franchisees from hiring full-time managers to run their outlets.

Comment: Unless you have a great deal of experience in the business you have chosen or in managing similar businesses, I feel strongly that you should initially commit your personal time and energies to make the system work. After you have developed a full understanding of the business and have competent, trusted staff members who can assume day-to-day operations, then consider delegating these responsibilities. Running the business through a manager can be fraught with peril unless you have mastered all aspects of the business and there are strong economic incentives and sufficient safeguards to ensure the manager will perform as desired.

27. **Conversions Encouraged: Yes.** This section pertains primarily to sole proprietorships or "mom and pop" operations. To the extent that there truly are centralized operating savings associated with the franchise, the most logical people to join a franchise system are sole practitioners who are working hard but only eking out a living. The implementation of proven systems and marketing clout could significantly reduce operating costs and increase profits.

Comment: The franchisor has the option of 1) actively encouraging such independent operators to become members of the franchise team, 2) seeking out franchisees with limited or no applied experience or 3) going after both groups. Concerned that it will be very difficult to break independent operators of the bad habits they have picked up over the years, many only choose course two. "They will continue to do things their way. They won't, or can't, accept corporate direction," they might say to themselves. Others are simply selective in the conversions they allow. In many cases, the franchise fee is reduced or eliminated for conversions.

28. **Area Development Agreements: Yes** means that Blimpie offers an area development agreement. Area development agreements are more fully described in Chapter One. Essentially, they allow an investor or investment group to develop an entire area or region. The schedule for development is clearly spelled out in the area development agreement. (Note: "Var." means varies and "Neg." means negotiable.)

Comment: Area development agreements represent an opportunity for the franchisor to choose a single franchisee or investment group to develop an entire area. The franchisee's qualifications should be strong and include proven business experience and the financial depth to pull it off. An area development agreement represents a great opportunity for an investor to tie up a large geographical area and develop a concept that may not have proven itself on a national basis. Keep in mind that this is a quantum leap from making an investment in a single franchise and is relevant only to those with development experience and deep pockets.

29. **Sub-Franchising Contracts: Yes.** Blimpie grants sub-franchising agreements. (See Chapter One for a more thorough explanation.) Like area development agreements, sub-franchising allows an investor or investment group to develop an entire area or region. The difference is that the sub-franchisor becomes a self-contained business, responsible for all relations with franchisees within its area, from initial training to on-going support. Franchisees pay their royalties to the sub-franchisor, who in turn pays a portion to the master franchisor.

Comment: Sub-franchising is used primarily by smaller franchisors who have a relatively easy concept and who are prepared to sell a portion of the future growth of their business to someone for some front-end cash and a percentage of the future royalties they receive from their franchisees.

30. **Expand in Territory: Yes.** Under conditions spelled out in the franchise agreement, Blimpie will allow its franchisees to expand within their exclusive territory.

Comment: Some franchisors define the franchisee's exclusive territory so tightly that there would never be room to open additional outlets within an area. Others provide a larger area in the hopes that the franchisee will do well and have the incentive to open additional units. There are clearly economic benefits to both parties from having franchisees with multiple units. There is no question that it is in your best interest to have the option to expand once you have proven to both yourself and the franchisor that you can manage the business successfully. Many would concur that the real profits in franchising come from managing multiple units rather than being locked into a single franchise in a single location. Additional fees may or may not be required with these additional units.

31. **Space Needs: 12,000 SF; FS, SF, SC, RM.** The average Blimpie's retail outlet will require 12,000 square feet in a Free-Standing (FS) building, Storefront (SF), Strip Center (SC) or Regional Mall (RM). Other types of leased space might be a Convenience Store (C-store) location, Executive Suite (ES), Home-Based (HB), Industrial Park (IP), Kiosk (KI), Office Building (OB), Power Center (PC), or Warehouse (WH).

Comment: Armed with the rough space requirements, you can better project your annual occupancy costs. It should be relatively easy to get comparable rental rates for the type of space required. As annual rent and related expenses can be as high as 15% of your annual sales, be as accurate as possible in your projections.

Franchisor Support and Training Provided

32. **Financial Assistance Provided: Yes (I)** notes that Blimpie is indirectly (I) involved in providing financial assistance. Indirect assistance might include making introductions to the franchisor's financial contacts, providing financial templates for preparing a business plan or actually assisting in the loan application process. In some cases, the franchisor becomes a co-signer on a financial obligation (equipment lease, space lease, etc.). Other franchisors are (D) directly involved in the process. In this case, the assistance may include a lease or loan made directly by the franchisor. Any loan would generally be secured by some form of collateral. A very common form of assistance is a note for all or part of the initial franchise fee. Yes (B) indicates that the franchisor provides both direct and indirect financial assistance. The level of assistance will generally depend upon the relative strengths of the franchisee.

Comment: The best of all possible worlds is one in which the franchisor has enough confidence in the business and in you to co-sign notes on the building and equipment leases and allow you to pay off the franchise fee over a specified period of time. Depending upon your qualifications, this could happen. Most likely, however, the franchisor will only give you some assistance in raising the necessary capital to start the business. Increasingly, franchisors are testing a franchisee's business acumen by letting him or her assume an increasing level of personal responsibility in securing financing. The objective is to find out early in the process how competent a franchisee really is.

33. **Site Selection Assistance: Yes** means that Blimpie will assist the franchisee in selecting a site location. While the phrase "location, location, location" may be hackneyed, its importance should not be discounted, especially when a business depends upon retail traffic counts and accessibility. If a business is home- or warehouse-based, assistance in this area is of negligible or minor importance.

Comment: Since you will be locked into a lease for a minimum of three, and probably five, years, optimal site selection is absolutely essential. Even if you were somehow able to sub-lease and extricate yourself from a bad lease or bad location, the franchise agreement may not allow you to move to another location. Accordingly, it is imperative that you get it right the first time.

If a franchisor is truly interested in your success, it should treat your choice of a site with the same care it would use in choosing a company-owned site. Keep in mind that many firms provide excellent demographic data on existing locations at a very reasonable cost.

34. **Lease Negotiations Assistance: Yes.** Once a site is selected, Blimpie will be actively involved in negotiating the terms of the lease.

Comment: Given the complexity of negotiating a lease, an increasing number of franchisors are taking an active role in lease negotiations. There are far too many trade-offs that must be considered — terms, percentage rents, tenant improvements, pass-throughs, kick-out clauses, etc. This responsibility is best left to the professionals. If the franchisor doesn't have the capacity to support you directly, enlist the help of a well-recommended broker. The penalties for signing a bad long-term lease are very severe.

35. **Co-operative Advertising: Yes.** This refers to the existence of a joint advertising program in which the franchisor and franchisees each contribute to promote the company's products and/or services (usually within the franchisee's specific territory).

Comment: Co-op advertising is a common and mutually-beneficial effort. By agreeing to split part of the advertising costs, whether for television,

51

radio or direct mail, the franchisor is not only supporting the franchisee, but guaranteeing itself royalties from the incremental sales. A franchisor that is not intimately involved with the advertising campaign — particularly when it is an important part of the business — may not be fully committed to your overall success.

36. Franchisee Assoc./Member: Yes/Yes. This response notes that the Blimpie system does include an active association made up of Blimpie franchisees and that the franchisor is also a member of the franchisee association.

Comment: The empowerment of franchisees has become a major rallying cry within the industry over the past three years. Various states have recently passed laws favoring franchisee rights, and the subject has been widely discussed in congressional staff hearings. Political groups even represent franchisee rights on a national basis. Similarly, the IFA is now actively courting franchisees to become active members. Whether they are equal members remains to be seen.

Franchisees have also significantly increased their clout with respect with the franchisor. If a franchise is to grow and be successful in the long term, it is critical that the franchisor and its franchisees mutually agree they are partners rather than adversaries.

37. Size of Corporate Staff: 100. Blimpie has 100 full-time employees on its staff to support its operating units.

Comment: There are no magic ratios that tell you whether the franchisor has enough staff to provide the proper level of support. It would appear, however, that Blimpie's staff of 100 is adequate to support 1,220 operating units. Less clear is whether a staff of three, including the company president and his wife, can adequately support 15 fledgling franchisees in the field.

Many younger franchises may be managed by a skeleton staff, assisted by outside consultants who perform various management functions during the start-up phase. From the perspective of the franchisee, it is essential that the franchisor have actual in-house franchising experience, and that the franchisee not be forced to rely on outside consultants to make the system work. Whereas a full-time, salaried employee will probably have the franchisee's objectives in mind, an outside consultant may easily not have the same priorities. Franchising is a unique form of business that requires specific skills and experience — skills and experience that are markedly different from those required to manage a non-franchised business. If you are thinking about establishing a long-term relationship with a firm just starting out in franchising, you should insist that the franchisor prove that it has an experienced, professional team on board and in place to provide the necessary levels of support to all concerned.

38. On-Going Support: B,C,D,E,F,G,H,I. Like initial training, the on-going support services provided by the franchisor are of paramount importance. Having a solid and responsive team behind you can certainly make your life much easier and allow you to concentrate your energies on other areas. As is noted below, the franchisors were asked to indicate their support for nine separate on-going services:

Service Provided	Included	At Add'l. in Fees	NA Cost
Central Data Processing	A	a	NA
Central Purchasing	B	b	NA
Field Operations Evaluation	C	c	NA
Field Training	D	d	NA
Initial Store Opening	E	e	NA
Inventory Control	F	f	NA
Franchisee Newsletter	G	g	NA
Regional or National Meetings	H	h	NA
800 Telephone Hotline	I	i	NA

If the franchisor provides the service at no additional cost to the franchisee (as indicated by letters A–I), a capital letter was used to indicate this. If the service is provided, but only at an additional cost, a lower case letter was used. If the franchisor responded with a NA, or failed to note an answer for a particular service, the corresponding letter was omitted from the data sheet.

39. Training: 80 Hours in Atlanta, GA; 120 Hours in Local Franchise.

Comment: Assuming that the underlying business concept is sound and competitive, adequate training and on-going support are among the most important determinants of your success as a franchisee. The initial training should be as lengthy and as "hands-on" as necessary to allow the franchisee to operate alone and with confidence. Obviously, every potential situation cannot be covered in any training program. But the franchisee should come away with a basic understanding of how the business operates and where to go to resolve problems when they come up. Depending on the business, there should be operating manuals, procedural manuals, company policies, training videos, (800) help-lines, etc. It may be helpful at the outset to establish how satisfied recent franchisees are with a company's training. I would also have a clear understanding about how often the company updates its manuals and training programs, the cost of sending additional employees through training, etc.

Remember, you are part of an organization that you are paying (in the form of a franchise fee and on-going royalties) to support you. Training is the first step. On-going support is the second step.

Specific Expansion Plans

40. **U.S.: All United States.** Blimpie is currently focusing its growth on the entire United States. Alternatively, the franchisor could have listed particular states or regions into which it wished to expand.

41. **Canada: All Canada.** Blimpie is currently seeking additional franchisees in Canada. Specific markets or provinces could have also been indicated.

42. **Overseas: Yes.** Blimpie is currently expanding overseas.

Comment: You will note that many smaller companies with less than 15 operating units suggest that they will concurrently expand throughout the U.S., Canada and internationally. In many cases, these are the same companies that foresee a 50+% growth rate in operating units over the next 12 months. The chances of this happening are negligible. As a prospective franchisee, you should be wary of any company that thinks it can expand throughout the world without a solid base of experience, staff and financial resources. Even if adequate financing is available, the demands on existing management will be extreme. New management cannot adequately fill the void until they are able to fully understand the system and absorb the corporate culture. If management's end objective is expansion for its own sake rather than by design, the existing franchisees will suffer.

Note: The statistics noted in the profiles preceding each company's analysis are the result of data provided by the franchisors themselves by way of a detailed questionnaire. Similarly, the data in the summary comparisons in the Introduction Chapter were taken from the company profile data. The figures used throughout each company's analysis, however, were generally taken from the UFOCs. In many cases, the UFOCs, which are only printed annually, contain information that is somewhat out of date. This is especially true with regard to the number of operating units and the current level of investment. A visit to our website at www.worldfranchising.com should provide current data.

೫೨

If you have not already done so, please invest some modest time to read Chapter 1 — 30 Minute Overview.

Recommended Reading

My strong sense is that every potential franchisee should be well-versed in the underlying fundamentals of the franchising industry before he or she commits to the way of life it involves. The better you understand the industry, the better prepared you will be to take maximum advantage of the relationship with your franchisor. There is no doubt that it will also place you in a better position to negotiate the franchise agreement — the conditions of which will dictate every facet of your life as a franchisee for the term of the agreement. The few extra dollars spent on educating yourself could well translate into tens of thousand of dollars to the bottom line in the years ahead.

In addition to general franchising publications, we have included several special interest books that relate to specific, but critical, parts of the startup and on-going management process— site selection, hiring and managing minimum wage employees, preparing accurate cash flow projections, developing comprehensive business and/or marketing plans, etc.

We have also attempted to make the purchasing process easier by allowing readers to purchase the books directly from Source Book Publications, either via our 800-line or our website at www.sourcebookpublications.com. All of the books are currently available in inventory and are generally sent the same day an order is received. A 15% discount is available on all orders over $100.00. See page **62** for an order form. Your complete satisfaction is 100% guaranteed on all books.

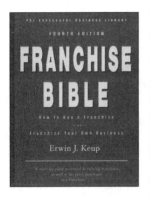

Franchise Bible: A Comprehensive Guide, 4th Edition, Keup, Oasis Press. 2000. 318 pp. $27.95.

This recently updated classic is equally useful for prospective franchisees and franchisors alike. The comprehensive guide and workbook explain in detail what the franchise system entails and the precise benefits it offers. The book features the new franchise laws that became effective January, 1995. To assist the prospective franchisee in rating a potential franchisor, Keup provides necessary checklists and forms. Also noted are the franchisor's contractual obligations to the franchisee and what the franchisee should expect from the franchisor in the way of services and support.

Tips & Traps When Buying a Franchise, Revised 2nd Edition, Tomzack, Source Book Publications. 1999. 236 pp. $19.95.

Many a novice franchisee is shocked to discover that the road to success in franchising is full of hidden costs, inflated revenue promises, reneged marketing support and worse. In this candid, hard-hitting book, Tomzack steers potential franchisees around the pitfalls and guides them in making a smart, lucrative purchase. Topics include: matching a franchise with personal finances and lifestyle, avoiding the five most common pitfalls, choosing a prime location, asking the right questions, etc.

Databases

Franchisor Database, Source Book Publications. (800) 841-0873 or (510) 839-5471.

Listing of over 2,800 active North American franchisors. 27 fields of information per company: full address, telephone/800/fax numbers, Internet address, email address, contact/title/salutation, president/title/salutation, # of franchised units, # of company-owned units, # total units, IFA/CFA Member, etc. 45 industry categories. Unlimited use.

Guaranteed deliverability — $0.50 rebate for any returned mailings. $1,200 for initial database, $150 per quarter for updates.

Directories

Bond's Franchise Guide — 2006 Edition, Bond/Hinh, Source Book Publications, 2006. 528 pp. $29.95.

This annual directory offers the prospective franchisee detailed profiles of over 1,000 franchises, as well as listings of franchise attorneys, consultants and service providers. The companies are divided into 45 distinct business categories for easy comparison. The data represents the most up-to-date, comprehensive and reliable information about this dynamic industry.

Minority Franchise Guide — 2006 Edition, Bond/Hinh, Source Book Publications, 2006. 336 pp. $19.95.

The only minority franchising directory! Contains detailed profiles and company logos of over 550 forward-looking franchisors that encourage and actively support the inclusion of minority franchisees. It also includes a listing of resources available to prospective minority franchisees.

Earnings Claims

"How Much Can I Make?", Bond/Kimmel, Source Book Publications. 2006. 368 pp. $29.95.

The single most important task for a prospective investor is to prepare a realistic cash flow statement that accurately reflects the economic potential of that business. *"How Much Can I Make?"* is an invaluable insider's guide that details historical sales, expense and/or profit data on actual franchise operations, **as provided by the franchisors themselves**. Whether you plan to buy a franchise or start your own business, these actual performances statistics will ensure that you have a realistic starting point in determining how much you can expect to make in a similar business. 116 current earnings claim statements, in their entirety, are included for the food-service, retail and service-based industries. Unfortunately, less than 20% of franchisors provide such projections/guidelines to prospective franchisees. *"How Much Can I Make?"* includes roughly half of the total universe of earnings claim statements available. The list of companies includes household names such as McDonald's and Baskin Robbins to newer, smaller franchises with only a few operating units. Any serious investor would be shortsighted not to take full advantage of this extraordinary resource.

International Franchising

International Herald Tribune International Franchise Guide, Bond/Thompson, Source Book Publications. 1999. 192 pp. $29.95.

This annual publication, sponsored by the International Herald Tribune, is the definitive guide to international franchising. It lists comprehensive, in-depth profiles of major franchisors who are committed to promote and support overseas expansion. Details specific geographic areas of desired expansion for each company, country by country — as well as the number of units in each foreign country as of the date of publication. Geared specifically to the needs and requirements of prospective international area developers, master franchisees and investors. Investors must be prepared to assume responsibility for the development of large geographic areas. Also listed are international franchise consultants, attorneys and service providers. Covers 32 distinct business categories.

Franchise Rankings

Bond's Top 50 Food-Service Franchises, Bond/Schiller, Source Book Publications, 2000. 288 pp. $19.95.

In response to the constantly asked question, *"What are the best franchises?"*, Bond's book focuses on the top 50 food-service franchises. Over 500 food-service systems were evaluated for inclusion. Companies were analyzed on the basis of historical performance, brand identification, market dynamics, franchisee satisfaction, the level of training and on-going support, financial stability, etc. Detailed four to five page profiles on each company, as well as key statistics and industry overview. All companies are proven performers and most have a national presence. Excellent starting point for someone focusing on the food-service industry.

Bond's Top 50 Retail Franchises, Bond/Schiller/Tong, Source Book Publications, 2001. 288 pp. $19.95.

In response to the constantly asked question, *"What are the best franchises?"*, Bond's book focuses on the top 50 retail franchises. Over 350 retail systems were evaluated for inclusion. Companies were analyzed on the basis of historical performance, brand identification, market dynamics, franchisee satisfaction, the level of training and on-going support, financial stability, etc. Detailed four to five page profiles on each company, as well as key statistics and industry overview. All companies are proven performers and most have a national presence. Excellent starting point for someone focusing on the retail industry.

Bond's Top 50 Service-Based Franchises, Bond/Schiller, Source Book Publications, 2001. 300 pp. $19.95.

In response to the constantly asked question, *"What are the best franchises?"*, Bond's book focuses on the top 50 service-based franchises. Over 400 service-based systems were evaluated for inclusion. Companies were analyzed on the basis of historical performance, brand identification, market dynamics, franchisee satisfaction, the level of training and on-going support, financial stability, etc. Detailed four to five page profiles on each company, as well as key statistics and industry overview. All companies are proven performers and most have a national presence. Excellent starting point for someone focusing on the service-based industry.

Site Selection

Location, Location, Location: How to Select the Best Site for Your Business, Salvaneschi, Oasis Press. 2000. 252 pp. $24.95.

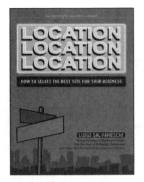

Whether you are searching for a new business site or relocating an existing business, you have the power to dramatically increase your profits by choosing the right location. For any business that depends on a customer's ability to find it, location is the most important ingredient for success. Learn how to: spot the essential characteristics of the best location; understand why and how people move from one point to another; analyze and learn from your competitor's business; and learn about the retail trading zone and how to use it to capture the most customers.

Other

The Economics of Franchising, Blair/Lafontaine, Cambridge University Press. 2005. 338 pp. $45.00.

The Economics of Franchising describes how and why franchising works. It also analyses the economic tensions that contribute to conflict in the franchisor-franchisee relationship. The treatment includes a great deal of empirical evidence on franchising, its importance in various segments of the economy, the terms of franchise contracts, and what we know about how all these have evolved over time, especially in the US market. The economic analysis of the franchisor-franchisee relationship begins with the observation that for franchisors, franchising is a contractual alternative to vertical integration. Subsequently, the tensions that arise between a franchisor and its franchisees, who in fact are owners of independent businesses, are examined in turn. In particular the authors discuss issues related to product quality control, tying arrangements, pricing, location and territories, advertising, and termination and renewals.

From Ice Cream to the Internet, Shane. 2005. 256 pp. $29.95.

Franchising can offer businesses a powerful new source of growth and improved financial performance. Now, Dr. Scott A. Shane helps businesses systematically asses the pros and cons of franchising, and offers proven best practices for building a successful system. *From Ice Cream to the Internet* focuses squarely on the strategic issues and challenges faced by franchisors. Shane answers key questions such as : What do the winners do differently? How does franchising affect your ability to compete with firms that don't? Shane then presents proven principles for every facet of franchising success: designing the system, recruiting, selecting, managing and supporting franchisees; establishing territories and pricing; managing expansion; and more.

The Franchise Bookstore
Order Form

Call (800) 841-0873 or (510) 839-5471; or FAX (510) 839-2104

Item #	Title	Price	Qty.	Total

Basic postage (1 Book)	**$7.00**
Each additional book add $4.00	
California tax @ 8.25% (if CA resident)	
Total due in U.S. dollars	
Deduct 15% if total due is over $100.00	
Net amount due in U.S. dollars	

Please include credit card number and expiration date for all charge card orders! Checks should be made payable to Source Book Publications. All prices are in U.S. dollars.

Mailing Information: All books shipped by USPS Priority Mail (2nd Day Air). Please print clearly and include your phone number in case we need to contact you. Postage and handling rates are for shipping within the U.S. Please call for international rates.

☐ **Check enclosed or**

Charge my:

☐ American Express   ☐ MasterCard   ☐ VISA

Card #:_____

Expiration Date:_____

Signature:_____

Name:_____   Title:_____

Company:_____   Telephone No.: ( )_____

Address:_____   State/Prov.:_____ Zip:_____

City: _____

Special Offer — Save 15%

*If your total order above exceeds $100.00,
deduct 15% from your bill.*

Please send order to:
Source Book Publications
1814 Franklin St., Ste. 815, Oakland, CA 94612
Satisfaction Guaranteed. If not fully satisfied,
return for a prompt, 100% refund.

Food Service 4

Auntie Anne's Hand-Rolled Soft Pretzels

Hand-Rolled Soft Pretzels

160-A, Rt. 41
Gap, PA 17527
Tel: (717) 442-4766
Fax: (717) 442-4139
E-Mail: lindae@auntieannesinc.com
Web Site: www.auntieannes.com
Ms. Linda Engels, Franchise Support Rep.

Our motto is: To serve a fresh, hot, golden-brown pretzel with friendly, courteous customer service in a sparkling clean store.

BACKGROUND: IFA MEMBER
Established: 1988; 1st Franchised: 1989
Franchised Units: 825
Company-Owned Units: 36
Total Units: 861
Dist.: US-706; CAN-0; O'seas-155
  North America: 44 States
  Density: 75 in PA, 53 in CA, 46 in NY
Projected New Units (12 Months): 50
Qualifications: 4, 2, 2, 2, 3, 5
Registered: All States

FINANCIAL/TERMS:
Cash Investment: $192.6-382.5K
Total Investment: $192.6-382.5K
Minimum Net Worth: $350K
Fees: Franchise — $30K
  Royalty — 7%; Ad. — 1%
Earnings Claim Statement: No
Term of Contract (Years): 10/10
Avg. # Of Employees: 4 FT, 4 PT
Passive Ownership: Allowed
Encourage Conversions: NA
Area Develop. Agreements: No
Sub-Franchising Contracts: No
Expand In Territory: No
Space Needs: 400-600 SF; FS

SUPPORT & TRAINING PROVIDED:
Financial Assistance Provided: Yes(I)
Site Selection Assistance: Yes
Lease Negotiation Assistance: Yes
Co-Operative Advertising: Yes
Franchisee Assoc./Member: Yes/Yes
Size Of Corporate Staff: 150
On-Going Support: B,C,D,E,G,H,I
Training: 2 Weeks Gap, PA.

SPECIFIC EXPANSION PLANS:
US: All United States
Canada: All Canada
Overseas: All Countries

All Auntie Anne's Hand-Rolled Soft Pretzels stores produce, from dough mixing to baking, their famous fresh, hot, golden brown, hand-rolled pretzels right in the store. A classic blue-and-white checkered design and the prominent use of the color white creates a clean and bright atmosphere that welcomes customers. The smell of baking Auntie Anne's pretzels draws customers and entertains them with the sight of employees rolling and twisting pretzel dough by hand.

A variety of pretzels are offered, including Original, Whole Wheat, Garlic, Cinnamon Sugar, Sour Cream and Onion, Sesame, Almond, Glazin' Raisin, Parmesan Herb, Maple Crumb and Jalapeno. Six of these pretzels have five grams of fat or less, perfect for the health-conscious consumer. Dipping sauces such as Cheese, Hot Salsa Cheese are Chocolate are also offered on the side, providing the perfect complement to the pretzel.

After 15 years in business, there are more than 800 franchises operating under the multiple brands owned by Auntie Anne's, with locations in 44 states and 11 international territories. An Auntie Anne's franchise is available as an in-line single unit, dual unit with other brands and a kiosk single unit.

Operating Units	12/31/2002	12/31/2003	12/31/2004
Franchised	533	568	593
% Change	--	6.6%	4.4%
Company-Owned	23	26	23
% Change	--	13.0%	-11.5%
Total	556	594	616
% Change	--	6.8%	3.7%
Franchised as % of Total	95.86%	95.62%	96.27%

Investment Required
The fee for an Auntie Anne's franchise is $30,000.

Auntie Anne's provides the following range of investments required to

open your initial franchise. The range assumes that all items are paid for in cash. To the extent that you choose to finance any of these expense items, your front-end investment could be substantially reduced.

Item	Established Low Range	Established High Range
Franchise Fee	$30,000	$30,000
Business Permits and Licenses	$100	$500
Equipment	$40,000	$64,000
Grand Opening Advertising	$500	$2,500
Insurance	$400	$2,500
Inventory	$3,300	$4,000
Lease, Utility, Deposits	$4,000	$7,000
Leasehold Improvements, Furniture, Fixtures, Signs	$96,500	$205,000
Professional Fees	$2,000	$10,000
Training	$750	$6,000
Additional Funds (for 3 months)	$15,000	$51,000
Total Investment	$192,550	$382,500

On-Going Expenses
Auntie Anne's franchisees pay a continuing services and royalty fee equaling 7% of gross sales and an advertising and marketing fund fee equaling 1% of gross sales.

What You Get—Training and Support
Auntie Anne's passionately adheres to a three-pronged philosophy in all of its concepts: Provide premium products and friendly, courteous service in a sparkling clean store. New franchisees are given three days of training in the classroom and two days in the store, along with supplementary training. Up to seven days of on-site training is provided after the store is opened.

An experienced staff provides assistance in site selection, lease negotiation, store layout and design. Auntie Anne's maintains advantageous relationships with developers and facility management firms throughout the world. In addition, a network of corporate and regional employees provides support in operations, general business issues and marketing in the form of site visits and constant communication.

Territory
Auntie Anne's does not grant exclusive territories.

Baskin Robbins

130 Royall St.
Canton, MA 02021
Tel: (781) 737-3842
Fax: (781) 737-4842
E-Mail: james.franks@dunkinbrands.com
Web Site: www.dunkin-baskin.com
Mr. James Franks, Director of Franchising

BASKIN-ROBBINS develops, operates and franchises retail stores that sell ice cream, frozen yogurt and other approved services. In some markets, BASKIN-ROBBINS, together with TOGO'S and/or DUNKIN' DONUTS, offers multiple brand combinations of the three brands. TOGO'S, BASKIN-ROBBINS and DUNKIN' DONUTS are all subsidiaries of Dunkin' Brands, Inc.

BACKGROUND: IFA MEMBER
Established: 1946; 1st Franchised: 1948
Franchised Units: 4,700
Company-Owned Units: 4
Total Units: 4,704
Dist.: US-2,490; CAN-620; O'seas-1,594
North America: 41 States
Density: 554 in CA, 195 in IL, 181 NY
Projected New Units (12 Months): 27
Qualifications: , , , , ,

Registered: All States

FINANCIAL/TERMS:
Cash Investment: $145.8-527.8K
Total Investment: $145.7-527.8K
Minimum Net Worth: $400K/Unit
Fees: Franchise — $40K
  Royalty — 5-5.9%; Ad. — 5%
Earnings Claim Statement: Yes
Term of Contract (Years): 20
Avg. # Of Employees: NA
Passive Ownership: Allowed
Encourage Conversions: NR
Area Develop. Agreements: Yes/3-5
Sub-Franchising Contracts: No
Expand In Territory: Yes
Space Needs: NR SF; FS, SF, SC, RM

SUPPORT & TRAINING PROVIDED:
Financial Assistance Provided: Yes(I)
Lease Negotiation Assistance: Yes
Co-Operative Advertising: Yes
Franchisee Assoc./Member: Yes/No
Size Of Corporate Staff: NA
On-Going Support: B,C,D,G,H,I
Training: 51 Days in Randolph, MA; 3.5 Days at another Location.

SPECIFIC EXPANSION PLANS:
US: All Regions
Canada: All Canada
Overseas: All Countries

Baskin-Robbins is one of the top ice cream chains, with 5,000 stores worldwide. Since its opening in 1946, customers have delighted in its library of flavors (approaching 1,000 distinctive tastes) and extensive range of offerings, from traditional treats like ice cream cones, cakes and sundaes to newer innovations like shakes and its signature Blasts.

Baskin-Robbins proudly serves more than 3.7 million people every week in the United States alone. It is part of the Dunkin' Brands family, which also includes Dunkin' Donuts and Togo's. Each brand has its own unique appeal, meaning that brands can combine forces – uniting two or three of the brands in a single store using a complementary daypart strategy – to expand your customer base.

Operating Units	8/31/2002	8/30/2003	8/28/2004
Franchised	1,257	1,177	1,140
% Change	--	-6.4%	-3.1%
Company-Owned	0	0	0
% Change	--	0.0%	0.0%
Total	1,257	1,177	1,140
% Change	--	-6.4%	-3.1%
Franchised as % of Total	100.00%	100.00%	100.00%

Investment Required
The fee for a Baskin-Robbins franchise is $30,000.

Baskin-Robbins provides the following range of investments required to open your initial franchise. The range assumes that all items are paid for in cash. To the extent that you choose to finance any of these expense items, your front-end investment could be substantially reduced.

Item	Established Low Range	Established High Range
Franchise Fee	$30,000	$30,000

Advertising	$3,000	$3,000
Licenses, Permits, Fees, Deposits	$3,500	$5,500
Opening Costs	$14,900	$45,100
Equipment, Fixtures, Signs, Uniforms	$40,400	$149,200
Insurance	$4,500	$15,000
Inventory	$4,000	$5,500
Real Estate	$10,000	$160,000
Training Expenses	$1,000	$20,500
Additional Funds (for 3 months)	$30,900	$77,300
Total Investment	$142,200	$511,100

On-Going Expenses

Baskin-Robbins franchisees pay on-going franchise fees equal to 5 to 5.9% of gross sales and continuing advertising fees equal to 5% of gross sales.

What You Get—Training and Support

Dunkin' Brands has a wealth of knowledge available to help franchisees succeed, a result of more than 143 years of total franchising experience. The extensive system for support has over 1,100 corporate employees to support franchisees around the world.

Dunkin' Brands offers comprehensive training, as well as operating manuals, that includes techniques, procedures, recommendations and guidelines. Continual support is provided with marketing, operational improvements, equipment procurement and employee training, and the Dunkin' Brands Market Optimization Model assists in locating the markets with the largest potential for brand growth.

Territory

Baskin-Robbins does not grant exclusive territories.

Big Apple Bagels

500 Lake Cook Rd., # 475
Deerfield, IL 60015
Tel: (800) 251-6101 (847) 948-7520
Fax: (847) 405-8140
E-Mail: tcervini@babcorp.com
Web Site: www.babcorp.com
Mr. Anthony S. Cervini, Director of Development

Bakery-café featuring three brands, fresh-from-scratch Big Apple Bagels and My Favorite Muffin, and freshly roasted Brewster's specialty coffee. Our product offering covers many day parts with a delicious assortment of made-to-order gourmet sandwiches, salads, soups, espresso beverages, and fruit smoothies. Franchisees can develop beyond their stores with corporate catering and gift basket opportunities, as well as wholesaling opportunities within their market area.

BACKGROUND: IFA MEMBER
Established: 1992; 1st Franchised: 1993
Franchised Units: 121
Company-Owned Units 1
Total Units: 122
Dist.: US-121; CAN-0; O'seas-1
North America: 21 States
Density: 39 in MI, 20 in WI, 10 in IL

Projected New Units (12 Months): 10
Qualifications: 3, 4, 3, 3, 3, 5
Registered: All States

FINANCIAL/TERMS:
Cash Investment: $60K
Total Investment: $239-368K
Minimum Net Worth: $250K
Fees: Franchise — $25K
 Royalty — 5%; Ad. — 1%
Earnings Claim Statement: No
Term of Contract (Years): 10/10
Avg. # Of Employees: 3 FT, 11 PT
Passive Ownership: Allowed
Encourage Conversions: Yes
Area Develop. Agreements: Yes/Varies
Sub-Franchising Contracts: No
Expand In Territory: Yes
Space Needs: 1,500-1,800 SF; SC

SUPPORT & TRAINING PROVIDED:
Financial Assistance Provided: No
Site Selection Assistance: Yes
Lease Negotiation Assistance: Yes
Co-Operative Advertising: No
Franchisee Assoc./Member: No
Size Of Corporate Staff: 20
On-Going Support: C,D,E,F,G,H,I
Training: 2 Weeks Milwaukee, WI; 5 Days Store Location Prior to Opening.

SPECIFIC EXPANSION PLANS:
US: All United States
Canada: All Canada
Overseas: All Countries

Big Apple Bagels stores feature a menu with unlimited appeal for all kinds of customers at any time of the day. Stores offer not only their exclusive brand of freshly baked bagels, but also muffins by My Favorite Muffin, gourmet and specialty sandwiches, salads, breakfast sandwiches, specialty drinks and Brewster's brewed coffees. Bagels can be accompanied with creamy cheese spreads or turned into a deli sandwich.

Every store has the advantage of being three businesses combined into one by functioning as a retail center, a production facility where bagels are freshly baked from scratch and a wholesale distributorship that sells products in bulk to local businesses and organizations.

Operating Units	11/30/2003	11/30/2004	11/30/2005
Franchised	165	163	145
% Change	--	-1.2%	-11%
Company-Owned	2	2	2
% Change	--	0.0%	0.0%
Total	167	165	147
% Change	--	-1.2%	-0.9%
Franchised as % of Total	98.80%	98.79%	98.64%

Investment Required

The fee for a Big Apple Bagels franchise varies by store type. Fees are as follows: $25,000 for a production store, $15,000 for a satellite store, $10,000 for a kiosk and $5,000 for a cart.

Big Apple Bagels provides the following range of investments required to open your initial franchise. The range assumes that all items are paid for in cash. To the extent that you choose to finance any of these expense items, your front-end investment could be substantially reduced. The following quotes apply to the opening of a production store.

Item	Established Low Range	Established High Range
Franchise Fee	$25,000	$25,000
Franchise Fee Deposit	$10,000	$10,000
Training	$1,600	$3,200
Optional Equipment	$0	$10,000
Deposits, Rent, Prepaid Expenses	$6,500	$15,000

Furniture, Fixtures, Equipment, Signs	$85,000	$120,000
Insurance	$5,200	$7,200
Leasehold Improvements	$85,000	$145,000
Opening Inventory, Supplies, Grand Opening	$10,000	$13,000
Professional Fees	$2,500	$7,000
Additional Funds (for 3 months)	$7,500	$22,100
Total Investment	$228,300	$377,500

On-Going Expenses

Big Apple Bagels franchisees pay a royalty fee equaling 5% of gross revenues, a marketing fund fee equaling 2% of gross revenues and local advertising fees equaling 2% of gross revenues.

What You Get—Training and Support

Support prior to opening includes assistance with site selection, store design and layout, purchasing coordination and a marketing campaign for the grand opening. The training program for franchisees offers instruction in both in-store and classroom training, marketing techniques, employee management, financial aspects of the business and operational training on-site before the franchisee's store has opened.

Big Apple Bagels offers continual marketing and promotional support by providing ad slicks that can be used directly in local media, point-of-purchase materials and year-round marketing strategies. Online support includes an e-mail program, which keeps franchisees up-to-date with the latest news and gives them the opportunity to submit feedback, and a secure online resource center with downloads and online sales reporting. Big Apple Bagels has also researched and negotiated the fairest prices for quality products from reliable companies to supply its franchisees.

Territory

Big Apple Bagels does not grant exclusive territories.

Blimpie

7730 E. Greenway Rd., # 104
Scottsdale, AZ 85260
Tel: (770) 984-2707 + 123
Fax: (770) 933-6109
E-Mail: jwcampbell@kahalacorp.com
Web Site: www.blimpie.com
Mr. John W. Campbell, VP Global Franchising

International submarine sandwich chain, serving fresh-sliced, high-quality meats and cheeses on fresh-baked bread. Also offering an assortment of fresh-made salads and other quality products.

BACKGROUND: IFA MEMBER
Established: 1964;   1st Franchised: 1977
Franchised Units: 1,210
Company-Owned Units   10
Total Units: 1,220
Dist.:   US-1,210; CAN-0; O'seas-10
 North America: 50 States
 Density: 209 in FL, 193 in GA
Projected New Units (12 Months):   NR
Qualifications: 4, 3, 2, 2, 2, 5
Registered: CA,FL,HI,IL,IN,MI,MN,NY,ND,OR,RI
 ,SD,WA,WI

FINANCIAL/TERMS:
Cash Investment:	$25-100K
Total Investment:	$75-250K
Minimum Net Worth:	$100K
Fees: Franchise —	$10-18K
Royalty — 6%;	Ad. — 4%
Earnings Claim Statement:	No
Term of Contract (Years):	20/5
Avg. # Of Employees:	4 FT, 8 PT
Passive Ownership:	Discouraged
Encourage Conversions:	Yes
Area Develop. Agreements:	Yes
Sub-Franchising Contracts:	Yes
Expand In Territory:	Yes
Space Needs: 1,200 SF; FS, SF, SC, RM	

SUPPORT & TRAINING PROVIDED:
Financial Assistance Provided:	Yes(I)
Site Selection Assistance:	Yes
Lease Negotiation Assistance:	Yes
Co-Operative Advertising:	Yes
Franchisee Assoc./Member:	Yes/Yes
Size Of Corporate Staff:	100+
On-Going Support:	B,C,D,E,F,G,H,I
Training: 80 Hours in Atlanta, GA; 120 Hours in Local Franchise.	

SPECIFIC EXPANSION PLANS:
US:	All United States
Canada:	All Canada
Overseas:	All Countries

With over forty years of experience in selling submarine style sandwiches with the highest quality meats, cheeses, and toppings on freshly baked breads, Blimpie has thrived due to its flexible and popular concept. Traditional restaurants can be found in free-standing buildings, strip centers and shopping malls. Blimpie also reaches a wide group of customers through its placement in non-traditional locations, including convenience stores, gas-station food marts, universities, hospitals, stadiums, kiosks and vending machines.

Blimpie is dedicated to creating a "consistent, quality experience for every customer." Their most recent innovation is a program called "The Next

Great Step," which improves each restaurant's merchandising, décor and menu variety.

Operating Units	6/30/2002	6/30/2003	6/30/2004
Franchised	1,871	1,647	1,410
% Change	--	-12.0%	-14.4%
Company-Owned	0	0	6
% Change	--	0.0%	N/A
Total	1,871	1,647	1,416
% Change	--	-12.0%	-14.0%
Franchised as % of Total	100.00%	100.00%	99.58%

Investment Required
The fee for a Blimpie franchise is $18,000 for a traditional restaurant and $10,000 for a non-traditional restaurant.

Blimpie provides the following range of investments required to open your initial franchise. The range assumes that all items are paid for in cash. To the extent that you choose to finance any of these expense items, your front-end investment could be substantially reduced.

Item	Established Low Range	Established High Range
Franchise Fee	$10,000	$18,000
Construction Costs	$50,000	$110,000
Equipment, Fixtures, Signs	$35,000	$80,000
Insurance	$3,850	$9,300
Grand Opening/First Year Operations Program	$3,000	$3,000
Inventory	$5,000	$10,000
Miscellaneous	$5,000	$9,000
Rental Fees/Deposits	$3,400	$16,000

Training Expenses	$950	$2,500
Additional Funds (for 3 months)	$15,000	$30,000
Total Investment	$131,200	$287,800

On-Going Expenses

Blimpie franchisees pay royalties equal to 6% of gross revenue, advertising fees equal to 4% of gross revenue, an initial program fee of $40 per week for the first 50 weeks of operation and financial services/administration fees of $300 to $500 per month.

What You Get—Training and Support

The Blimpie training program begins with 80 hours of direct experience in a local Blimpie restaurant, followed by two weeks of formal instruction at Blimpie University and concluding with 40 additional on-site hours at an additional Blimpie restaurant. Blimpie University teaches our franchisees valuable marketing, accounting, personnel management, cost management and customer relations skills.

A Blimpie representative will be on hand to address all business-related issues. Franchisees also receive continuing support from an array of materials to assist them in operations, such as quarterly newsletters, "how to" operating manuals and computer-based management systems. In addition, Blimpie provides lease negotiation assistance, national purchasing power and marketing programs that operate at the national, regional and local levels.

Territory

Blimpie does not grant exclusive territories.

Burger King Corporation

5505 Blue Lagoon Dr.
Miami, FL 33126
Tel: (866) KING-BKC
Fax: (305) 378-7721
E-Mail: franchiseinquiry@whopper.com
Web Site: www.burgerking.com
Franchise Development, Franchisor

Our Vision: We proudly serve the best burgers in the business, plus a variety of real, authentic foods - all freshly prepared - just the way you want it! BURG-ER KING ® Corporation operates more than 11,000 restaurants in all 50 states and in 60 countries around the world. 90% of the BURGER KING ® restaurants are owned and operated by independent franchisees, many of them family-owned operations that have been in business for decades.

BACKGROUND: IFA MEMBER
Established: 1954;
1st Franchised: 1961
Franchised Units: 9,913
Company-Owned Units 1,228
Total Units: 11,141
Dist.: US-7,134; CAN-500; O'seas-3,507
North America: 50 States, 9 Provinces
Density: NR

Projected New Units (12 Months): NR
Qualifications: , , , , ,
Registered: All States and AB

FINANCIAL/TERMS:
Cash Investment: $Varies/UFOC
Total Investment: $Varies/UFOC
Minimum Net Worth: $1.5MM
Fees: Franchise — $50K
  Royalty — 4.5%; Ad. — 4%
Earnings Claim Statement: Yes
Term of Contract (Years): 20
Avg. # Of Employees: 15 FT, 35 PT
Passive Ownership: Allowed
Encourage Conversions: Yes
Area Develop. Agreements: No
Sub-Franchising Contracts: No
Expand In Territory: Yes
Space Needs: 3,600 SF; FS, SF, RM

SUPPORT & TRAINING PROVIDED:
Financial Assistance Provided: No
Site Selection Assistance: Yes
Lease Negotiation Assistance: Yes
Co-Operative Advertising: No
Franchisee Assoc./Member: Yes/Yes
Size Of Corporate Staff: 928
On-Going Support: B,C,D,E,F,H
Training: 400 Hours in Restaurant; 700 Hours.

SPECIFIC EXPANSION PLANS:
US: All United States
Canada: All Canada
Overseas: All Countries

Since 1954, Burger King Corporation has helped shape the fast-food industry by empowering guests to make their own dining decisions. BURGER KING® prides itself on providing guests with customized selections of quality food, served hot and fresh at a reasonable price and in a friendly environment—as embodied by their signature HAVE IT YOUR WAY® campaign. Menu offerings include well-known products like the WHOPPER® sandwich, as well as a complete line of breakfast items, salads, BK VEGGIE® Burger and desserts. Newer products, such as the premium Angus Steak Burger, BK™ Chicken Fries, the TENDERCRISP®

75

and TENDERGRILL™ Chicken Sandwiches and BK JOE® coffee, have
enabled BURGER KING restaurants to customize guests' orders and
appeal to a broader customer base.

With more than 11,000 restaurants worldwide in more than 60 countries,
the BURGER KING® brand is one of the world's most widely recognized
consumer brands.

Operating Units	6/30/2003	6/30/2004	6/30/2005
Franchised	7,278	6,980	6,693
% Change	--	-4.1%	-4.1%
Company-Owned	611	642	689
% Change	--	5.1%	7.3%
Total	7,889	7,622	7,382
% Change	--	-3.4%	-3.1%
Franchised as % of Total	92.26%	91.58%	90.67%

Investment Required
The fee for a Burger King franchise is $50,000.

Burger King provides the following range of investments required to open
your initial franchise. The range assumes that all items are paid for in cash.
To the extent that you choose to finance any of these expense items, your
front-end investment could be substantially reduced.

Burger King offers a variety of restaurant facility configurations that vary
in initial investment. The following set of figures is for a free-standing
ROC 40/60 facility that seats approximately 40-60 and sits on a half acre
of land.

Item	Established Low Range	Established High Range
Franchise Fee	$50,000	$50,000

Business Licenses, Utility Deposits, Lease Deposits and Payments	$10,000	$20,000
Cash and Inventory Control System	$35,000	$50,000
Décor Package	$20,000	$40,000
Equipment	$150,000	$200,000
Insurance	$14,000	$22,000
Opening Inventory	$6,000	$8,000
Playground Equipment	$135,000	$245,000
Real Estate/Building/ Landscaping/ Improvement Fees	$760,000	$1,530,000
Signage & Drive-Thru	$30,000	$50,000
Training Expenses/Pre-Opening Wages	$52,000	$81,000
Additional Funds	$45,000	$90,000
Total Investment	$1,172,000	$2,141,000

On-Going Expenses

Burger King franchisees pay a royalty fee equal to 4.5% of monthly gross revenues and advertising fees equal to 4% of monthly gross revenues.

What You Get—Training and Support

A trained restaurant team is critical to any new restaurant's operational success. Before any new restaurant can open, all managers have to be certified. Your Field Training Specialist can assist you in developing your plan to meet this training requirement. Your Franchise Business Leader is your primary contact who will assist you in developing your restaurant opening plan.

Territory

Burger King Corporation does not grant exclusive territories.

Carl's Jr.

Carl's Jr.

6307 Carpinteria Ave., # A
Carpinteria, CA 93013
Tel: (866) 253-7655 (805) 745-7842
Fax: (714) 780-6320
E-Mail: chopkins@ckr.com
Web Site: www.carlsjr.com
Mr. Craig Hopkins, Director Franchise Sales

CARL'S JR. restaurants are located predominantly in the Western United States and have long been known as the place to go for premium quality, juicy and delicious charbroiled burgers. CARL'S JR. restaurants offer superior food quality, a diverse menu focused on burgers, premium dining selections at reasonable prices and attentive customer service to create a quality dining experience for its customers.

BACKGROUND:	IFA MEMBER
Established: 1979;	1st Franchised: 1984
Franchised Units:	580
Company-Owned Units	426
Total Units:	1,006
Dist.:	US-1,006; CAN-0; O'seas-0
North America:	NR
Density:	NR

Projected New Units (12 Months): NR
Qualifications: 4, 4, 4, 2, 2, 5
Registered: CA,OR,WA

FINANCIAL/TERMS:
Cash Investment:	$300K
Total Investment:	$913K-1.354MM
Minimum Net Worth:	$1MM
Fees: Franchise —	$35K
Royalty — 4%;	Ad. — 5.25%
Earnings Claim Statement:	No
Term of Contract (Years):	20
Avg. # Of Employees:	12 FT, 4 PT
Passive Ownership:	Not Allowed
Encourage Conversions:	Yes
Area Develop. Agreements:	Yes/Varies
Sub-Franchising Contracts:	No
Expand In Territory:	No
Space Needs: NR SF; NR	

SUPPORT & TRAINING PROVIDED:
Financial Assistance Provided:	No
Site Selection Assistance:	No
Lease Negotiation Assistance:	No
Co-Operative Advertising:	Yes
Franchisee Assoc./Member:	No
Size Of Corporate Staff:	NR
On-Going Support:	B,C,D,E,G,H,I
Training: 12 Weeks.	

SPECIFIC EXPANSION PLANS:
US:	All United States
Canada:	All Canada
Overseas:	All Countries

Carl's Jr. is widely known for bringing sit-down restaurant quality burgers to fast-food customers, such as the Six Dollar Burger Line, which goes with 100% Angus beef and all the fixings. Breakfast woes can be conquered by The Breakfast Burger—a dinner plate breakfast on a bun. Other favorites includes charbroiled and crispy chicken sandwiches and, for those watching their waistline, entrée salads and low-carb selections.

Carl's Jr. was the first in the industry to offer cushioned seats, carpeted dining rooms, music and partial dining-room service, combining the best features of casual dining with the convenience and affordability of fast food. Carl's Jr. now offers dual-branding with the Green Burrito, a Mexican quick-service concept, so franchisees may increase menu variety and widen customer appeal.

Operating Units	1/27/2003	1/26/2004	1/31/2005
Franchised	547	580	586
% Change	--	6.0%	1.0%
Company-Owned	440	426	428
% Change	--	-3.2%	0.5%
Total	987	1,006	1,014
% Change	--	1.9%	0.8%
Franchised as % of Total	55.42%	57.65%	57.79%

Investment Required
The fee for a Carl's Jr. franchise is $35,000.

Carl's Jr. provides the following range of investments required to open your initial franchise. The range assumes that all items are paid for in cash. To the extent that you choose to finance any of these expense items, your front-end investment could be substantially reduced.

Item	Established Low Range	Established High Range
Franchise Fee	$10,000	$35,000
Building/Site Improvements	$450,000	$650,000
Equipment	$240,000	$300,000
Initial Training	Variable	Variable
Point of Sale System	$20,000	$40,000
Pre-Opening Costs	$23,500	$31,700
Signage	$15,000	$90,000

Additional Funds (for 3 months)	$162,000	$220,000
Total Investment	$920,500	$1,366,700

On-Going Expenses
Carl's Jr. franchisees pay a royalty fee equal to up to 4% of gross sales and an advertising fee equal to 5.25% of gross sales.

What You Get—Training and Support
Franchisee training takes 12 weeks to complete, and includes in-restaurant training at an actual Carl's Jr. location and classroom instruction at designated training facilities. Instruction is provided by experienced restaurant managers, and subjects include leadership, managing fundamentals and managing business operations.

Franchisees also receive site-selection assistance and marketing support via print, radio and television advertisements.

Territory
Carl's Jr. grants exclusive territories on a limited basis.

Carvel Corporation

200 Glenridge Point Pkwy., # 200
Atlanta, GA 30342-1450
Tel: (800) 227-8353 (404) 255-3250
Fax: (404) 255-4978
E-Mail: ghill@focusbrands.com
Web Site: www.carvel.com
Mr. Geoff Hill, SVP Franchise Sales/Development

The nation's first retail ice cream franchise, CARVEL is the leading manufacturer of uniquely shaped ice cream cakes, and a leading provider of premium soft serve and hand-dipped ice cream products. Since the company's founding in 1934, CARVEL has become one of the best-loved and most recognized names in the industry. With products made fresh daily in the store, CARVEL has more than 540 franchised and foodservice locations, as well as its famous ice cream cakes in over 8,400 supermarket outlets.

BACKGROUND:	IFA MEMBER
Established: 1934;	1st Franchised: 1947
Franchised Units:	538
Company-Owned Units	0
Total Units:	538
Dist.:	US-510; CAN-0; O'seas-28
North America:	25 States, 1 Province
Density:	217 in NY, 52 in NJ,29 in CT

Projected New Units (12 Months):	60	Space Needs: 1,200-1,500 SF; FS, SC, RM, KI, PC
Qualifications: 5, 5, 3, 3, 3, 5		
Registered: CA,MD,NY,RI,VA		**SUPPORT & TRAINING PROVIDED:**
		Financial Assistance Provided: Yes(I)
FINANCIAL/TERMS:		Site Selection Assistance: Yes
Cash Investment:	$100K	Lease Negotiation Assistance: No
Total Investment:	$300K	Co-Operative Advertising: Yes
Minimum Net Worth:	$300K	Franchisee Assoc./Member: Yes/Yes
Fees: Franchise —	$30K	Size Of Corporate Staff: 100
Royalty — $1.82/Gal.;	Ad. — $1.62/Gal.	On-Going Support: B,C,D,E,G,H,I
Earnings Claim Statement:	Yes	Training: 10 Days Atlanta, GA.
Term of Contract (Years):	20	
Avg. # Of Employees:	2 FT, 6 PT	**SPECIFIC EXPANSION PLANS:**
Passive Ownership:	Not Allowed	US:All Exc.WA,OR,ID,UT,MT,WY,ND,SD,KS,MS,
Encourage Conversions:	Yes	NM
Area Develop. Agreements:	No	Canada: All Canada
Sub-Franchising Contracts:	No	Overseas: South & Central America, Asia, Middle
Expand In Territory:	Yes	East, Europe, Africa

Carvel has made itself known as "America's Freshest Ice Cream," successfully developing quality products in soft ice cream, hand-dipped ice cream, ice cream cakes and novelties. Only the freshest and best ingredients are used in their ice cream mix, and the special production techniques result in the creamy, rich products for which Carvel is famous.

With brand awareness of over 90% in core markets, Carvel continues to build on the strength of its name by expanding worldwide. It also has a devoted research and development team that constantly strives to create enticing new products that match Carvel's past innovations. Since 1934, Carvel has been a pioneer in the ice cream and franchising industry, from its developments in production equipment and manufacturing processes to its refinement in franchisee training.

Operating Units	12/31/2002	12/31/2003	12/31/2004
Franchised	367	384	425
% Change	--	4.6%	10.7%
Company-Owned	0	0	0
% Change	--	0.0%	0.0%
Total	367	384	425
% Change	--	4.6%	10.7%

Franchised as % of Total	100.00%	100.00%	100.00%

Investment Required
The fee for a Carvel franchise is $30,000.

Carvel provides the following range of investments required to open your initial franchise. The range assumes that all items are paid for in cash. To the extent that you choose to finance any of these expense items, your front-end investment could be substantially reduced.

Item	Established Low Range	Established High Range
Franchise Fee	$30,000	$30,000
Construction Build-Out	$85,000	$185,000
Architect	$3,000	$10,500
Equipment, Fixtures, Signs	$94,000	$112,000
Molds, Small Wares	$10,000	$10,000
Inventory	$7,624	$7,624
Permits/Deposits/Insurance	$4,500	$11,500
Training Expenses	$1,750	$2,000
Additional Funds (for 3 months)	$10,800	$19,300
Total Investment	$246,674	$387,924

On-Going Expenses
The franchisee pays a continuing royalty of $1.82 per liquid gallon of mix purchased for a full store, with a minimum annual payment of $11,820. The franchisee also pays advertising contribution fees of $1.62 per liquid gallon, with a minimum annual payment of $10,530.

What You Get—Training and Support

Tom Carvel founded the Carvel College of Ice Cream Knowledge in 1949. Also known as the "Sundae School," it continues to educate new franchisees about operating their own Carvel franchise. Carvel also provides ongoing field training, on-site assistance with store openings, regular consultation visits (up to three a year), business analyses and quality control inspections.

Carvel also offers support in local marketing, public relations and site selection, as well as a toll-free helpline to handle any other franchisee queries.

Territory
Carvel does not grant exclusive territories.

Dunkin' Donuts

130 Royall St., 2 West B
Canton, MA 02021
Tel: (800) 777-9983
Fax:
E-Mail: lynette.mckee@dunkinbrands.com
Web Site: www.dunkinbrandsfranchising.com
Ms. Lynette McKee, Vice President Franchising

Founded in 1950, today DUNKIN' DONUTS is the #1 retailer of coffee-by-the-cup in America, selling 2.7 million cups a day, nearly 1 billion cups a year. DUNKIN' DONUTS is also the largest coffee and baked goods chain in the world and sells more donuts, coffee and bagels than any other quick-service restaurant in America. DUNKIN' DONUTS has more than 6,500 shops in 29 countries worldwide. Based in Canton, MA, DUNKIN' DONUTS is a subsidiary of DUNKIN' BRANDS.

BACKGROUND:	IFA MEMBER
Established: 1950;	1st Franchised: 1955
Franchised Units:	6,590

Company-Owned Units	0
Total Units:	6,590
Dist.:	US-4,815; CAN-500; O'seas-1,275
North America:	39 States
Density:	490 in MA, 359 in NY, 237 IL
Projected New Units (12 Months):	350
Qualifications: 5, 4, 2, 2, 5, 4	
Registered: CA,FL,IL,IN,MD,MI,MN,NY,OR,RI,VA,WA,WI,DC	

FINANCIAL/TERMS:

Cash Investment:	$184K-1.7MM
Total Investment:	$633-1,700MM
Minimum Net Worth:	$1.5MM/Unit
Fees: Franchise —	$40-80K
Royalty — 5.9%;	Ad. — 5%
Earnings Claim Statement:	Yes
Term of Contract (Years):	20
Avg. # Of Employees:	NR
Passive Ownership:	Allowed
Encourage Conversions:	Yes
Area Develop. Agreements:	Yes/5
Sub-Franchising Contracts:	No
Expand In Territory:	Yes
Space Needs: NR SF; FS, SF, SC, RM	

SUPPORT & TRAINING PROVIDED:

83

Financial Assistance Provided:	Yes(I)	Training: 51 Days in Randolph, MA; 3.5 Days in another Location.
Site Selection Assistance:	NA	
Lease Negotiation Assistance:	Yes	
Co-Operative Advertising:	Yes	**SPECIFIC EXPANSION PLANS:**
Franchisee Assoc./Member:	Yes/No	US: All Regions
Size Of Corporate Staff:	NR	Canada: PQ, ON
On-Going Support:	B,C,E,G,H,I	Overseas: All Countries

Dunkin' Donuts is the top retailer of coffee by the cup in America, with almost 1 billion cups sold every year. William Rosenberg founded the company in Massachusetts in 1950. Since then, Dunkin' Donuts has become famous for not just its donuts, but also its menu of various baked goods, such as muffins, bagels and MUNCHKINS® donut holes. Its beverages are also popular, and include basics like fresh, hot coffee (nine flavors available), as well as proprietary drinks like COOLATTA®. As the largest coffee and baked goods chain in the world, Dunkin' Donuts sells 4 million donuts and 2.7 million cups of coffee every day. Its 6,000 outlets around the world, about 4,400 of which are located in North America, have built strong, international brand recognition and market presence.

As part of Dunkin' Brands, a family that also includes Baskin-Robbins and Togo's, franchisees have the opportunity to develop stores that combine Dunkin' Donuts with another brand to expand their customer bases. Such innovative combo stores have redefined the quick-service experience for customers and establish the framework for future growth.

Operating Units	8/31/2002	8/30/2003	8/28/2004
Franchised	3,183	3,151	3,274
% Change	--	-1.0%	3.9%
Company-Owned	0	0	0
% Change	--	0.0%	0.0%
Total	3,183	3,151	3,274
% Change	--	-1.0%	3.9%
Franchised as % of Total	100.00%	100.00%	100.00%

Investment Required

The fees for traditional Dunkin' Donuts franchises range from $40,000 to $80,000. Non -traditional stores fees range from $10,000 to $60,000. Traditional stores include the following types: manufacturing/retail outlet, satellite, in-line, free-standing or non-traditional. Non-traditional stores are alternative points of distribution outlets that are typically located in another host establishment, such as stadiums.

Dunkin' Donuts provides the following range of investments required to open your initial franchise. The range assumes that all items are paid for in cash. To the extent that you choose to finance any of these expense items, your front-end investment could be substantially reduced. Non-traditional investment figures are not included below.

Item	Established Low Range	Established High Range
Franchise Fee	$40,000	$80,000
Marketing	$5,000	$5,000
Building/Site Development Costs	$80,000	$870,000
Add'l Development Costs	$17,000	$90,000
Equipment, Fixtures, Signs	$110,400	$369,200
Insurance	$4,500	$15,000
Inventory	$3,000	$15,000
Licenses, Permits, Fees	$3,500	$5,500
Miscellaneous Opening Costs	$12,200	$54,100
Training Expenses	$2,000	$35,500
Additional Funds (for 3 months)	$77,300	$175,600
Total Investment	$354,900	$1,714,900

On-Going Expenses

Dunkin' Donuts franchisees pay on-going franchise fees equal to 5 to 5.9%

of gross sales and continuing advertising fees equal to 5% of gross sales.

What You Get—Training and Support
Franchisees have access to the immense operating and training system that supports all 12,000 Dunkin' Brands' distribution points worldwide. Training and support covers the following: brand orientation, in-store evaluation, integrated brand training for combination storefronts, production, shift leader certification, basic management and human resources.

Territory
Dunkin' Donuts does not grant exclusive territories.

El Pollo Loco

3333 Michelson Dr., # 550
Irvine, CA 92612-0680
Tel: (800) 997-6556 (949) 399-2055
Fax: (949) 399-2025
E-Mail: mcontreras@elpolloloco.com
Web Site: www.elpolloloco.com
Mr. Marcelino Contreras, Director Franchise Development

EL POLLO LOCO is the nation's leading quick-service restaurant chain specializing in flame-grilled chicken. Offering a fresh, wholesome alternative to traditional fast food, EL POLLO LOCO serves its famous citrus-marinated, flame-grilled chicken with warm tortillas, fresh salsas and a variety of accompaniments. Fresh Mexican entrees (signature grilled burritos, Pollo Bowls, Pollo Salads, etc.) also served. All feature the delicious citrus-marinated, flame-grilled chicken that put us on the map.

BACKGROUND: IFA MEMBER

Established: 1975;	1st Franchised: 1983
Franchised Units:	191
Company-Owned Units	142
Total Units:	333
Dist.:	US-329; CAN-0; O'seas-4
North America:	5 States
Density:	299 in CA, 13 in NV,11 in AZ
Projected New Units (12 Months):	25
Qualifications: 5, 5, 5, 3, 3, 5	
Registered: All States Except VA	

FINANCIAL/TERMS:

Cash Investment:	$250K
Total Investment:	$425-630
Minimum Net Worth:	$500K
Fees: Franchise —	$40K
Royalty — 4%;	Ad. — 5%
Earnings Claim Statement:	Yes
Term of Contract (Years):	20
Avg. # Of Employees:	8 FT, 17 PT
Passive Ownership:	Discouraged
Encourage Conversions:	Yes
Area Develop. Agreements:	Yes/Varies
Sub-Franchising Contracts:	No
Expand In Territory:	Yes
Space Needs: 2,400 SF; FS, SF, SC	

SUPPORT & TRAINING PROVIDED:

Financial Assistance Provided:	Yes
Site Selection Assistance:	Yes
Lease Negotiation Assistance:	No

Co-Operative Advertising:	No	**SPECIFIC EXPANSION PLANS:**	
Franchisee Assoc./Member:	Yes/Yes	US:	West, Southwest,Upper Midwest, Northeast
Size Of Corporate Staff:	142	Canada:	No
On-Going Support:	B,C,D,E,G,H,I	Overseas:	No
Training: 6 Weeks in Southern CA.			

El Pollo Loco, Spanish for "The Crazy Chicken," is the leading quick-service restaurant franchise specializing in flame-grilled chicken – chicken marinated in special herbs, spices and citrus juices and served with warm tortillas and fresh salsas. El Pollo Loco truly delivers on the dining trends consumers want today: healthy food, open-fire cooking, bold flavors and the ability to customize their meals according to their particular tastes. What makes this opportunity irresistible is the strength of their numbers combined with the depth of experience within their management team.

While El Pollo Loco has been located primarily in the Southwest, the company has just started to expand nationwide. Development has already begun for a Chicago store, scheduled to open in October 2005. El Pollo Loco is set to continue its expansion and growth in the marketplace with new products and compelling marketing.

Operating Units	12/31/2002	12/31/2003	12/31/2004
Franchised	171	178	185
% Change	--	4.1%	3.9%
Company-Owned	134	136	137
% Change	--	1.5%	0.7%
Total	305	314	322
% Change	--	3.0%	2.5%
Franchised as % of Total	56.07%	56.69%	57.45%

Investment Required
The fee for an El Pollo Loco franchise is $40,000.

El Pollo Loco provides the following range of investments required to

open your initial franchise. The range assumes that all items are paid for in cash. To the extent that you choose to finance any of these expense items, your front-end investment could be substantially reduced.

Item	Established Low Range	Established High Range
Franchise Fee	$40,000	$40,000
Lease Payment/Deposit	$5,000	$10,000
Architectural Design	$15,000	$35,000
Equipment, Fixtures, Furnishings, Signs	$281,000	$340,000
Computer System	$30,000	$50,000
Training Expenses (Per Manager)	$5,000	$15,000
Opening Inventory and Supplies	$9,000	$12,500
Insurance	$3,000	$6,000
Grand Opening Fee	$5,000	$10,000
Additional Funds (for 3 months)	$25,000	$100,000
Total Investment	$418,000	$618,500

On-Going Expenses
El Pollo Loco franchisees pay a royalty fee equal to 4% of monthly gross sales and an advertising fee equal to 4% or 5% of monthly gross revenues.

What You Get—Training and Support
Throughout the site-selection process, franchisees receive advice and assistance from experienced El Pollo Loco staff. Franchisees and their managers go through six weeks of management training that readies them to handle the aspects of operating and managing an El Pollo Loco restaurant. Refresher courses are also offered.

Corporate staff will also be on hand for the grand opening and with promotions to build a customer base. After the restaurant has opened, they will continue to visit and give guidance and assistance. Franchisees also receive an operations manual that is updated regularly.

Territory
El Pollo Loco grants exclusive territories.

Friendly's Restaurants

1855 Boston Rd.
Wilbraham, MA 01095-1002
Tel: (800) 576-8088 (413) 543-2400
Fax: (413) 543-2820
E-Mail: laurel.adams@friendlys.com
Web Site: www.friendlys.com
Ms. Laurel Adams, Franchise Development Manager

FRIENDLY'S is a full-service restaurant chain with ice cream a key point of difference. FRIENDLY'S has experienced growth in every year since 2000. The franchisee will receive support, including training, marketing, site selection, restaurant openings and on-going operational assistance.

BACKGROUND: IFA MEMBER
Established: 1935;   1st Franchised: 1997
Franchised Units: 206
Company-Owned Units   <u>314</u>
Total Units: 520
Dist.:   US-520; CAN-0; O'seas-0
North America: 16 States
Density: 122 in MA, 115 in NY, 66 PA
Projected New Units (12 Months):   10
Qualifications: 5, , 5, , , 4

Registered: FL,IL,IN,MD,NY,RI,VA

FINANCIAL/TERMS:
Cash Investment:	$400-500K
Total Investment:	$499K-1.95MM
Minimum Net Worth:	$650K-1.5MMLiq
Fees: Franchise —	$30-35K
Royalty — 4%;	Ad. — 3%
Earnings Claim Statement:	Yes
Term of Contract (Years):	20/10-20
Avg. # Of Employees:	40 FT, 35 PT
Passive Ownership:	Not Allowed
Encourage Conversions:	Yes
Area Develop. Agreements:	Yes
Sub-Franchising Contracts:	No
Expand In Territory:	Yes
Space Needs: 4,100-4,500 SF; FS	

SUPPORT & TRAINING PROVIDED:
Financial Assistance Provided:	No
Site Selection Assistance:	Yes
Lease Negotiation Assistance:	No
Co-Operative Advertising:	No
Franchisee Assoc./Member:	No
Size Of Corporate Staff:	325
On-Going Support:	A,b,C,d,E,F,G,h
Training: 12 Weeks at the Corporate Training Center and in Individual Training Units.	

SPECIFIC EXPANSION PLANS:
US:	SE, NE, Mid-Atlantic
Canada:	No
Overseas:	No

At Friendly's, customers delight in signature sandwiches, entrees and desserts that feature the restaurants' legendary premium ice cream—created with fresh milk delivered daily, hot fudge made from imported Dutch chocolate and whipped topping made with fresh cream. Since 1935,

Friendly's core values have remained the same: "Good food, famous ice cream shop treats, fair prices and friendly service."

Friendly's Restaurants become an integral community meeting place where everyone is welcome. With smart marketing messages such as the award-winning "You & me & Friendly's" ad campaign, Friendly's is an attractive concept poised for growth. It enjoys more than 90% brand awareness, and continues to expand its customer base by revitalizing restaurants and adding new products.

Operating Units	12/31/2002	12/31/2003	12/31/2004
Franchised	156	157	188
% Change	--	0.6%	19.7%
Company-Owned	387	380	347
% Change	--	0.0%	0.0%
Total	543	537	535
% Change	--	-1.1%	-0.4%
Franchised as % of Total	28.73%	29.24%	35.14%

Investment Required
The fee for an initial Friendly's franchise is $35,000 for the first two restaurants and $30,000 for any thereafter.

Friendly's provides the following range of investments required to open your initial franchise. The range assumes that all items are paid for in cash. To the extent that you choose to finance any of these expense items, your front-end investment could be substantially reduced.

Item	Established Low Range	Established High Range
Franchise Fee	$30,000	$35,000
Construction	$60,300	$1,158,500

Pre-Opening/ Grand Opening, Opening Team Expenses	$35,200	$80,600
Furniture, Equipment, Signs	$144,000	$305,500
Inventory	$28,000	$43,000
Training Expenses	$11,000	$56,250
Additional Funds (for 3 months)	$190,100	$275,400
Total Investment	$498,500	$1,954,250

On-Going Expenses
The franchisee pays an ongoing royalty fee equal to 4% of net sales and a marketing fund fee equal to 3%.

What You Get—Training and Support
Friendly's franchisees receiving the following support: site evaluation and selection assistance, construction planning and development guidance, product purchasing programs, ongoing support in operations and product research/development, staff training resources, reliable marketing and advertising strategies and a cost-efficient distribution system.

Territory
Friendly's Franchise Agreements do not grant exclusive territories. Friendly's Development Agreements grant territories with limited exclusivity.

Great Wraps

Tel: (888) 489-7277 (404) 248-9900 + 16
Fax: (404) 248-0180
E-Mail: franchise@greatwraps.com
Web Site: www.greatwraps.com
Mr. Dan Reed, Director Franchise Development

GREAT WRAPS is the #1 Hot Wrapped Sandwich & Grilled Sub Franchise, and is experiencing rapid growth. That's because we offer a franchise oppor-

4 Executive Park E., # 315
Atlanta, GA 30329

tunity that is unique and proven . . . and provides tremendous growth potential. We feature a powerful menu that is fresher and tastier than traditional fast food-like the Santa Fe Chicken Wrap, our signature GyroWrap, BuffaloWrap and Grilled PhillyCheesesteaks. Our operation is extremely efficient and so simple to learn, you don't even need prior food experience.

BACKGROUND: IFA MEMBER
Established: 1978; 1st Franchised: 1986
Franchised Units: 86
Company-Owned Units 1
Total Units: 87
Dist.: US-87; CAN-0; O'seas-0
  North America: 23 States
  Density: 29 in GA, 13 in CA, 6 in FL
Projected New Units (12 Months): 35
Qualifications: 5, 3, 3, 3, 4, 4
Registered: CA,IL,MD,MI,NY,VA

FINANCIAL/TERMS:
Cash Investment: $70-80K
Total Investment: $210-310K
Minimum Net Worth: $250K
Fees: Franchise — $19.5K

Royalty — 5.5%; Ad. — .5%
Earnings Claim Statement: No
Term of Contract (Years): 15/10
Avg. # Of Employees: 5 FT, 6 PT
Passive Ownership: Discouraged
Encourage Conversions: Yes
Area Develop. Agreements: Yes/15 Yrs.+
Sub-Franchising Contracts: Yes
Expand In Territory: Yes
Space Needs: 600-1,500 SF; RM, SC, Airport, Univer.

SUPPORT & TRAINING PROVIDED:
Financial Assistance Provided: Yes(I)
Site Selection Assistance: Yes
Lease Negotiation Assistance: Yes
Co-Operative Advertising: Yes
Franchisee Assoc./Member: Yes
Size Of Corporate Staff: 13
On-Going Support: B,C,D,E,G,H
Training: 3 Weeks Atlanta, GA.

SPECIFIC EXPANSION PLANS:
US: Nationwide
Canada: No
Overseas: No

Great Wraps is the #1 Hot Wrapped Sandwich and Grilled Sub franchise in the industry, and it is experiencing rapid growth. That's because Great Wraps is leading a whole new food category, and entrepreneurs are anxious to jump on-board. They want to capitalize on the general food trend in which customers are looking beyond traditional fast food burgers, pizzas and subs, and more towards better and healthier alternatives. That's where Great Wraps excels. It features a unique menu combination of Hot Wraps (like their Santa Fe Chicken Wrap®, Gyro Wrap® and the Buffalo Bill), Grilled Philly Cheesesteaks and Grilled Flatbread Sandwiches. Great Wraps uses fresh-cooked meats, melted cheeses, fresh-cut produce and tasty sauces to produce sandwiches that are truly at cut above.

The mission of Great Wraps is to always sharpen their edge, which is strives to achieve by keeping their concept current, providing franchises with the most efficient "turnkey" store-opening package, and developing effective marketing support programs. Great Wraps has geared up for continued explosive growth and expansion, as its fresh and exciting concept continues to catch on.

Operating Units	12/31/2003	12/31/2004	12/31/2005
Franchised	53	65	83
% Change	--	22.6%	28.7%
Company-Owned	1	1	1
% Change	--	0.0%	0.0%
Total	54	66	84
% Change	--	22.2%	28.3%
Franchised as % of Total	98.15%	98.48%	98.8%

Investment Required
The fee for a Great Wraps franchise is $19,500.

Great Wraps provides the following range of investments required to open your initial franchise. The range assumes that all items are paid for in cash. To the extent that you choose to finance any of these expense items, your front-end investment could be substantially reduced.

Item	Established Low Range	Established High Range
Franchise Fee	$19,500	$19,500
Equipment, Furniture, Signage, Menu	$58,000	$82,000
Construction	$100,000	$170,000
Architectural Fees/ Security Deposit	$9,200	$18,000
Opening Inventory	$5,000	$5,000
Grand Opening Advertising	$2,500	$2,500
Insurance	$4,500	$4,500

Training Costs	$3,000	$3,000
Professional Fees	$1,000	$2,800
Additional Funds (for 2 months)	$12,500	$12,500
Total Investment	$215,200	$319,800

On-Going Expenses
Great Wraps franchisees pay a royalty fee equal to 5.5% of weekly net sales and a weekly advertising fee ranging from 0.5% to 2% of sales.

What You Get—Training and Support
Great Wraps provides site-selection assistance, and can adjust its store layout for almost any location. A director of store development assists franchisees with store construction, with eye toward reducing hassle, minimizing cost and maximizing quality. Once a site has been selected and a design confirmed, the store can be open and operating within 10-12 weeks.

Franchisees don't need prior experience with food, and are taught everything they need to know through the S.T.A.R. Training program, which continues on an ongoing basis. Great Wraps, as the first wrapped sandwich franchise, has more than 15 years of experience from which to offer support. Franchisees receive low prices for ingredients and supplies through group-buying contracts. In addition, Great Wraps offers several marketing programs, including one for the grand opening, and a comprehensive marketing manual.

Territory
Great Wraps does not grant exclusive territories.

KFC

P. O. Box 34550, 1900 Colonel Sanders Ln.
Louisville, KY 40213
Tel: (866) 2YUM-YUM (502) 874-8300
Fax: (502) 874-8848
E-Mail: 2yumyum@yum.com
Web Site: www.yumfranchises.com
Ms. Leigh Anne Lochner, Franchise Specialist

World's largest quick-service restaurant with a chicken-dominant menu. KFC offers full-service restaurants and non-traditional express units for captive markets.

BACKGROUND:	IFA MEMBER
Established: 1939;	1st Franchised: 1952
Franchised Units:	4,277
Company-Owned Units	1,248
Total Units:	5,525
Dist.:	US-5,525; CAN-0; O'seas-0
North America:	50 States,10 Provinces
Density:	CA, TX, IL
Projected New Units (12 Months):	100
Qualifications: 5, 4, 5, 3, 3, 5	

Registered: All States

FINANCIAL/TERMS:

Cash Investment:	$NR
Total Investment:	$1.1-1.7MM
Minimum Net Worth:	$1MM
Fees: Franchise —	$25K
Royalty — 4% or $600/Mo.;	Ad. — 5%
Earnings Claim Statement:	No
Term of Contract (Years):	20
Avg. # Of Employees:	2 FT, 22 PT
Passive Ownership:	Not Allowed
Encourage Conversions:	No
Area Develop. Agreements:	No
Sub-Franchising Contracts:	No
Expand In Territory:	Yes
Space Needs: 2,000-3,000 SF; FS	

SUPPORT & TRAINING PROVIDED:

Financial Assistance Provided:	No
Site Selection Assistance:	Yes
Lease Negotiation Assistance:	No
Co-Operative Advertising:	Yes
Franchisee Assoc./Member:	Yes/Yes
Size Of Corporate Staff:	820
On-Going Support:	C,d,E,G,h,I
Training: 10-16 Weeks of Training.	

SPECIFIC EXPANSION PLANS:

US:	All United States
Canada:	All Canada
Overseas:	All Countries

KFC is the most popular chicken restaurant around the world. KFC is famous for its Original Recipe and Extra Crispy chicken, as well as its homestyle side dishes. Almost 8 million customers sample KFC food every day in more than 11,000 restaurants in 80 countries around the world. KFC is also part of the Yum! Brands family, the largest restaurant company in the world with over 32,500 units. Family members include A & W Restaurants, Long John Silver's, Pizza Hut and Taco Bell. Multi-branding opportunities are available to expand a franchise's customer appeal and market share.

Operating Units	12/31/2002	12/31/2003	12/31/2004
Franchised	4,150	4,229	4,202
% Change	--	1.9%	-0.6%
Company-Owned	1,308	1,300	1,248
% Change	--	-0.6%	-4.0%
Total	5,458	5,529	5,450
% Change	--	1.3%	-1.4%
Franchised as % of Total	76.04%	76.49%	77.10%

Investment Required

The initial fee for a KFC franchise is $25,000.

KFC provides the following range of investments required to open your initial franchise. The range assumes that all items are paid for in cash. To the extent that you choose to finance any of these expense items, your front-end investment could be substantially reduced.

Item	Established Low Range	Established High Range
Franchise Fee	$25,000	$25,000
Real Property	$500,000	$850,000
Construction/Leasehold Improvements	$325,000	$500,000
Equipment/Signage	$250,000	$300,000
Opening Advertising	$5,000	$5,000
Opening Inventory	$10,000	$10,000
Initial Training	$2,300	$2,300
Other Costs and Additional Funds (for 3 months)	$25,000	$40,000
Total Investment	$1,142,300	$1,732,300

On-Going Expenses

KFC franchisees pay a royalty fee equal to 4% of gross revenues (minimum of $600 per month), a local advertising fee equal to 3% of gross revenues and a national cooperative advertising fee equal to 2% of gross revenues.

What You Get—Training and Support

All Yum! Franchisees receive extensive training, support and marketing. Yum! spends more than $600 million a year on consumer advertising. Multi-branding opportunities for KFC are offered with Taco Bell, Pizza Hut, Long John Silver's and A&W Restaurants.

Franchise recruiters walk interested candidates through the entire process of becoming a franchisee, providing information on the site registration process, start-up costs, training and the sites with the greatest development potential. Franchisees are later assigned Franchise Business Coaches or Franchise Business Leaders who provide support as operations begin. Each franchisee completes Management Team Training, and is offered further training opportunities and support through the Yum! University.

KFC franchisees also benefit from the tremendous purchasing power of the Yum! family. UFPC provides supply chain management services for all Yum! brands, and since March of 1999, UFPC has saved Yum! more than $539.6 million. UFPC reduces suppliers' costs by negotiating costs, making volume purchase deals and assuming other procurement functions and risks.

Territory

KFC does not grant exclusive territories. Franchisees get a protected area with a radius of 1½ miles or containing a population of 30,000 people, whichever is smaller.

The Krystal Company

1 Union Square, Fl. 9
Chattanooga, TN 37402-2505
Tel: (800) 458-5912
Fax: (423) 757-1588
E-Mail: cstringer@krystalco.com
Web Site: www.krystal.com
Ms. Carolyn Stringer, Assistant to President

The KRYSTAL COMPANY, a 'cultural icon' in the Southeast, is a unique brand with 72 years of success as a niche franchisor, we provide quality service and thoughtful leadership to our franchise partners. We are an innovative, forward-looking franchisor who is looking for highly motivated operators. We offer a protected development territory, requiring a minimum 3-restaurant development agreement, minimum liquidity of $650K and a net worth of $1.2 million. KRYSTAL, fresh, hot, small and square.

BACKGROUND: IFA MEMBER
Established: 1932;   1st Franchised: 1990
Franchised Units: 188
Company-Owned Units   <u>248</u>
Total Units: 436
Dist.:   US-436; CAN-0; O'seas-0
   North America: 15 States
   Density: 104 in GA, 105 in TN, 53 AL

Projected New Units (12 Months):   25
Qualifications: 5, 4, 5, 2, 2, 5
Registered: FL, VA

FINANCIAL/TERMS:

Cash Investment:	$200-300K/Rest
Total Investment:	$900K-1.3MM
Minimum Net Worth:	$1.2MM
Fees: Franchise —	$32.5K
Royalty — 4.5%;	Ad. — 4%
Earnings Claim Statement:	No
Term of Contract (Years):	20/20
Avg. # Of Employees:	12-15 FT, 15 PT
Passive Ownership:	Allowed
Encourage Conversions:	Yes
Area Develop. Agreements:	No
Sub-Franchising Contracts:	No
Expand In Territory:	Yes
Space Needs: 1,300-2,200 SF; FS,SC,C-Store	

SUPPORT & TRAINING PROVIDED:

Financial Assistance Provided:	No
Site Selection Assistance:	Yes
Lease Negotiation Assistance:	No
Co-Operative Advertising:	Yes
Franchisee Assoc./Member:	Yes/No
Size Of Corporate Staff:	100
On-Going Support:	A,B,C,D,E,F,G,H,I

Training: 4 Weeks Company Store; 1 Week Corporate Computer Center.

SPECIFIC EXPANSION PLANS:

US:	SE,TX,OK,VA,NC,SC,WV,FL
Canada:	No
Overseas:	No

Krystal was founded in 1932 and is the second-oldest quick-serve restaurant in the country. Krystal's menu features the Krystal hamburger, a fresh, hot, small and uniquely square product with its own niche in the burger industry.

To customers, Krystal is famous for the "little food with the big taste," but to franchisees Krystal offers even bigger opportunities. Krystal has introduced a new, contemporary restaurant design that pays homage to the traditional Krystal look, but is more efficient to build. Its menu has also been streamlined, using the original Krystal burger to gain a stronger marketing position. In addition, Krystal is aggressively pursuing expansion by granting multiunit franchises, providing franchisees with the perfect growth vehicles.

Operating Units	12/31/2001	12/31/2002	12/31/2003
Franchised	166	176	175
% Change	--	6.0%	-0.6%
Company-Owned	246	245	244
% Change	--	-0.4%	-0.4%
Total	412	421	419
% Change	--	2.2%	-0.5%
Franchised as % of Total	40.29%	41.81%	41.77%

Investment Required
The fee for a Krystal franchise is $32,500.

Krystal provides the following range of investments required to open your initial franchise. The range assumes that all items are paid for in cash.
To the extent that you choose to finance any of these expense items, your front-end investment could be substantially reduced.

Item	Established Low Range	Established High Range
Franchise Fee	$32,500	$32,500
Construction Costs	$224,900	$392,000
Equipment	$149,100	$274,000
Grand Opening Advertising	$5,000	$5,000
Inventory	$12,500	$15,500
Miscellaneous Development	$24,500	$45,000

Miscellaneous Opening Costs	$10,500	$11,500
Site Development	$77,000	$250,000
Training Expenses	$14,000	$18,000
Additional Funds (for 2 months)	$10,500	$11,500
Total Investment (not including land)	$560,500	$1,055,000

On-Going Expenses
Krystal franchisees pay a royalty fee equal to 4.5% of weekly gross receipts and an advertising fee equal to 4% of weekly gross receipts.

What You Get—Training and Support
With so much importance placed on the design of Krystal restaurants, Krystal's Pre-Construction Management Program saves franchisees much time and energy by facilitating pre-construction activities from site selection through construction. Franchisees will be able to plan for a timely and efficient restaurant opening while Krystal manages the details of architecture, site engineering, contracting bid solicitations and other construction-related matters.

Franchisees will simultaneously receive ongoing field support, access to a corporate management team keyed in to the latest food-service innovations, comprehensive corporate and on-site training for themselves and key managers, and marketing materials and strategies. It all adds up to a comprehensive support system that enables franchisees to open and operate their Krystal restaurant efficiently and successfully.

Territory
Krystal grants exclusive multiunit territories.

La Salsa Fresh Mexican Grill

6307 Carpinteria Ave., # A
Carpinteria, CA 93013
Tel: (866) 253-7655 (805) 745-7843
Fax: (714) 780-6320
E-Mail: rbasinger@ckr.com
Web Site: www.lasalsa.com
Mr. Ron Basinger, VP Franchise Sales

A fast, casual restaurant chain, specializing in hand-crafted Mexican favorites and appealing to health-conscious individuals with discriminating taste.

BACKGROUND: IFA MEMBER
Established: 1979; 1st Franchised: 1989
Franchised Units: 41
Company-Owned Units 61
Total Units: 102
Dist.: US-102; CAN-0; O'seas-0
  North America: NR
  Density: 62 in CA, 5 in AZ, 4 in FL
Projected New Units (12 Months): 25
Qualifications: 4, 4, 4, 2, 2, 5
Registered: CA,FL,IL,IN,MD,MI,MN,NY,VA,WA,
  WI

FINANCIAL/TERMS:
Cash Investment: $NR
Total Investment: $431-612K
Minimum Net Worth: $1.2MM
Fees: Franchise — $30K 1st
  Royalty — 5%; Ad. — 3%
Earnings Claim Statement: No
Term of Contract (Years): 10
Avg. # Of Employees: 12 FT, 4 PT
Passive Ownership: Not Allowed
Encourage Conversions: Yes
Area Develop. Agreements: Yes/Varies
Sub-Franchising Contracts: No
Expand In Territory: No
Space Needs: 2,500 SF; SF, SC, RM

SUPPORT & TRAINING PROVIDED:
Financial Assistance Provided: No
Site Selection Assistance: No
Lease Negotiation Assistance: No
Co-Operative Advertising: Yes
Franchisee Assoc./Member: No
Size Of Corporate Staff: NR
On-Going Support: B,C,D,E,G,H,I
Training: 5 Weeks.

SPECIFIC EXPANSION PLANS:
US: All United States
Canada: All Canada
Overseas: NR

La Salsa is a fresh Mexican food chain that has been providing tacos, burritos, taquitos and other specialties in a quick and casual setting since 1979. A prominent part of La Salsa is its display kitchen, which allows customers to see their food prepared fresh with quality ingredients and customized to their preferences. La Salsa's personalized approach provides customers with a unique, dependable dining experience.

La Salsa's charbroiled cooking and quality ingredients set it apart from the competition. Customers are attracted to La Salsa's charbroiled preparation of items like tender sirloin steak and marinated chicken breast, as well as its fresh produce, seven salsa varieties and sauces. In fact, some of La Salsa's best franchise owners actually began as customers.

Operating Units	1/27/2003	1/26/2004	1/31/2004
Franchised	42	41	39
% Change	--	-2.4%	-4.9%
Company-Owned	57	61	62
% Change	--	7.0%	1.6%
Total	99	102	101
% Change	--	3.0%	-1.0%
Franchised as % of Total	42.42%	40.20%	38.61%

Investment Required
The fee for a La Salsa franchise is $30,000.

La Salsa provides the following range of investments required to open your initial franchise. The range assumes that all items are paid for in cash. To the extent that you choose to finance any of these expense items, your front-end investment could be substantially reduced.

Item	Established Low Range	Established High Range
Franchise Fee	$30,000	$30,000
Building and Site Improvements	$180,000	$300,000
Equipment	$180,000	$200,000
Signage	$8,000	$12,000
Grand Opening Advertising	$5,000	$5,000
Training Expenses	$16,000	$18,000
Opening Inventories	$3,000	$5,000
Pre-Opening Expenses	$14,000	$30,000

Additional Funds (for 3 months)	$15,000	$32,000
Total Investment (not including Real Estate)	$451,000	$632,000

On-Going Expenses
La Salsa franchisees pay a royalty fee equal to 5% of gross sales and an advertising fee equal to 5% of gross sales. Other expenses cover the cost of point-of-purchase advertising materials, management training fees and materials, and grand opening support.

What You Get—Training and Support
La Salsa understands the importance of a good location, and finds that a franchise can work well in a variety of spots, including in-line strip centers, small free-standing villages and downtown business districts. La Salsa typically focuses on areas with high visibility in a high-traffic retail center. Their trademark modern, inviting atmosphere and stylish, colorful décor appeals to both lunch and dinner patrons.

La Salsa gives franchisees thorough support in the following areas before and after opening: marketing, real estate, construction, management training and restaurant "opening team" assistance.

Territory
La Salsa does not grant exclusive territories.

Long John Silver's

P. O. Box 34550, 1900 Colonel Sanders Ln.
Louisville, KY 40213
Tel: (866) 2YUM-YUM (502) 874-8300
Fax: (502) 874-8848
E-Mail: 2yumyum@yum.com
Web Site: www.yumfranchises.com
Ms. Leigh Anne Lochner, Franchise Specialist

LONG JOHN SILVER'S is the largest, quick-service

seafood restaurant chain in the world. We continue to aggressively grow with new units and sales. Opportunities are available in new and existing markets and with our sister brand, A & W in our new co-brand facilities.

BACKGROUND: IFA MEMBER
Established: 1969; 1st Franchised: 1969
Franchised Units: 500
Company-Owned Units <u>700</u>
Total Units: 1,200
Dist.: US-1,200; CAN-0; O'seas-0
 North America: 35 States
 Density: 185 in TX, 114 in OH, 101 IN
Projected New Units (12 Months): NR
Qualifications: 5, 5, 3, 4, 5, 5
Registered: ALL

FINANCIAL/TERMS:
Cash Investment: $NR
Total Investment: $1.0-1.3MM
Minimum Net Worth: $1MM/360 Liq.
Fees: Franchise — $20K
 Royalty — 6% Gr. Receipts; Ad. — 4% Gr. Rec.
Earnings Claim Statement: Yes

Term of Contract (Years): 20
Avg. # Of Employees: NR
Passive Ownership: Discouraged
Encourage Conversions: NR
Area Develop. Agreements: NR
Sub-Franchising Contracts: No
Expand In Territory: Yes
Space Needs: NR SF; FS, C-Store, Food Court

SUPPORT & TRAINING PROVIDED:
Financial Assistance Provided: No
Site Selection Assistance: Yes
Lease Negotiation Assistance: NR
Co-Operative Advertising: Yes
Franchisee Assoc./Member: Yes
Size Of Corporate Staff: NR
On-Going Support: C,D,E,G,h,I
Training: 10-16 Weeks of Training.

SPECIFIC EXPANSION PLANS:
US: All United States
Canada: All Canada
Overseas: Asia, Europe, Caribbean, Latin America, Middle East

Long John Silver's is the nation's largest and most dominant quick-service seafood restaurant chain. Its menu features batter-dipped fish, chicken and shrimp, while also offering popular sides such as fries, coleslaw and hushpuppies. The chain was founded in 1969, and today has more than 1,200 restaurants that serve almost four million customers each week. Long John Silver's enjoys the highest market share in its category and aims to increase its dominance through its "Fish First" strategy for franchise expansion.

As part of the Yum! corporate family, Long John Silver's franchisees can utilize the power of multibranding and add another powerhouse brand to their restaurants. This doubles menu offerings and, consequently, broadens the customer base. Research indicates that consumers prefer multi-brand restaurants, and Yum! franchisees are uniquely positioned to take advantage of this preference. The combination that currently offers the best growth opportunity is an A & W Restaurant paired with Long John

Silver's. A & W has been an all-American icon for more than eighty years. A family favorite in the quick-service restaurant industry, its restaurants are recognized for their hamburgers, juicy hot dogs and famous draft A & W Root Beer.

Together these two brands give franchisees a unique one-two punch in the ever-competitive quick-service marketplace.

Operating Units	12/25/2002	12/24/2003	12/22/2004
Franchised	495	532	583
% Change	--	7.5%	9.6%
Company-Owned	742	759	817
% Change	--	2.3%	7.6%
Total	1,237	1,291	1,400
% Change	--	4.4%	8.4%
Franchised as % of Total	40.02%	41.21%	41.64%

Investment Required
The fee for a Long John Silver's franchise is $20,000.

Long John Silver's provides the following range of investments required to open your initial franchise. The range assumes that all items are paid for in cash. To the extent that you choose to finance any of these expense items, your front-end investment could be substantially reduced.

Item	Established Low Range	Established High Range
Franchise Fee	$20,000	$20,000
Construction Costs	$335,000	$515,000
Deposits/Other Expenses	$3,000	$30,000
Furnishings, Fixtures & Equipment	$125,000	$270,000
Opening Inventory	$10,000	$20,000

Opening-Related Advertising	$3,000	$5,000
Real Estate	$150,000	$550,000
Signage	$30,000	$60,000
Training Expenses	$10,000	$25,000
Additional Funds (for 3 months)	$100,000	$200,000
Total Investment	$786,000	$1,695,000

On-Going Expenses

Long John Silver's franchisees pay on-going royalty fees equaling 5% of total gross sales and advertising fees equaling an additional 5% of gross sales.

What You Get—Training and Support

Franchisees go through Management Team Training before opening their restaurant. Opening a single-brand store requires six to eight weeks of training for key restaurant personnel, while multibrand training depends on the franchisee's prior level of experience in the quick-service restaurant industry and ranges from 12 to 18 weeks. Franchise Business Coaches and Franchise Business Leaders alert franchisees of important news and initiatives, organize regional training sessions and give advice to the franchisee as they open their store.

Yum! University supports the education and installment of Yum! leadership programs for franchisees. Franchisees can take courses in HR College, Leading Change, Ops College, Coaching Leaders, Multibrand Operations, Development College and Finance College.

Long John Silver's, like all Yum! brands, has an annual promotional calendar that offers a variety of special offers throughout the year to grab customers' interests. In addition, national marketing news is shared and local coordinated activities are carried out regularly.

Territory
Long John Silver's grants exclusive territories.

Maui Wowi Hawaiian Coffees and Smoothies

5445 DTC Parkway, # 1050
Greenwood Village, CO 80111
Tel: ((877) 849-6992 (303) 781-7800
Fax: (303) 781-2438
E-Mail: leads@mauiwowi.com
Web Site: www.mauiwowi.com
Mr. Mike Garcia, Franchise Development Coord.

Ranked as # 175 in Inc 500, with over 350 locations, MAUI WOWI is the #1 largest smoothie/coffee franchise in the world. With 24/7 support and extensive training, MAUI WOWI offers a simple, profitable and flexible business model. MAUI WOWI has thousands of locations and events throughout the country waiting for a MAUI WOWI franchise owner. Because of our flexibility, low investment and variety of business models, MAUI WOWI is the fastest-growing franchise.

BACKGROUND:	IFA MEMBER
Established: 1983;	1st Franchised: 1997
Franchised Units:	350
Company-Owned Units	0
Total Units:	350
Dist.:	US-350; CAN-0; O'seas-0
North America:	43 States
Density:	NR

Projected New Units (12 Months):	250-300
Qualifications: 2, 2, 1, 1, 1, 5	
Registered: All States	

FINANCIAL/TERMS:	
Cash Investment:	$50K+
Total Investment:	$70-300K
Minimum Net Worth:	$250K
Fees: Franchise —	$29.5-59.5K
Royalty — 0%;	Ad. — 2%
Earnings Claim Statement:	Yes
Term of Contract (Years):	10
Avg. # Of Employees:	2 FT
Passive Ownership:	Allowed
Encourage Conversions:	Yes
Area Develop. Agreements:	Yes
Sub-Franchising Contracts:	No
Expand In Territory:	Yes
Space Needs: 100 SF; HB, KI	

SUPPORT & TRAINING PROVIDED:	
Financial Assistance Provided:	Yes(I)
Site Selection Assistance:	Yes
Lease Negotiation Assistance:	Yes
Co-Operative Advertising:	Yes
Franchisee Assoc./Member:	No
Size Of Corporate Staff:	30
On-Going Support:	B,C,D,E,F,G,H,I
Training: 5 Days in Denver, CO.	

SPECIFIC EXPANSION PLANS:	
US:	All United States
Canada:	All Canada
Overseas:	All Countries

Over the last 23 years, Maui Wowi Hawaiian has created the proven recipe for franchise success, offering you the opportunity to join the smoothie and coffee revolution and enjoy an escape from the typical career. The largest Hawaiian Coffee/Smoothie franchise in the United States since

1997, Maui Wowi Hawaiian has over 350 units in operation and over 600 more licensed to be developed. Maui Wowi Hawaiian offers a simple, profitable and flexible business model. There are thousands of locations and events throughout the country waiting for a Maui Wowi Hawaiian franchise operator! Because of it's flexibility, low investment, and variety of business models, Maui Wowi Hawaiian is one of the fastest growing franchises in the world.

Maui Wowi Hawaiian is famous for its fresh fruit smoothies, a blend of the customer's fresh fruit puree of choice with an exclusive custom design non-fat yogurt, banana and ice. The Maui Wowi Hawaiian coffee beverage line is a premiere coffee experience. The blends are derived from four Hawaiian islands – Kona, Maui, Kauai and Molokai. Each blend has a distinct taste that is used for freshly brewed coffees and as the coffee base for our full line of Kona espresso, latte, cappuccino and their new iced coffee frozen blend line, Chillen'.

Maui Wowi Hawaiian products are sold in multi-business model formats of retail locations, specialty carts, semi-permanent kiosks, and catering units to allow franchise operators to open multiple locations at a reasonable cost. Due to Maui Wowi Hawaiian's flexibility and low start-up cost, the franchise organization is one of the fastest-growing franchises worldwide.

Operating Units	12/31/2002	12/31/2003	12/31/2004
Franchised	150	180	195
% Change	--	20.0%	8.3%
Company-Owned	0	0	0
% Change	--	0.0%	0.0%
Total	150	180	195
% Change	--	20.0%	8.3%
Franchised as % of Total	100.00%	100.00%	100.00%

Investment Required

The fee for a Maui Wowi Hawaiian franchise starts as low as $27,500.

Maui Wowi Hawaiian provides the following range of investments required to open your initial franchise. The range assumes that all items are paid for in cash. To the extent that you choose to finance any of these expense items, your front-end investment could be substantially reduced.

Item	Established Low Range	Established High Range
Franchise Fee	$27,500	$59,500
Training Expenses	$0	$2,950
Construction	$75,000	$250,000
Optional Equipment	$0	$16,865
Turn Key Location Fee	$13,000	$13,000
Miscellaneous Opening Costs	$500	$25,000
Commercial Broker's Fee	$0	$15,000
Additional Funds (for 3 months)	$0	$35,000
Total Investment (not including Real Estate)	$116,000	$417,315

On-Going Expenses

Maui Wowi Hawaiian franchisees pay a marketing fee equal to 12% of the purchase price of Maui Wowi Hawaiian exclusive product lines and equipment. This fee is included in the list price.

What You Get—Training and Support

Maui Wowi Hawaiian Mainland (corporate headquarters) provides franchisees with an experienced team of professionals to provide all necessary support in real estate development, operations, training, marketing and compliance support. Franchise mentors are also available to help new franchisees achieve their goals. Dedicated departments with seasoned professionals provide support with real estate acquisition, working with health departments, equipment, strategic market development, staffing and general business operations. Maui Wowi Hawaiian franchisees thus can freely reap the benefits of a simple, yet flexible concept, a recognized brand name, a quality product, equipment developed with 23 years of experience and support every step of the way.

Territory
Maui Wowi Hawaiian grants exclusive territories for Directors of Regional Support (area developers).

The Melting Pot Restaurant

8810 Twin Lakes Blvd.
Tampa, FL 33614
Tel: (800) 783-0867 + 108 (813) 881-0055
Fax: (813) 367-0076
E-Mail: dana@meltingpot.com
Web Site: www.meltingpot.com
Mr. Dan N. Addison, Director Franchise Sales

The largest fondue-based restaurant system in the world. Franchise provides numerous areas of expertise and assistance to new and established owners. Large percentage of existing owners become multi-unit operators. A unique dining format that is often referred to as a "fun and gotta be experienced" event.

BACKGROUND:	IFA MEMBER
Established: 1975;	1st Franchised: 1984
Franchised Units:	95
Company-Owned Units	6
Total Units:	101
Dist.:	US-101; CAN-0; O'seas-0
North America:	33 States

Density:	20 in FL, 5 in CA, 5 in TX
Projected New Units (12 Months):	20
Qualifications: 5, 5, 3, 3, 3, 5	
Registered: CA,FL,IL,IN,MD,MI,MN,NY,OR,RI,VA,WA,WI,DC	

FINANCIAL/TERMS:	
Cash Investment:	$200-250K
Total Investment:	$595K-1.1MM
Minimum Net Worth:	$500K
Fees: Franchise —	$35K
Royalty — 4.5%;	Ad. — .5%
Earnings Claim Statement:	Yes
Term of Contract (Years):	10/10
Avg. # Of Employees:	10-20 FT, 5-20 PT
Passive Ownership:	Not Allowed
Encourage Conversions:	No
Area Develop. Agreements:	Yes
Sub-Franchising Contracts:	No
Expand In Territory:	No
Space Needs: 4,000-6,000 SF; FS, SC	

SUPPORT & TRAINING PROVIDED:	
Financial Assistance Provided:	Yes(I)
Site Selection Assistance:	Yes
Lease Negotiation Assistance:	Yes
Co-Operative Advertising:	Yes
Franchisee Assoc./Member:	No
Size Of Corporate Staff:	50
On-Going Support:	A,b,C,D,E,F,G,h,I
Training: 7 Weeks, Tampa, FL.	

SPECIFIC EXPANSION PLANS:		Canada:	No
US:	All US Except ND,SD	Overseas:	No

The Melting Pot is the nation's leading fondue restaurant chain. Guests can choose from four tasty fondue cooking styles and a variety of entrees, including beef, chicken, duck, shrimp, scallops, lobster and more. A special dipping sauce accompanies each dish. The Melting Pot restaurants use only the finest quality cheeses, which have been carefully aged to meet Melting Pot standards. Servers season the fondue to customers' personal preferences. Desserts include a variety of decadent chocolate fondue recipes.

The Melting Pot offers a completely unique dining experience that has been a proven success since 1975. A convenient advantage is that it does not require any chefs, ovens or fryers. Conveniently for the owner, the restaurant is only open for dinner and there is little, if any, direct competition within its niche market. As The Melting Pot now opens 15-17 new locations every year, it is the perfect time for people to try to "dip into something different."

Operating Units	3/31/2003	3/31/2004	3/31/2005
Franchised	65	71	87
% Change	--	9.2%	22.5%
Company-Owned	4	4	5
% Change	--	0.0%	25.0%
Total	69	75	92
% Change	--	8.7%	22.7%
Franchised as % of Total	94.20%	94.67%	94.57%

Investment Required
The fee for a The Melting Pot franchise is $35,000.

The Melting Pot provides the following range of investments required to

open your initial franchise. The range assumes that all items are paid for in cash. To the extent that you choose to finance any of these expense items, your front-end investment could be substantially reduced.

Item	Established Low Range	Established High Range
Franchise Fee	$35,000	$35,000
Real Estate Improvements	$250,000	$500,000
Equipment, Furniture, Fixtures and Signage	$230,800	$360,800
Deposits	$12,000	$25,000
Opening Inventory, Supplies, Proprietary Products	$20,000	$58,500
Grand Opening Advertising	$8,000	$15,000
Training Expenses	$10,000	$19,000
Licenses	$6,000	$10,000
Insurance	$3,000	$6,000
Legal	$2,000	$6,000
Additional Funds (for 3 months)	$48,000	$95,000
Total Investment (Not including Real Estate)	$598,800	$1,011,303

On-Going Expenses

The Melting Pot franchisees pay a royalty fee equal to 4.5% of monthly gross revenue, a central advertising fund fee equal to up to 1.5% of gross revenue (a maximum of $22,500 per year), and a local advertising fee equal to 3% of gross revenue.

What You Get—Training and Support

With the extensive training and support that the Melting Pot provides, franchisees are not required to have any restaurant experience.

The Melting Pot Franchise Support Center has a development team with professionals who specialize in site selection, food service and interior design. The design of each Melting Pot restaurant is customized by the design team to reflect the franchisee's personality and the surrounding local neighborhood. A complete set of design drawings is provided for layout, equipment specifications, interior-design details and finish selections.

Franchisees complete a 7-week training program that covers all operations, including equipment orders, from the kitchen to the dining room to the bar. A team of trainers assists with grand openings, as well as supplying ongoing assistance with daily training tips and other support.

The Melting Pot has an innovative program called Training Champions, where each restaurant selects a representative who monitors the training of new employees and ensures consistency. These Training Champions earn national certification in food safety and handling techniques and receive daily updates and insights through online training.

Territory
The Melting Pot grants exclusive territories.

Mrs. Fields Cookies

Mr. Dara Dejbakhsh, EVP Operations/Development

Premier retail cookie business with 'uncompromising quality,' 94% brand recognition, easy to operate, flexible designs and store options that operate in traditional and non-traditional venues.

2855 E. Cottonwood Pkwy., # 400
Salt Lake City, UT 84121-7050
Tel: (800) 343-5377 (801) 736-5600
Fax: (801) 736-5936
E-Mail: darad@mrsfields.com
Web Site: www.mrsfieldsfranchise.com

BACKGROUND:	IFA MEMBER
Established: 1977;	1st Franchised: 1990
Franchised Units:	372
Company-Owned Units	59
Total Units:	431
Dist.:	US-354; CAN-0; O'seas-77
North America:	43 States, 1 Province
Density:	103 in CA, 30 in MI,25 in IL

Projected New Units (12 Months):	38	Expand In Territory:	Yes

Projected New Units (12 Months): 38
Qualifications: 4, 4, 2, 2, 2, 5
Registered: All States Except VA

FINANCIAL/TERMS:
Cash Investment: $10-73.5K
Total Investment: $162.4-247.1K
Minimum Net Worth: $150K/75K LIQ
Fees: Franchise — $30K
  Royalty — 6%; Ad. — 1%
Earnings Claim Statement: Yes
Term of Contract (Years): 7/7
Avg. # Of Employees: 3 FT, 2 PT
Passive Ownership: Not Allowed
Encourage Conversions: Yes
Area Develop. Agreements: No
Sub-Franchising Contracts: No

Expand In Territory: Yes
Space Needs: 600-900 SF; RM, SC, SF, Stadium

SUPPORT & TRAINING PROVIDED:
Financial Assistance Provided: No
Site Selection Assistance: Yes
Lease Negotiation Assistance: Yes
Co-Operative Advertising: No
Franchisee Assoc./Member: Yes/Yes
Size Of Corporate Staff: 100+
On-Going Support: A,B,C,D,E,F,G,H,I
Training: In Salt Lake City, UT.

SPECIFIC EXPANSION PLANS:
US: All United States
Canada: All Canada
Overseas: NR

Debbi Fields opened the first store Mrs. Fields in Palo Alto, California, more than 20 years ago. And now, with an astonishing 94% name-recognition rate, Mrs. Fields Cookies is the world's premier chain of cookie stores. Tasty, freshly baked delights include signature cookies and brownies, as well as muffins, bagels and croissants, and continuing experiments with new products keep the brand fresh and exciting. Mrs. Fields has over 3,000 distribution outlets around the world, enabling it to accomplish the goal of "indulging the world with a sweet treat and a warm smile."

Operating Units	12/28/2002	1/3/2004	1/1/2005
Franchised	277	317	360
% Change	--	14.4%	13.6%
Company-Owned	122	75	26
% Change	--	-38.5%	-65.3%
Total	399	392	386
% Change	--	-1.8%	-1.5%
Franchised as % of Total	69.42%	80.87%	93.26%

Investment Required
The fee for a Mrs. Fields franchise is $30,000.

Mrs. Fields provides the following range of investments required to open your initial franchise. The range assumes that all items are paid for in cash. To the extent that you choose to finance any of these expense items, your front-end investment could be substantially reduced. The following figures refer to the construction of a new Mrs. Fields store.

Item	Established Low Range	Established High Range
Franchise Fee	$30,000	$30,000
Training Expenses	$2,900	$3,600
Improvements	$125,000	$175,000
Opening Inventory	$1,000	$5,000
Grand Opening	$5,000	$5,000
Miscellaneous Fees/ Deposits	$5,500	$9,000
Coffee Preparation Equipment	$2,500	$4,000
Computer Equipment	$0	$7,500
Additional Funds (for 3 months)	$8,000	$12,000
Total Investment (not including Real Estate)	$179,900	$251,100

On-Going Expenses
Mrs. Fields franchisees pay a royalty fee equal to 6% of monthly gross revenue, marketing fees equal to 1% to 3% of monthly gross revenue and a cooperative advertising fee that may equal up to 3% of monthly gross revenue.

What You Get—Training and Support
In Mrs. Fields' in-depth training program, franchisees experience both classroom and on-the-job training. After the store is opened, the extensive and experienced support staff provides various operational assistance, covering areas such as customer service, hiring and training personnel, store set-up and product display, baking procedures, merchandising,

promotion and advertising.

Territory
Mrs. Fields does not grant exclusive territories.

Pretzel Time

FRESHNESS WITH A TWIST!™

2855 E. Cottonwood Pkwy., # 400
Salt Lake City, UT 84121-7037
Tel: (800) 343-5377 (801) 736-5600
Fax: (801) 736-5936
E-Mail: donl@mrsfields.com
Web Site: www.mrsfieldsfranchise.com
Ms. Dara Dejbakhsh, EVP Operations/Development

'Freshness With A Twist.' Retail pretzel stores, offering a healthy snack alternative that is freshly mixed, rolled and baked. Store options are available for traditional and non-traditional venues.

BACKGROUND: IFA MEMBER
Established: 1991;   1st Franchised: 1992
Franchised Units: 178
Company-Owned Units   54
Total Units: 232
Dist.:   US-228; CAN-0; O'seas-4
 North America: 37 States, 2 Provinces
 Density: 25 in NY, 21 in CA, 15 in TX
Projected New Units (12 Months):   21
Qualifications: , , , , ,
Registered: All States

FINANCIAL/TERMS:

Cash Investment:	$175-250K
Total Investment:	$107-238.5K
Minimum Net Worth:	$150K/75K LIQ
Fees: Franchise —	$25K
Royalty — 7%;	Ad. — 1%
Earnings Claim Statement:	Yes
Term of Contract (Years):	7/7
Avg. # Of Employees:	3 FT, 2 PT
Passive Ownership:	Discouraged
Encourage Conversions:	Yes
Area Develop. Agreements:	Yes/3
Sub-Franchising Contracts:	No
Expand In Territory:	Yes
Space Needs: 400-800 SF; RM	

SUPPORT & TRAINING PROVIDED:

Financial Assistance Provided:	No
Site Selection Assistance:	Yes
Lease Negotiation Assistance:	Yes
Co-Operative Advertising:	No
Franchisee Assoc./Member:	Yes
Size Of Corporate Staff:	100+
On-Going Support:	B,C,D,E,F,G,H,I
Training: 6 Days Salt Lake City, UT.	

SPECIFIC EXPANSION PLANS:

US:	All United States
Canada:	All Canada
Overseas:	NR

Pretzel Time offers customers "freshness with a twist!" Its famous soft pretzels were introduced in 1991, and Pretzel Time has grown steadily since, supported by consumers' growing attachment to more healthful fresh-baked goods. Buyers are attracted to the reasonable price and low-fat content of Pretzel Time pretzels, and can customize an order with a variety of toppings or lemonade on the side. The current menu includes classic pretzels, the pizza pretzel, the ham-and-cheese pretzel and specialty items like the Cinnamon Twist. At each of its 300 locations in shopping centers nationwide, Pretzel Time is always aiming to keep the menu exciting with its in-house research and development team.

Pretzel Time is now part of the Mrs. Fields family and franchisees have the opportunity to co-brand with other Mrs. Fields brands and attract a larger customer base.

Operating Units	12/28/2002	1/3/2004	1/1/2005
Franchised	163	172	188
% Change	--	5.5%	9.3%
Company-Owned	79	54	33
% Change	--	-31.6%	-38.9%
Total	242	226	221
% Change	--	-6.6%	-2.2%
Franchised as % of Total	67.36%	76.11%	85.07%

Investment Required
The fee for a Pretzel Time franchise is $25,000.

Pretzel Time provides the following range of investments required to open your initial franchise. The range assumes that all items are paid for in cash. To the extent that you choose to finance any of these expense items, your front-end investment could be substantially reduced. The following figures refer to the construction of a new Pretzel Time store.

Item	Established Low Range	Established High Range
Franchise Fee	$25,000	$25,000
Training Expenses	$1,500	$3,000
Improvements/Equipment	$75,000	$250,000

Opening Inventory	$1,000	$5,000
Grand Opening	$5,000	$5,000
Miscellaneous Fees/ Deposits	$1,500	$6,500
Insurance	$2,500	$3,500
Computer Equipment	$0	$7,500
Additional Funds (for 3 months)	$8,000	$12,000
Total Investment (not including Real Estate)	$119,500	$317,500

On-Going Expenses

Pretzel Time franchisees pay a royalty fee equal to 7% of monthly gross revenue, marketing fees equal to 1 to 3% of monthly gross revenue and a cooperative advertising fee that may equal up to 3% of monthly gross revenue.

What You Get—Training and Support

Since being acquired by Mrs. Fields Famous Brands in 1996, the support system for Pretzel Time franchisees has been refined and strengthened. Franchisees receive support in the form of store-site selection, employee training programs and franchisee orientation. Franchisees may choose to open an in-line store, kiosks or extended product-line kiosks that can be adapted to fit into airport concourses, office building lobbies, stadiums, hospitals or universities.

Franchisees must complete an extensive training program with both classroom and in-store instruction to open and operate a Pretzel Time store. Ongoing support includes: customer service, hiring and training personnel, store set-up and product display, baking procedures, merchandising, promotion and advertising.

Territory

Pretzel Time does not grant exclusive territories.

Rita's Italian Ice

1525 Ford Rd.
Bensalem, PA 19020-4505
Tel: (800) 677-7482 (215) 633-9899
Fax: (215) 633-9922
E-Mail: s.miele@ritascorp.com
Web Site: www.ritasice.com
Mr. Steve Miele, Franchise Licensing Manager

Retail outlets selling Italian ices, old-fashioned frozen custard, misto shakes and layered gelati, as well as other cool treats.

BACKGROUND: IFA MEMBER
Established: 1984; 1st Franchised: 1989
Franchised Units: 341
Company-Owned Units 1
Total Units: 342
Dist.: US-342; CAN-0; O'seas-0
North America: 12 States
Density: PA, NJ, MD
Projected New Units (12 Months): 100
Qualifications: 5, 3, 2, 3, 5, 5
Registered: RI,MD,NY,VA

FINANCIAL/TERMS:
Cash Investment: $75K
Total Investment: $164.4-340K
Minimum Net Worth: $250K
Fees: Franchise — $34K
  Royalty — 6.5%; Ad. — 2.5%
Earnings Claim Statement: Yes
Term of Contract (Years): 10/10
Avg. # Of Employees: 1 FT, 9 PT
Passive Ownership: Discouraged
Encourage Conversions: Yes
Area Develop. Agreements: Yes
Sub-Franchising Contracts: No
Expand In Territory: Yes
Space Needs: 600-1,500 SF; FS, SC, KI, RM, Univ.

SUPPORT & TRAINING PROVIDED:
Financial Assistance Provided: Yes(I)
Site Selection Assistance: Yes
Lease Negotiation Assistance: Yes
Co-Operative Advertising: Yes
Franchisee Assoc./Member: No
Size Of Corporate Staff: 60
On-Going Support: B,C,D,E,F,G,H,I
Training: 6 Days Corporate Office; 2-4 Days On-Site.

SPECIFIC EXPANSION PLANS:
US: East of Mississippi
Canada: No
Overseas: No

Rita's features Ices, Cones, Shakes and other Cool Stuff. Rita's Italian Ices are made fresh daily and available in more than 30 different flavors. Rita's old-fashioned Frozen Custard, available in chocolate and vanilla, can be served in either a cone or a cup. Rita's famous Gelati provides frozen dessert fans with the best of both worlds with its layers of Italian Ice and Frozen Custard. Rita's Misto, the coolest name in shakes, is a blend of Italian Ice and creamy custard that, when blended, forms a refreshing treat that can be enjoyed on the go. Rita's also offers Cream Ices for those who prefer a treat that is smoother and richer than Italian Ice, but not as heavy as traditional ice cream.

Today Rita's is the nation's largest Italian Ice chain with more than 340 locations operating throughout the East Coast and as far west as Ohio. Rita's was founded by Bob Tumolo in the summer of 1984. He began by experimenting with his mother's help with recipes for Italian Water Ice. The response for the final result was overwhelming. In May of 2005, Rita's was purchased by Pittsburgh-based McKnight and Capital Partners under the direction of CEO Jim Rudolph. Today Rita's has more than 340 stores in 12 states and has an aggressive growth plan of 1,500 stores by 2,010.

Operating Units	12/31/2003	12/31/2004	12/31/2005
Franchised	279	309	341
% Change	--	10.75%	10.4%
Company-Owned	1	1	1
% Change	--	0.0%	0.0%
Total	280	310	342
% Change	--	10.71%	10.32%
Franchised as % of Total	99.64%	99.68%	99.71%

Investment Required
The fee for a Rita's Italian Ice franchise is $27,500.

Rita's provides the following range of investments required to open your initial franchise. The range assumes that all items are paid for in cash. To the extent that you choose to finance any of these expense items, your front-end investment could be substantially reduced.

Item	Established Low Range	Established High Range
Franchise Fee	$30,000	$30,000
Lease Deposit & Leasehold Improvements	$51,200	$169,000
Equipment	$57,000	$70,000

Signs & Awnings	$7,700	$20,000
Initial Inventory	$4,800	$6,000
Advertising	$1,900	$1,900
Additional Funds (for 3 months)	$11,800	$43,100
Total Investment	$164,400	$340,000

On-Going Expenses
Rita's Italian Ice franchisees pay a royalty fee equal to 6.5% of estimated and/or gross sales, an advertising fee equal to 2.5% of estimated and/or gross sales or $100 and an annual advisory council fee of $150.

What You Get—Training and Support
Training is divided into two phases, with six days at a corporate training center and two to four days at the franchisee's location for the grand opening. Training covers production, quality control, inventory control, advertising concepts and strategies, and general business practices. Franchisees also receive corporate assistance with site selection, lease negotiation, store design and development, and the equipment package required to operate the store. Franchisees also receive proprietary recipes, ongoing support and a professionally managed marketing program.

Territory
Rita's Italian Ice grants exclusive territories.

Shake's Frozen Custard

244 W. Dickson St.
Fayetteville, AR 72701-5221
Tel: (866) 742-5648 (479) 587-9115
Fax: (479) 587-0780
E-Mail: toddosborne@shakesfrozencustard.com
Web Site: www.shakesfrozencustard.com
Mr. Todd Osborne, Development Specialist

SHAKE'S FROZEN CUSTARD is where friends gather, couples fall in love, and people of all ages come to enjoy the vibrant nostalgic atmosphere of the 50's. Featuring an extensive menu consisting of our one-of-a-kind, delicious frozen custard and a wide variety of innovative concepts, SHAKE'S is a rapidly growing franchise system. With intensive training and continuous support, we will always ensure your business is operating to its maximum potential.

BACKGROUND:

Established: 1991;	1st Franchised: 1999
Franchised Units:	42
Company-Owned Units	3
Total Units:	45
Dist.:	US-45; CAN-0; O'seas-0
North America:	8 States
Density:	12 in AR, 8 in MO, 7 in TX
Projected New Units (12 Months):	25
Qualifications: 4, 4, 2, 1, 3, 5	
Registered: FL,IL,IN,VA,WI	

FINANCIAL/TERMS:

Cash Investment:	$50-250K
Total Investment:	$166-800K
Minimum Net Worth:	$250K
Fees: Franchise —	$30K

Royalty — 5%;	Ad. — 3%
Earnings Claim Statement:	Yes
Term of Contract (Years):	15/5
Avg. # Of Employees:	3 FT, 12 PT
Passive Ownership:	Discouraged
Encourage Conversions:	No
Area Develop. Agreements:	Yes/15
Sub-Franchising Contracts:	No
Expand In Territory:	Yes
Space Needs: 1,200 SF; FS	

SUPPORT & TRAINING PROVIDED:

Financial Assistance Provided:	Yes(I)
Site Selection Assistance:	Yes
Lease Negotiation Assistance:	Yes
Co-Operative Advertising:	Yes
Franchisee Assoc./Member:	Yes
Size Of Corporate Staff:	10
On-Going Support:	A,B,C,D,E,F,G,h
Training: 2 Weeks in Fayetteville, AR.	

SPECIFIC EXPANSION PLANS:

US:	South, SE, SW, Midwest
Canada:	No
Overseas:	No

If you're looking for a franchise that provides families with a wholesome experience using wholesome ingredients, consider Shake's Frozen Custard, a retro-style creamery driven by three core principles: quality, service and cleanliness. The winner of numerous "best of" designations within the areas it serves, Shake's uses high-quality ingredients, exclusive recipes and custom toppings to create its signature product – a smooth, creamy, additive-free ice cream whipped up hourly.

Shake's offers a variety of facility layouts – all designed to lure customers with a fishbowl effect using strategically placed interactive sites and viewing stations – to accommodate most sites, including a double drive-thru facility the company likens to an ice cream-dispensing factory; a single drive-thru facility similar to the double facility but requiring less land space; and end-cap facilities that can be tailored to fit strip centers and other attached structures.

Operating Units	12/31/2003	12/31/2004	12/31/2005
Franchised	39	39	42
% Change	--	0.0%	7.7%
Company-Owned	2	2	3
% Change	--	0.0%	50%
Total	41	41	45
% Change	--	0.0%	9.8%
Franchised as % of Total	95.12%	95.12%	93.3%

Investment Required

The fee for a Shake's Frozen Custard franchise is $30,000.

Shake's Frozen Custard provides the following range of investments required to open your initial franchise. The range assumes that all items are paid for in cash. To the extent that you choose to finance any of these expense items, your front-end investment could be substantially reduced.

Item	Established Low Range	Established High Range
Franchise fee	$30,000	$30,000
Rent/real estate acquisition and improvements	Varies	Varies
Equipment, signage, point-of-sale systems	$100,000	$180,000
Inventory and supplies	$7,000	$20,000
Prepaid expenses/deposits	$5,000	$15,000
Additional funds (for three months)	$20,000	$50,000
Total	$162,000	$295,000

On-Going Expenses

Shake's Frozen Custard franchisees pay a royalty fee equal to 5% of weekly gross sales, a marketing fee equal to up to 3% of gross sales and a local marketing fee equal to up to 1.5% of gross sales.

What You Get—Training and Support
The Shake's training program consists of two weeks of comprehensive classroom and one-on-one instruction in recipes, production and ordering.

Territory
Shake's Frozen Custard grants exclusive territories generally encompassing a 3-mile radius around the franchisees' locations.

Uno Chicago Grill

100 Charles Park Rd.
Boston, MA 02132-4985
Tel: (877) 855-8667 (617) 218-5200
Fax: (617) 218-5376
E-Mail: fred.houston@unos.com
Web Site: www.unos.com
Mr. Fred Houston, VP Franchising

A full-service casual theme restaurant with a brand name signature product - UNO's Original Chicago Deep Dish Pizza. A full varied menu with broad appeal featuring steak, shrimp and pasta. A flair for fun including a bar and comfortable décor in a facility that attracts guests of all ages.

BACKGROUND:

	IFA MEMBER
Established: 1943;	1st Franchised: 1979
Franchised Units:	89
Company-Owned Units	122
Total Units:	211
Dist.:	US-207; CAN-0; O'seas-4
North America:	32 States
Density:	31 in NY, 30 in MA, 15 in VA
Projected New Units (12 Months):	16

Qualifications: 5, 5, 5, 3, 4, 4

Registered: All States

FINANCIAL/TERMS:

Cash Investment:	$700K
Total Investment:	$1.3-2.7MM
Minimum Net Worth:	$3MM
Fees: Franchise —	$40K
Royalty — 5%;	Ad. — 1%
Earnings Claim Statement:	Yes
Term of Contract (Years):	20/10
Avg. # Of Employees:	40 FT, 40 PT
Passive Ownership:	Allowed
Encourage Conversions:	Yes
Area Develop. Agreements:	Yes
Sub-Franchising Contracts:	No
Expand In Territory:	Yes
Space Needs: 5,800 SF; FS, SC	

SUPPORT & TRAINING PROVIDED:

Financial Assistance Provided:	Yes(I)
Site Selection Assistance:	Yes
Lease Negotiation Assistance:	Yes
Co-Operative Advertising:	Yes
Franchisee Assoc./Member:	Yes/Yes
Size Of Corporate Staff:	135
On-Going Support:	a,B,C,D,E,F,G,H,I

Training: 12 Weeks in a Training Restaurant; 2 Weeks On-Site Staff Training.

SPECIFIC EXPANSION PLANS:

US:	All United States
Canada:	All Canada

Overseas: Asia, South and Central America, Europe

Founded in Chicago in 1943, Pizzeria Uno was a casual restaurant known for its deep-dish pizza. More than 60 years later and going by the new moniker Uno Chicago Grill, the restaurant still evokes the style and memory of Old Chicago and it's still known for its pizza, but now it has even more to offer with a menu that includes steak, ribs, salads, pasta, soups, sandwiches, desserts and a full bar.

An Uno Chicago Grill franchise is for those who think on the big side. General requirements for an Uno site include a 1.8-acre lot and a population of 50,000 with a median household income of $40,000 within a 5-mile radius. The company is especially interested in franchisees who would like to open multiple Uno Chicago Grill locations.

Operating Units	12/31/2002	12/31/2003	12/31/2004
Franchised	73	72	82
% Change	--	-1.4%	13.9%
Company-Owned	116	118	125
% Change	--	1.7%	5.9%
Total	189	190	207
% Change	--	0.5%	8.9%
Franchised as % of Total	38.62%	37.0%	39.61%

Investment Required
The fee for an Uno Chicago Grill franchise is $35,000 plus a $5,000 territorial fee per restaurant.

Uno Chicago Grill provides the following range of investments required to open your initial franchise. The range assumes that all items are paid for in cash. To the extent that you choose to finance any of these expense items, your front-end investment could be substantially reduced.

Item	Established Low Range	Established High Range

Franchise fee	$35,000	$35,000
Leasehold improvements	$500,000	$1,300,000
Furniture, fixtures and equipment	$350,000	$500,000
Site work	$50,000	$500,000
Initial inventory	$10,000	$20,000
Point-of-sale computer hardware and software	$30,000	$35,000
Supplies (for 3 months)	$1,000	$3,000
Business permits	$1,000	$20,000
Liquor license	Varies	Varies
Insurance deposits and premiums (for 1st year)	$12,000	$20,000
Architect fees	$20,000	$40,000
Other professional fees	$2,500	$10,000
Site lease	$15,000	$30,000
Utility deposits	$1,000	$5,000
Advertising and promotion	$1,000	$5,000
Additional funds (for 3 months)	$75,000	$150,000
Total	$1,103,500	$2,673,000

On-Going Expenses

Uno Chicago Grill franchisees pay a royalty fee equal to 5% of gross sales, and a marketing fee equal to 1% of gross sales. Minimum local advertising costs equal to up to 2% of gross sales and a systemwide marketing and media fund fee equal to up to 1% of gross sales. Other costs include local advertising association fees, if applicable, and an advertising and promotion materials fee.

What You Get—Training and Support

Uno Chicago Grill's outpouring of support begins on-site before the restaurant even exists. Starting with site-selection assistance, Uno Chicago Grill guides franchisees through the design and construction process, working with the contractor and providing the architect with adaptable prototype plans. This support is then complemented by three visits to the under-construction site. When opening time rolls around, a pre-opening team arrives to train staff and provide opening assistance. Regional directors later conduct reviews and provide field resources. For assistance with point-of-sale systems, support is on call 24 hours a day.

For every Uno Chicago Grill manager, the franchisor offers a no-cost training program that lasts for eight to 12 weeks and is catered to meet each individual manager's needs. Among the topics studied by new managers: kitchen, bar and dining-room operations, purchasing, accounting, employee relations and computer systems. Workbooks and training systems allow for self-paced, ongoing learning opportunities. Offered seminars cover interviewing and employee-retention techniques.

On the marketing side, a variety of supplies are available to franchisees, including quarterly promotions, media buying and analysis, in-store point-of-purchase materials and newspaper inserts. The marketing department produces two new menus each year, conducts research and develops radio and television ads and appetizer, drink and dessert merchandising pieces.

Uno Chicago Grill also maintains an in-house art department.

Territory
Uno Chicago Grill grants exclusive territories based on market evaluations of demographics and growth trends, the penetration of the Uno business system and its competitors and the availability of appropriate restaurant sites.

Wienerschnitzel/ Tastee Freez

4440 Von Karman Ave., # 222
Newport Beach, CA 92660
Tel: (800) 764-9353 + 609 (949) 851-2609
Fax: (949) 851-2618
E-Mail: lhughes@galardigroup.com
Web Site: www.wienerschnitzel.com
Mr. Lowry Hughes, Vice President Operations

WIENERSCHNITZEL is the world's largest quick service hot dog restaurant chain with over 350 locations selling 90 million hot dogs annually. We are interested in developing new franchisees throughout California, the Southwest and Pacific Northwest.

BACKGROUND: IFA MEMBER
Established: 1961; 1st Franchised: 1965
Franchised Units: 350
Company-Owned Units: 0
Total Units: 350
Dist.: US-350; CAN-0; O'seas-0
  North America: 11 States
  Density: 228 in CA, 51 in TX, 14 in A
Projected New Units (12 Months): 35
Qualifications: 4, 3, 3, 2, 1, 4

Registered: CA,IL,OR,WA

FINANCIAL/TERMS:
Cash Investment: $150-250K
Total Investment: $135K-1.2MM
Minimum Net Worth: $500-700K
Fees: Franchise — $36K
  Royalty — 5%; Ad. — 3-5%
Earnings Claim Statement: No
Term of Contract (Years): 20/1-20
Avg. # Of Employees: 1-3 FT, 25-30 PT
Passive Ownership: Discouraged
Encourage Conversions: Yes
Area Develop. Agreements: No
Sub-Franchising Contracts: No
Expand In Territory: Yes
Space Needs: 20,000 SF; FS

SUPPORT & TRAINING PROVIDED:
Financial Assistance Provided: Yes(I)
Site Selection Assistance: Yes
Lease Negotiation Assistance: No
Co-Operative Advertising: Yes
Franchisee Assoc./Member: Yes/Yes
Size Of Corporate Staff: 48
On-Going Support: A,B,C,D,E,F,G,H,I
Training: NR

SPECIFIC EXPANSION PLANS:
US: SW, W, NW
Canada: No
Overseas: No

Wienerschnitzel is, arguably, fast-food royalty. The world's largest chili, corn and hot dog chain was founded by a former Taco Bell employee and was named by the wife of the Mexican food franchise's founder.

The first store opened on the Pacific Coast Highway in 1961, and seven years later, the Der Wienerschnitzel name (the "Der" was dropped in 1977) was emblazoned on 200 restaurants, which were popular sites for car clubs, inspiring the drive-thrus that are now a staple of the fast-food industry.

Then, in 2003, Wienerschnitzel added another fast-food legend to its lineup with the acquisition of Tastee Freez, whose signature soft-serve ice cream, first offered in 1950, actually outdates the Wienerschnitzel brand.

Wienerschnitzel offers three dining-room store types varying in size from 1,250-2,000 square feet. Drive-thru locations are only considered in fair-weather climates.

Operating Units	12/31/2002	12/31/2003	12/31/2004
Franchised	55	59	62
% Change	--	7.3%	5.1%
Company-Owned	0	0	0
% Change	--	0.0%	0.0%
Total	55	59	62
% Change	--	7.3%	5.1%
Franchised as % of Total	100.00%	100.00%	100.00%

Investment Required
The fee for a Wienerschnitzel franchise is $32,000. Additional units are available at a cost of $15,000-$32,000. Franchisees can open a Wiener-schnitzel co-branded with a Tastee-Freez for an additional cost of $5,000, which includes training.

Wienerschnitzel provides the following range of investments required to open your initial franchise. The range assumes that all items are paid for in cash. To the extent that you choose to finance any of these expense items, your front-end investment could be substantially reduced. The following figures refer to the opening of a full franchise.

Item	Established Low Range	Established High Range
Franchise fee	$2,500	$32,000
Rent	$1,500	$23,500
Equipment, furniture, furnishings, fixtures	$112,500	$175,000
Opening inventory	$5,000	$8,000
Training	$2,000	$4,500
Insurance	$4,000	$5,800
Uniforms	$1,500	$1,500
Security deposit	$2,000	$32,000
Real estate improvements	$0	$750,000
Advertising fee (for 3 months)	$3,600	$18,000
Miscellaneous opening costs	$1,500	$1,500
Total	$136,100	$10,518,000

On-Going Expenses

Wienerschnitzel franchisees pay a national advertising fee equal to 1% of gross sales, a local advertising fee equal to 3-5% of gross sales and a service fee equal to 5% of gross sales. Additional costs include those for manager and new employee training, management certification and a management-development program.

What You Get—Training and Support

Wienerschnitzel training lasts six weeks, during which operators learn how to run daily business with lessons that cover basic floor skills, paperwork, ordering and receiving, labor laws, team training, accounting, sanitation, inventory, customer complaints, interviewing, marketing and preventive maintenance. The training is intense, but thorough. During six-day workweeks, new franchisees will spend 10 hours a day in learning situations, not including time for additional reading and home study. After five days in the classroom, franchisees move to operating restaurants, where they complete the training process. That is, unless they are also opening a Tastee Freeze unit, in which case additional training is provided on-site three weeks before opening.

Architecturally, Wienerschnitzel provides assistance with prototype building drawings, equipment, computer and sign vendors and site review and approval based on demographics, traffic reports and aerial photos. Ongoing assistance with daily operations, training and marketing are also provided.

Territory
Wienerschnitzel grants exclusive territories encompassing the area within a ½-mile radius of the franchisee's restaurant, or within 1 mile along the same street.

Wing Zone

900 Circle 75 Pkwy., # 930
Atlanta, GA 30339-3084
Tel: (877) 946-4966 (404) 875-5045
Fax: (404) 875-6631
E-Mail: stan@wingzone.com
Web Site: www.wingzone.com
Mr. Stan Friedman, Executive Vice President

Delivery and take-out of 25 taste-tempting flavors of fresh, cooked-to-order Buffalo wings. We also feature chicken fingers, grilled or fried chicken sandwiches, half-pound burgers, salads, sides, appetizers and desserts - all delivered hot and fresh to your door. A great opportunity in urban and suburban markets, near apartments, campuses, military bases, hospitals and offices.

BACKGROUND: IFA MEMBER
Established: 1991;   1st Franchised: 1999
Franchised Units: 111

Company-Owned Units	2
Total Units:	113
Dist.:	US-113; CAN-0; O'seas-0
North America:	24 States
Density:	10 in LA, 10 in NC, 9 in FL
Projected New Units (12 Months):	30
Qualifications: 5, 5, 5, 5, 1, 5	
Registered: FL,MD,MI,NY,OR,RI,VA,WA,DC	

FINANCIAL/TERMS:

Cash Investment:	$60-75K
Total Investment:	$176-249K
Minimum Net Worth:	$200K
Fees: Franchise —	$25K
Royalty — 5%;	Ad. — 0.5%
Earnings Claim Statement:	Yes
Term of Contract (Years):	10/10
Avg. # Of Employees:	5 FT, 10 PT
Passive Ownership:	Not Allowed
Encourage Conversions:	No
Area Develop. Agreements:	Yes
Sub-Franchising Contracts:	No
Expand In Territory:	Yes
Space Needs: 1,200 SF; SF, SC	

SUPPORT & TRAINING PROVIDED:

Financial Assistance Provided:	Yes(I)	Training: 12 Days Atlanta, GA; 10 Days In-Store.
Site Selection Assistance:	Yes	
Lease Negotiation Assistance:	Yes	**SPECIFIC EXPANSION PLANS:**
Co-Operative Advertising:	No	US:　　　　　　　　　　　SE, NE, MW, SW
Franchisee Assoc./Member:	Yes/Yes	Canada:　　　　　　　　　　Near Border
Size Of Corporate Staff:	12	Overseas:　　　　　　　　　　　　No
On-Going Support:	B,C,D,E,F,G,H,I	

Are you tired of pizza? You're probably not the only one. While the take-out and delivery market is expected to rake in $200 billion in the next five years, evening and late-night diners still have few choices beyond the usual pepperoni pie.

It's a hole in the market that Wing Zone is perfectly positioned to fill. Offering 25 flavors of jumbo buffalo wings as well as sandwiches, chicken fingers, burgers and sides, Wing Zone, which started in a fraternity-house-kitchen at the University of Florida in 1991, is now filling stomachs in 24 states with its signature sauces.

Offering only take-out and delivery service and catering mostly to college and urban communities (where late-night bookworms and party animals are always on the prowl for a good meal), Wing Zone franchises require low overhead and only about 1,000 to 1,200 square feet of space.

Operating Units	9/30/2003	9/30/2004	9/30/2005
Franchised	42	57	69
% Change	--	35.7%	21.1%
Company-Owned	2	2	2
% Change	--	0.0%	0.0%
Total	44	59	71
% Change	--	34.1%	20.3%
Franchised as % of Total	95.45%	96.61%	97.18%

Investment Required
The fee for a Wing Zone franchise is $25,000.

Wing Zone provides the following range of investments required to open your initial franchise. The range assumes that all items are paid for in cash. To the extent that you choose to finance any of these expense items, your front-end investment could be substantially reduced.

Item	Established Low Range	Established High Range
Franchise fee	$20,000	$25,000
Leasehold improvements	$40,000	$80,000
Equipment/Systems	$51,000	$59,500
Signs	$6,000	$8,000
Initial inventory	$4,000	$4,000
Computer point-of-sale system, office equipment, furniture and supplies	$18,000	$18,000
Grand opening marketing	$5,000	$5,000
Start-up marketing	$3,000	$3,000
Insurance	$2,000	$3,500
Real estate costs	$4,000	$8,000
Architectural plans	$4,000	$8,000
Utility deposits	$1,000	$2,500
Uniforms	$1,000	$1,000
Drop safe and lock	$1,000	$1,500
Your out-of-pocket initial training expenses	$1,000	$3,000
Operating cost (for 3 months)	$15,000	$19,000
Total	$176,000	$249,000

On-Going Expenses

Wing Zone franchisees pay a royalty fee equal to 5% of gross sales, advertising fees equal to up to 5% of gross sales and a marketing development fee equal to 0.5-1% of gross sales. Additional costs include a daily $400 per-person charge for refresher training.

What You Get—Training and Support

When Wing Zone franchisees set out to build their businesses, the franchisor pitches in to help out with territory demographics, site selection, lease negotiation, staffing, architectural and build-out requirements and signage.

Training for a franchisee and up to three other people takes place at the corporate center and on-site with instruction focusing on food preparation, delivery operations and the point-of-sale computer system.

After the unit opens, Wing Zone maintains quality control through visitations and inspections of the franchisee's unit. The company also makes recommendations regarding inventory and labor costs. Ongoing consultation and marketing support is also available by phone.

Additional assistance comes with the equipment package, marketing programs, volume printing of menus, door hangers, magnets and direct mailings, product and procedure research and development, an intranet and national contracts for food supplies.

Territory

Wing Zone grants exclusive territories, the size of which depends on a unit's location. In rural areas, franchisees are granted territories encompassing a 3-mile radius around their unit. In urban areas, franchisees are granted territories encompassing a ½-mile radius around their unit.

Retail 5

7-Eleven

2711 N. Haskell Ave., 34th Fl.
Dallas, TX 75204-2911
Tel: (800) 255-0711 (214) 828-7764
Fax: (214) 841-6776
E-Mail: jwebbj01@7-11.com
Web Site: www.7-eleven.com
Ms. Joanne Webb-Joyce, Dir. National Franchise
 Sales

7-ELEVEN stores were born from the simple concept of giving people 'what they want, when and where they want it.' This idea gave rise to the entire convenience store industry. While this formula still works today, customers' needs are changing at an accelerating pace. We are meeting this challenge with an infrastructure of daily distribution of fresh perishables, regional production of fresh foods and pastries and an information system that greatly improves ordering and merchandising decisions.

BACKGROUND: IFA MEMBER
Established: 1927;   1st Franchised: 1964
Franchised Units: 25,139
Company-Owned Units: 2,377
Total Units: 27,516
Dist.:   US-5,788; CAN-488; O'seas-21,240
 North America: 36 States, 5 Provinces
 Density: 1,219 in CA, 614 VA, 542 FL

Projected New Units (12 Months):   150
Qualifications: 4, 4, 3, 3, 5, 5
Registered: CA,IL,IN,MD,MI,NY,OR,RI,VA,WA,
 WI

FINANCIAL/TERMS:
Cash Investment: $111K
Total Investment: $Varies
Minimum Net Worth: $15K
Fees: Franchise — $91K
 Royalty — NA;   Ad. — NA
Earnings Claim Statement: No
Term of Contract (Years):   15
Avg. # Of Employees: 5 FT, 5 PT
Passive Ownership: Not Allowed
Encourage Conversions: NA
Area Develop. Agreements: No
Sub-Franchising Contracts: No
Expand In Territory: No
Space Needs: 2,400 SF; FS, SC

SUPPORT & TRAINING PROVIDED:
Financial Assistance Provided: Yes(D)
Site Selection Assistance: NA
Lease Negotiation Assistance: NA
Co-Operative Advertising: No
Franchisee Assoc./Member: Yes/Yes
Size Of Corporate Staff: 1,000
On-Going Support: A,B,C,D,E,F,G,H,I
Training: 6 Weeks at Various Training Stores throughout US.

SPECIFIC EXPANSION PLANS:
US: NW,SW,MW,NE, Great Lakes
Canada: No
Overseas: No

7-Eleven, the "friendly little store that's just around the corner," has built a strong reputation for operating stores similar to family-owned businesses but designed to grow with innovative features. Open 24 hours a day, seven days a week, 7-Eleven re-defines "convenience," with more than 25,000 franchises worldwide. An industry leader for more than 77 years, 7-Eleven has been successfully franchising for more than 40 years.

Operating Units	12/31/2002	12/31/2003	12/31/2004
Franchised	3,276	3,338	3,422
% Change	--	1.9%	2.5%
Company-Owned	2,264	2,241	2,230
% Change	--	0.0%	0.0%
Total	5,540	5,579	5,652
% Change	--	0.7%	1.3%
Franchised as % of Total	59.13%	59.83%	60.54%

Investment Required
The franchise fee for a 7-Eleven store depends on the franchised store's gross profits for the past year, i.e. the fee is higher for locations that generate more revenue. The fee for a store with sales less than $200,000 in 12 months is fixed at $10,000. Stores with sales of $200,001 to $250,000 have a fee equal to 5% of the store's historical sales volume, stores with sales between $250,001 and $350,000 have a fee of 15%, stores with sales of $350,000 to $450,000 have a fee of 20% and stores with sales exceeding $450,000 have a fee of 25%. Fees for brand new store locations are determined by the average gross profits of nearby locations. The fee can be reduced or waived depending on a franchisee's experience. Financing is also available.

7-Eleven provides the following range of investments required to open your initial franchise. The range assumes that all items are paid for in cash. To the extent that you choose to finance any of these expense items, your front-end investment could be substantially reduced.

Item	Established Low Range	Established High Range
Franchise Fee	$0	$371,100
Store Supplies	$250	$2,000
Cash Register Fund	$100	$10,000
Inventory	$30,794	$85,063
Licenses & Permits	$100	$3,000
Real Estate	To be decided	To be decided
Training Expenses	$0	$2,677
Additional Funds (for 3 months)	$156,252	$558,472
Total Investment	$187,546	$1,032,312

On-Going Expenses
7-Eleven franchisees pay on-going fees equal to 50% of gross profit and advertising fees that vary based on total gross profit. Stores with monthly rents exceeding $10,000 per month must also pay monthly fees equal to 50% of those occupancy costs.

What You Get—Training and Support
With a proven system of operation, a recognizable name, inventory financing and modern equipment, 7-Eleven provides a store and a system that is ready for a new franchisee to step right into. This system includes training, counseling, accounting, financial reports, advertising and merchandising support. Franchisees select the area where they would like to operate a store before they begin the training program.

Costs such as building and equipment rental, utilities and property taxes are paid by the franchisor using funds obtained from franchisee fees. After opening, 7-Eleven provides general business advice and support, and local and national franchisee advisory councils are also available to provide assistance.

Territory
7-Eleven does not grant exclusive territories.

Aaron's Sales & Lease Ownership

309 E. Paces Ferry Rd., N. E.
Atlanta, GA 30305-2377
Tel: (800) 551-6015 (678) 402-3445
Fax: (678) 402-3540
E-Mail: jim.thrash@aaronrents.com
Web Site: www.aaronsfranchise.com
Mr. Jim Thrash, Director of Franchising

AARON'S SALES & LEASE OWNERSHIP is one of the fastest-growing retail companies in the U.S., specializing in furniture, electronics and appliances. AARON'S SALES & LEASE OWNERSHIP offers franchisees the expertise, advantages and support of a well-established company, plus the opportunity to realize a significant financial return in a booming market segment.

BACKGROUND: IFA MEMBER
Established: 1955;   1st Franchised: 1992
Franchised Units: 383
Company-Owned Units   766
Total Units: 1,149
Dist.:   US-1,144; CAN-5; O'seas-0
North America: 47 States
Density: TX, FL, GA
Projected New Units (12 Months):   80
Qualifications: 5, 5, 1, 4, 5, 5
Registered: CA,FL,HI,IL,IN,MI,NY,ND,OR,RI,SD, VA,WA,WI

FINANCIAL/TERMS:
Cash Investment: $300K
Total Investment: $254-559K
Minimum Net Worth: $450K
Fees: Franchise — $50K
   Royalty — 6%;   Ad. — 2.5%
Earnings Claim Statement: Yes
Term of Contract (Years):   10/10
Avg. # Of Employees: 6 FT
Passive Ownership: Allowed
Encourage Conversions: NA
Area Develop. Agreements: Yes/Varies
Sub-Franchising Contracts: No
Expand In Territory: Yes
Space Needs: 8,000 SF; SC

SUPPORT & TRAINING PROVIDED:
Financial Assistance Provided: Yes(I)
Site Selection Assistance: Yes
Lease Negotiation Assistance: Yes
Co-Operative Advertising: Yes
Franchisee Assoc./Member: Yes
Size Of Corporate Staff: 3,500
On-Going Support: A,B,C,D,E,F,H,I
Training: 3 Weeks Corporate Headquarters; 2 Weeks Minimum On-Site; On-Going Varies.

SPECIFIC EXPANSION PLANS:
US: All United States
Canada: All Canada
Overseas: All Countries

Aaron's Sales and Lease Ownership is a unique retail business that both leases and sells products such as electronics, furniture and appliances. Serving millions of customers who are without credit or who prefer leasing to outright buying – Aaron's offers customers items at prices comparable to those of traditional retailers, as well as benefits such as no-cost repair services, no credit checks and no debt obligation.

Aaron's provides customers with the win-win choice between buying and leasing a quality product at a reasonable price. Aaron's occupies a unique niche in the marketplace with a large customer base. Over 30% of the 96 million households in the United States match the profile of the average leasing customer, which feeds the country's most consistently growing market – the consumer durable goods leasing market.

Operating Units	12/31/2002	12/31/2003	12/31/2004
Franchised	232	287	357
% Change	--	23.7%	24.4%
Company-Owned	387	489	616
% Change	--	26.4%	26.0%
Total	619	776	973
% Change	--	25.4%	25.4%
Franchised as % of Total	37.48%	36.98%	36.69%

Investment Required
The fee for an Aaron's franchise is $50,000.

Aaron's provides the following range of investments required to open your initial franchise. The range assumes that all items are paid for in cash. To the extent that you choose to finance any of these expense items, your front-end investment could be substantially reduced.

Item	Established Low Range	Established High Range
Franchise Fee	$50,000	$50,000
Advertising	$2,000	$5,000
Delivery Vehicle	$1,100	$5,500
Equipment, Fixtures, Signs	$12,570	$17,680
Insurance	$6,500	$11,000
Inventory	$120,000	$160,000

Real Estate/Improvements	$6,000	$141,000
Training Expenses	$500	$3,800
Additional Funds (for 6-15 months)	$70,000	$180,000
Total Investment	$268,670	$573,980

On-Going Expenses

Aaron's franchisees pay royalties equal to 6% of gross revenue; advertising production fees equal to the lesser of two amounts, 0.5% of gross revenue or $3,750 per year; and regional media fees equal to the lesser of two amounts, 2% or $15,000 per year. Additional fees payable by the franchisee include advertising agency funding and consulting services.

What You Get—Training and Support

Aaron's University, a series of in-depth training sessions held in a different city every week. Franchise principals are required to attend one session per month, and they must finish at least three before opening their Aaron's locations. Trainers monitor progress and give exams to ensure proficiency.

New franchisees will be instructed in a variety of topics, including: personnel selection and training, store design, computer software operation, promotional programs, lease negotiation, inventory management, product marketing and customized management resources such as Aaron's Customer Tracking System.

Franchisees are trained on-the-job by Aaron's Franchise Field Consultants, who are dedicated to facilitating the process of opening and running your business. After a store is open, the consultant will act as a personal liaison with Aaron's Franchise Support Center. Additional franchisee benefits include advanced training seminars, a technical support line, inventory financing assistance and an in-house advertising agency for the Aaron's brand.

Territory
Aaron's grants exclusive territories.

The Athlete's Foot

1412 Oakbrook Dr., # 100
Norcross, GA 30093
Tel: (800) 524-6444 (770) 514-4523
Fax: (770) 514-4903
E-Mail: franchiseinfo@theathletesfoot.com
Web Site: www.theathletesfoot.com
Mr. Peter Franetovich, Director Franchise Sales

THE ATHLETE'S FOOT, with more than 600 stores in 45 countries, is the leading international franchisor of name-brand athletic footwear. As a franchisee, you will benefit from headquarters' support, including training, advertising, product selection, special vendor discount programs, continual footwear research and much more.

BACKGROUND: IFA MEMBER
Established: 1971; 1st Franchised: 1972
Franchised Units: 593
Company-Owned Units: 1
Total Units: 594
Dist.: US-239; CAN-2; O'seas-353
North America: 47 States, 1 Province
Density: NR
Projected New Units (12 Months): 120
Qualifications: 4, 5, 3, 3, 2, 5

Registered: All States

FINANCIAL/TERMS:
Cash Investment: $70K Min.
Total Investment: $200-450K
Minimum Net Worth: $200K
Fees: Franchise — $39.9K
 Royalty — 3.5-5%; Ad. — 1%
Earnings Claim Statement: No
Term of Contract (Years): 10/5
Avg. # Of Employees: 2 FT, 6 PT
Passive Ownership: Discouraged
Encourage Conversions: Yes
Area Develop. Agreements: Yes/10
Sub-Franchising Contracts: Yes
Expand In Territory: Yes
Space Needs: 1,200-2,800 SF; FS, SF, SC, RM

SUPPORT & TRAINING PROVIDED:
Financial Assistance Provided: Yes(I)
Site Selection Assistance: Yes
Lease Negotiation Assistance: Yes
Co-Operative Advertising: No
Franchisee Assoc./Member: Yes/Yes
Size Of Corporate Staff: 25
On-Going Support: B,C,D,E,f,G,H,I
Training: 1 Week at Headquarters in Atlanta; 1 Wk. Prior to and during Opening on Location; On-Going.

SPECIFIC EXPANSION PLANS:
US: All United States
Canada: All Canada
Overseas: All Countries

Athlete's Foot is the world's premier franchisor of athletic footwear stores, with more than 30 years of franchising experience in over 40 countries. It is a recognizable yet flexible concept that fits into malls, strip centers and streetfront locations in both large and small cities. Its brand-name strength translates to appeal across diverse demographics, and its global buying power and unique business model allows franchisees to tailor their inventory of footwear and apparel to local tastes.

To assist customers in finding the best-fitting footwear at every store, Athlete's Foot's FitPrint System both measures and analyzes each person's foot and factors in arch type and pressure points. This proprietary technology is used to find the ideal shoe for customers and provides the franchisee with a competitive edge in the marketplace.

Operating Units	12/31/2002	12/31/2003	7/31/2004
Franchised	170	182	199
% Change	--	7.1%	9.3%
Company-Owned	175	149	130
% Change	--	-14.9%	-12.8%
Total	345	331	329
% Change	--	-4.1%	-0.6%
Franchised as % of Total	49.28%	54.98%	60.49%

Investment Required
The fee for an Athlete's Foot franchise is $39,900.

Athlete's Foot provides the following range of investments required to open your initial franchise. The range assumes that all items are paid for in cash. To the extent that you choose to finance any of these expense items, your front-end investment could be substantially reduced.

Item	Established Low Range	Established High Range
Franchise Fee	$39,900	$39,900
Advertising	$7,500	$23,500
Equipment, Fixtures, Signs	$40,000	$70,000
Inventory Control System	$8,000	$10,000
Opening Costs	$30,000	$60,000
Opening Inventory	$50,000	$150,000

Real Estate, Improvements, Fees	$21,000	$88,000
Training Expenses	$3,000	$8,000
Total Investment	$199,400	$449,400

On-Going Expenses
Athlete's Foot franchisees pay royalties equal to 5% of net sales and marketing support fund fees equal to 1% of net sales.

What You Get—Training and Support
Franchisees go through "New Owner Training" at corporate headquarters and on-site training at their own store location. Operations managers make visits and provide consultation on improving efficiency and profits. Franchisees are given assistance with site selection, lease negotiation, marketing materials and opening inventory management. Athlete's Foot provides focused training on inventory control, shoplifting prevention, sales and customer satisfaction.

Many associates become certified "Fit Technicians" to ensure proficiency in fitting shoes and knowledge of the Athlete's Foot product line. An advanced training program, the "Master Fit Technician" certification is also available to augment an already-certified associate's skills and knowledge. This level of required competency at all franchise locations sets the Athlete's Foot name apart from the rest of the industry.

Territory
Athlete's Foot grants protected territories.

Aussie Pet Mobile|

34189 Pacific Coast Hwy., # 203
Dana Point, CA 92629-2814
Tel: (949) 234-0680
Fax: (949) 234-0688
E-Mail: dlouy@aussiepetmobile.com
Web Site: www.aussiepetmobile.com
Mr. David Louy, VP Franchise Sales

AUSSIE PET MOBILE is an internationally proven franchise system of mobile pet grooming with new U.S. headquarters in Orange County, CA. We pride ourselves on our innovative van design, heated hydrobath and a 15-step grooming maintenance process. No experience is required. The AUSSIE PET MOBILE franchise package includes a comprehensive training course. Franchisees enjoy a protected territory with regional and national advertising support. Individual owner-operator and multi-unit programs available.

BACKGROUND: IFA MEMBER
Established: 1996;   1st Franchised: 1997
Franchised Units: 346
Company-Owned Units   4
Total Units: 350
Dist.:   US-280; CAN-1; O'seas-69

North America:	24 States
Density:	CA, CO, VA
Projected New Units (12 Months):	NR
Qualifications: 4, 4, 2, 3, 4, 5	
Registered: All States Except ND	

FINANCIAL/TERMS:

Cash Investment:	$60-200K
Total Investment:	$60-241.4K
Minimum Net Worth:	$125-750K
Fees: Franchise —	$35-125K
Royalty — 8%;	Ad. — 4%
Earnings Claim Statement:	Yes
Term of Contract (Years):	10/10
Avg. # Of Employees:	Varies
Passive Ownership:	Allowed
Encourage Conversions:	No
Area Develop. Agreements:	Yes/10
Sub-Franchising Contracts:	No
Expand In Territory:	Yes
Space Needs: NR SF; NA	

SUPPORT & TRAINING PROVIDED:

Financial Assistance Provided:	Yes(I)
Site Selection Assistance:	NA
Lease Negotiation Assistance:	NA
Co-Operative Advertising:	Yes
Franchisee Assoc./Member:	Yes/Yes
Size Of Corporate Staff:	20
On-Going Support:	A,B,C,D,E,F,G,H,I

Training: 10 Days for Employees; 3 Days Franchisees; 3 Days Advanced Employees.

SPECIFIC EXPANSION PLANS:

US:	All United States
Canada:	All Canada
Overseas:	UK, Europe, Mexico

Aussie Pet Mobile is the world's first mobile pet grooming service franchise. Essentially a pet grooming spa on wheels, Aussie Pet Mobile conveniently helps busy families with the difficult job of keeping their pets bathed and groomed. The customized Mercedes sprinter van arrives right at the owners' home, and inside pets receive a 15-step spa treatment that includes shampooing, massaging, blow drying, brushing, nail clipping and cleaning of the eyes and ears.

In addition, it is possible to own an Aussie Pet Mobile franchise and maintain another career simultaneously, as franchisees are offered flexibility and freedom in how involved they are in day-to-day operations.

Aussie Pet Mobile has enjoyed much success in Australia, where it was created, as well as in the United States, where pet-care spending has increased from $16 billion in 1993 to nearly $36 billion in 2004. Aussie Pet Mobile franchisees benefit from growing brand awareness, strong marketing and a lack of branded competition in the marketplace. By offering convenience and flexibility for the booming pet-care industry, Aussie Pet Mobile has created a niche for itself and has thrived in all economic climates with high levels of repeat business.

Operating Units	12/31/2002	12/31/2003	12/31/2004
Franchised	86	106	111
% Change	--	23.3%	4.7%
Company-Owned	0	0	5
% Change	--	0.0%	N/A
Total	86	106	116
% Change	--	23.3%	9.4%
Franchised as % of Total	100.00%	100.00%	95.69%

Investment Required
The fee for an Aussie Pet Mobile franchise territory ranges from $25,000 to $35,000.

Aussie Pet Mobile provides the following range of investments required to open your initial franchise. The range assumes that all items are paid for in cash. To the extent that you choose to finance any of these expense items, your front-end investment could be substantially reduced.

Item	Established Low Range	Established High Range

Franchise Fee	$35,000	$125,000
Advertising	$5,000	$9,000
Business Expenses	$350	$350
Equipment	$25,000	$75,000
Insurance	$750	$750
Opening Inventory	$1,000	$1,000
Sprinter Van	$2,250	$2,250
Training	$3,200	$3,000
Additional Funds (for 3 months)	$4,000	$13,000
Total Investment	$76,550	$229,350

On-Going Expenses
Aussie Pet Mobile franchisees pay a royalty fee equal to the greater of 8% of monthly gross volume or a minimum royalty of $547, and advertising fees equal to the greater of 4% of monthly gross revenues or a minimum fee of $274. When franchisee's revenue reaches $15,000 per month, the royalty drops to 5% and advertising drops to 3% retroactively.

What You Get—Training and Support
Aussie Pet Mobile offers four levels of financial investment for new franchisees. Extensive training is available for both franchisees and groomers, and the mobile nature of the business means no real estate is required. Aussie Pet Mobile franchisees also enjoy PR and marketing support.

Aussie Pet Mobile's national call center operates 24 hours a day, 7 days a week, 365 days a year; managing new customer inquiries and transferring them to the franchisee in their area. Aussie Pet Mobile also produces a quarterly newsletter to inform franchisees of new training opportunities, announce expansion details and developments and recognize outstanding franchisees. Ongoing support includes a groomer helpline and a van helpline.

Territory
Aussie Pet Mobile grants exclusive territories.

Baby USA

793 Springer Dr.
Lombard, IL 60148
Tel: (800) 323-4198 (630) 652-0600
Fax: (630) 652-9080
E-Mail: franchise@usababy.com
Web Site: www.usababy.com
Mr. James L. Courtney, Sr. Dir. Market Devel.

USA BABY is North America's leading specialty retailer of infant and juvenile furniture and accessories. Franchisees receive market evaluation, site selection, store design, financing, opening, advertising, merchandising and on-going operational support. Exclusive territories and substantial single, multi-unit and area development opportunities exist for candidates with a passion for serving customers, developing employee teams and participating in a proven retail environment.

BACKGROUND:

Established: 1975;	1st Franchised: 1986
Franchised Units:	70
Company-Owned Units	0
Total Units:	70
Dist.:	US-69; CAN-0; O'seas-1
North America:	22 States
Density:	8 in IL, 6 in IL, 6 in CA
Projected New Units (12 Months):	12

Qualifications: 4, 4, 1, 3, 2, 5
Registered: CA,FL,HI,IL,IN,MD,MI,MN,NY,VA,WA,WI

FINANCIAL/TERMS:

Cash Investment:	$120-170K
Total Investment:	$450-650K
Minimum Net Worth:	$180K
Fees: Franchise —	$42.5K
Royalty — 3%;	Ad. — 5%
Earnings Claim Statement:	Yes
Term of Contract (Years):	10/10
Avg. # Of Employees:	5 FT, 4 PT
Passive Ownership:	Not Allowed
Encourage Conversions:	Yes
Area Develop. Agreements:	Yes/Varies
Sub-Franchising Contracts:	No
Expand In Territory:	Yes
Space Needs: 10,000-12,000 SF; SC	

SUPPORT & TRAINING PROVIDED:

Financial Assistance Provided:	Yes(I)
Site Selection Assistance:	Yes
Lease Negotiation Assistance:	Yes
Co-Operative Advertising:	NA
Franchisee Assoc./Member:	Yes/Yes
Size Of Corporate Staff:	18
On-Going Support:	C,D,E,G,H,I

Training: 8 Days Corporate Office/Store; 4 Days Pre-Opening; 4 Days Opening; 4-5 Days Post-Opening.

SPECIFIC EXPANSION PLANS:

US:	All United States
Canada:	All Canada
Overseas:	No

As America's leading specialty retailer of furniture and accessories for infants and young children, Baby USA stores appeal to doting new parents. Designer room vignettes display products as they would actually be used and show parents what their baby's nursery is capable of becoming. An extensive variety of fabrics and finishes cater to each customer's individual tastes, and 15-year warranties guarantee the quality of all Baby USA furniture. Baby USA streamlines the process of preparing for a new baby by providing a baby registry, a no-charge layaway program and hassle-free returns.

Baby USA is positioned for stronger growth in the future as the baby industry continues to boom. Child-related businesses are projected to remain in the top 15 fastest-growing industries of 2005. Baby USA stores carry many products only available through exclusive contracts with manufacturers, giving them an edge in this competitive market, and offer competitive pricing to benefit the customer and the franchisee.

Operating Units	12/31/2001	12/31/2002	12/31/2003
Franchised	59	66	64
% Change	--	11.9%	-3.0%
Company-Owned	0	0	0
% Change	--	0.0%	0.0%
Total	59	66	64
% Change	--	11.9%	-3.0%
Franchised as % of Total	100.00%	100.00%	100.00%

Investment Required
The fee for a Baby USA franchise ranges from $23,400 to $60,200 depending on the population of the franchise's territory.

Baby USA provides the following range of investments required to open your initial franchise. The range assumes that all items are paid for in cash. To the extent that you choose to finance any of these expense items, your front-end investment could be substantially reduced.

Item	Established Low Range	Established High Range
Franchise Fee	$23,400	$60,200
Computer	$2,000	$32,000
Equipment, Fixtures, Signs	$63,000	$119,000

Insurance	$2,000	$4,000
Inventory	$185,000	$250,000
Lease Deposits, Improvements	$40,000	$110,000
Rent	$3,500	$10,500
Training Expenses	$2,000	$3,000
Additional Funds	$50,000	$100,000
Total Investment	$370,900	$688,700

On-Going Expenses

Baby USA franchisees pay royalties equal to 1.5 to 3% of gross receipts, local advertising fees equal to 5% of gross receipts and insurance fees of $2,000 to $4,000.

What You Get—Training and Support

Baby USA provides two weeks of focused training and discusses topics such as marketing, merchandising, sales, store layout and employment management. A Chief Merchandising Officer assists franchisees in strategic planning and merchandise organization to help them achieve the highest possible volume sales.

Baby USA also gives franchisees the tools to form a solid business plan, financial assistance through third-party lenders, coordination assistance with the site selection process and help designing attractive stores.

After a store is opened, Baby USA makes one-on-one advisory visits to franchisee stores as part of its Franchise Health Check Program to ensure that operations are successful and to offer suggestions for improvement.

Territory

Baby USA grants exclusive territories.

Cartridge World

6460 Hollis St.
Emeryville, CA 94608
Tel: (866) 473-5623 (510) 594-9900
Fax: (510) 594-9991
E-Mail: jdring@cartridgeworld.com
Web Site: www.cartridgeworldusa.com
Mr. John Dring, Executive Vice President/COO

CARTRIDGE WORLD is the leader in printer cartridge refilling. Our business strategy combines the skilled process of refilling printer cartridges for inkjet and laser printers, photocopy and fax machines with knowledgeable and fast customer service, convenient retail locations and savings to the customer of up to 50%. CARTRIDGE WORLD, which dominates its market, has become one of the fastest-growing franchise concepts in the world. Named #1 in its market by Entrepreneur Magazine.

BACKGROUND: IFA MEMBER
Established: 1997;   1st Franchised: 2002
Franchised Units: 1,143
Company-Owned Units   0
Total Units: 1,143
Dist.:   US-360; CAN-14; O'seas-769
  North America: 41 States, 3 Provinces
  Density: 40 in CA, 34 in TX, 30 in NJ
Projected New Units (12 Months):   350

Qualifications: 4, 5, 3, 3, 2, 5
Registered: All States and AB

FINANCIAL/TERMS:

Cash Investment:	$30K
Total Investment:	$104-172K
Minimum Net Worth:	$250-350K
Fees: Franchise —	$30K
Royalty — 6%;	Ad. — 2%
Earnings Claim Statement:	No
Term of Contract (Years):	10/10
Avg. # Of Employees:	1 FT, 1 PT
Passive Ownership:	Discouraged
Encourage Conversions:	Yes
Area Develop. Agreements:	No
Sub-Franchising Contracts:	Yes
Expand In Territory:	Yes
Space Needs: NR SF; FS, SF, SC	

SUPPORT & TRAINING PROVIDED:

Financial Assistance Provided:	Yes(I)
Site Selection Assistance:	Yes
Lease Negotiation Assistance:	Yes
Co-Operative Advertising:	Yes
Franchisee Assoc./Member:	Yes/Yes
Size Of Corporate Staff:	30
On-Going Support:	B,C,D,E,F,G,H,I
Training: 2 Weeks Emeryville, CA; 2 Weeks In-Store Field Training.	

SPECIFIC EXPANSION PLANS:

US:	All United States
Canada:	All Canada
Overseas:	All Countries

Cartridge World's primary business is refilling empty printer cartridges, whether for inkjet or laser printers, photocopiers or fax machines, using black or color ink. With the increased use of computers and printers at work and home, ink and toner are needed on a steady basis. The growth of digital-camera use has led to a similar increase in inkjet photo printers, and the need to recycle has also pushed up demand for Cartridge World's convenient and cost-saving services. Cartridge World also aims to be a one-stop shop for printer needs, also providing the devices themselves, new cartridges, specialty paper, fax supplies and technical advice.

Customers save up to 50% by refilling a used cartridge instead of buying a new one. More than 70% of people throw their used ones away and buy new ones—an incredible amount of potential for the Cartridge World industry as awareness of its services spreads.

Operating Units	12/31/2003	12/31/2004	12/31/2005
Franchised	10	108	360
% Change	--	980.0%	233.0%
Company-Owned	0	0	0
% Change	--	0.0%	0.0%
Total	10	108	360
% Change	--	980.0%	233.0%
Franchised as % of Total	100.00%	100.00%	100.00%

Investment Required

The fee for a Cartridge World franchise is $30,000.

Cartridge World provides the following range of investments required to open your initial franchise. The range assumes that all items are paid for in cash. To the extent that you choose to finance any of these expense items, your front-end investment could be substantially reduced.

Item	Established Low Range	Established High Range
Franchise Fee	$30,000	$30,000
Equipment	$27,000	$29,000
Opening Inventory	$9,000	$9,000
Furnishings, Fixtures, Signs, Computer Equipment	$9,000	$21,000
Business Licenses/ Expenses	$300	$800
Grand Opening Package	$7,000	$7,000

Insurance	$1,000	$1,500
Real Estate/Construction	$5,500	$29,000
Misc. Funds	$1,000	$5,000
Other Costs and Additional Funds (for 3 months)	$14,300	$39,800
Total Investment	$104,100	$172,100

On-Going Expenses
Cartridge World franchisees pay a royalty fee equal to 6% of gross volume on all other goods and services and an advertising fund fee equal to 2% of gross volume on all other goods and services.

What You Get—Training and Support
Franchisees receive in-store training as well as training at corporate headquarters in Emeryville, California. They receive design assistance with the store construction and get ongoing support and technical advice both by phone and through an exclusive franchisee website. Annual meetings and seminars keep franchisees up to date with the latest news and technologies. Even without previous experience, new franchisees can learn all the necessary specialized skills for handling printer cartridges in their training sessions.

Franchisees also receive a business operations manual, computer software and information on purchasing, stock control, administration, bookkeeping, sales and marketing.

Territory
Cartridge World grants exclusive territories for a specific period of time.

EmbroidMe|

2121 Vista Pkwy.
West Palm Beach, FL 334411
Tel: (800) 727-6720 (561) 868-1453
Fax: (561) 640-6062
E-Mail: franchise@embroidme.com
Web Site: www.embroidme.com
Franchise Development Team,

The custom apparel and merchandise industry is exploding and embroidery is everywhere. To capitalize on this explosion, EMBROIDME has launched a revolution in the custom embroidery industry. At EMBROIDME, we are 'casually dressing America,' not only in our retail showrooms and through our corporate marketing program, but across the internet as well. We invite you to learn more about our unique, turn-key EMBROIDME concept, system and cutting edge franchise. Call 800/727-6720 or www. EmbroidMe.com.

BACKGROUND: IFA MEMBER
Established: 2000; 1st Franchised: 2001
Franchised Units: 300
Company-Owned Units: 0
Total Units: 300
Dist.: US-285; CAN-10; O'seas-5
  North America: 21 States, 1 Province
  Density: 24 in TX, 13 in CA, 12 in FL
Projected New Units (12 Months): 85

Qualifications: 3, 3, 2, 2, 1, 4
Registered: All States

FINANCIAL/TERMS:
Cash Investment: $50-60K
Total Investment: $155-160K
Minimum Net Worth: $50K
Fees: Franchise — $39.5K
  Royalty — 5%/$40K Cap.; Ad. — 1%
Earnings Claim Statement: No
Term of Contract (Years): 35/35
Avg. # Of Employees: 3 FT
Passive Ownership: Discouraged
Encourage Conversions: Yes
Area Develop. Agreements: Yes/Varies
Sub-Franchising Contracts: No
Expand In Territory: Yes
Space Needs: 1,300-1,500 SF; SC

SUPPORT & TRAINING PROVIDED:
Financial Assistance Provided: Yes(I)
Site Selection Assistance: Yes
Lease Negotiation Assistance: Yes
Co-Operative Advertising: Yes
Franchisee Assoc./Member: No
Size Of Corporate Staff: 150
On-Going Support: C,D,E,F,G,H,I
Training: 2 Weeks West Palm Beach, FL; 2 Weeks Franchisee's Location (1 Wk. Technical, 1 Wk. Mktg.)

SPECIFIC EXPANSION PLANS:
US: All United States
Canada: All Canada
Overseas: All Countries

EmbroidMe is a custom embroidery business that produces customized apparel for corporations and private organizations and provides promotional merchandise and specialty items for advertising. The customer base also includes restaurants, schools, clubs, churches, trade shows, bars and any group interested in presenting a united identity.

EmbroidMe showrooms showcase the range of colors, sizes and styles available for the casual apparel. Among the products offered are polo shirts, T-shirts, denim wear, hats, sweatshirts, sports attire, uniforms, robes, fleeces, jackets, bags, totes, aprons and towels. Additional accessories and gifts are also showcased. The entire production center is housed in the store, allowing EmbroidMe franchisees to fulfill an order "personally, professionally and punctually."

Operating Units	12/31/2002	12/31/2003	12/31/2004
Franchised	66	127	182
% Change	--	92.4%	43.3%
Company-Owned	0	0	0
% Change	--	0.0%	0.0%
Total	66	127	182
% Change	--	92.4%	43.3%
Franchised as % of Total	100.00%	100.00%	100.00%

Investment Required

The fee for an EmbroidMe franchise is $37,500, or $19,500 if buying a conversion or an additional unit.

EmbroidMe provides the following range of investments required to open your initial franchise. The range assumes that all items are paid for in cash. To the extent that you choose to finance any of these expense items, your front-end investment could be substantially reduced.

Item	Established Low Range	Established High Range
Franchise Fee	$19,500	$37,500
Training Expenses	$210	$490
Equipment Deposit (if leased)	$4,800	$5,500
Equipment Package (if purchasing outright)	$121,323	$121,323
Advertisements	$300	$1,500

Insurance	$750	$2,000
Security/Utility Deposits and Licenses	$500	$3,000
Opening Supplies	$500	$1,500
Additional Funds (for 0-6 months)	$20,000	$55,000
Total Investment (if leasing equipment)	$46,560	$106,490
Total Investment (if purchasing equipment)	$163,083	$222,313

On-Going Expenses
EmbroidMe franchisees pay a royalty fee equal to 5% of gross revenue and an advertising fee equal to 1% of gross revenue.

What You Get—Training and Support
No previous experience is required to operate EmbroidMe equipment. Franchisees receive classroom and on-the-job training that begins with two weeks at EmbroidMe's training headquarters, where they will be instructed not only in operating equipment, but also computer design technology, marketing strategies, merchandising systems and business management. Franchisees gain assistance with financing, site selection, lease negotiations, store design, on-going merchandising and field support, websites and more. They also benefit from EmbroidMe's bulk purchasing power, a company newsletter, direct mail programs, promotional materials and a toll-free support number.

EmbroidMe has a strong Internet presence that allows customers to access online, network-wide services that transfer them to an EmbroidMe store nearby. In addition, EmbroidMe works to increase its website traffic through heavy advertising with major Internet search engines.

Territory
EmbroidMe grants exclusive territories.

FASTFRAME

EXPERT PICTURE FRAMING

1200 Lawrence Dr., # 300
Newbury Park, CA 91320-1234
Tel: (800) 333-3225 (805) 498-4463
Fax: (805) 498-8983
E-Mail: brenda@fastframe.com
Web Site: www.fastframe.com
Ms. Brenda Hales, Franchise Development

FASTFRAME is the largest and fastest-growing custom picture framing franchise in the world. With over 300 locations, we maintain our leadership in the industry by recruiting business partners who are both qualified and passionate about our industry. We strive to provide our franchisees with an all-inclusive and uncomplicated process whereby they can easily become a part of this very enjoyable business. FASTFRAME has built its reputation of high quality craftsmanship and customer satisfaction.

BACKGROUND: | IFA MEMBER
Established: 1986; | 1st Franchised: 1987
Franchised Units: | 315
Company-Owned Units | 1
Total Units: | 316
Dist.: | US-306; CAN-0; O'seas-10
  North America: | 35 States
  Density: | 76 in CA, 22 in IL, 22 in TX
Projected New Units (12 Months): | 40

Qualifications: 5, 4, 1, 1, 1, 5
Registered: All States Except ND and SD.

FINANCIAL/TERMS:
Cash Investment:	$40-50K
Total Investment:	$105-150K
Minimum Net Worth:	$150K
Fees: Franchise —	$25K
Royalty — 7.5%;	Ad. — 3%
Earnings Claim Statement:	No
Term of Contract (Years):	10/10
Avg. # Of Employees:	1 FT, 2 PT
Passive Ownership:	NR
Encourage Conversions:	Yes
Area Develop. Agreements:	No
Sub-Franchising Contracts:	NR
Expand In Territory:	Yes
Space Needs: 1,200-1,500 SF; FS, SF, SC	

SUPPORT & TRAINING PROVIDED:
Financial Assistance Provided:	Yes(I)
Site Selection Assistance:	Yes
Lease Negotiation Assistance:	Yes
Co-Operative Advertising:	Yes
Franchisee Assoc./Member:	Yes/Yes
Size Of Corporate Staff:	23
On-Going Support:	A,B,C,D,E,F,G,H,I
Training: 2 Weeks at Newbury Park, CA; 1 Week at On-Site.	

SPECIFIC EXPANSION PLANS:
US:	All United States
Canada:	No
Overseas:	No

FASTFRAME is the largest—and fastest-growing—custom picture-framing franchise in the world. Franchisees enjoy high margins, low staff requirements, sociable hours and a strong repeat customer base. FAST-FRAME guarantees that customers will be satisfied with the completed product, or they will redesign the piece in the same price range free of charge within 30 days of the sale. Only a low, non-perishable inventory is necessary, and franchisees benefit from running a "good news business" that is non-seasonal.

FASTFRAME also offers a satellite program, where franchisees operate an additional store that is smaller and has no production facility. No inventory is required and only one employee is needed to operate it, reducing costs by utilizing the services of the full-service location.

Operating Units	9/30/2002	9/30/2003	9/30/2004
Franchised	214	260	295
% Change	--	21.5%	13.5%
Company-Owned	1	4	1
% Change	--	0.0%	0.0%
Total	215	264	296
% Change	--	22.8%	12.1%
Franchised as % of Total	99.53%	98.48%	99.66%

Investment Required
The fee for a FASTFRAME franchise is $25,000.

FASTFRAME provides the following range of investments required to open your initial franchise. The range assumes that all items are paid for in cash. To the extent that you choose to finance any of these expense items, your front-end investment could be substantially reduced.

Item	Established Low Range	Established High Range
Franchise Fee	$25,000	$25,000
Equipment	$18,400	$19,400
Initial Inventory/Supplies/ Misc.	$8,500	$13,000
Leasehold Improvements, Signage, Fixtures, Displays	$8,000	$40,000
Opening Fee/Marketing Expenses	$29,800	$29,800

Travel Expenses	$6,000	$8,000
Additional Funds (for 3 months)	$10,000	$15,000
Total Investment	$105,700	$150,200

On-Going Expenses

FASTFRAME franchisees pay a royalty fee equal to 7.5% of gross sales and an advertising fee equal to 3% of gross sales.

What You Get—Training and Support

Franchisees go through two weeks of training prior to the opening of the store and have one week of in-store training once it opens. Franchisees receive a demographic study; a legal review of the lease; blueprints; and assistance with contractors, lease negotiation, site selection, construction and the grand opening. FASTFRAME also creates grand-opening marketing, as well as providing a business plan and on-going support.

New employee training is included at no cost. FASTFRAME continues to support franchisees by making store visits and coordinating in-store group meetings, regional meetings and national conventions.

FASTFRAME maintains an in-house marketing department and provides professionally designed advertising materials and programs. With a strong online presence, FASTFRAME efficiently directs customers to individual stores located near them, as well as provides franchisees with a FAST-FRAME intranet.

Territory

FASTFRAME grants exclusive territories.

Foot Solutions

2359 Windy Hill Rd., # 220
Marietta, GA 30067
Tel: (866) 338-2597 (770) 955-0099
Fax: (770) 953-6270
E-Mail: fscorp@footsolutions.com
Web Site: www.footsolutions.com
Ms. Lisa Levine, Leads Processor

Health and wellness specialty retail franchise that focuses on foot care, including computer scanning of feet, with a unique 10 step process and total fit system. We carry shoes designed and built to fit the shape of the foot. Shoes that look good and feel good along with custom insoles for proper balance and support.

BACKGROUND:	IFA MEMBER
Established: 2000;	1st Franchised: 2000
Franchised Units:	182
Company-Owned Units	1
Total Units:	183
Dist.:	US-163; CAN-16; O'seas-4
North America:	29 States, 3 Provinces
Density:	15 in CA, 14 in TX, 11 in GA
Projected New Units (12 Months):	80
Qualifications: 3, 3, 1, 2, 3, 3	

Registered: CA,HI,IL,IN,MD,MN,NY,ND,RI,SD,VA,WA,WI

FINANCIAL/TERMS:

Cash Investment:	$50-65K
Total Investment:	$200-240K
Minimum Net Worth:	$300-500K
Fees: Franchise —	$27.5K
Royalty — 5%;	Ad. — 2%
Earnings Claim Statement:	No
Term of Contract (Years):	20/10/10
Avg. # Of Employees:	2-3 FT
Passive Ownership:	Allowed
Encourage Conversions:	Yes
Area Develop. Agreements:	Yes - Intl.
Sub-Franchising Contracts:	No
Expand In Territory:	Yes
Space Needs: 1,000-1,500 SF; SC	

SUPPORT & TRAINING PROVIDED:

Financial Assistance Provided:	Yes(I)
Site Selection Assistance:	Yes
Lease Negotiation Assistance:	Yes
Co-Operative Advertising:	Yes
Franchisee Assoc./Member:	Yes/Yes
Size Of Corporate Staff:	31
On-Going Support:	b,C,D,E,G,H,I
Training: 2 Weeks Marietta, GA; 1 Week in Field.	

SPECIFIC EXPANSION PLANS:

US:	All United States
Canada:	All Canada
Overseas:	All Countries

Foot Solutions provides valuable services for people with sore and tired feet by analyzing their foot problems, customizing insoles and orthotics and giving them a perfect fit. The company targets customers over the age of 40—the fastest growing segment of the market. Foot Solutions serves anyone whose active lifestyle makes them susceptible to foot-related problems. From sophisticated European comfort shoes to unique health and wellness shoes that help people correct posture, lose weight, and tone legs, glutes and tummies, Foot Solutions has something for everyone, even those hard-to-fit people. Foot Solutions has a number of exclusive products as well as a number of branded products.

The use of computer scanning and biomechanical balancing allows customers to see how they can reduce or eliminate pain. With the latest technology and foot-scanning equipment, custom insoles and orthotics can be offered at half the cost of similar units in one-sixth the average turnaround time. The average customer spends $200 and many see positive results from their Foot Solutions experience right in the store.

The success of Foot Solutions results from referrals with network marketing systems, educational infomercials and radio commercials, as well as referrals from the medical community and satisfied customers. Franchisees enjoy a high level of referrals and repeat business and a low level of competition due to the uniqueness of its services and its focus on health and wellness, which is at the beginning of its life cycle.

Operating Units	12/31/2003	12/31/2004	12/31/2005
Franchised	87	138	183
% Change	--	58.6%	32.6%
Company-Owned	1	1	1
% Change	--	0.0%	0.0%
Total	88	139	184
% Change	--	58.0%	32.4%
Franchised as % of Total	98.86%	99.28%	99.46%

Investment Required
The fee for an initial Foot Solutions franchise is $27,500.

Foot Solutions provides the following range of investments required to open your initial franchise. The range assumes that all items are paid for in cash. To the extent that you choose to finance any of these expense items, your front-end investment could be substantially reduced.

Item	Established Low Range	Established High Range

Franchise Fee	$27,500	$27,500
Advertising	$6,000	$10,000
Point of Sale System	$4,200	$5,000
Equipment, Fixtures, Signs	$20,000	$43,000
Insurance	$1,600	$2,400
Inventory	$72,000	$72,500
Real Estate	$18,000	$25,000
Training Expenses	$3,000	$5,400
Miscellaneous Opening Costs	$4,000	$6,000
Working Capital	$30,000	$40,000
Total Investment *	$186,300	$236,800

* Average Total Investment is $200,000.

On-Going Expenses

The franchisee pays an ongoing royalty fee equal to 5% of total net sales and a national advertising fee equal to 2% of total net sales. Other fees include a grand-opening advertising fee or $6,000 for both your initial investment and jump-starting your business.

What You Get—Training and Support

Foot Solutions provides franchisees with: training at corporate centers and in the field for both franchisee and staff; operations manuals and videos; guidelines for managing operations, work flow, recordkeeping, start-up inventory products, tools, merchandise delivery and inventory control; and online support through an exclusive Foot Solutions website. Foot Solutions will also assist in preparing a loan portfolio, designing and opening the store, installing and testing equipment and advertising copy. The Foot Solutions training facility is certified by the Board for Certification of Pedorthist.

Franchisees would receive field set up support for three days, grand opening support for three days, and follow up visits.

Territory

Foot Solutions grants exclusive territories with protected territory of at least 100,000 people per location.

KaBloom

The power of fresh flowers.®

250 First Ave., # 102, 1st Needham Pl.
Needham, MA -2494
Tel: (800) KABLOOM (781) 455-1102
Fax: (781) 455-6721
E-Mail: lflaherty@kabloom.com
Web Site: www.kabloom.com
Mr. Larry Flaherty, Director of Franchising

KABLOOM is the US's largest, fastest-growing and only national retail storefront florist. KABLOOM blends basic retailing fundamentals and merchandising with the European philosophy of fresh flowers in people's daily lives. With 110 stores open by 12/2004, 125+ franchisees in 30 states have bought the rights to open 350+ stores over the next few years. Flowers are FedExed to your store within 48 to 72 hours of having been cut. Strong walk-in business, weddings, funerals, weekly clients-the list is endless.

BACKGROUND:

Established: 1998;	1st Franchised: 2002
Franchised Units:	100
Company-Owned Units	5
Total Units:	105
Dist.:	US-105; CAN-0; O'seas-0
North America:	29 States, DC
Density:	32 in MA, 10 in FL, 9 in NJ
Projected New Units (12 Months):	25-50+

IFA MEMBER

Qualifications: 4, 2, 1, 2, 5, 5
Registered: CA,FL,IL,IN,MI,MN,NY,OR,RI,VA,WA,WI,DC

FINANCIAL/TERMS:

Cash Investment:	$75K
Total Investment:	$169.5-266K
Minimum Net Worth:	$200K
Fees: Franchise —	$30K 1st Store
Royalty — 5.5-4% Varies;	Ad. — 4%
Earnings Claim Statement:	No
Term of Contract (Years):	10/5/5/5
Avg. # Of Employees:	3 FT or PT
Passive Ownership:	Discouraged
Encourage Conversions:	Yes
Area Develop. Agreements:	Yes/TBD
Sub-Franchising Contracts:	No
Expand In Territory:	Yes
Space Needs: 700-1,400 SF; FS, SF, SC	

SUPPORT & TRAINING PROVIDED:

Financial Assistance Provided:	No
Site Selection Assistance:	Yes
Lease Negotiation Assistance:	Yes
Co-Operative Advertising:	Yes
Franchisee Assoc./Member:	No
Size Of Corporate Staff:	10
On-Going Support:	A,B,C,D,E,F,G,H,I
Training: 3 Weeks Total at Store and Home Office.	

SPECIFIC EXPANSION PLANS:

US:	All US Exc. AK, HI, ND and SD.
Canada:	No
Overseas:	No

KaBloom is a rapidly growing chain of flower shops known for their colorful, fresh and prominent floral displays. Opened in 1998, KaBloom has experienced superb growth, with more than 100 stores nationwide and more on the way. The KaBloom brand name has the competitive advantage in a marketplace where most competitors are small, independent mom-and-pop retailers.

KaBloom differentiates itself from mass-market retailers by fulfilling all the needs of every customer, regardless of the occasion. The success of KaBloom's walk-in service and customer demand for other services has led the franchise to expand its services to include deliveries, weddings, wire orders and funerals. Due to its popularity, KaBloom has also begun to develop store-within-a-store outlets, such as those in supermarket floral sections.

Operating Units	12/31/2002	12/31/2003	12/31/2004
Franchised	19	44	100
% Change	--	131.6%	127.3%
Company-Owned	12	10	N/A
% Change	--	-16.7%	N/A
Total	31	54	100
% Change	--	74.2%	85.2%
Franchised as % of Total	61.29%	81.48%	100.00%

Investment Required
The fee for a KaBloom franchise is $30,000.

KaBloom provides the following range of investments required to open your initial franchise. The range assumes that all items are paid for in cash. To the extent that you choose to finance any of these expense items, your front-end investment could be substantially reduced.

Item	Established Low Range	Established High Range
Franchise Fee	$30,000	$30,000
Rent and Deposits	$0	$10,500
Construction Costs	$100,000	$141,000

Furniture and Equipment	$1,000	$5,000
Opening Inventory	$8,000	$12,500
Hardware Software	$0	$20,000
Marketing Introduction Program	$7,500	$20,000
Insurance	$2,000	$2,500
Delivery Vehicle	$0	$400
Other Costs and Additional Funds	$27,550	$60,500
Total Investment	$176,050	$302,400

On-Going Expenses

KaBloom franchisees pay a royalty fee that ranges from 4.5% to 5.5% of gross sales, an advertising fee equal to 3% of gross sales and a local advertising fee equal to 1% of gross sales. Other ongoing fees include those for cooperative advertising funds, communication systems and membership in the Society of American Florists.

What You Get—Training and Support

Franchisees receive insightful site-selection assistance: Scouts visit a candidate site to monitor traffic, and if it is sufficiently high, KaBloom examines nearby stores to see if a KaBloom store will be a good fit for the location. Throughout the process, KaBloom also considers demographics, accessibility and local ordinances.

KaBloom trains store personnel at every level and in every quarter of the year. Five weeks of training in both stores and classrooms cover sales skills, business operations and floral design techniques. Franchisees also benefit from the lower prices secured through Kabloom's volume-purchasing power, a centralized distribution center and a sophisticated order-entry system. KaBloom's corporate personnel also provides assistance with store openings, corporate marketing resources, branding and general everyday guidance.

Territory
KaBloom grants exclusive territories.

Merkinstock

P. O. Box 12488
Oakland, CA 94604
Tel: (510) 839-5462
Fax: (510) 839-2104
E-Mail: sourcebook@earthlink.net
Web Site: www.merkinstock.com
Mr. Jeffrey A. Elder, President

World's largest selection of merkins - both natural and synthetic. Over 35 models, 15 color selections. Custom fitting in discrete environment. Also custom dyeing. Guaranteed satisfaction. 15 stores in Far East and Europe prove that concept is ripe for aggressive expansion into the U. S. market. Looking for entrepreneurs with the desire to succeed.

BACKGROUND:

Established: 1992;	1st Franchised: 1995
Franchised Units:	52
Company-Owned Units	7
Total Units:	59
Dist.:	US-42; CAN-2; O'seas-15
North America:	2 States, 1 Province
Density:	2 in CA, 1 in NV
Projected New Units (12 Months):	10
Qualifications: 3, 5, 4, 2, 3, 5	

Registered: CA

FINANCIAL/TERMS:

Cash Investment:	$90K
Total Investment:	$150K
Minimum Net Worth:	$250K
Fees: Franchise —	$20K
Royalty — 6%;	Ad. — 2%
Earnings Claim Statement:	Yes
Term of Contract (Years):	15/15
Avg. # Of Employees:	2 FT
Passive Ownership:	Not Allowed
Encourage Conversions:	Yes
Area Develop. Agreements:	Yes/15
Sub-Franchising Contracts:	Yes
Expand In Territory:	No
Space Needs: 1,200 SF; FS, SC, RM	

SUPPORT & TRAINING PROVIDED:

Financial Assistance Provided:	Yes(D)
Site Selection Assistance:	Yes
Lease Negotiation Assistance:	Yes
Co-Operative Advertising:	Yes
Franchisee Assoc./Member:	No
Size Of Corporate Staff:	4
On-Going Support:	a,B,C,D,E,f,G,G,I

Training: 3 Weeks Headquarters; 2 Weeks On-Site; On-Going.

SPECIFIC EXPANSION PLANS:

US:	All United States
Canada:	All Canada
Overseas:	All Countries

Merkinstock has brought back the popular usage of merkins as a decorative form of self-expression and personality, rather than simply a physical necessity. Merkinstock currently possesses the largest variety of colors, materials and designs in the industry with styles to suit any personality and need.

The Merkinstock brand is widely associated with personal creativity and customization, allowing customers to pick and choose their own combinations of available merkin models. The company invests tremendously in customer service, providing sales representatives sensitive and discrete enough to make any customer feel comfortable.

In 1992, founders Sydney and Bob Anning invented a line of merkins that added more spunk and inspiration to the drab, conservative merkins traditionally offered. The Annings began franchising in 1995, and have led a merkin revolution in the process. Market response to this new retail segment has been astounding in Europe and Asia and American markets show promising increases in the number of operating units and revenue gross. Now, with the popularity of body piercings and tattoos waning, merkins are perched to become the next big thing in body decoration and personalization the world over.

Operating Units	12/31/2003	12/31/2004	12/31/2005
Franchised	28	43	52
% Change	--	53.57%	20.93%
Company-Owned	10	10	7
% Change	--	0.0%	0.0%
Total	38	53	59
% Change	--	39.47%	11.32%
Franchised as % of Total	73.36%	81.13%	88.13%

Investment Required
The fee for a Merkinstock franchise is $20,000.

Merkinstock provides the following range of investments required to open your initial franchise. The range assumes that all items are paid for in cash. To the extent that you choose to finance any of these expense items, your front-end investment could be substantially reduced.

Item	Established Low Range	Established High Range
Franchise Fee	$25,500	$45,000
Advertising	$6,500	$18,500
Equipment, Fixtures, Signs	$30,000	$50,000
Inventory Control System	$5,000	$8,000
Opening Costs	$24,300	$75,600
Opening Inventory	$64,000	$135,000
Real Estate, Improvements, Fees	$25,000	$65,000
Training Expenses	$6,000	$6,000
Total Investment	$186,300	$403,100

On-Going Expenses

Merkinstock franchisees pay royalties equaling 6% and advertising contributions equaling 2.9% of gross revenue.

What You Get—Training and Support

As Merkinstock values its customer service orientation, the company provides a comprehensive training program designed to familiarize you with basic business management, merkin history and the Merkinstock product line. The program is free, but all travel, lodging and meal expenses must be paid by the franchisee. The program lasts approximately three weeks. Successful completion of the program is based upon the customization of your own merkin and your ability to properly attach, adjust and clean the merkin in the presence of a trained Merkinstock employee.

Merkinstock's support system is both strong and loving. Each year, a large convention brings franchisees together in a weekend bonding event. During the convention, franchisees share their opinions on the latest merkin models as well as tips on how to better serve their customers' needs. Merkinstock also encourages franchisees to submit their ideas for new models. In addition to the annual convention, franchisees receive support and assistance from their assigned Merkinstock experts, who will periodically visit their stores to evaluate the business's performance and product quality.

The company relies primarily upon foot traffic, word-of-mouth recommendations and gossip to gain exposure and promotion. While relaxing social rules may accommodate the emergence of merkins into the conventional marketplace, Merkinstock's marketing department believes that national advertising campaigns in major media forms would upset the delicate balance between the need for and acceptance of merkins as a major retail item and the private nature of their use. Accordingly, advertising funds are focused solely on the printing of catalogues, accompanying instructions and point-of-sale and store design displays.

Territory
Merkinstock grants exclusive territories.

Merle Norman Cosmetics

9130 Bellanca Ave.
Los Angeles, CA 90045-4710
Tel: (800) 421-6648 (310) 641-3000
Fax: (310) 337-2370
E-Mail: claporta@merlenorman.com
Web Site: www.merlenorman.com
Ms. Carol LaPorta, VP Studio Development

MERLE NORMAN COSMETICS is a specialty retail store, selling scientifically developed, state-of-the-art cosmetic products, using the 'free make over' and 'try before you buy' complete customer satisfaction methods of selling.

BACKGROUND:
Established: 1931; IFA MEMBER
1st Franchised: 1989
Franchised Units: 1,936

Company-Owned Units	4
Total Units:	1,940
Dist.:	US-1,831; CAN-90; O'seas-19
North America:	50 States,10 Provinces
Density:	260 in TX, 113 in GA, 99 AL
Projected New Units (12 Months):	120
Qualifications: 3, 4, 3, 3, 4, 4	
Registered: All States	
FINANCIAL/TERMS:	
Cash Investment:	$NR
Total Investment:	$28.6-155.9K
Minimum Net Worth:	$NR
Fees: Franchise —	$0
Royalty — 0%;	Ad. — 0%
Earnings Claim Statement:	Yes
Term of Contract (Years):	10
Avg. # Of Employees:	2 FT, 2-5 PT
Passive Ownership:	Discouraged
Encourage Conversions:	No
Area Develop. Agreements:	No
Sub-Franchising Contracts:	No
Expand In Territory:	Yes

Space Needs: 450-800 SF; SC, RM		Size Of Corporate Staff:	630
		On-Going Support:	a,B,C,D,E,F,G,H,I
SUPPORT & TRAINING PROVIDED:		Training: 2 Weeks Los Angeles, CA.	
Financial Assistance Provided:	Yes(I)		
Site Selection Assistance:	Yes	**SPECIFIC EXPANSION PLANS:**	
Lease Negotiation Assistance:	Yes	US:	All United States
Co-Operative Advertising:	Yes	Canada:	All CAN Except Quebec
Franchisee Assoc./Member:	No	Overseas:	All Countries

The cosmetics industry is a perennial strong performer, generating billions of dollars in sales every year. Merle Norman Cosmetic Studios present the perfect opportunity to enter the retail cosmetics industry, with a nationally recognized brand and a network of 2,000 studios.

Merle Norman has carved out its niche by offering a private setting for customers to receive personal treatment, removing the department-store distractions. Studios are located in both mall and non-mall locations, and have bright, inviting and elegant interiors that offer user-friendly displays. The complete Merle Norman Cosmetics line fulfills a wide range of skin care and makeup needs, and products are easily accessible through the store's "Try Before You Buy" policy. Customers receive the attention of an experienced Beauty Consultant, who offers a free skin-type analysis and will address any personal concerns for a skin-care or color makeover. The combination of personalized treatment and quality products creates strong loyalty to and repeat business for the Merle Norman brand.

Operating Units	12/31/2002	12/31/2003	12/31/2004
Franchised	1,880	1,883	1,917
% Change	--	0.2%	1.8%
Company-Owned	7	6	5
% Change	--	-14.3%	-16.7%
Total	1,887	1,889	1,922
% Change	--	0.1%	1.7%
Franchised as % of Total	99.63%	99.68%	99.74%

Investment Required

There is no fee for a Merle Norman franchise; however, franchisees must purchase an initial package of Merle Norman products. The prices for the initial package ranges from approximately $10,774 to $23,662.

Merle Norman provides the following range of investments required to open your initial franchise. The range assumes that all items are paid for in cash. To the extent that you choose to finance any of these expense items, your front-end investment could be substantially reduced. The following figures refer to a mall location.

Item	Established Low Range	Established High Range
Initial Package of Real Inventory and Supplies	$10,774	$23,662
Computer	$1,800	$4,900
Deposits, Insurance and Other Costs	$12,800	$29,300
Studio Costs	$17,980	$95,000
Training Expenses	$1,500	$3,000
Total Investment (not including Real Estate)	$44,854	$155,862

On-Going Expenses

The only on-going costs are for purchases of additional Merle Norman products at wholesale prices.

What You Get—Training and Support

Franchisees receive training at corporate headquarters in managing a Merle Norman Studio. Training includes instruction in product knowledge, makeup application, sales, studio management, personnel and the point-of-sale system. Field training classes are offered on staffing, recruiting and more. Beauty consultants can be certified for Home Office Training on their own with *The Box* training kit.

Support begins with assistance with site selection, lease review, studio design and layout, and continues with promotion for the grand opening. After the Studio has opened, regional business consultants can meet with franchisees to assist in specific merchandising and business-related issues. Daily support is provided by a regional specialist at corporate headquarters. Franchisees also receive access to a broad selection of marketing materials for multiple media, from television and radio to press releases and product brochures. Merle Norman reimburses 60% of approved marketing costs for franchisees that participate in the co-op program.

Territory
Merle Norman does not grant exclusive territories.

More Space Place

America's Murphy Bed Store®

5040 140th Ave. N.
Clearwater, FL 33760-3735
Tel: (888) 731-3051 + 14 (727) 539-1611
Fax: (727) 524-6382
E-Mail: mjuarez@morespaceplace.com
Web Site: www.morespaceplace.com
Mr. Marty Juarez, Vice President Franchising

One of America's Top 100 Franchise Opportunities! (as listed in Bond's Top 100 Franchises, 2004 and 2005). We create beautiful living spaces for our customers. Picture an elegant home office that converts into an extra bedroom. With our professionally installed Murphy bed and custom-designed office, it can happen. With us, you can fashionably design closets, entertainment centers, utility rooms and garages and turn spare bedrooms into multi-purpose rooms.

BACKGROUND:
Established: 1989;   1st Franchised: 1993

Franchised Units:	35
Company-Owned Units	3
Total Units:	38
Dist.:	US-38; CAN-0; O'seas-0
North America:	12 States
Density:	22 in FL, 3 in TX, 3 in SC
Projected New Units (12 Months):	12
Qualifications: 4, 4, 1, 3, 2, 5	
Registered: CA,FL,IL,MD,MI,MN,NY,RI,VA,WI	

FINANCIAL/TERMS:

Cash Investment:	$40-60K
Total Investment:	$128.5-194K
Minimum Net Worth:	$150K
Fees: Franchise —	$18-29.5K
Royalty — 4.5%;	Ad. — 2.5%
Earnings Claim Statement:	No
Term of Contract (Years):	10/10
Avg. # Of Employees:	3 FT, 1 PT
Passive Ownership:	Discouraged
Encourage Conversions:	Yes
Area Develop. Agreements:	Yes/10
Sub-Franchising Contracts:	No
Expand In Territory:	Yes
Space Needs: 1,400-2,000 SF; FS, SF, SC	

SUPPORT & TRAINING PROVIDED:

Financial Assistance Provided:	Yes
Site Selection Assistance:	Yes

Lease Negotiation Assistance:	Yes	Days On-Site.
Co-Operative Advertising:	No	
Franchisee Assoc./Member:	No	**SPECIFIC EXPANSION PLANS:**
Size Of Corporate Staff:	55	US: All United States
On-Going Support:	B,C,D,E,F,G,H,I	Canada: No
Training: 12 Days Headquarters Clearwater, FL; 6		Overseas: No

As the nation's largest wall-bed retailer, More Space Place makes room for the way customers live, with a variety of smart, yet stylish room solutions that can be customized for a space of any size. Retractable beds offered include panel beds, side beds and the versatile Murphy bed, which can be folded into a closet. These beds can be used in a number of space-saving layouts, such as a room that becomes a home office by day and a guest bedroom by night. And bedrooms are not the only space that can be transformed, creating more demand for More Space Place services; entertainment systems, closets, pantries, garages, art studios and computer rooms can all be customized to fit customers' needs.

Design consultants incorporate all the ideas, preferences and needs of the customer into the final design. Custom modular systems are carefully crafted to meet More Space Place's high standards and specifications, using only quality materials and the services of professionals to manage construction and installation.

Operating Units	6/30/2003	6/30/2004	6/30/2005
Franchised	19	22	28
% Change	--	15.8%	27.3%
Company-Owned	3	3	3
% Change	--	0.0%	0.0%
Total	22	25	31
% Change	--	13.6%	24%
Franchised as % of Total	86.64%	88%	90.3%

Investment Required
The fee for a More Space Place franchise is $29,500.

More Space Place provides the following range of investments required to open your initial franchise. The range assumes that all items are paid for in cash. To the extent that you choose to finance any of these expense items, your front-end investment could be substantially reduced.

Item	Established Low Range	Established High Range
Franchise Fee	$18,000	$29,500
Training Expenses	$1,500	$2,500
Real Estate Improvements/ Architectural Costs	$20,000	$38,000
Office Equipment, Computer, Supplies	$3,000	$4,500
Pallet Lifter	$600	$4,500
Van or Trailer	$1,600	$4,700
Signage	$5,000	$12,000
Grand Opening	$32,500	$46,500
Architect's Fee & Engineering Costs	$0	$3,000
Misc. Operating Costs	$4,000	$5,000
Insurance	$1,800	$2,800
Additional Funds/ Working Capital	$25,000	$35,000
Total Investment	$113,000	$188,000

On-Going Expenses
More Space Place franchisees pay a royalty fee equal to the greater of 4.5% of gross revenue or $500 per month, a national advertising contribution fee equal to the greater of 2.5% of gross revenue or $500 per month, a regional advertising contribution fee equal to the greater of 2.5% of gross revenue or $500 per month, and a local advertising fee equal to the greater of 7% of gross revenue or $2,500 per month.

What You Get—Training and Support

Franchisees receive a comprehensive start-up package that includes financing options, site-selection support, showroom design and specifications, product selection, lifetime owner and personnel training and a product line with thousands of variations.

Additional support is provided for furniture selection, start-up, accounting setup, product knowledge, sales training, advertising and marketing. Franchisees also benefit from a powerful CAD system, a product ordering and inventory system, minimal standing inventory, a single-source supplier, new product development and acquisition, group purchasing power and manufacturer product guarantees.

Territory

More Space Place grants exclusive territories with a minimum estimated population of 150,000 and development territories to those franchises qualified to open multiple units.

Motophoto

MOTOPHOTO

4444 Lake Center Dr.
Dayton, OH 45426-3868
Tel: (800) 733-6686 (937) 854-6686
Fax: (937) 854-0140
E-Mail: franchise@motophoto.com
Web Site: www.motophoto.com
Mr. Joseph M. O'Hara, Vice President

MOTOPHOTO is a crisp, up-scale, "clicks and mortar" specialty retailer in the exploding digital photography and digital portrait studio marketplaces. Consumers and Prosumers experience the MOTOPHOTO difference through precisely blending the versatility of digital products and services with the convenience of in-store, kiosk, or on-line interactions. Nearly a quarter century of franchising experience translates to superior franchisee training and exceptional ongoing business support.

BACKGROUND:	IFA MEMBER
Established: 1981;	1st Franchised: 1982
Franchised Units:	141
Company-Owned Units	3
Total Units:	144
Dist.:	US-117; CAN-27; O'seas-0
North America:	19 States, 1 Province
Density:	24 in NJ, 12 in VA, 9 in OK
Projected New Units (12 Months):	10
Qualifications: 4, 4, 1, 2, 4, 4	
Registered: CA,IL,MD,MI,NY,VA	

FINANCIAL/TERMS:	
Cash Investment:	$40-60K
Total Investment:	$225-275K
Minimum Net Worth:	$250K
Fees: Franchise —	$35K
Royalty — 6%;	Ad. — 0.5%
Earnings Claim Statement:	No
Term of Contract (Years):	10/10
Avg. # Of Employees:	3 FT, 3 PT

Passive Ownership:	Discouraged	Co-Operative Advertising:	Yes
Encourage Conversions:	Yes	Franchisee Assoc./Member:	No
Area Develop. Agreements:	No	Size Of Corporate Staff:	9
Sub-Franchising Contracts:	No	On-Going Support:	C,D,E,h,I
Expand In Territory:	No	Training: 9 Days Dayton, OH; 3-5 Days Regional	
Space Needs: 1,200-1,400 SF; SC		Training Center; 1 Week Franchisee's Store.	
SUPPORT & TRAINING PROVIDED:		**SPECIFIC EXPANSION PLANS:**	
Financial Assistance Provided:	Yes(I)	US:	Florida Only.
Site Selection Assistance:	Yes	Canada:	ON
Lease Negotiation Assistance:	Yes	Overseas:	No

MotoPhoto provides one-hour film development, restoration of old or damaged photos, passport photos, digital photography and 35mm photo conversions. Services such as personal photography have created substantial "add-on" business, and MotoPhoto also appeals to corporate customers who seek material for marketing brochures and annual reports. As added bonuses for customers, MotoPhoto offers portrait proofs within one hour and its stores are equipped with digital applications that endow customers with increased options for photo enhancing and digital transfers.

A dominant franchise in a $15.6 billion industry, MotoPhoto provides security through the strength of its brand name and more than 75 years of experience in the imaging industry and in franchising – as reflected in their growth from 20 stores in 1982 to more than 144 today. Franchisees receive an additional competitive edge by being able to operate their stores within protected territories.

Operating Units	12/31/2002	12/31/2003	12/31/2004
Franchised	233	205	166
% Change	--	-12.0%	-19.0%
Company-Owned	0	0	6
% Change	--	0.0%	N/A
Total	233	205	172
% Change	--	-12.0%	-16.1%
Franchised as % of Total	100.00%	100.00%	96.51%

Investment Required

The fee to renew a MotoPhoto franchise is $1,750. Transfer fees are paid by the seller.

MotoPhoto provides the following range of investments required to open your initial franchise. The range assumes that all items are paid for in cash. To the extent that you choose to finance any of these expense items, your front-end investment could be substantially reduced. The following figures refer to a store that is transferred to the franchisee.

Item	Established Low Range	Established High Range
Franchise Fee	$0	$0
Professional Fees	$2,700	$2,700
Store Refurbishment/ Rental Deposits	$2,500	$28,300
Equipment	$0	$135,800
Additional Portrait Equipment	$0	$16,600
Opening Advertising	$3,000	$3,000
Merchandise	$0	$5,000
Initial Training	$1,800	$3,600
Other Costs and Additional Funds (for 3 months)	$4,000	$24,000
Total Investment	$14,000	$219,000

On-Going Expenses

MotoPhoto franchisees pay a royalty fee equal to 6% of net retail sales plus 3% of net wholesale sales; an ongoing advertising fee equal to 0.5% of net retail sales; a cooperative/local advertising fee equal to 5.5% of net retail sales; and a regional/national advertising fund fee of up to 2.5% of combined net retail sales.

What You Get—Training and Support

Franchisees receive support in areas such as design and construction, training, marketing, information systems and purchasing. Site-selection assistance and five weeks of training (two spent in a formal learning environment and three on the job) are also provided. Franchisees also benefit from discounts made possible through corporate contracts with vendors. MotoPhoto encourages its franchisees to suggest new ideas that are evaluated, tested and then shared with all other franchisees. Franchisees enjoy the opportunity to work with a group of entrepreneurial franchisees and an experienced franchisor management provides all other support.

Territory
MotoPhoto grants exclusive territories.

Party America

980 Atlantic Ave., # 103
Alameda, CA 94501
Tel: (510) 747-1800 + 283
Fax: (510) 747-1810
E-Mail: franchising@partyamerica.com
Web Site: www.partyamerica.com
Mr. Dave Crane, VP Franchise Development

PARTY AMERICA, the 2004 Party Retailer of the Year, is the premier party specialty retailer that captures the "Party Experience" by offering the most comprehensive everyday and seasonal merchandise needed to throw a great party!

BACKGROUND:	IFA MEMBER
Established: 1980;	1st Franchised: 1987
Franchised Units:	62
Company-Owned Units	226
Total Units:	288
Dist.:	US-287; CAN-0; O'seas-1
North America:	46 States
Density:	40 in CA, 21 in MN, 16 in CO

Projected New Units (12 Months): 10
Qualifications: 5, 4, 3, 4, 4, 5
Registered: All States Except Hawaii

FINANCIAL/TERMS:	
Cash Investment:	$150K
Total Investment:	$335-500K
Minimum Net Worth:	$400K
Fees: Franchise —	$25K
Royalty — 4%;	Ad. — 4%
Earnings Claim Statement:	Yes
Term of Contract (Years):	10/10
Avg. # Of Employees:	4 FT, 6 PT
Passive Ownership:	Allowed
Encourage Conversions:	Yes
Area Develop. Agreements:	Yes/5
Sub-Franchising Contracts:	Yes
Expand In Territory:	Yes
Space Needs: 6,000-10,000 SF; SF, SC, Power Ctr.	

SUPPORT & TRAINING PROVIDED:	
Financial Assistance Provided:	Yes(I)
Site Selection Assistance:	Yes
Lease Negotiation Assistance:	Yes
Co-Operative Advertising:	NA
Franchisee Assoc./Member:	Yes
Size Of Corporate Staff:	100
On-Going Support:	C,D,E,G,H
Training: 1-5 Days Alameda, CA.	

SPECIFIC EXPANSION PLANS: US: All United States	Canada: Overseas:	All Canada All Countries

Party America is a specialty retail chain – one of the fastest growing in America – that that offers seasonal and everyday supplies for all kinds of parties and celebrations. From birthdays to weddings to baby showers and more, products include decorations, catering supplies and paper products. Whether a customer is looking for gift boxes, decor accents or even serving trays, Party America aims to satisfy all entertaining needs.

Party America has over 208 company-owned stores and 62 franchises, and is the second-largest party supply retailer in the country.

Operating Units	1/31/2004	1/31/2005	1/31/2006
Franchised	58	58	62
% Change	--	0.0%	6.9%
Company-Owned	63	64	208
% Change	--	1.6%	225%
Total	121	122	270
% Change	--	0.8%	121.3%
Franchised as % of Total	47.93%	47.54%	22.96%

Investment Required
The fee for a Party America franchise is $25,000.

Party America provides the following range of investments required to open your initial franchise. The range assumes that all items are paid for in cash. To the extent that you choose to finance any of these expense items, your front-end investment could be substantially reduced.

Item	Established Low Range	Established High Range
Franchise Fee	$25,000	$25,000

Real Estate/Improvements	$0	$0
Equipment and Fixtures	$29,000	$100,000
Signs	$8,000	$18,000
Computer Equipment	$15,000	$20,000
Deposits/Business Licenses	$3,800	$12,500
Grand Opening	$5,000	$5,000
Opening Inventory	$125,000	$200,000
Additional Funds (for 3 months)	$40,000	$80,000
Total Investment	$250,800	$460,500

On-Going Expenses

Party America franchisees pay a royalty fee equal to 4% of gross sales up to $2 million and 2% of gross sales over $2 million. Franchisees must have a local advertising program that is equal to the greater 4% of general sales.

What You Get—Training and Support

From the start, Party America franchisees receive assistance with site selection, store layout and merchandise selection. Everyday and seasonal buying teams monitor products for quality control and keep inventory up to date throughout the year as more than a dozen holiday and theme celebrations take place. Franchisees also benefit from Party America's purchasing power in corporately negotiated contracts with vendors.

In addition to providing merchandise and management training, Party America gives franchisees access to the company intranet site, holds franchise meetings and makes field visits to stores. Franchisees are also trained to operate a computerized point-of-sale system that handles inventory and cash management control, purchasing and receiving functions, and reporting and analysis needs. As for marketing, sixteen direct mail and newspaper inserts are produced every year to promote Party America's offerings and brand.

Territory
Party America grants exclusive territories

Wild Bird Center

7370 MacArthur Blvd.
Glen Echo, MD 20812-1200
Tel: (800) 945-3247 (301) 229-9585
Fax: (301) 320-6154
E-Mail: georgejr@wildbird.com
Web Site: www.wildbird.com
Mr. George H. Petrides, Jr., Director Franchise Development

A WBCA franchise is more than a store; it is a valued community resource. The story of THE WILD BIRD CENTERS OF AMERICA, Inc. is one of enthusiasm about wild birds and a professional approach to the birding market. The customer enjoys friendly, personal service in a peaceful environment with the feel of a relaxing backyard. The owner provides this service with the help of highly efficient systems and support.

BACKGROUND:	IFA MEMBER
Established: 1985;	1st Franchised: 1988
Franchised Units:	92
Company-Owned Units	0
Total Units:	92
Dist.:	US-92; CAN-0; O'seas-0
North America:	31 States, 1 Province

Density: 10 in MD, 8 in CA, 8 in VA
Projected New Units (12 Months): 15
Qualifications: 5, 4, 2, 4, 2, 5
Registered: All Except HI

FINANCIAL/TERMS:

Cash Investment:	$35-50K
Total Investment:	$89-144K
Minimum Net Worth:	$150K
Fees: Franchise —	$18K
Royalty — 3-4%;	Ad. — .5%
Earnings Claim Statement:	Yes
Term of Contract (Years):	10
Avg. # Of Employees:	1 FT, 2 PT
Passive Ownership:	Discouraged
Encourage Conversions:	No
Area Develop. Agreements:	No
Sub-Franchising Contracts:	No
Expand In Territory:	No
Space Needs: 1,500-2,400 SF; SC	

SUPPORT & TRAINING PROVIDED:

Financial Assistance Provided:	Yes(I)
Site Selection Assistance:	Yes
Lease Negotiation Assistance:	Yes
Co-Operative Advertising:	Yes
Franchisee Assoc./Member:	Yes/Yes
Size Of Corporate Staff:	15
On-Going Support:	C,d,E,F,G,h,I
Training: 6 Days Home Office; 1 Day On Site.	

SPECIFIC EXPANSION PLANS:

US:	All United States
Canada:	All Canada
Overseas:	No

Owning a Wild Bird Center franchise is like running a business out of your own back yard. In shops filled with plants, birdbaths, bird feeders and even ponds, Wild Bird Center franchisees cater to local birdlovers with products and tips designed to keep back yards healthy and the birdwatching plentiful and fulfilling.

Americans spent $2.6 billion on birdseed alone in 2001, and Wild Bird Center's product line extends far beyond your typical wild bird food. The store's offerings include top-quality, exclusive birdseed blends as well as feeders, nest boxes, binoculars and spotting scopes.

In line with the friendly backyard environment, each Wild Bird Center also fills a niche in the community by hosting educational events such as monthly birdwalks, demonstrations, seminars and children's programs. Corporate partnerships further Wild Bird Center's goal of maintaining healthy natural habitats. The franchisor has teamed up with groups such as the Cornell Laboratory of Ornithology, the National Bluebird Society, the National Bird-Feeding Society and the wild bird feeding institute.

Operating Units	12/31/2002	12/31/2003	12/31/2004
Franchised	82	83	91
% Change	--	1.2%	9.6%
Company-Owned	2	2	1
% Change	--	0.0%	-50.0%
Total	84	85	92
% Change	--	1.2%	8.2%
Franchised as % of Total	97.62%	97.65%	98.91%

Investment Required
The fee for a Wild Bird Centers franchise is $18,000.

Wild Bird Centers provides the following range of investments required to open your initial franchise. The range assumes that all items are paid for in cash. To the extent that you choose to finance any of these expense items, your front-end investment could be substantially reduced.

Item	Established Low Range	Established High Range
Franchise fee	$18,000	$18,000

Initial training fee	$2,000	$2,000
Opening inventory	$30,000	$40,000
Real estate and improvements	As incurred	As incurred
Store interior fit-up (including design fees)	$18,000	$30,000
Signage	$2,000	$6,000
Office supplies	$500	$500
Opening advertising (for 3 months)	$2,000	$4,000
Licenses	$200	$500
Legal and accounting fees (including organizational expenses)	$750	$1,500
Computer system and electronic credit card system	$7,500	$10,000
Telephone system	$300	$500
Fax machine	$150	$300
Insurance premiums (for 3 months)	$250	$1,000
Utility deposits	$250	$500
Travel and living expenses while training	$1,000	$1,500
Miscellaneous opening costs	$1,000	$3,000
Working capital (for 3 months)	$2,500	$5,000
Total	$86,150	$124,300

On-Going Expenses

Wild Bird Center franchisees pay a royalty fee equal to 3-4% of gross sales (depending on market size), a promotion fee equal to 0.5% of gross sales and a cooperative marketing fee of $2,700 a year. Other costs include a $2,000 lump-sum fee for training.

What You Get—Training and Support

Wild Bird Center support includes a 7-day training program; the fruits of constant scientific and consumer testing and research into proprietary bird-seeds and feeders; in-store décor that mixes hard data about customer-traffic patterns with wooden fixtures, colors and lighting that offset and highlight products for sale; and an internal intranet site with discussion groups, product information and company documents. In addition, a customized point-of-sale register system increases efficiency and enables accurate keeping of advertising and marketing lists that detail customers' buying and contact information.

For further training, Wild Bird Center manuals cover selling techniques, promotion and community outreach, scientific studies, advertising, visual merchandising, and computer and store operations.

Just as each Wild Bird Center becomes part of its local community, each Wild Bird Center also joins a systemwide community with their fellow centers. Franchisees contribute photographs and articles to the Wild Bird News newsletter, swap ideas for advertising, merchandising and community programs, even refer customers to one another and work together to get the right product in a customer's hands.

Territory

Wild Bird Center grants exclusive territories with populations of approximately 50,000 to 250,000 people within areas encompassing approximately 25 to 100 square miles.

Wild Birds Unlimited

	11711 N. College Ave., # 146
	Carmel, IN 46032-5634
	Tel: (888) 730-7108 (317) 571-7100
	Fax: (317) 208-4050
	E-Mail: gilkersonl@wbu.com
	Web Site: www.wbu.com
	Ms. Linda Gilkerson, Manager Franchise Development

WILD BIRDS UNLIMITED is North America's original and largest group of retail stores catering to the backyard birdfeeding and nature enthusiast. We currently have over 300 stores in the U. S. and Canada. Stores provide birdseed, feeders, houses, optics and nature-related gifts. Additionally, stores provide extensive educational programs regarding backyard birdfeeding. Franchisees are provided an all-inclusive support system.

BACKGROUND: IFA MEMBER
Established: 1981;   1st Franchised: 1983

Franchised Units:	315
Company-Owned Units	0
Total Units:	315
Dist.:	US-302; CAN-13; O'seas-0
North America:	42 States, 3 Provinces
Density:	23 in TX, 17 in MI, 15 in IL
Projected New Units (12 Months):	15

Qualifications: 5, 5, 1, 3, 2, 5
Registered: CA,FL,IL,IN,MD,MI,MN,NY,OR,RI,VA,WA,WI,DC

FINANCIAL/TERMS:

Cash Investment:	$25-35K
Total Investment:	$99-155K
Minimum Net Worth:	$150K

Fees: Franchise —	$18K
Royalty — 4%;	Ad. — .5%
Earnings Claim Statement:	Yes
Term of Contract (Years):	10/5
Avg. # Of Employees:	2 FT, 4 PT
Passive Ownership:	Not Allowed
Encourage Conversions:	NA
Area Develop. Agreements:	No
Sub-Franchising Contracts:	No
Expand In Territory:	Yes
Space Needs: 1,400-1,800 SF; FS, SC	

SUPPORT & TRAINING PROVIDED:

Financial Assistance Provided:	Yes(I)
Site Selection Assistance:	Yes
Lease Negotiation Assistance:	Yes
Co-Operative Advertising:	No
Franchisee Assoc./Member:	Yes/Yes
Size Of Corporate Staff:	43
On-Going Support:	C,D,E,F,G,H,I

Training: 6 Days in Indianapolis, IN; 1 Day at Store Site.

SPECIFIC EXPANSION PLANS:

US:	All United States
Canada:	All Canada
Overseas:	No

When most people think of hobby stores, they imagine model airplanes and train sets. But what about the 66 million people that the U.S. Fish and Wildlife Service says venture outdoors to spend their free time feeding birds and watching wildlife?

Since 1981, Wild Birds Unlimited has focused on catering to the interests and needs of those nature hobbyists. WBU franchisees occupy a bird-feeding market worth $4.3 billion a year, offering bird-feeding and wildlife-watching enthusiasts with supplies and resources while simultaneously encouraging nature appreciation and environmental preservation.

But they do more than encourage. As part of WBU's Pathways to Nature conservation fund, which is co-sponsored by the national Fish and Wildlife Foundation, each WBU store donates part of its proceeds to fund education, conservation and wildlife-viewing projects at refuges and parks.

As a dispenser of information and the exclusive source for special bird-feeding products, Wild Birds Unlimited maintains a community presence that is enhanced by its partnerships with groups such as the Cornell Laboratory of Ornithology, Bird Studies Canada, the Canadian Wildlife Federation, the Organization for Bat Conservation and the American Camping Association.

Operating Units	12/31/2002	12/31/2003	12/31/2004
Franchised	279	295	303
% Change	--	5.7%	2.7%
Company-Owned	0	0	0
% Change	--	0.0%	0.0%
Total	279	295	303
% Change	--	5.7%	2.7%
Franchised as % of Total	100.00%	100.00%	100.00%

Investment Required
The fee for a Wild Birds Unlimited franchise is $18,000. The fee for an additional store is $9,000.

Wild Birds Unlimited provides the following range of investments required to open your initial franchise. The range assumes that all items are paid for in cash. To the extent that you choose to finance any of these expense items, your front-end investment could be substantially reduced.

Item	Established Low Range	Established High Range
Franchise fee	$18,000	$18,000
Training	$2,000	$2,000
Travel, meals, lodging	$1,000	$3,000
Lease deposit	$2,500	$4,500
First month's rent	$2,500	$4,500
Leasehold improvements	$6,471	$19,801

Insurance (1st quarter)	$200	$600
Legal/accounting	$750	$2,000
Office equipment	$3,549	$7,732
Signs	$2,880	$7,000
Advertising	$6,007	$12,383
Retail fixtures	$11,616	$15,831
Opening inventory	$24,000	$32,000
Miscellaneous expenses	$4,097	$8,272
Additional funds (for 3 months)	$5,000	$15,000
Total	$90,570	$152,619

On-Going Expenses

Wild Birds Unlimited franchisees pay a royalty fee equal to 4% of gross sales, a local advertising fee equal to 2% of gross sales, a regional and local advertising co-op fee equal to a maximum of 2% of gross sales, an advertising fund fee equal to 0.5% of gross sales (maximum of $2,500 a year) and an annual fee for point-of-sale software.

What You Get—Training and Support

Right off the bat, WBU franchisees benefit from one-on-one field consulting and are given site-selection and lease-negotiation assistance. Online forecasting tools provide checklists for site selection, and WBU staff review the age, income, family-type and lifestyle demographics of proposed locations. Training covers store operations as well as the retail industry – topics such as floor-plan layout, marketing, purchasing, human resources, finance, information systems and trends.

Before a store's opening, a customized financial plan is prepared with franchisees, and after opening, support continues through yearly visits from a regional consultant who reviews the franchisee's operations.

Online, WBU franchisees can access sales summaries, operational and product news and marketing ideas, in addition to order customized materials and supplies. Each location is also given a Web page with a link from the franchisor's main site. Additional learning opportunities are also online, including product updates, nature education and customer-service resources.

Franchisees also receive regular updates on marketing and product development. Print advertising, online information and partnership development is customized for franchisees' markets and marketing guides, direct mail, print advertising, newsletter templates, display suggestions, public relations and education-outreach ideas, special purchasing programs and trend updates are season-tailored. WBU also prepares ads, in-store signs and in-store video presentations for franchisee use.

Every month, WBU conducts a financial analysis comparing sales figures from all WBU stores to help franchisees understand the market and gauge their performances. A financial forecaster tool is also available, as are special services for handling backroom management, cash flow, operational issues, multiple-store management and store transfers, human resources and visual merchandising.

A human resources system helps train employees and includes advice about recruiting, selecting and training employees, while store-manager training consists of optional reading, projects and discussions at WBU's franchise support center. To build knowledge about the interests of WBU customers, a self-administered bird-feeding specialist program is offered in print or on CD-ROM and covers the basics about the hobby and WBU's core products.

A toll-free phone line and e-mail communications are other sources of assistance.

Territory
Wild Birds Unlimited grants exclusive territories.

Service-Based 6

Action International

Business Coaching

5670 Wynn Rd., Suite A & C
Las Vegas, NV 89118-2356
Tel: (888) 483-2828 (702) 795-3188
Fax: (702) 795-3183
E-Mail: malcolmgordon@action-international.com
Web Site: www.action-international.com
Mr. Malcolm Gordon, U S Sales Manager

ACTION INTERNATIONAL is one of the fastest-growing franchises (#16 Entrepreneur Mag., 2/04) and is the largest business coaching company in the world. The company was established in 1993 in Australia by Brad Sugars. Brad recognized early that most owners of small- to medium-sized businesses were unaware of how to effectively grow their businesses and achieve their goals. He developed a comprehensive system and methodology to assist this group. There are now 700 franchisees in 19 countries.

BACKGROUND: IFA MEMBER
Established: 1993; 1st Franchised: 1997
Franchised Units: 600
Company-Owned Units 1
Total Units: 601
Dist.: US-121; CAN-60; O'seas-420
North America: 25 States, 3 Provinces
Density: 23 in PA, 22 in NJ, 14 in GA
Projected New Units (12 Months): 180

Qualifications: 4, 3, 3, 3, 4, 5
Registered: FL,IL,IN,MD,MI,MN,NY,RI,SD,VA,WI,DC

FINANCIAL/TERMS:
Cash Investment: $75-89K
Total Investment: $75-89K
Minimum Net Worth: $100K
Fees: Franchise — $50K
 Royalty — 5%; Ad. — 5%
Earnings Claim Statement: No
Term of Contract (Years): 5/5
Avg. # Of Employees: 1 FT
Passive Ownership: Not Allowed
Encourage Conversions: NA
Area Develop. Agreements: Yes
Sub-Franchising Contracts: No
Expand In Territory: Yes
Space Needs: NA SF; HB

SUPPORT & TRAINING PROVIDED:
Financial Assistance Provided: Yes(I)
Site Selection Assistance: NA
Lease Negotiation Assistance: NA
Co-Operative Advertising: No
Franchisee Assoc./Member: No
Size Of Corporate Staff: 10
On-Going Support: A,B,C,D,E,F,G,H,I
Training: 10 Days Las Vegas, NV.

SPECIFIC EXPANSION PLANS:
US: All United States
Canada: All Canada
Overseas: AU, UK, Ireland, GR, FR, MX, Singapore, India, Malaysia, Spain, NZ

Action International is a business training and coaching program geared toward owners of small and medium-sized businesses who, as they expand, need assistance becoming more competitive. Through uniquely designed business methodologies, Action International teaches them how to improve their operations, offering expertise in lead generation, prospect client conversion and increasing interaction with clients.

A potential market of more than 5.7 million small business owners exists in the United States alone. Many of these owners want more than survival—they want to succeed. But many lack the sales, marketing and management tools to make this possible. Each Action International Business Coach spends a full 12 months mentoring a business and helping its operators achieve specific goals, in addition to increasing overall revenues and efficiency. Action International was founded in 1993 and has grown steadily ever since, attesting to the potential of an industry that is still largely untapped.

Operating Units	6/30/2002	6/30/2003	6/30/2004
Franchised	58	94	145
% Change	--	62.1%	54.3%
Company-Owned	0	0	0
% Change	--	0.0%	0.0%
Total	58	94	145
% Change	--	62.1%	54.3%
Franchised as % of Total	100.00%	100.00%	100.00%

Investment Required

The fee is $50,000 for a Primary Licensed Consultant franchise; the fee is $30,000 for an Associate Licensed Consultant franchise. Franchisees designated as a Primary Licensed Consultant have additional income opportunities but require approval and a minimum of one year's operation as an Associate Licensed Consultant to conduct business. Fees and total investment estimates differ for each designation.

Action International provides the following range of investments required to open your initial franchise. The range assumes that all items are paid for in cash. To the extent that you choose to finance any of these expense items, your front-end investment could be substantially reduced.

Item	Established Low Range	Established High Range
Franchise Fee	$30,000 (Associate)	$50,000 (Primary)
Additional Funds	$5,000	$7,500
Annual Conference	$0	$2,000
Insurance	$1,000	$1,500
Marketing, Inventory	$1,000	$2,500
Office Equipment	$0	$4,000
Training	$25,000	$25,000
Total Investment	$62,000 (Associate)	$92,500 (Primary)

On-Going Expenses

Action International franchisees designated as Primary Licensed Consultants pay royalties equaling $1,500 per month; Associate Licensed Consultants pay $1,000 per month. Marketing and advertising production fees equal 5% of Gross Revenues. Additional fees include facility and speaker fees at seminars and the cost of Action International products.

What You Get—Training and Support

Ten days of exhaustive training covers all facets of becoming an Action International franchisee. Experts are flown in from around the world to manage sessions. Franchisees are instructed on everything they will be doing as a Business Coach, as well as how to market their franchise and obtain clients. They will also learn how to recognize problems in businesses, how to develop solutions and how to best mentor the client in implementing the strategies.

Franchisees receive ongoing support and access to the recommendations of more than 700 other franchisees and will take part in biweekly conference calls with other coaches and a Master Franchisee. In addition, the experience gained in operating an Action International franchise helps franchisees coach their clientele, other business owners who would prefer learning from men and women who have run their own business.

Territory
Action International does not grant exclusive territories.

Allegra Print & Imaging

21680 Haggerty Rd., #105S
Northville, MI 48167
Tel: (888) 258-2730 (248) 596-8600
Fax: (248) 596-8601
E-Mail: meredithz@allegranetwork.com
Web Site: www.allegranetwork.com
Ms. Meredith Zielinski, Development Program Manager

As one of the largest printing franchises in the world, ALLEGRA NETWORK links more than 400 locations in the US, Canada and Japan. This January marks the 20th year that ALLEGRA has ranked among Entrepreneur Mag's Annual 500. ALLEGRA NETWORK's premier brand, ALLEGRA PRINT & IMAGING offers full-service print and graphic communications services including full-color printing, graphic design, digital color copying, mailing services, high sped output, online file transfer and many other services.

BACKGROUND:

	IFA MEMBER
Established: 1976;	1st Franchised: 1977
Franchised Units:	450
Company-Owned Units	0
Total Units:	450
Dist.:	US-450; CAN-0; O'seas-0
North America:	42 States, 3 Provinces

Density:	63 in MI, 34 in IL, 31 in MN
Projected New Units (12 Months):	12
Qualifications: 5, 2, 1, 2, 2, 2	
Registered: All States	

FINANCIAL/TERMS:

Cash Investment:	$40K+
Total Investment:	$155.6-279K
Minimum Net Worth:	$200K
Fees: Franchise —	$30K
Royalty — 3.6-6%;	Ad. — 1-2%
Earnings Claim Statement:	No
Term of Contract (Years):	20/20
Avg. # Of Employees:	3 FT, 1 PT
Passive Ownership:	Not Allowed
Encourage Conversions:	Yes
Area Develop. Agreements:	No
Sub-Franchising Contracts:	Yes
Expand In Territory:	Yes
Space Needs: 1,200 SF; FS, SF, SC	

SUPPORT & TRAINING PROVIDED:

Financial Assistance Provided:	Yes
Site Selection Assistance:	Yes
Lease Negotiation Assistance:	Yes
Co-Operative Advertising:	Yes
Franchisee Assoc./Member:	Yes/Yes
Size Of Corporate Staff:	50+
On-Going Support:	C,D,E,F,G,h,I
Training: 2 Weeks at Home Office; 1 Week On-Site; On-Going	

SPECIFIC EXPANSION PLANS:

US:	All United States
Canada:	All Canada
Overseas:	No

Allegra Print & Imaging centers provide printing services for small and medium-sized businesses and organizations primarily based in a franchisee's local community. Allegra offers technological advances such as full-color digital printing, print-on-demand capabilities and custom websites that allow franchisees to receive customer orders online. Allegra has a strong online presence convenient for the growing number of Internet-savvy customers who need professionally printed communications for their own customers.

As one of the largest franchised printing companies in the world, Allegra is positioned perfectly to take advantage of the growing market for digital color printing. With median center sales of $671,000 a year and almost 500 printing centers in North America alone, Allegra enjoys stable growth from year to year.

Operating Units	12/31/2002	12/31/2003	12/31/2004
Franchised	451	416	386
% Change	--	-7.8%	-7.2%
Company-Owned	0	0	0
% Change	--	0.0%	0.0%
Total	451	416	386
% Change	--	-7.8%	-7.2%
Franchised as % of Total	100.00%	100.00%	100.00%

Investment Required
The fee for an Allegra franchise is $30,000.

Allegra provides the following range of investments required to open your initial franchise. The range assumes that all items are paid for in cash. To the extent that you choose to finance any of these expense items, your front-end investment could be substantially reduced.

Item	Established Low Range	Established High Range
Franchise Fee	$30,000	$30,000
Additional Funds (for 12 months)	$50,000	$75,000
Business Licenses/Permits	$100	$1,000
Equipment	$97,456	$146,873
Fixtures, Furniture, Signs	$16,200	$19,000
Insurance	$1,200	$2,000
Leasehold Improvements	$2,500	$10,000
Real Estate, Utilities	$2,500	$7,500
Total Investment	$199,956	$291,373

On-Going Expenses

Allegra franchisees pay royalties equal to 6% of total monthly receipts (maximum of $65,330); national marketing fund fees equal to 1% of total monthly receipts (maximum of $6,540); MarketSmart payments ranging from $0.56-0.66 per piece of direct mail; local advertising cooperative fees equal to 1% of total monthly receipts; and Internet Service fees of $40 per month and a one-time set-up charge of $400.

What You Get—Training and Support

The base for Allegra's franchisee support system is a 40-person corporate staff and 12 regional Allegra professionals. Allegra's Annual Operating Ratio Study analyzes finances to improve franchisee performance, and performance groups assist franchisees with expansion and profitability. Allegra also provides each franchisee with a customizable website to tap into the online market.

The six-person Allegra Technology Group provides immediate answers to questions about all aspects of running an Allegra franchise. They manage a toll-free support phoneline for inquiries about equipment and the management of daily printing operations. They also keep Allegra on the cutting edge of graphics printing by testing new products, exploring methods to improve daily and sharing their discoveries and knowledge in publications distributed throughout the year.

Territory
Allegra grants exclusive territories.

AlphaGraphics

alphagraphics®

DESIGN ■ COPY ■ PRINT

268 S. State St., # 300
Salt Lake City, UT 84111-2048
Tel: (800) 955-6246 (801) 595-7270
Fax: (801) 595-7271
E-Mail: opportunity@alphagraphics.com
Web Site: www.alphagraphics.com
Mr. Keith M. Gerson, VP of Marketing & Development

At ALPHAGRAPHICS, we work with people to plan, produce and manage their visual communications, enabling them to achieve their goals more effectively and confidently. The ALPHAGRAPHICS network is comprised of nearly 300 business centers located throughout the US and 9 other countries. Our business centers offer complete visual communications solutions, including design, copying, printing, digital archiving, finishing, mailing services, oversized printing and promotional items. Trained/experienced staff.

BACKGROUND: IFA MEMBER
Established: 1970; 1st Franchised: 1980
Franchised Units: 266
Company-Owned Units 0
Total Units: 266
Dist.: US-231; CAN-0; O'seas-35
North America: 38 States
Density: 25 in TX, 24 in IL, 24 in CA
Projected New Units (12 Months): 24

Qualifications: 4, 5, 1, 3, 3, 5
Registered: All States

FINANCIAL/TERMS:
Cash Investment: $75-100K
Total Investment: $225.7-366.7K
Minimum Net Worth: $300K
Fees: Franchise — $25.9K
 Royalty — 1.5-8%; Ad. — 2.5%
Earnings Claim Statement: Yes
Term of Contract (Years): 20/20
Avg. # Of Employees: 5 FT
Passive Ownership: Not Allowed
Encourage Conversions: Yes
Area Develop. Agreements: Yes
Sub-Franchising Contracts: No
Expand In Territory: Yes
Space Needs: 1,200-3,000 SF; FS, SC, SC

SUPPORT & TRAINING PROVIDED:
Financial Assistance Provided: Yes(I)
Site Selection Assistance: Yes
Lease Negotiation Assistance: No
Co-Operative Advertising: Yes
Franchisee Assoc./Member: No/No
Size Of Corporate Staff: 94
On-Going Support: b,C,D,E,G,H,I
Training: 4 Weeks Salt Lake City, UT Service Center

SPECIFIC EXPANSION PLANS:
US: All United States
Canada: All Canada
Overseas: Spain, Italy, France, Germany, Benelux, Austria

AlphaGraphics is the "gold standard of quick-print franchise stores," providing print services to local businesses and document management to global Internet customers. AlphaGraphics fills a variety of basic needs for businesses, from high-speed and high-volume copying to high-quality offset printing, as well as promotional items, digital color prints and scanning. The proprietary AlphaLink network connects all AlphaGraphics centers so that documents in need of printing can be transferred electronically around the world whenever necessary. AlphaGraphics also looks beyond printing, offering businesses crucial growth services such as website design and management.

AlphaGraphics provides convenience printing, which is the swiftest growing part of the billion-dollar printing industry. AlphaGraphics has a global presence as a one-stop place for designing, printing and managing electronic documents.

Operating Units	6/30/2002	6/30/2003	6/30/2004
Franchised	242	241	244
% Change	--	-0.4%	1.2%
Company-Owned	0	0	0
% Change	--	0.0%	0.0%
Total	242	241	244
% Change	--	-0.4%	1.2%
Franchised as % of Total	100.00%	100.00%	100.00%

Investment Required
The fee for an AlphaGraphics franchise is $25,900.

AlphaGraphics provides the following range of investments required to open your initial franchise. The range assumes that all items are paid for in cash. To the extent that you choose to finance any of these expense items, your front-end investment could be substantially reduced.

Item	Established Low Range	Established High Range
Franchise Fee	$25,900	$25,900
Finance Costs	$4,500	$12,000
Furniture, Fixtures, Signs, Equipment	$109,575	$109,575
Insurance	$1,600	$4,000
ISO, Other Fees	$5,150	$5,150
Marketing	$15,000	$15,000
Miscellaneous	$14,000	$29,000
Real Estate	$20,000	$60,000
Training, Grand Opening	$24,000	$24,000
Additional Funds (for 12 months)	$53,394	$82,094
Total Investment	$273,119	$366,719

On-Going Expenses

AlphaGraphics franchisees pay royalties equal to 1.5 to 8% of gross sales, local marketing fees equal to 1 to 2%, regional marketing fees up to 2% and multi-regional marketing fees equal to 0.5%. Additional training or assistance is available for $750-$900 a day.

What You Get—Training and Support

New franchisees begin with four weeks of exhaustive training at Alpha-Graphics corporate headquarters in Salt Lake City. Franchisees are instructed in all aspects of running an AlphaGraphics center: managing the business, running daily operations and developing a customer base. They are given access to efficient management systems and tools that are easy to operate and designed for growth.

The AlphaGraphics Integrated Marketing Program is a proprietary system that gives franchisees an edge in formulating marketing programs for prospective and current customers. The software assists in customizing promotions that target the needs and preferences of clients, as well as monitoring success rates. AlphaGraphics marketing consultants are also available to provide training and make on-site visits.

In 1997, AlphaGraphics became the first—and still the only—quick-print shop to earn an ISO 9000 certification for meeting international quality management and assurance standards in its franchising process and store-operating and performance-monitoring systems. These standards apply to all AlphaGraphics locations around the world, which are linked through the AlphaLink communications system. The network provides franchise support and training through the free exchange of ideas among all connected franchisees.

Territory
AlphaGraphics grants protected territories encompassing approximately 1,200 to 2,500 businesses.

The Alternative Board

THE ALTERNATIVE BOARD®
Achieve Success with Peer Advice and Coaching

1640 Grant St., # 200
Denver, CO 80203
Tel: (800) 727-0126 (303) 839-1200
Fax: (303) 839-0012
E-Mail: salesinfo@tabboards.com
Web Site: www.tabboards.com
Ms. Kris Vollrath, Franchise Support Manager

THE ALTERNATIVE BOARD (TAB) is seeking entrepreneurs, business consultants or transitioning executives who are looking to start or expand their own business. As a TAB-Certified Facilitator, you will chair monthly group meetings of owners, CEOs and presidents of privately-owned companies. In addition to facilitating these monthly meetings, you will provide individual coaching sessions using proprietary processes and tools.

BACKGROUND:	IFA MEMBER
Established: 1990;	1st Franchised: 1996
Franchised Units:	154
Company-Owned Units	8
Total Units:	162
Dist.:	US-149; CAN-12; O'seas-1
North America:	38 States, 4 Provinces
Density:	NR
Projected New Units (12 Months):	75
Qualifications: 3, 5, 5, 5, 4, 5	
Registered: All States	

FINANCIAL/TERMS:	
Cash Investment:	$44.3-105.9K
Total Investment:	$44.3-105.9K
Minimum Net Worth:	$200K
Fees: Franchise —	$25-55K
Royalty — 35%/$1.5-4.5K/Mo;	Ad. — 1%/$100-400
Earnings Claim Statement:	No
Term of Contract (Years):	10/10

Avg. # Of Employees:	1 FT	Lease Negotiation Assistance:	NA
Passive Ownership:	Not Allowed	Co-Operative Advertising:	No
Encourage Conversions:	NA	Franchisee Assoc./Member:	Yes/Yes
Area Develop. Agreements:	No	Size Of Corporate Staff:	28
Sub-Franchising Contracts:	No	On-Going Support:	A,C,D,G,H,I
Expand In Territory:	Yes	Training: 6 Days Denver, CO.	
Space Needs: NA SF; HB, Exec.Suite			
		SPECIFIC EXPANSION PLANS:	
SUPPORT & TRAINING PROVIDED:		US:	All United States
Financial Assistance Provided:	No	Canada:	All Canada
Site Selection Assistance:	NA	Overseas:	All Countries

The Alternative Board® (TAB) franchisee manages peer advisory boards of up to 12 owners, CEOs and presidents of privately owned, non-competing businesses. The franchisee chairs monthly group meetings, in which participants discuss the problems they face and the opportunities they encounter and receive feedback from other experienced businesspeople, as well as you, the facilitator. Franchisees also become certified coaches to provide one-on-one coaching and further assist members in achieving their desired success and goals.

TAB has helped businesses excel since 1990 by offering services such as strategic planning, advice for both business and personal issues, objective feedback, skill development and a confidential and supportive environment where business ideas flow and peers can hold each other accountable for their own businesses.

TAB provides nationwide exposure and local promotional assistance, making cold calls unnecessary. Additional members are gained through marketing campaigns and group informational meetings. Franchisees earn revenue through fees paid by members of their peer groups, including initiation and diagnostic fees, monthly membership dues and charges for additional coaching and consulting.

Operating Units	12/31/2003	12/31/2004	12/31/05
Franchised	86	101	142
% Change	--	17.4%	40.6%

Company-Owned	11	5	8
% Change	--	-54.5%	60%
Total	97	106	150
% Change	--	9.3%	41.5%
Franchised as % of Total	88.66%	95.28%	94.7%

Investment Required

The fee for a The Alternative Board® franchise ranges from $25,000 to $55,000, depending on the size of the territory.

The Alternative Board® requires the following range of investments to open your initial franchise.

Item	Established Low Range	Established High Range
Franchise Fee	$25,000	$55,000
Business Coach Fees	$300	$1,400
Deposits/Licenses, Accounting/Professional Fees	$0	$2,100
Equipment, Fixtures, Signs	$0	$1,350
Kick-Off Campaign	$3,600	$18,000
Supplies, Stationery, Cards	$325	$600
TAB Membership Developer Fees/Expenses	$3,000	$11,000
Training Fee	$9,000	$12,000
Additional Funds (for 3 months)	$1,000	$2,000
Total Investment	$42,225	$103,450

On-Going Expenses

The Alternative Board® franchisees pay royalties equal to 35% of the membership dues they receive or until the election of a monthly flat fee ranging from $1,500 to $4,500 (depending on the territory size); $200 or 50% of all business assessment fees, whichever is greater; a member administration and support fee of $10 per member per month; member marketing campaign charges of $3.60 per prospect; and contractor license fees equaling $1,000 per month per territory. Additional fees include a marketing development fee, an international conference fee and charges for TAB promotional materials, the cost of which varies by territory.

What You Get—Training and Support

A personal coach who has already acted as a successful facilitator will be assigned to each franchisee. They will act as mentors and give feedback throughout the first twelve months of becoming a certified facilitator. Franchisees become familiar with Strategic Business Leadership® procedures that define goals and develop strategies to maximize results within a reasonable time period. All new facilitators are given six days of training at the corporate headquarters, where they are instructed in all aspects of running a TAB franchise. In addition to learning how to run meetings, coach privately and gain new members, franchisees are given access to resources such as the TAB Confidential Manual and over 100 PowerPoint presentations for use at their monthly membership meetings. Facilitators also learn to analyze their members' business operations using an online business assessment tool for one-on-one coaching sessions.

TAB promotes communication between facilitators and board members by providing an online hotline where facilitators around the world exchange tips, ideas and perfected methods. One monthly newsletter, accessible both online and in print, is provided for board members and facilitators. International Facilitator conferences also take place every year, allowing franchisees to share their best practices with one another and learn new techniques from the corporate staff.

Territory

The Alternative Board® grants exclusive territories.

American Leak Detection

THE ORIGINAL LEAK SPECIALISTS™

888 Research Dr., # 100, P.O. Box 1701
Palm Springs, CA 92262
Tel: (800) 755-6697 (760) 320-9991
Fax: (760) 320-1288
E-Mail: sbangs@americanleakdetection.com
Web Site: www.americanleakdetection.com
Ms. Sheila Bangs, Director Franchise Development

Electronic detection of water, drain, gas, waste, and sewer leaks under concrete slabs of homes, commercial buildings, pools, spas, fountains, etc. with equipment commissioned/patented/manufactured by company.

BACKGROUND: IFA MEMBER
Established: 1974; 1st Franchised: 1985
Franchised Units: 307
Company-Owned Units <u>6</u>
Total Units: 313
Dist.: US-238; CAN-8; O'seas-67
  North America: 41 States, 3 Provinces
  Density: 71 in CA, 35 in FL, 15 in TX
Projected New Units (12 Months): 4
Qualifications: 3, 3, 2, 2, 2, 3
Registered: All States and AB

FINANCIAL/TERMS:

Cash Investment:	$58-120K
Total Investment:	$85-150K
Minimum Net Worth:	$Varies
Fees: Franchise —	$57.5K
Royalty — 6-10%;	Ad. — NA
Earnings Claim Statement:	No
Term of Contract (Years):	10/10
Avg. # Of Employees:	1-4 FT, 2 PT
Passive Ownership:	Discouraged
Encourage Conversions:	NA
Area Develop. Agreements:	No
Sub-Franchising Contracts:	No
Expand In Territory:	Yes
Space Needs: NR SF; NR	

SUPPORT & TRAINING PROVIDED:

Financial Assistance Provided:	Yes(D)
Site Selection Assistance:	NA
Lease Negotiation Assistance:	NA
Co-Operative Advertising:	Yes
Franchisee Assoc./Member:	Yes/Yes
Size Of Corporate Staff:	34
On-Going Support:	a,B,C,D,f,G,H,I
Training: 6-10 Weeks Palm Springs, CA.	

SPECIFIC EXPANSION PLANS:

US:	Northeast, Midwest
Canada:	MB, SK
Overseas: Western Europe, Japan, Mexico, Australia	

For over 30 years, American Leak Detection has been the world leader in the detection of hidden water and sewer leaks. We have set the standard for non-invasive leak detection and repair with our proprietary methods and state-of-the-art technology.

From swimming pools cracks to concealed plumbing systems, the smallest leak or pipe defect is located with the most advanced, sophisticated electronic devices – without bashing holes in walls or digging up yards.

Our franchisees receive extensive training, excellent methodologies and access to a world-class R&D department. Our company recently merged with Plain Sight Systems, a company consisting of scientists, engineers, and mathematicians centered at Yale University. Together, we are building our next generation of internet, lead generation and leak detection tools that will continue to make American Leak Detection the leader in the industry.

Operating Units	9/30/2003	9/30/2004	9/30/2005
Franchised	151	155	148
% Change	--	2.6%	-4.5%
Company-Owned	2	4	2
% Change	--	100.0%	-100.0%
Total	153	159	150
% Change	--	3.9%	-5.7%
Franchised as % of Total	98.69%	97.48%	98.7%

Investment Required
The fee for an initial American Leak Detection franchise ranges from $57,500 to $100,000, depending on the population of the franchise's designated territory. American Leak Detection provides up to 50% of financing, depending on a franchisee's credit.

American Leak Detection provides the following range of investments required to open your initial franchise. The range assumes that all items are paid for in cash. To the extent that you choose to finance any of these expense items, your front-end investment could be substantially reduced.

Item	Established Low Range	Established High Range
Franchise Fee	$57,500	$100,000

Business Licenses/Taxes	$0	$2,250
Insurance	$750	$3,000
Supplies	$375	$6,300
Vehicle	$0	$20,000
Other Costs & Additional Funds (for 3 months)	$12,630	$23,500
Total Investment	$71,255	$155,050

On-Going Expenses

The franchisee pays an ongoing royalty fee ranging from 6 to 10% of adjusted gross volume.

What You Get—Training and Support

Training starts with six weeks of training in management, marketing, accounting and on-the-job techniques. A monthly newsletter keeps franchisees up-to-date, and a four-day convention takes place annually for franchisees to communicate ideas and generate new ones.

American Leak Detection's research and development department continually works to improve and update equipment, while the marketing staff assists with press coverage. A website is maintained for the exclusive use of franchisees, which means that franchisees benefit from instantaneous communication and support from fellow team members. Follow-up training and marketing assistance is provided after the business opens, and employee training programs are customized for each franchisee's needs.

Territory

American Leak Detection grants exclusive territories.

AmeriSpec Home Inspection Service

HOME INSPECTION SERVICE
Number One in North America

889 Ridge Lake Blvd.
Memphis, TN 38120-9421
Tel: (800) 426-2270 (901) 820-8500
Fax: (901) 820-8520
E-Mail: sales@amerispec.com
Web Site: www.amerispecfranchise.com
Ms. Theresa Westphall, Sales Coordinator

AMERISPEC delivers productivity enhancing tools to our owners like feature-rich personal Websites, branded email accounts, secure web delivery for reports and contact management software specifically designed to manage a home inspection business. A private intranet permits two-way communication with and among our owners. Consider our extensive training, the acclaimed and recognized 'AMERISPEC REPORT,' our on-going educational support and the package is complete.

BACKGROUND:

	IFA MEMBER
Established: 1987;	1st Franchised: 1988
Franchised Units:	360
Company-Owned Units	2
Total Units:	362
Dist.:	US-282; CAN-80; O'seas-0
North America:	48 States, 8 Provinces
Density:	24 in CA, 16 in FL, 11 in IL
Projected New Units (12 Months):	25

Qualifications: 3, 3, 3, 3, 1, 5
Registered: All States

FINANCIAL/TERMS:

Cash Investment:	$10-15K
Total Investment:	$24.6-63.5K
Minimum Net Worth:	$25K
Fees: Franchise —	$18-26.9K
Royalty — 7%;	Ad. — 3%
Earnings Claim Statement:	No
Term of Contract (Years):	5/5
Avg. # Of Employees:	1 FT, 2 PT
Passive Ownership:	Allowed
Encourage Conversions:	Yes
Area Develop. Agreements:	No
Sub-Franchising Contracts:	No
Expand In Territory:	Yes
Space Needs: NA SF; HB	

SUPPORT & TRAINING PROVIDED:

Financial Assistance Provided:	Yes(D)
Site Selection Assistance:	NA
Lease Negotiation Assistance:	NA
Co-Operative Advertising:	Yes
Franchisee Assoc./Member:	No
Size Of Corporate Staff:	45
On-Going Support:	C,D,E,G,h,I
Training: 2 Weeks Memphis, TN.	

SPECIFIC EXPANSION PLANS:

US:	All United States
Canada:	All Canada
Overseas:	No

AmeriSpec Home Inspection Service conducts home inspections for homeowners, prospective homeowners and realtors. Inspections cover more than 400 areas in the home and all adhere to AmeriSpec's Standards of Excellence. Their goal is to provide the most complete home inspection. Proprietary software such as the AmeriSpec Home Inspector and tools such as the AmeriSpec Report facilitate the process of preparing reports for clients.

AmeriSpec carries out more than 150,000 inspections a year from more than 360 locations in North America, and has completed more than 1.5 million since 1987. Part of the extensive ServiceMaster network, Ameri-Spec franchisees benefit from financial assistance from the ServiceMaster Acceptance Company, as well as other services.

Operating Units	12/31/2002	12/31/2003	12/31/2004
Franchised	287	300	314
% Change	--	4.5%	4.7%
Company-Owned	2	2	2
% Change	--	0.0%	0.0%
Total	289	302	316
% Change	--	4.5%	4.6%
Franchised as % of Total	99.31%	99.34%	99.37%

Investment Required
The fee for an initial AmeriSpec franchise is $29,900.

AmeriSpec provides the following range of investments required to open your initial franchise. The range assumes that all items are paid for in cash. To the extent that you choose to finance any of these expense items, your front-end investment could be substantially reduced.

Item	Established Low Range	Established High Range
Franchise Fee	$17,910	$29,900
AmeriSpec Report	$450	$450
Computer System/ Equipment	$200	$4,000
Equipment/Furniture	$500	$2,500
Field Inspection Hardware/Accessories	$250	$2,000
Marketing	$500	$1,700

Miscellaneous Opening Costs	$4,000	$8,500
Opening Promotional Expenses	$1,500	$2,500
Training Expenses	$750	$1,250
Additional Funds (for 3 months)	$500	$12,000
Total Investment	$26,560	$64,800

On-Going Expenses

The franchisee pays an ongoing earned service fee of 7% of gross receipts (minimum of $250 per month) and an advertising contribution fee equaling 3% of gross receipts (minimum of $125 per month).

What You Get—Training and Support

During pre-training, franchisees are introduced to an AmeriSpec Business Consultant who will support them as they go through the process of opening an AmeriSpec franchise. Study materials will be provided and pre-training objectives will be established for the franchisee to fulfill.

Franchisees then go through the AmeriSpec Management Institute with two weeks of training at the AmeriSpec Training Center in Memphis, Tennessee. The first week's instruction details the steps taken in conducting a home inspection, in addition to how to format, prepare and present a report to clients and use AmeriSpec Home Inspector software. Franchisees practice inspections on a full-scale and fully working model of a home and learn to apply AmeriSpec's Standards of Excellence. The second week covers the marketing and managing aspects of the franchise, providing computer, software and Internet setup and training. Franchisees also learn how to analyze their own market's needs, formulate marketing strategies, manage daily operations, determine pricing and create short- and long-term business plans.

Take-home materials are also provided, such as the AmeriSpec Smart Start program, a helpful outline of the steps a franchisee should take from week to week that helps franchisees avoid common mistakes. The AmeriSpec Home Study System expands the franchisee's knowledge of the home through ten modules that contain 4,000 pages of text, 1,500 illustrations and over 17 hours of video.

Territory

AmeriSpec grants Standard territories encompassing approximately 4,000 annual residential real estate transactions and Alternate territories encompassing approximately 1,000 to 2,000 annual real estate transactions.

Century 21 Real Estate

1 Campus Dr.
Parsippany, NJ 07054
Tel: (877) 221-2765 (973) 428-9700
Fax: (973) 496-5806
E-Mail: brien.mcmahon@cendant.com
Web Site: www.century21.com
Mr. Brien McMahon, EVP Franchise Sales

With more than 143,000 broker and sales associates worldwide, the CENTURY 21 ® system is the world's largest residential real estate organization, providing comprehensive training, management, administrative and marketing support for its members.

BACKGROUND: IFA MEMBER
Established: 1972; 1st Franchised: 1972
Franchised Units: 7,680
Company-Owned Units 0
Total Units: 7,680
Dist.: US-4,340; CAN-359; O'seas-2,981
North America: 50 States, DC
Density: 546 in CA, 383 in FL, 268 TX
Projected New Units (12 Months): NR
Qualifications: 4, 4, 5, 4, 4, 4
Registered: All States and AB

FINANCIAL/TERMS:

Cash Investment:	$NR
Total Investment:	$11.6-522.4K
Minimum Net Worth:	$25K
Fees: Franchise —	$NR
Royalty — 6%;	Ad. — 2%
Earnings Claim Statement:	No
Term of Contract (Years):	10
Avg. # Of Employees:	Varies
Passive Ownership:	Not Allowed
Encourage Conversions:	Yes
Area Develop. Agreements:	No
Sub-Franchising Contracts:	No
Expand In Territory:	Yes
Space Needs: 1,000 SF; FS, SF, SC	

SUPPORT & TRAINING PROVIDED:

Financial Assistance Provided:	No
Site Selection Assistance:	No
Lease Negotiation Assistance:	No
Co-Operative Advertising:	Yes
Franchisee Assoc./Member:	Yes/Yes
Size Of Corporate Staff:	NR
On-Going Support:	A,C,D,E,G,H,I
Training: 5 Days in Parsippany, NJ; 3-7 Sessions on Telephone; 1 Day On-Site.	

SPECIFIC EXPANSION PLANS:

US:	All United States
Canada:	All Canada
Overseas:	All Countries

With more than 143,000 broker and sales associates worldwide, the Century 21® system is the world's largest residential real estate organization, providing comprehensive training, management, administrative and marketing support for its members.

Operating Units	12/31/2003	12/31/2004	12/31/2005
Franchised	6,628	7,222	7,877
% Change	--	9.0%	9.1%
Company-Owned	0	0	0
% Change	--	0.0%	0.0%
Total	6,628	7,222	7,877
% Change	--	9.0%	9.1%
Franchised as % of Total	100.00%	100.00%	100.00%

Investment Required
The fee for a Century 21® franchise is $25,000.

Century 21 Real Estate LLC provides the following range of investments required to open your initial franchise. The range assumes that all items are paid for in cash. To the extent that you choose to finance any of these expense items, your front-end investment could be substantially reduced.

Item	Established Low Range	Established High Range
Franchise Fee	$0	$25,000
Advertising (for 3 months)	$1,623	$28,750
Brokers Council Fees	$105	$1,500
Equipment/Fixtures	$0	$122,332
Office Supplies	$3,200	$19,700
Service Fees	$1,500	$170,129
Signs	$5,000	$24,000
Training and Promotion	$237	$33,100

Other Operating Expenses (for 3 months)	$48	$98,000
Total Investment	$11,713	$522,511

On-Going Expenses
Century 21® franchisees pay a royalty fee equal to 6% of gross income, with a minimum of $562 per month and a maximum of $1,300 per month, and national advertising fund fees equal to 2% of monthly gross income. Additional fees include varying brokers council fees and an International Management Academy fee of $1,800.

What You Get—Training and Support
Century 21 provides new franchisees with the following: live and self-paced web-based classes through the award-winning Century 21® Learning System, direct instruction and guidance from a local broker's office, affordable beginning and advanced courses to further develop field knowledge, software to manage daily operations, and financial and marketing tools such as the Century 21® Learning System Virtual Solution Series, which provides PowerPoint tutorials and digital photography guidance. Additional valuable services include networking events where franchisees interact with and learn from peers.

With one of the most recognized names in the real estate industry, the Century 21 System is dedicated to maintaining the strength of its brand name through national television, radio, print and online marketing campaigns. Franchisees benefit from personalized advertising materials and programs targeting different demographics including specialty and emerging markets (new construction, mature moves, first-time homeowners, luxury and more). Additionally, to help System members maintain their relationships with customers, programs such as the Century 21® System's Quality Service Survey, Preferred Client Club and Century 21® Connections were established.

Territory
The Century 21 System grants protected territories with a quarter-mile

radius. Franchisees are not prohibited from seeking listings or buyers in any area.

Children's Orchard

900 Victors Way, # 200
Ann Arbor, MI 48108
Tel: (800) 999-5437 + 222 (734) 994-9199 + 222
Fax: (734) 994-9323
E-Mail: campaign364@mail.emaximation.com
Web Site: www.childorch.com
Mr. Taylor Bond, President

Upscale children's retail/resale stores, featuring clothing, toys, furniture, equipment, books and parenting products. We buy top-brand items from area families by appointment, and re-sell in boutique-style stores, along with top-quality new children's items from nearly 200 suppliers. These are large volume stores selling thousands of items per week.

BACKGROUND: IFA MEMBER
Established: 1980; 1st Franchised: 1985
Franchised Units: 85
Company-Owned Units 1
Total Units: 86
Dist.: US-86; CAN-0; O'seas-0
 North America: 22 States
 Density: 18 in CA, 14 in MA, 6 in MI
Projected New Units (12 Months): 15
Qualifications: 5, 3, 2, 4, 2, 5
Registered: All Except HI,ND,RI,SD

FINANCIAL/TERMS:
Cash Investment: $30-50K
Total Investment: $72.5-158K
Minimum Net Worth: $200K
Fees: Franchise — $22.5K
 Royalty — 5%; Ad. — 1%
Earnings Claim Statement: No
Term of Contract (Years): 10
Avg. # Of Employees: 1 FT, 3 PT
Passive Ownership: Discouraged
Encourage Conversions: Yes
Area Develop. Agreements: Yes/Open
Sub-Franchising Contracts: No
Expand In Territory: No
Space Needs: 1,200-2,000 SF; SF, SC

SUPPORT & TRAINING PROVIDED:
Financial Assistance Provided: Yes(I)
Site Selection Assistance: Yes
Lease Negotiation Assistance: Yes
Co-Operative Advertising: Yes
Franchisee Assoc./Member: Yes/Yes
Size Of Corporate Staff: 15
On-Going Support: B,C,D,E,F,G,H,I
Training: 12 Days Training in Ann Arbor, MI.

SPECIFIC EXPANSION PLANS:
US: All US Except HI, AK
Canada: No
Overseas: No

Children's Orchard benefits from the huge, and growing, market for children's clothing, furniture, and toys. Larger than the entire market for fast food, it exceeds $200 billion dollars . . . and it's getting bigger. Every year there are nearly 200,000 more children than the previous year. And, with parents facing increasing pressure on their disposable income, Upscale Resale presents them with a terrific value alternative.

A fast growing market is certainly important in selecting a business opportunity but it's not the only attribute to consider. Strong gross margins and inventory turnover are key investment considerations that Children's Orchard owners measured when making their decision to open their own Children's Orchard store. As you learn more about the Children's Orchard opportunity and review our documentation and talk with Children's Orchard owners, you'll be able to get a clear idea of what to expect from your investment and what it takes to get there.

Operating Units	12/31/2003	12/31/2004	12/31/2005
Franchised	84	84	94
% Change	--	0.0%	10.6
Company-Owned	2	1	1
% Change	--	-100.0%	0.0%
Total	86	84	95
% Change	--	-2.3%	11.6%
Franchised as % of Total	97.67%	98.8%	98.9%

Investment Required
The fee for a Children's Orchard franchise is $25,000.

When determining the amount of capital you'll need to invest to open and operate a Children's Orchard business, you'll need to take into consideration a number of factors. These include: the region of the country in which you'll be opening the store, the size of the space you select, and the amount of any improvement allowance your landlord may provide to cover build-out expenses.

Your budget for the first few months of opening and operating your business should be in the range of $115,600-$197,000. This includes the cost of items such as:

Item	Established Low Range	Established High Range
Franchise Fee	$25,000	$25,000
Equipment, Fixtures, Signs, Supplies	$27,400	$43,000
Inventory	$20,000	$35,000
Leasehold Improvements/ Interior Buildout	$5,000	$30,000
Rent/Lease Deposits	$2,000	$15,000
Training / Travel	$1,200	$4,000
Additional Funds (for 1st year)	$35,000	$45,000
Total Investment	$115,600	$197,000

Working capital needs vary significantly. Ultimately, you will need sufficient working capital to cover the business's expenses while you build its sales to reach its cash break-even point. The higher your cash break-even, the more working capital you will want to include in your initial investment budget.

In most instances, to finance the business through a lending institution, you will need to have at least $40,000 in cash available and a personal net worth of at least $225,000. You will also need to have an outside income to cover your living expenses while the business is in its development phase.

On-Going Expenses
Children's Orchard franchisees pay on-going royalty fees equal to 5% of gross sales or $2,500 per calendar quarter, whichever is greater; and advertising fees equal to 1% of gross sales or $500 per calendar quarter, whichever is greater.

What You Get—Training and Support
Entrepreneurs join franchise systems for a variety of reasons. One of the

most common is that they don't want to "re-invent the wheel." Nor do we think they should. In fact, a key advantage of joining a mature franchise like Children's Orchard is that our years of retail and franchising experience have positioned us to know what is needed, and when, to help new franchisees every step of the way. We've taken our 25+ years of experience, combined it with a skilled and talented support team, and given them one goal: provide the tools and guidance that Children's Orchard owners need to open, operate, and grow their own Children's Orchard store. Here are some of the key ways in which we meet that goal:

- Comprehensive assistance in selecting a site and negotiating a lease.
- A thorough two-week initial training program.
- A "paint by numbers" process for your store's design, décor, and merchandizing.
- Comprehensive assistance in inventory selection, purchasing, and display.
- Professionally developed Grand Opening program.
- Professionally managed public relations.
- Ongoing support through regular phone contact and store visits.
- Sources of supply for unique "new" inventory, equipment, and supplies.
- Sophisticated and franchisee friendly technology that includes 24/7 support through our web-based franchise network.
- Thorough analysis of your business's financial results.
- Ongoing training and inventory assistance at bi-annual national meetings.

Territory
Children's Orchard grants exclusive territories.

Choice Hotels International

C H O I C E   H O T E L S   I N T E R N A T I O N A L

10750 Columbia Pike
Silver Spring, MD 20901-4427
Tel: (800) 547-0007 (301) 592-5000
Fax: (301) 592-6205
E-Mail: franchise_sales@choicehotels.com
Web Site: www.choicehotelsfranchise.com
Mr. Ron Burgett, VP Franchise Sales

CHOICE HOTELS is the leading hotel franchisor with more than 60 years' experience in developing brands and services that optimize hotel performance. Our single focus is on enhancing the return on investment for our owners and growing our brands strategically. Brands include COMFORT INN, COMFORT SUITES, QUALITY, SLEEP INN, CLARION, MAINSTAY SUITES, ECONO LODGE, and RODEWAY INN, and our new boutique brand extension, CLARION COLLECTION. Either convert an existing location or build a new one.

BACKGROUND: IFA MEMBER
Established: 1941;   1st Franchised: 1962
Franchised Units: 5,000
Company-Owned Units   3
Total Units: 5,003
Dist.:   US-3,829; CAN-260; O'seas-914
  North America: 50 States,10 Provinces
  Density: 258 in TX, 251 in CA, 205 FL
Projected New Units (12 Months):   400+

Qualifications: 4, 4, 4, 2, 1, 1
Registered: All States

FINANCIAL/TERMS:

Cash Investment:	$20-30% Costs
Total Investment:	$2-10MM
Minimum Net Worth:	$Varies
Fees: Franchise —	$25-50K
Royalty — 2.75-5.1%;	Ad. — 1.75% Rev.
Earnings Claim Statement:	Yes
Term of Contract (Years):	20/5
Avg. # Of Employees:	Varies
Passive Ownership:	Allowed
Encourage Conversions:	Yes
Area Develop. Agreements:	No
Sub-Franchising Contracts:	No
Expand In Territory:	Yes
Space Needs: 31,000-33,000 SF; FS	

SUPPORT & TRAINING PROVIDED:

Financial Assistance Provided:	Yes(B)
Site Selection Assistance:	Yes
Lease Negotiation Assistance:	Yes
Co-Operative Advertising:	Yes
Franchisee Assoc./Member:	Yes/Yes
Size Of Corporate Staff:	1,500
On-Going Support:	A,B,C,D,F,G,h,I
Training: 1 Day (on Aspects of Operation).	

SPECIFIC EXPANSION PLANS:

US:	All United States
Canada:	All Canada
Overseas:	All Countries

Choice Hotels International is one of the largest hotel franchisors in the world with more than 5,000 hotels, inns, all-suites, extended stay and resort properties open in 43 countries. Choice Hotel's diverse portfolio meets the needs of today's developers and value-minded travelers. Comfort Inn®, Comfort Suite®, Quality®, Sleep Inn®, Clarion®, MainStay Suites®, Econo Lodges®, Rodeway Inn®, Suburban® and their new upscale all-suites brand Cambria Suites™.

With over 60 years of experience in the hotel industry, Choice Hotels offers franchisees a comprehensive support system that includes operational systems, technology support and marketing programs. Choice Hotels International is committed to supporting franchisees by increasing reservations and reducing operating costs.

In 2004, Choice Hotels Central Revenue System booked over $1.4 billion in room revenue – with over 55 million occupied room nights. By offering guests loyalty programs with rewards such as Choice Privileges, Ea$y Choice and Airline Miles, Choice guests benefit and so do franchisees.

Operating Units	12/31/2003	12/31/2004	12/31/2005
Franchised	4,810	4,977	5210
% Change	--	3.5%	4.9%
Company-Owned	0	0	0
% Change	--	0.0%	0.0%
Total	4,810	4,977	5,200
% Change	--	3.5%	4.9%
Franchised as % of Total	100.00%	100.00%	100.00%

Investment Required
The fee for a Choice Hotels International franchise is $500 per room with a range of $25,000 to $60,000.

Choice Hotels International provides the following range of investments required to open your initial franchise. The range assumes that all items are paid for in cash. To the extent that you choose to finance any of these expense items, your front-end investment could be substantially reduced. Costs will vary depending on the brand chosen. The list below is not exhaustive as each brand has a separate list of required investments.

Item	Established Low Range	Established High Range

Franchise Fee ($500/ room, $50,000 minimum)	$25,000	$60,000
Construction/Architecture	$1,100,000	$5,700,000
Furniture, Fixtures, Equipment, Signs	$160,000	$1,100,000
Hotel Internet Access	$14,000	$25,000
Insurance (Construction, General, Workers)	$80,000	$275,000
Opening Inventory	$40,000	$300,000
Pre-Opening Advertising	$0	$60,000
Real Estate	Not Determinable	Not Determinable
Salaries	$40,000	$100,000
Working Capital	$119,517	$275,000
Other Costs and Additional Funds (for 3 Months)	$75,000	$175,000
Total Investment	$1,653,517	$8,070,000
Total Cost Per Room	$41,337	$80,700

On-Going Expenses

In general, Choice Hotels International franchisees pay a royalty fee starting at 3.5% of the preceding month's gross room revenue (GRR), a marketing fee starting at 1.25% of the preceding month's GRR, a reservation fee equal to 1.75% of the preceding month's GRR and a data communications fee of $140 a month. Fees vary depending on brand. The Rodeway brand offers a flat per room, per month fee that combines the fees for royalties, marketing and reservations.

What You Get—Training and Support

A staff of 300 franchise services professionals located throughout the country is dedicated to providing franchisees in their regions with all the support they need. Franchisees receive assistance with the design, construction, opening and operating of a hotel. A five-day orientation program provides the necessary skills for managing a hotel, as well as how to formulate a marketing program and familiarize oneself with Choice Hotels' extensive franchisee resources. Franchise Service Directors will visit hotels to train staff in guest satisfaction, reward programs, housekeeping, maintenance and front-desk management. After a hotel opens, they will continue to offer support and advice to improve revenue. Additional specialized training programs, regional training days and annual conventions are also conducted.

Choice Hotels International understands that revenue begins with attracting the attention of desired guests, and it accomplishes this through extensive national and local marketing, partnerships with other well-known brands and promotional opportunities. Advertisements appear on national TV and radio, in national consumer and trade publications and on major Internet sites. Marketing brochures can be customized for each franchisee's hotel, and franchisees receive assistance with press releases and graphic design. In 2004 alone, Choice Hotels International spent more than $50 million on advertising.

Territory
Choice Hotels International does not grant exclusive territories.

Coldwell Banker Real Estate

1 Campus Dr.
Parsippany, NJ 07054
Tel: (973) 359-5757
Fax: (973) 359-5908
E-Mail: david.hardy@cendant.com
Web Site: www.coldwellbanker.com
Mr. David Hardy, SVP Business Development

For 99 years, the COLDWELL BANKER (TM) organization has been the premiere provider of full-service real estate. With more than 3,600 independently and company owned and operated residential real estate offices with approximately 120,000 sales associates globally, the company is an industry leader.

BACKGROUND:	IFA MEMBER
Established: 1981;	1st Franchised: 1981
Franchised Units:	2,600
Company-Owned Units	900
Total Units:	3,500
Dist.:	US-3,044; CAN-217; O'seas-239
North America:	50 States, DC
Density:	380 in CA, 255 in FL, 159 TX

217

Projected New Units (12 Months):	NR	Space Needs: 1,000 SF; FS, SF, SC	
Qualifications: 4, 4, 5, 4, 4, 4			
Registered: All States and AB		**SUPPORT & TRAINING PROVIDED:**	
		Financial Assistance Provided:	No
FINANCIAL/TERMS:		Site Selection Assistance:	No
Cash Investment:	$NR	Lease Negotiation Assistance:	No
Total Investment:	$23.5-477.3K	Co-Operative Advertising:	Yes
Minimum Net Worth:	$25K	Franchisee Assoc./Member:	Yes
Fees: Franchise —	$NR	Size Of Corporate Staff:	100
Royalty — 6%;	Ad. — 2.5%	On-Going Support:	A,C,D,E,G,H,I
Earnings Claim Statement:	No	Training: 4 Days in Parsippany, NJ; 1-2 Days On-	
Term of Contract (Years):	10	Site; Varies via Internet.	
Avg. # Of Employees:	Varies		
Passive Ownership:	Not Allowed	**SPECIFIC EXPANSION PLANS:**	
Encourage Conversions:	Yes	US:	All United States
Area Develop. Agreements:	No	Canada:	All Canada
Sub-Franchising Contracts:	No	Overseas:	All Countries
Expand In Territory:	Yes		

For 100 years, the Coldwell Banker™ organization has been the premiere provider of full-service real estate. With nearly 4,000 independently and company-owned and operated residential real estate offices with approximately 126,400 sales associates globally, the company is an industry leader.

Operating Units	12/31/2003	12/31/2004	12/31/2005
Franchised	2,595	2,769	2,892
% Change	--	6.7%	4.4%
Company-Owned	891	883	943
% Change	--	0.0%	6.8%
Total	3,486	3,652	3,835
% Change	--	4.8%	5.0%
Franchised as % of Total	74.44%	75.82%	75.4%

Investment Required

The fee for a Coldwell Banker franchise ranges from $13,000 to $25,000, depending on the size of the franchisee's market.

Coldwell Banker provides the following range of investments required to

open your initial franchise. The range assumes that all items are paid for in cash. To the extent that you choose to finance any of these expense items, your front-end investment could be substantially reduced.

Item	Established Low Range	Established High Range
Franchise Fee	$13,000	$25,000
Building/Yard/Open House/Misc. Rider Signs	$3,500	$26,050
Computer Equipment	$1,000	$4,000
Insurance	$300	$1,000
Printed Materials/Name Badges	$5,220	$7,800
Training Costs	$200	$2,700
Other Costs and Additional Funds (for 3 months)	$250	$3,500
Total Investment	$23,470	$70,050

On-Going Expenses

Coldwell Banker franchisees pay a royalty fee equal to 6% of gross revenue and national advertising fund fees equal to 2.5% of gross revenue monthly, with a minimum of $542 and a maximum of $1,084.

What You Get—Training and Support

The Coldwell Banker® University offers training in multiple formats: a classroom environment, national events, tele-classes, CD-ROMs and online virtual classrooms. Continuing education credit is also available online for instruction 24 hours a day. Online resources keep franchisees on the cutting edge. The LeadRouter™ program enables franchisees to manage leads efficiently and provide clients with quicker responses. CBNet, an online portal, provides franchisees with marketing tools, presentations, further training and the latest news and events.

National television campaigns and promotion in newspapers and magazines increase brand awareness, direct leads to franchisees and reinforce the image of Coldwell Banker as the authority on real estate. Coldwell Banker provides an extensive catalog of marketing tools that franchisees can personalize and customize to suit their needs.

Territory
Coldwell Banker does not grant exclusive territories.

Comfort Keepers

6640 Poe Ave., # 200
Dayton, OH 45414-2600
Tel: (888) 329-1368 (937) 264-1933 + 320
Fax: (937) 264-3103
E-Mail: comfortmf@franchisehub.com
Web Site: www.comfortkeepers.com
Mr. Larry France, Manager, Franchise Development

COMFORT KEEPERS is the service leader, with 97.3% client satisfaction. We provide non-medical, in-home care, such as companionship, meal preparation, light housekeeping, grocery and clothing shopping, grooming and assistance with recreational activities for the elderly and others who need assistance in daily living.

BACKGROUND:

	IFA MEMBER
Established: 1999;	1st Franchised: 1999
Franchised Units:	530
Company-Owned Units	0
Total Units:	530
Dist.:	US-502; CAN-23; O'seas-5
North America:	45 States, 3 Provinces
Density:	50 in FL, 39 in CA, 37 in OH
Projected New Units (12 Months):	102
Qualifications: 5, 5, 2, 3, 3, 4	

Registered: All States

FINANCIAL/TERMS:

Cash Investment:	$40-65K
Total Investment:	$40-65K Min.
Minimum Net Worth:	$75K
Fees: Franchise —	$23.2K
Royalty — 5/4/3% Desc.;	Ad. — 0%
Earnings Claim Statement:	No
Term of Contract (Years):	10/10
Avg. # Of Employees:	2 FT + Caregivers
Passive Ownership:	Not Allowed
Encourage Conversions:	Yes
Area Develop. Agreements:	No
Sub-Franchising Contracts:	No
Expand In Territory:	Yes
Space Needs: 600-800 SF; HB, Office Space	

SUPPORT & TRAINING PROVIDED:

Financial Assistance Provided:	Yes(I)
Site Selection Assistance:	No
Lease Negotiation Assistance:	No
Co-Operative Advertising:	No
Franchisee Assoc./Member:	Yes
Size Of Corporate Staff:	28
On-Going Support:	B,C,D,G,h,I
Training: 1 Week Dayton, OH and On-Going.	

SPECIFIC EXPANSION PLANS:

US:	All United States
Canada:	All Canada
Overseas:	All Countries

Comfort Keepers was founded to help people stay in their own homes and give them the highest quality of care. It not only provides in-home care to thousands in North America, but it delivers it with compassion. Caregivers are all carefully screened and are required to have compassion and a sincere interest in providing support. Caregivers follow the highest standards, which includes a philosophy of always providing "excellent care" and always "doing the right thing."

The number of Americans turning 65 is continually rising. The issue of aging adults who would prefer to stay in their own home but need some assistance is one that increasingly concerns their children, who frequently do not live nearby. The need for senior service care will continue to grow and, with hundreds of locations already in place around the world, the network of Comfort Keepers can easily offer a helping hand.

Operating Units	2/28/2003	12/31/2003	12/31/2004
Franchised	338	393	438
% Change	--	16.3%	11.5%
Company-Owned	1	0	0
% Change	--	-100.0%	0.0%
Total	339	393	438
% Change	--	15.9%	11.5%
Franchised as % of Total	99.71%	100.00%	100.00%

Investment Required
The fee for a Comfort Keepers franchise is $23,225.

Comfort Keepers provides the following range of investments required to open your initial franchise. The range assumes that all items are paid for in cash. To the extent that you choose to finance any of these expense items, your front-end investment could be substantially reduced.

Item	Established Low Range	Established High Range
Franchise fee	$23,225	$23,225

Business Premises	$0	$2,000
Furniture and Equipment	$1,000	$3,000
Insurance	$1,650	$1,800
Advertising, Marketing and Promotion	$6,000	$9,000
Organizational Expenses/ Supplies/Printing	$750	$1,275
Telephone, bank & other deposits	$250	$600
Employment Screening	$150	$300
Additional funds (working capital)	$11,500	$25,500
Total	$44,525	$66,700

On-Going Expenses

Comfort Keepers franchisees pay a royalty fee based on monthly gross revenues. If revenue is $28,928 or less, fee is 5%; if $28,929 to $46,730, fee is $1,397.50 plus 4% of gross revenue over $28,928; if $46,731 or more, fee is $2,085.50 plus 3% of gross revenue over $46,730. Other fees include a national advertising contribution fee not less than 0.5% nor more than 2% of monthly gross revenue, and a local advertising fee equal to $500 per month minimum.

What You Get—Training and Support

Franchisees complete a comprehensive 5-day training course that helps them jump start their business operations. Corporate headquarters provide on-going support, and regional operations managers give hands-on assistance to increase business growth. Franchisees can exchange ideas with other franchisees at state, regional and national meetings. The network of hundreds of Comfort Keepers around the world produces collective knowledge and understanding among franchisees. Comfort Keepers also maintains a franchisee website, which offers a library, training resources, news, information and online communication opportunities with other owners.

Advertising guidance and support is also provided at the local and national levels, with assistance from a leading PR firm. Comfort Keepers gives franchisees a guidebook that outlines the marketing process, as well as recruitment advertisements, templates for print advertisements, recruitment advertisements, ready-to-print press releases and more.

Territory
Comfort Keepers grants exclusive territories.

Cottman Transmission Systems

201 Gibraltar Rd., # 150
Horsham, PA 19044
Tel: (800) 394-6116 (215) 643-5885
Fax: (215) 956-0340
E-Mail: barry@cottman.com
Web Site: www.cottman.com
Mr. Barry Auchenbach, VP Franchise Development

Automotive service franchise with centers nationwide. A market leader with opportunities for solid growth. A highly supportive company that offers intensive training, outstanding advertising and on-site support. A forty+-year reputation of treating customers with fairness, integrity and honesty. No automotive experience required.

BACKGROUND:	IFA MEMBER
Established: 1962;	1st Franchised: 1964
Franchised Units:	405
Company-Owned Units	6
Total Units:	411
Dist.:	US-405; CAN-4; O'seas-2
North America:	43 States, 2 Provinces
Density:	PA, TX, NJ
Projected New Units (12 Months):	60
Qualifications: 4, 4, 1, 2, 3, 3	
Registered: CA,FL,IL,IN,MD,MI,MN,NY,OR,RI,S	

D,VA,WA,WI,DC,AB

FINANCIAL/TERMS:	
Cash Investment:	$60K
Total Investment:	$161-209K
Minimum Net Worth:	$200K
Fees: Franchise —	$31.5K
Royalty — 7.5%;	Ad. — $730/Wk.
Earnings Claim Statement:	Yes
Term of Contract (Years):	15/15
Avg. # Of Employees:	3 FT
Passive Ownership:	Not Allowed
Encourage Conversions:	Yes
Area Develop. Agreements:	Yes/4
Sub-Franchising Contracts:	Yes
Expand In Territory:	Yes
Space Needs: 3,000-4,000 SF; FS,SC, Auto Mall	

SUPPORT & TRAINING PROVIDED:	
Financial Assistance Provided:	Yes(I)
Site Selection Assistance:	Yes
Lease Negotiation Assistance:	Yes
Co-Operative Advertising:	No
Franchisee Assoc./Member:	No
Size Of Corporate Staff:	70
On-Going Support:	C,D,E,F,G,H,I
Training: 6 Weeks Extensive On-Site Training.	

SPECIFIC EXPANSION PLANS:	
US:	All United States
Canada:	All Canada
Overseas:	Open

223

Cottman Transmission has been America's transmission specialist since 1962. Cottman's mission statement is to "promote dynamic corporate and personal growth in a family atmosphere through integrity, professionalism and caring service to our customers, our dealers and to ourselves." Cottman prides itself on its 97% customer satisfaction rating and dealership-quality services that are completed quickly and at rates that are 15% lower than dealership costs.

As the prices of new cars continue to rise and changing economic conditions lead more Americans to keep each car around longer, the car maintenance and repair industry continues to grow. After more than four decades and more than 400 locations nationwide, Cottman Transmission is strong, stable and still growing fast, having opened 100 new stores since 2001.

Operating Units	12/31/2003	9/30/2004	9/30/2005
Franchised	355	353	365
% Change	--	-0.6%	3.4%
Company-Owned	33	39	35
% Change	--	18.2%	-10.3%
Total	388	392	400
% Change	--	1.0%	2.0%
Franchised as % of Total	91.49%	90.05%	91.25%

Investment Required
The fee for a Cottman Transmission franchise is $31,500.

Cottman Transmission provides the following range of investments required to open your initial franchise. The range assumes that all items are paid for in cash. To the extent that you choose to finance any of these expense items, your front-end investment could be substantially reduced.

Item	Established Low Range	Established High Range

Franchise Fee	$31,500	$31,500
Training Expenses	$11,500	$12,200
Deposits	$8,500	$12,000
Equipment	$44,000	$59,000
Leasehold Improvements	$12,500	$20,000
Insurance	$3,000	$4,000
Professional Fees	$3,000	$5,000
Computer system/software	$2,500	$3,500
Initial Supply Package	$1,000	$1,000
Opening Inventory	$2,000	$2,000
Grand Opening Advertising	$2,000	$2,000
Telemarketing Fund	$1,000	$1,000
Exterior Sign Package	$4,000	$10,000
Interior Design Package	$4,500	$5,500
Working Capital	$30,000	$40,000
Total Investment	$161,000	$208,700

On-Going Expenses

Cottman Transmission franchisees pay ongoing royalty fees equal to 7.5% of total gross sales and advertising fees equal to $730.

What You Get—Training and Support

Training begins with a three-week program in Cottman's corporate offices in Horsham, PA. Thereafter, there is an additional 6-week on-site training program for the franchisee and staff. Cottman encourages franchisees to act as members of a family, communicating and working together for the good of the whole. Cottman's yearly convention provides opportunities for franchisees to exchange ideas with Cottman management. The convention also provides a forum for Cottman to incentify existing franchisees with programs for growth.

Each member of the expanding Cottman family benefits from Cottman's

Home Office Support. The Home Office provides the latest news and updates in transmission technology, in addition to staffing a technical hotline, distributing monthly newsletters and directing field operations managers to franchisees in need of support. Cottman also assists with site selection and design, personnel management, advertising and sales.

Territory

Cottman Transmission grants exclusive territories.

Coverall Cleaning Concepts

5201 Congress Ave., # 275
Boca Raton, FL 33487
Tel: (800) 537-3371 (561) 922-2690
Fax: (561) 922-2495
E-Mail: info@coverall.com
Web Site: www.coverall.com
Mr. Jack Caughey, VP Business Development

Commercial cleaning franchise which includes comprehensive training, equipment, billing and collection services, and an initial customer base. With an affordable down payment as low as $1,500, COVERALL CLEANING CONCEPTS provides a combination of business programs and support systems that focus on meeting the franchisees and customers alike. Master and territory franchises are also available.

BACKGROUND: IFA MEMBER

Established: 1985;	1st Franchised: 1985
Franchised Units:	7,085
Company-Owned Units	0
Total Units:	7,085
Dist.:	US-6,536; CAN-233; O'seas-316
North America:	32 States, 2 Provinces
Density:	1,296 CA, 1,054 FL, 750 OH

Projected New Units (12 Months): 1817
Qualifications: 3, 3, 2, 2, 3, 5
Registered: All States Except SD

FINANCIAL/TERMS:

Cash Investment:	$1.5-25.2K
Total Investment:	$6.2-36K
Minimum Net Worth:	$1.5K
Fees: Franchise —	$6.2-32.2K
Royalty — 5%;	Ad. — 0%
Earnings Claim Statement:	No
Term of Contract (Years):	20/20
Avg. # Of Employees:	1-2 FT, 2-3 PT
Passive Ownership:	Allowed
Encourage Conversions:	Yes
Area Develop. Agreements:	Yes/20
Sub-Franchising Contracts:	Yes
Expand In Territory:	Yes
Space Needs: NA SF; NA	

SUPPORT & TRAINING PROVIDED:

Financial Assistance Provided:	Yes(D)
Site Selection Assistance:	Yes
Lease Negotiation Assistance:	No
Co-Operative Advertising:	Yes
Franchisee Assoc./Member:	No/No
Size Of Corporate Staff:	90
On-Going Support:	A,B,C,D,G,H,I
Training: 40 Hours at Local Regional Support Center.	

SPECIFIC EXPANSION PLANS:

US: All United States

Canada:		All Canada	Overseas:	All Countries

Coverall Cleaning Concepts has brought about a revolution by applying successful business models to the specific needs of the commercial cleaning industry. Backed by an extensive support system and multi-faceted training programs, Coverall Cleaning Concepts successfully utilizes the most advanced technologies and provides janitorial services from more than 8,500 Franchise Owners around the world.

While the commercial cleaning industry is largely served by small-scale operations, the Coverall Cleaning Concepts Franchise Program gives individual entrepreneurs the chance to succeed while providing them with a recognizable brand name and access to large national accounts.

Operating Units	12/31/2003	12/31/2004	12/31/2005
Franchised	7,403	8,451	8,953
% Change	--	14.2%	5.8%
Company-Owned	0	0	0
% Change	--	0.0%	0.0%
Total	7,403	8,451	8,953
% Change	--	14.2%	5.8%
Franchised as % of Total	100.00%	100.00%	100.00%

Investment Required
The fee for a Coverall Cleaning Concepts Franchise ranges from $6,000 to $32,200, depending on the volume of business desired by a franchisee.

Coverall Cleaning Concepts provides the following range of investments required to open your initial franchise. The range assumes that all items are paid for in cash. To the extent that you choose to finance any of these expense items, your front-end investment could be substantially reduced.

Item	Established Low Range	Established High Range
Franchise Fee	$6,000	$32,200
Business License/Permits	$25	$120
Office Supplies/ Equipment	$0	$100
Misc. Pre-Opening	$0	$200
Insurance	$52/Month	$345/Month
Uniforms	$0	$100
Additional Funds (for 4 months)	$266	$3,200
Total Investment	$6,291	$35,920

On-Going Expenses

Coverall franchisees pay on-going royalty fees equal to 5% of gross monthly billings, management fees equal to 10% of gross monthly billings, general liability insurance costs of $52 to $345 a month and franchise owner insurance coverage equal to 2.4% of gross monthly billings. Additional fees include extra sales and marketing fees, premium account fees, retraining fees and a referral fee for special one-time services like window cleaning or floor refinishing.

What You Get—Training and Support

Services are provided throughout the three phases of each franchise's development: start-up, operation and growth.

In the first phase, a 10-step training program covers all aspects of the business, including innovations in cleaning methods and equipment, management, environmental concerns and safety precautions. Coverall Cleaning Concepts has an advantageous alliance with Procter & Gamble, the largest consumer products company in the world, which supplies all cleaning products at a discounted price.

During the operating phase, Franchise Owners receive the assistance of the Coverall Cleaning Concepts Regional Support Center, which manages customer bills and provides customer service and direct support via on-call professionals.

Finally, in the growth phase, Coverall Cleaning Concepts continues to update training materials, communicate new developments, provide advanced certification programs and assist in continuing to expand the business through marketing and a Franchise Referral Program.

Territory
Coverall Cleaning Concepts' Master Franchise Program offers the exclusive developmental rights to operate the Coverall Cleaning Concepts system in an entire metropolitan area. A Coverall Cleaning Concepts Master Franchise Owner gains access to Coverall's proven franchise program and will be permitted to sell and support janitorial franchises in an exclusive market on an ongoing basis.

Crestcom International, LTD.

6900 E. Belleview Ave., # 300
Greenwood Village, CO 80111-1619
Tel: (888) 273-7826 (303) 267-8200
Fax: (303) 267-8207
E-Mail: franchiseinfo@crestcom.com
Web Site: www.crestcom.com
Mr. Kelly Krause, VP International Marketing

CRESTCOM franchisees market and deliver world-renowned training in leadership, customer service, sales and management development. CRESTCOM uses a unique combination of video instruction and live facilitation to teach these skills. Thousands of organizations use CRESTCOM training, from multinational giants to small, local firms. The company is active in 45+ countries and has materials in over 20 languages.

BACKGROUND:	IFA MEMBER
Established: 1987;	1st Franchised: 1992
Franchised Units:	149
Company-Owned Units	0
Total Units:	149
Dist.:	US-58; CAN-15; O'seas-76
North America:	25 States, 4 Provinces
Density:	NR
Projected New Units (12 Months):	20
Qualifications: 4, 5, 2, 4, 5, 5	
Registered: All States	

FINANCIAL/TERMS:	
Cash Investment:	$12.5-61.5K
Total Investment:	$26.6-88.4K
Minimum Net Worth:	$NR
Fees: Franchise —	$39.5-59.5K
Royalty — 1.5%;	Ad. — NA
Earnings Claim Statement:	Yes

Term of Contract (Years):	7/7/7	Lease Negotiation Assistance:	NA
Avg. # Of Employees:	2-5 FT	Co-Operative Advertising:	No
Passive Ownership:	Discouraged	Franchisee Assoc./Member:	Yes
Encourage Conversions:	NA	Size Of Corporate Staff:	15
Area Develop. Agreements:	No	On-Going Support:	D,G,H
Sub-Franchising Contracts:	No	Training: 7-10 Days Denver, CO, Phoenix, AZ or	
Expand In Territory:	Yes	Sacramento, CA.	
Space Needs: NR SF; SF, HB			
		SPECIFIC EXPANSION PLANS:	
SUPPORT & TRAINING PROVIDED:		US:	All United States
Financial Assistance Provided:	Yes	Canada:	All Canada
Site Selection Assistance:	NA	Overseas:	All Countries

Crestcom International has emerged as a world leader in providing cutting-edge training solutions. Crestcom Franchisees market and deliver training in the area of Sales, Recruiting, Customer Service and particularly Management Skills Development.

Each month Crestcom Franchisees train thousands of executives and managers from more than 150 major cities in nearly 50 countries. Crestcom clients range from small local companies to organizations with thousands of employees.

Crestcom's training and support allows potential Franchisees to participate in the companies Initial Training program, attend an actual Crestcom class, and accompany an exiting Franchisee on sales calls before deciding whether to acquire a Franchise.

Operating Units	12/31/2002	12/31/2003	12/31/2004
Franchised	47	58	62
% Change	--	23.4%	6.9%
Company-Owned	0	0	0
% Change	--	0.0%	0.0%
Total	47	58	62
% Change	--	23.4%	6.9%
Franchised as % of Total	100.00%	100.00%	100.00%

Investment Required

The fee for a Crestcom franchise is $12,500 for an associate franchise and $61,500 for a Standard Franchise.

Crestcom provides the following range of investments required to open your initial franchise. The range assumes that all items are paid for in cash. To the extent that you choose to finance any of these expense items, your front-end investment could be substantially reduced.

Item	Established Low Range	Established High Range
Franchise Fee	$12,500	$61,500
Insurance	$600	$1,800
Legal and Accounting	$500	$1,500
Marketing Program	$6,000	$6,000
Mentor Program	$0	$2,500
Office Lease Costs/ Equipment/Supplies	$425	$3,430
Seminar Expense	$200	$900
Shipping Costs; Initial Inventory	$200	$800
Training Expenses	$1,120	$2,550
Additional Funds (for 3 months)	$5,000	$8,775
Total Investment	$26,545	$89,755

On-Going Expenses

Crestcom franchisees pay a royalty fee equal to 1.5% of gross revenue and a distribution fee equal to 34% of gross revenue. Other ongoing fees include the cost of materials and a new materials surcharge.

What You Get—Training and Support

When new Franchisees acquire a Crestcom Franchise they receive the right to own, operate and subject to certain conditions or sell their business. They receive an initial supply of Crestcom material and training and

Three-quarters of the population dreams of being independent, but lack the tools to achieve their goals on their own. That's why the Entrepreneur's Source exists. The Entrepreneur's Source consultants provide an array of information about self-employment, franchising, education and training. Consultants expose 95% of their clients to businesses and options they never knew or properly considered.

Consultants assist small businesses, a sector with much unrealized potential, by offering them expansion through franchising. By focusing on the possibilities of franchising, consultants are not limited to any particular industry. New consultants are not required to have prior franchising experience, and, with The Entrepreneur's Source's flexible concept, low overhead and global marketplace, consultants have the tools to succeed and the potential to keep growing.

Operating Units	12/31/2001	12/31/2002	12/31/2003
Franchised	94	194	251
% Change	--	106.4%	29.4%
Company-Owned	0	0	0
% Change	--	0.0%	0.0%
Total	94	194	251
% Change	--	106.4%	29.4%
Franchised as % of Total	100.00%	100.00%	100.00%

Investment Required
The fee for an Entrepreneur's Source franchise is $49,000.

The Entrepreneur's Source provides the following range of investments required to open your initial franchise. The range assumes that all items are paid for in cash. To the extent that you choose to finance any of these expense items, your front-end investment could be substantially reduced.

Item	Established Low Range	Established High Range
Franchise Fee	$49,000	$49,000
Training Expenses	$3,000	$4,500
Equipment	$3,000	$4,000
Marketing Aids	$1,300	$2,300
Miscellaneous Opening Costs	$1,000	$2,500
Brand Setup Fee	$9,000	$9,000
Intranet & Extranet Setup	$2,500	$2,500
Initial Training Fee	$10,000	$10,000
Additional Funds (for 6 months)	$8,700	$11,700
Total Investment (not including Real Estate)	$87,500	$95,500

On-Going Expenses
The Entrepreneur's Source franchisees pay on-going lead generation and support fees of $750 per month. Additional costs are for optional extra training or on-site assistance.

What You Get—Training and Support
Franchisees start off with a pre-training phase with a coach and then go on to the E-Source Academy, where they learn how to be a consultant, practice working with a client from first contact to placement and how to create a "Possibilities Profile" for them. Additional support is provided by national and regional offices, tele-coaching and national conferences.

The Entrepreneur's Source has a strong Internet presence that generates new clients for franchisees, and the latest technology, such as the Esource-Central system, provides the Internet tools and resources to communicate with other franchisees and remain up-to-date with the latest news. Targeted advertising materials are available at the international, national and regional levels.

While franchisees can start off in the Individual Office Program, the Entrepreneur's Source offers additional routes to growth. The Master Developer Program is for franchisees who wish to form a larger business with partners, and the International Master Licensing Program is for franchisees interested in helping The Entrepreneur's Source expand overseas.

Territory

The Entrepreneur's Source grants a saturation maximum.

ERA Franchise Systems

1 Campus Dr.
Parsippany, NJ 07054
Tel: (800) 869-1260 (973) 428-9700
Fax: (973) 496-7354
E-Mail: david.hardy@cendant.com
Web Site: www.era.com
Mr. David Hardy, SVP Business Development

A network of more than 2,840 offices and over 36,600 brokers and sales associates in the U. S. and 29 countries. As the innovator of the popular Sellers Security Plan and the ERA Answers Book, ERA has been developing quality products and services to members and consumers alike since 1971.

BACKGROUND: IFA MEMBER
Established: 1971;   1st Franchised: 1971
Franchised Units: 2,811
Company-Owned Units: 30
Total Units: 2,841
Dist.:   US-1,215; CAN-0; O'seas-1,626
  North America: 50 States
  Density: 124 in CA, 123 in FL, 68 NY
Projected New Units (12 Months):   NR
Qualifications: 4, 4, 5, 4, 4, 4

Registered: All States

FINANCIAL/TERMS:
Cash Investment:	$NR
Total Investment:	$42.7-205.9K
Minimum Net Worth:	$25K
Fees: Franchise —	$12.5-20K
Royalty — 6%;	Ad. — 2%
Earnings Claim Statement:	No
Term of Contract (Years):	10
Avg. # Of Employees:	Varies
Passive Ownership:	Not Allowed
Encourage Conversions:	Yes
Area Develop. Agreements:	No
Sub-Franchising Contracts:	No
Expand In Territory:	Yes
Space Needs: 1,000 SF; FS, SF, SC	

SUPPORT & TRAINING PROVIDED:
Financial Assistance Provided:	No
Site Selection Assistance:	No
Lease Negotiation Assistance:	No
Co-Operative Advertising:	Yes
Franchisee Assoc./Member:	Yes/Yes
Size Of Corporate Staff:	NR
On-Going Support:	A,C,D,E,G,H,I
Training: 1 Week in Parsippany, NJ; 3-4 Days On-Site	

SPECIFIC EXPANSION PLANS:
US:	All United States
Canada:	All Canada
Overseas:	All Countries

235

Since 1971, ERA Real Estate has been guiding people through the process of buying or selling their homes—one of the most important financial commitments they will ever make. A leading franchised brokerage networks with franchisees in 29 countries and territories, ERA Real Estate is made up of more than 36,600 brokers and sales associates. ERA Real Estate strives to offer customers everything that they could need or want.

ERA Real Estate maintains an award-winning website that allows buyers and sellers to access homes for sale using a virtual open house for every listing. ERA Real Estate was the first real-estate franchise to provide nationwide home warranties with its Home Protection Plan, which guards against unexpected repairs. ERA® also offers the Sellers Security Plan, a program that offers sellers a guaranteed price and sale date. In addition, ERA® clients have help with every aspect of their move and benefit from ERA Real Estate's partnerships with moving companies, hotels and other services.

Operating Units	12/31/2003	12/31/2004	12/31/2005
Franchised	2,474	2,601	2,813
% Change	--	5.1%	8.2%
Company-Owned	31	30	30
% Change	--	-3.2%	0.0%
Total	2,505	2,631	2,843
% Change	--	5.0%	8.1%
Franchised as % of Total	98.8%	98.9%	98.9%

Investment Required
The fee for an ERA® franchise ranges from $12,500 to $20,000 depending on the size of the market.

ERA Real Estate provides the following range of investments required to open your initial franchise. The range assumes that all items are paid for in cash. To the extent that you choose to finance any of these expense items, your front-end investment could be substantially reduced.

Item	Established Low Range	Established High Range
Franchise Fee	$20,000	$20,000
Advertising/Public Relations	$1,500	$20,000
Automobile Leases	$0	$1,000
Insurance	$200	$5,000
Legal/Accounting Fees	$300	$2,600
Misc. Opening Costs	$2,500	$7,500
Multiple Listing Service (Real Estate) Dues	$150	$600
Signs/Supplies/Furniture	$5,500	$55,000
Taxes	$50	$1,200
Training Expenses	$500	$3,000
Additional Funds	$12,000	$90,000
Total Investment	$42,700	$205,900

On-Going Expenses

ERA® franchisees pay a royalty fee equal to 6% of gross revenue (minimum fees range from $304 to $607 depending on market size) and an advertising fee equal to 2% of monthly gross revenues (a monthly minimum of $323 and maximum of $1,115). Other ongoing fees include an assignment fee of $5,000.

What You Get—Training and Support

The ERA® Top Gun Academy provides ERA® Sales Associates with eight weeks of intensive training in customer-service skills, presentations and techniques. Franchisees receive an online storefront on ERA.com, which allows them to post property details and office profiles and links to a personal website. Franchisees also receive exclusive access to local marketing materials, incentive programs, powerful prospecting tools and more. A franchisee-only Web site offers the latest news, training and marketing resources, while the ERA® On-Line Advertiser provides all kinds of media advertising templates that can be customized for each franchisee.

ERA Real Estate offers personalized, targeted programs for niche properties, such as the ERA® International Collection for luxury properties, the
ERA® Historical Real Estate Program for historical properties and the
ERA® Hispanic Marketing program for the burgeoning Latino market. A
national public relations program and nationwide advertising on TV, on
the radio and in print strengthen the brand and give ERA® franchisees
more exposure and recognition.

Territory
ERA Real Estate does not grant exclusive territories.

Express Personnel Services

8516 Northwest Expy.
Oklahoma City, OK 73162-5145
Tel: (877) 652-6400 (405) 840-5000
Fax: (405) 717-5665
E-Mail: franchising@expresspersonnel.com
Web Site: www.expressfranchising.com
Ms. Diane Carter, Manager of Franchise Admin.

If you have a passion for owning your business,
EXPRESS PERSONNEL SERVICES has a passion
for helping you succeed. EXPRESS PERSONNEL
SERVICES is a sales-focused, business-to-business
franchise. An EXPRESS PERSONNEL SERVICES
franchise has four profit centers in one franchise
agreement. EXPRESS provides three weeks of start-
up training and on-going online learning. EXPRESS
helps as many people as possible find good jobs by
helping as many clients as possible find good people.

BACKGROUND:	IFA MEMBER
Established: 1983;	1st Franchised: 1985
Franchised Units:	512
Company-Owned Units	0
Total Units:	512

Dist.:	US-482; CAN-20; O'seas-10
North America:	47 States
Density:	52 in TX, 31 in OK, 23 in WA
Projected New Units (12 Months):	100
Qualifications: 4, 4, 3, 4, 4, 4	
Registered: All States	

FINANCIAL/TERMS:	
Cash Investment:	$115-162K
Total Investment:	$115-162K
Minimum Net Worth:	$100K
Fees: Franchise —	$25K
Royalty — 8-9%;	Ad. — 0.6%
Earnings Claim Statement:	No
Term of Contract (Years):	5/5
Avg. # Of Employees:	3 FT
Passive Ownership:	Not Allowed
Encourage Conversions:	Yes
Area Develop. Agreements:	No
Sub-Franchising Contracts:	No
Expand In Territory:	Yes
Space Needs: 1,000-1,200 SF; SF, SC	

SUPPORT & TRAINING PROVIDED:	
Financial Assistance Provided:	No
Site Selection Assistance:	Yes
Lease Negotiation Assistance:	Yes
Co-Operative Advertising:	Yes
Franchisee Assoc./Member:	No
Size Of Corporate Staff:	190

On-Going Support:	A,C,D,E,G,H,I
Training: 2 Weeks Oklahoma City, OK HQ; Plus 1 Week Certified Training Office in Field.	

SPECIFIC EXPANSION PLANS:	
US:	All United States
Canada:	All CAN Except PQ
Overseas:	South Africa, Australi

Express Personnel Services delivers staffing support and HR services in over 500 offices in the United States, Canada, South Africa and Australia. Express is a sales-focused, business-to-business franchise with company sales totaling nearly $1.6 billion in 2005. An Express franchise consists of four service lines in one agreement, including temporary/flexible staffing, evaluation/direct hire, professional/contract staffing and business solutions. With a mission to help as many people as possible find good jobs and help as many clients as possible find good people, Express employs 325,000 people annually in light industrial, office services and professional positions.

Operating Units	12/31/2003	12/31/2004	9/15/2005
Franchised	326	338	494
% Change	--	3.7%	46.2%
Company-Owned	1	0	0
% Change	--	-100.0%	0.0%
Total	327	338	494
% Change	--	3.4%	46.2%
Franchised as % of Total	99.69%	100.00%	100.00%

Investment Required
The fee for an Express Personnel Services franchise is $25,000.

Express Personnel Services provides the following range of investments required to open your initial franchise. The range assumes that all items are paid for in cash. To the extent that you choose to finance any of these expense items, your front-end investment could be substantially reduced.

Item	Established Low Range	Established High Range
Franchise Fee	$25,000	$25,000
Lease/Deposits	$2,300	$4,000
Equipment, Fixtures, Signs	$27,300	$35,300
Insurance	$1,000	$3,500
Inventory	$750	$1,000
Leasehold Improvements	$2,000	$12,000
Training Expenses	$6,000	$6,000
Additional Funds	$50,000	$75,000
Total Investment	$114,350	$161,800

On-Going Expenses
The franchisee keeps 60% of the monthly gross margin, and Express Personnel Services takes care of the following on-going expenses: payroll processing, client invoicing and collections, risk-management administration and worker compensation.

What You Get—Training and Support
Prior to the office opening, new Express franchisees attend 10 days of sales, operations and business management instruction at Express Personnel's international headquarters in Oklahoma City, Okla. Five additional days are then spent in a certified regional field office to complete the training. Continual training is available through online classes and certification programs. Annually Express hosts regional Sales and Leadership Education Summits and the International Leadership Conference providing franchisees access to motivational speakers, educational forums and networking opportunities.

Express provides franchisees with:
- Proprietary front and back office software with critical reporting capabilities
- Toll-free franchisee assistance and technical support centers from 7 a.m. to 7 p.m. (CST)

- One dedicated field support specialist per every six franchisees
- Collateral sales materials at no charge
- Advertising and marketing campaigns at volume prices
- Comprehensive operation and management manuals
- Lifelong learning via Express University and regional training
- 100% financing of payroll for temporary associates

Territory
Express Personnel Services grants exclusive territories.

Fantastic Sams

Fantastic Sams

50 Dunham Rd.
Beverly, MA 01915
Tel: (978) 232-5600 +5626
Fax: (978) 232-5601
E-Mail: franchise@fantasticsams.com
Web Site: www.fantasticsams.com
Mr. Rich C. Pittius, SVP Franchise Development

FANTASTIC SAMS is the largest full-service hair care franchise, with over 1,350 salons worldwide. Our full service salons offer quality hair care services for the entire family, including cuts, perms and color. When you join the FANTASTIC SAMS family of franchisees, you'll receive both local and national support through on-going management training, educational programs and national conferences, as well as advertising and other benefits. No hair care experience required.

BACKGROUND: IFA MEMBER
Established: 1974;   1st Franchised: 1976
Franchised Units: 1,377
Company-Owned Units   0
Total Units: 1,377
Dist.:   US-1,344; CAN-18; O'seas-15
North America: 43 States, 4 Provinces
Density: 221 in CA, 102 in FL, 99 MI
Projected New Units (12 Months):   120
Qualifications: 5, 5, 1, 4, 1, 5

Registered: All States

FINANCIAL/TERMS:
Cash Investment: $50K
Total Investment: $138-193K
Minimum Net Worth: $250K
Fees: Franchise — $25-30K
  Royalty — $227/Wk.;   Ad. — $116/Wk.
Earnings Claim Statement: No
Term of Contract (Years):   10/10
Avg. # Of Employees: 8 FT
Passive Ownership: Allowed
Encourage Conversions: Yes
Area Develop. Agreements: Yes/10
Sub-Franchising Contracts: Yes
Expand In Territory: Yes
Space Needs: 1,200 SF; SC

SUPPORT & TRAINING PROVIDED:
Financial Assistance Provided: Yes
Site Selection Assistance: Yes
Lease Negotiation Assistance: Yes
Co-Operative Advertising: Yes
Franchisee Assoc./Member: No
Size Of Corporate Staff: 40
On-Going Support: c,d,E,F,H
Training: 5 Day Salon Fundamentals Class; On-Going within Region.

SPECIFIC EXPANSION PLANS:
US: All United States
Canada: All Canada
Overseas: Pacific Rim, UK, Australia

241

Fantastics Sams greets every guest with "honesty, integrity and respon-siveness," a commitment reflected at every level of the organization. In the booming multibillion-dollar haircare industry, Fantastic Sams provides convenient service as a one-stop shop for women, men and children of all ages. It provides a wide range of quality treatments—from cuts to color-ing—at an affordable price, and never requires appointments.

In addition, Fantastic Sams provides its own high-quality shampoo, con-ditioner and treatment products, such as Fantastic hair care and Fantastic Color.

Fantastic Sams caters to more than 550,000 guests a week in more than 1,350 salons worldwide. With over 30 years of business experience, it is one of the most recognized names in the haircare industry today.

Operating Units	6/30/2003	6/30/2004	6/30/2005
Franchised	1,285	1,311	1,338
% Change	--	2.0%	2.1%
Company-Owned	0	0	0
% Change	--	0.0%	0.0%
Total	1,285	1,311	1,338
% Change	--	2.0%	2.1%
Franchised as % of Total	100.00%	100.00%	100.00%

Investment Required
The fee for a Fantastic Sams franchise is $25,000.

Fantastic Sams provides the following range of investments required to open your initial franchise. The range assumes that all items are paid for in cash. To the extent that you choose to finance any of these expense items, your front-end investment could be substantially reduced.

Item	Established Low Range	Established High Range
Franchise Fee	$25,000	$30,000
Advertising	$10,000	$15,000
Leasehold Improvements	$0	$35,000
Equipment, Fixtures, Signs	$70,000	$55,000
Insurance	$1,000	$3,000
Inventory	$8,000	$10,000
Misc. Deposits	$6,500	$9,500
Salon Supplies	$2,500	$3,500
Training Expenses	$0	$2,500
Additional Funds (for 3 months)	$15,000	$30,000
Total Investment	$138,000	$193,500

On-Going Expenses

Fantastic Sams franchisees pay on-going license fees of $327.43 per week and a national advertising fund fee of $115.65 per week. Additional expenses include regional advertising fund fees and tanning service-related fees when applicable.

What You Get—Training and Support

Fantastic Sams new owner training program, Salon Fundamentals, is a one-week course that instructs new franchisees in: guest relations, employee management, marketing, technical knowledge, retailing and business management. Other programs support salons with their grand opening and marketing, research and development and computer management. Additional programs, including Salon Management 101 and 201, will coach managers in improving everyday tasks such as scheduling appointments and managing staff meetings. A key to the company's success is Fantastic Sams University, which is devoted to recruiting and training stylists and keeping them up-to-date in the most fashionable hair-styling techniques.

A staff of over 50 professional instructors offer on-going support in operations, products and promotions. National conferences play a key role in motivating franchisees, allowing them to network and gain more training. The Fantastic Sams name is given fresh exposure annually through coordinated efforts in national and regional advertising campaigns.

Territory
Fantastic Sams grants exclusive territories.

FasTracKids International, LTD.

"Enrichment Education for Tomorrow's Leaders"

6900 E. Belleview Ave., 1st Fl.
Greenwood Village, CO 80111-1619
Tel: (888) 576-6888 (303) 224-0200
Fax: (303) 224-0222
E-Mail: info@fastrackids.com
Web Site: www.fastrackids.com
Mr. Jim Gunlock, International Marketing Manager

FASTRACKIDS® INTERNATIONAL, recognized last year as one of the Top 10 New Franchises by Entrepreneur Magazine, has appointed over 220 licensees in 32 countries. Thousands of children have benefited from the technologically advanced FASTRACKIDS curriculum. Developed for children ages 3-6, FASTRACKIDS is designed to increase thinking and reasoning abilities while enhancing communication skills and self-esteem.

BACKGROUND:	IFA MEMBER
Established: 1998;	1st Franchised: 1998
Franchised Units:	200
Company-Owned Units	0
Total Units:	200

Dist.:	US-91; CAN-3; O'seas-106
North America:	23 States
Density:	CA, GA, NY
Projected New Units (12 Months):	55
Qualifications: 4, 4, 4, 4, 5, 5	
Registered: All States	

FINANCIAL/TERMS:	
Cash Investment:	$35.5K
Total Investment:	$78.9-188.9K
Minimum Net Worth:	$NR
Fees: Franchise —	$22K
Royalty — Varies;	Ad. — 0%
Earnings Claim Statement:	No
Term of Contract (Years):	5/20
Avg. # Of Employees:	1-5 FT
Passive Ownership:	Discouraged
Encourage Conversions:	NA
Area Develop. Agreements:	Yes/5
Sub-Franchising Contracts:	No
Expand In Territory:	Yes
Space Needs: 700 SF; NA	

SUPPORT & TRAINING PROVIDED:	
Financial Assistance Provided:	No
Site Selection Assistance:	Yes
Lease Negotiation Assistance:	Yes
Co-Operative Advertising:	Yes
Franchisee Assoc./Member:	No
Size Of Corporate Staff:	12
On-Going Support:	C,G,h,I
Training: 5 Days in Denver, CO.	

SPECIFIC EXPANSION PLANS:	Canada:	All Canada
US: All United States	Overseas:	All Countries

FasTracKids is an innovative education program designed to enrich the minds of preschool-age children still in the critical early years of development. Goals include: provide children with accelerated and enriched education; teach children how to apply and transfer knowledge; encourage creativity and brain development; develop speaking and communication skills; and stimulate leadership and personality development. Children complete the course by attending two-hour sessions four times a month for two years.

FasTracKids instructors use technologically advanced educational tools, such as the FasTrack Learning Station, which involves the use of CD-ROM-based lessons, LCD projection and an interactive white board. Hands-on activities, such as student-produced newscasts, draw children into the material and improve communication skills. Parents are encouraged to utilize the FasTracKids website to see what their children are learning and to learn how to supplement their children's education at home.

With more than 180 licensees in 24 countries, FasTracKids is one of the fastest-growing children's education franchises.

Operating Units	12/31/2002	12/31/2003	12/31/2004
Franchised	14	26	52
% Change	--	85.7%	100.0%
Company-Owned	0	0	0
% Change	--	0.0%	0.0%
Total	14	26	52
% Change	--	85.7%	100.0%
Franchised as % of Total	100.00%	100.00%	100.00%

Investment Required

The fee for a FasTracKids franchise is $21,500.

FasTracKids provides the following range of investments required to open your initial franchise. The range assumes that all items are paid for in cash. To the extent that you choose to finance any of these expense items, your front-end investment could be substantially reduced.

Item	Established Low Range	Established High Range
Franchise Fee	$22,000	$22,000
Build Out Expenses	$750	$75,000
Educational Package Access Fee	$7,500	$7,500
Furniture, Equipment, Supplies, Signs	$1,850	$19,600
Initial Training Expenses	$1,000	$2,550
Insurance	$0	$2,000
Legal and Accounting	$500	$5,400
Marketing/Promotion	$1,200	$11,000
Real Estate	$6,000	$6,000
Additional Funds (for 3 months)	$1,500	$30,000
Total Investment	$42,300	$181,050

On-Going Expenses

FasTracKids franchisees pay a royalty fee equal to 1.5% of gross revenue and a maintenance/usage fee equal to 11% of gross revenue. An advertising fee may be collected in the future that is up to 5% of the greater of gross revenue or a minimum enrollment fee for each student.

What You Get—Training and Support

FasTracKids licensees receive instructional materials that assist in the operation of a FasTracKids business; training on how to enroll students; FasTracKids classroom resources, such as the CD-ROM curriculum; and a procedures manual on managing and marketing the franchise.

On-going support includes a FasTracKids newsletter and an exclusive website for licensees. Regional seminars and an international conference are also planned to provide licensees with sales and marketing, tips on facilitating classes and the opportunity to improve business and instruction skills.

Territory
FasTracKids territories are based on the population of a specific geo-graphic area.

FASTSIGNS

FASTSIGNS®

2550 Midway Rd., # 150
Carrollton, TX 75006-2357
Tel: (800) 827-7446 + 283 (214) 346-5616
Fax: (972) 248-8201
E-Mail: bill.mcpherson@fastsigns.com
Web Site: www.franchise.fastsigns.com
Mr. Bill N. McPherson, VP Franchise Development

FASTSIGNS, the sign and graphic solutions pro-vider for businesses worldwide, continues to receive accolades as the premier business-to-business fran-chise concept. FASTSIGNS was recently named #1 in Business Services in Franchise Business Review's Top 50 and repeatedly in Entrepreneur Magazine for 15 years. Average per store gross sales has increased 13 of the last 14 years to $534,889 in 2004. Average per store gross sales has increased 13 of the last 14 years to $585,000 in 2005.

BACKGROUND: IFA MEMBER
Established: 1985;   1st Franchised: 1986
Franchised Units: 503
Company-Owned Units   0
Total Units: 503
Dist.:   US-421; CAN-13; O'seas-69
  North America: 45 States, 4 Provinces
  Density: 52 in TX, 36 in CA, 26 in FL

Projected New Units (12 Months):	30
Qualifications: 5, 4, 1, 2, 3, 5	
Registered: All States and AB	
FINANCIAL/TERMS:	
Cash Investment:	$75K
Total Investment:	$172 - 247K
Minimum Net Worth:	$240K
Fees: Franchise —	$25K
Royalty — 6%;	Ad. — 2%
Earnings Claim Statement:	Yes
Term of Contract (Years):	20/10
Avg. # Of Employees:	3 FT
Passive Ownership:	Not Allowed
Encourage Conversions:	Yes
Area Develop. Agreements:	Yes
Sub-Franchising Contracts:	Int
Expand In Territory:	Yes
Space Needs: 1,700 SF; SC	
SUPPORT & TRAINING PROVIDED:	
Financial Assistance Provided:	Yes(I)
Site Selection Assistance:	Yes
Lease Negotiation Assistance:	Yes
Co-Operative Advertising:	Yes
Franchisee Assoc./Member:	Yes
Size Of Corporate Staff:	94
On-Going Support:	C,D,E,G,H,I
Training: 2 Weeks in Dallas, TX; 2 Weeks On-Site.	

247

SPECIFIC EXPANSION PLANS:		Canada:	All Canada
US:	All United States	Overseas:	UK, New Zealand, Australia

FASTSIGNS, the sign and graphic solutions provider for businesses worldwide, continues to receive accolades as the premier business-to-business franchise concept. FASTSIGNS was recently named the #1 in Business Services in Franchise Business Review's Top 50 and has been featured in Entrepreneur Magazine's Annual 500 for 15 years. Average per store gross sales has increased 13 of the last 14 years to $585,000 in 2005. We're proud of our franchise owners and their remarkable success stories. Come join the team!

Operating Units	12/31/2003	12/31/2004	12/31/2005
Franchised	386	396	503
% Change	1.8%	2.6%	21.27%
Company-Owned	0	0	0
% Change	0.0%	0.0%	0.0%
Total	386	396	503
% Change	1.8%	2.6%	21.27%
Franchised as % of Total	100.00%	100.00%	100.00%

Investment Required
The fee for a FASTSIGNS franchise is $25,000.

FASTSIGNS provides the following range of investments required to open your initial franchise. The range assumes that all items are paid for in cash. To the extent that you choose to finance any of these expense items, your front-end investment could be substantially reduced.

Item	Established Low Range	Established High Range
Franchise Fee	$25,000	$25,000

Leasehold Improvements, Store Graphics, Architectural/Engineering	$35,875	$57,009
Furniture/Fixtures/ Signage	$14,641	$25,245
Lease/Utility Deposits	$3,500	$6,500
Initial Inventory	$5,244	$5,294
Advertising	$10,062	$19,628
Training Costs	$9,240	$17,365
Business Licenses/Permits & Insurance	$1,146	$2,000
Professional Fees	$2,400	$7,500
Other Costs and Additional Funds (for 3 months)	$102,586	$136,715
Total Investment	$209,694	$302,256

On-Going Expenses

FASTSIGNS franchisees pay a service fee equal to 6% of gross sales and a NAC fee equal to 2% of gross sales. Other fees include an undetermined advertising cooperative fee (equal to a maximum of 2% of gross sales) and the cost of various advertising and promotional materials.

What You Get—Training and Support

Franchisees go through a detailed three-week New Owner Training program, accompanied by online training, videos, manuals and field training. Marketing materials are customized for each store, while marketing experts help franchisees develop a focused marketing strategy. Franchisees also benefit from an exclusive online intranet that allows them to communicate with other franchisees and offers them further training and marketing resources; they can also develop their own unique online web catalog for their customers. State-of-the-art graphic design systems can be used to provide a variety of sign and graphics. Signs can be customized for any customer's need and are suitable for windows, walls, vehicles, trade show displays and indoor or outdoor displays.

FASTSIGNS offers site-selection assistance, grand opening support and a Franchise Services Team ready to help with every aspect of a franchisee's store. FASTSIGNS will also teach franchisees how to form business plans and cash flow/operating budget and advertising strategies, as well as how to analyze, understand and improve financial performance.

Territory
FASTSIGNS grants exclusive territories.

Fish Window Cleaning Services

200 Enchanted Pkwy.
Manchester, MO 63021
Tel: (877) 707-3474 (636) 530-7334
Fax: (636) 530-7856
E-Mail: fransales@fishwindowcleaning.com
Web Site: www.fishwindowcleaning.com
Mr. John English, VP Franchise Development

There is no glass ceiling when it comes to the potential you will have to grow your own unique service business in a large protected territory, specializing in year-round commercial and residential low-rise window cleaning. You can have the satisfaction of owning a business that requires no night or weekend work, backed by a franchisor with 27 years of experience.

BACKGROUND:	IFA MEMBER
Established: 1978;	1st Franchised: 1998
Franchised Units:	185
Company-Owned Units	1
Total Units:	186
Dist.:	US-186; CAN-0; O'seas-0

North America:	35 States
Density:	NR
Projected New Units (12 Months):	40
Qualifications: 4, 4, 1, 2, 3, 5	
Registered: All States	

FINANCIAL/TERMS:	
Cash Investment:	$66.4-127.6K
Total Investment:	$66.4-127.6K
Minimum Net Worth:	$100-200K
Fees: Franchise —	$24.9-49.9K
Royalty — 8-6%;	Ad. — 1%
Earnings Claim Statement:	Yes
Term of Contract (Years):	10
Avg. # Of Employees:	3-12 FT
Passive Ownership:	Discouraged
Encourage Conversions:	Yes
Area Develop. Agreements:	No
Sub-Franchising Contracts:	No
Expand In Territory:	Yes
Space Needs: NA SF; NA	

SUPPORT & TRAINING PROVIDED:	
Financial Assistance Provided:	Yes(I)
Site Selection Assistance:	Yes
Lease Negotiation Assistance:	Yes
Co-Operative Advertising:	Yes
Franchisee Assoc./Member:	Yes
Size Of Corporate Staff:	22
On-Going Support:	A,B,C,D,E,G,H,I

Training: 12 Days.	US:	All United States
	Canada:	Soon
SPECIFIC EXPANSION PLANS:	Overseas:	No

Fish Window Cleaning is a window-cleaning business that caters to homeowners and small businesses (with buildings three stories and under). As an experienced and proven franchisor with over 27 years of experience, Fish Window Cleaning intends to dominate the market and be "clearly seen" as the best and most respected window-cleaning company in the world.

Franchisees benefit from never-ending demand – every window needs cleaning – low start-up costs, high profit margin from repeat customers and a broad market of both commercial and residential buildings. The simple part of the business is cleaning glass, but Fish Window Cleaning also trains franchisees in operation organization. The turnkey nature of the business means franchisees can step right into running their businesses and are given ample support as they grow.

Operating Units	12/31/2002	12/31/2003	12/31/2004
Franchised	43	107	166
% Change	--	148.8%	55.1%
Company-Owned	1	1	1
% Change	--	0.0%	0.0%
Total	44	108	167
% Change	--	145.5%	54.6%
Franchised as % of Total	97.73%	99.07%	99.40%

Investment Required

The fee for a Fish Window Cleaning franchise varies by territory size. The fee for a small territory is $24,900; the fee for a standard territory is $29,900; and the fee for an executive territory is $49,900.

Fish Window Cleaning provides the following range of investments required to open your initial franchise. The range assumes that all items are paid for in cash. To the extent that you choose to finance any of these expense items, your front-end investment could be substantially reduced. The total investment depends on the size of the franchisee's territory; the following figures refer to a standard territory.

Item	Established Low Range	Established High Range
Franchise Fee	$29,900	$29,900
Attorney's Fees	$500	$2,000
Business Development/ Marketing	$9,000	$11,000
Equipment	$4,500	$5,000
Insurance/Business Licenses/Membership dues	$1,200	$1,800
Office Package	$20,200	$22,200
Office Space (3 months)	$1,200	$1,800
Training Expenses	$2,000	$4,000
Additional Funds (for 3 months)	$13,000	$17,000
Total Investment	$80,900	$94,100

On-Going Expenses

Fish Window Cleaning franchisees pay a royalty fee equal to 6-8% of total gross sales and an advertising fee equal to 1% of total gross sales. Other ongoing fees include a weekly technical support fee of $50 and monthly marketing fees that range from $1,600 to $3,800 depending on market size.

What You Get—Training and Support

Franchisees receive 2 weeks of training at corporate headquarters in St. Louis, Missouri, as well as comprehensive training documentation and an operations manual. A Window Cleaning Training Camp is provided for employees and managers. Franchisees receive access to an exclusive web-site, proprietary software to manage their business and their own personal webpage and e-mail. Franchisees also have access to a toll-free support number, annual and regional meetings and a newsletter. Once a franchisee begins operating his or her business, he or she will receive additional training in the form of a 2-day field visit and get help building a customer base. A Fish Window Cleaning representative accompanies the franchisee in selling, securing and setting up commercial accounts.

Territory
Fish Window Cleaning grants exclusive territories.

Furniture Medic

 FURNITURE MEDIC®

North America:	47 States,10 Provinces
Density:	38 in FL, 27 in CA, 22 in VA
Projected New Units (12 Months):	50

Qualifications: 4, 4, 2, 3, 3, 5
Registered: All States

3839 Forest Hill-Irene Rd.
Memphis, TN 38125-2502
Tel: (800) 255-9687 (901) 597-8600
Fax: (901) 597-8660
E-Mail: dmessenger@smclean.com
Web Site: www.furnituremedicfranchise.com
Mr. David Messenger, VP Market Expansion

FURNITURE MEDIC is a division of The Service-Master Company. It is the largest furniture and wood repair and restoration company in the world with over 600 franchises. Furniture Medic has unique products and processes which enable much of the work to be done on-site, reducing costs and saving time for its residential and commercial customers. Financing is provided for the initial franchise fees, start-up equipment and vehicles to qualified candidates through ServiceMaster Acceptance Company.

FINANCIAL/TERMS:

Cash Investment:	$15-25K
Total Investment:	$37-81.9K
Minimum Net Worth:	$50K
Fees: Franchise —	$24.5K
Royalty — 7%/$250 Min.;	Ad. — 1%/$50 Min.
Earnings Claim Statement:	No
Term of Contract (Years):	5/5
Avg. # Of Employees:	1 FT, 1 PT
Passive Ownership:	Not Allowed
Encourage Conversions:	NA
Area Develop. Agreements:	No
Sub-Franchising Contracts:	No
Expand In Territory:	Yes

Space Needs: NR SF; NA

BACKGROUND: IFA MEMBER

Established: 1992;	1st Franchised: 1992
Franchised Units:	595
Company-Owned Units:	0
Total Units:	595
Dist.:	US-420; CAN-71; O'seas-104

SUPPORT & TRAINING PROVIDED:

Financial Assistance Provided:	Yes(D)
Site Selection Assistance:	NA
Lease Negotiation Assistance:	No
Co-Operative Advertising:	No
Franchisee Assoc./Member:	Yes/Yes
Size Of Corporate Staff:	21
On-Going Support:	A,B,G,h,I

Training: 3 Weeks Memphis, TN. **SPECIFIC EXPANSION PLANS:**	US: Canada: Overseas:	Most metropolitan markets in US. All Canada All Countries

Furniture Medic provides the "prescription for damaged furniture." As the largest wood repair and restoration company in the world, Furniture Medic serves a variety of markets, from residential homes and business offices to the hospitality industry and furniture retailers. Furniture Medic is a flexible service that can provide direct assistance immediately and on-site.

Furniture Medic is part of the ServiceMaster family. Among the many benefits of this relationship is the ServiceMaster Acceptance Company, which provides financial assistance. Franchisees also gain lucrative opportunities through working with other ServiceMaster Clean Disaster Restoration franchisees. As part of the ServiceMaster network, Furniture Medic helped serve more than 12.5 million customers in 2004.

Operating Units	12/31/2002	12/31/2003	12/31/2004
Franchised	460	425	391
% Change	--	-7.6%	-8.0%
Company-Owned	0	0	0
% Change	--	0.0%	0.0%
Total	460	425	391
% Change	--	-7.6%	-8.0%
Franchised as % of Total	100.00%	100.00%	100.00%

Investment Required
The fee for an initial Furniture Medic franchise is $24,500.

Furniture Medic provides the following range of investments required to open your initial franchise. The range assumes that all items are paid for in cash. To the extent that you choose to finance any of these expense items, your front-end investment could be substantially reduced.

Item	Established Low Range	Established High Range
Franchise Fee	$4,900	$24,500
Marketing	$600	$3,000
Vehicle	$2,260	$25,644
Equipment, Fixtures, Signs	$445	$1,850
Insurance	$2,500	$4,500
Advertising Fund/ Royalty Fee (3 months)	$900	$900
Opening Package	$2,500	$12,500
Training Expenses	$1,000	$3,000
Additional Funds (for 3 months)	$2,000	$6,000
Total Investment	$17,105	$81,894

On-Going Expenses
The franchisee pays an ongoing royalty fee equal to the greater of $250 per month or 7% gross sales and a national advertising fund fee equal to the greater of $50 per month or 1% of gross sales.

What You Get—Training and Support
Furniture Medic provides an exhaustive three-week course to prepare franchisees for business ownership, opening their store and the National Service Academy. Two weeks of training follow at the National Service Academy. Three to four months after graduation, franchisees receive an additional week of training to further assess and hone technical skills, business plans, marketing and record keeping.

The franchisee fee covers the costs of all necessary tools, supplies, equipment, products and cases required for a Furniture Medic franchise, as well as helpful tools such as a notebook computer with proprietary software and management programs.

Territory
Furniture Medic does not grant exclusive territories.

Geeks on Call

814 Kempsville Rd., # 106
Norfolk, VA 23502
Tel: (888) 667-4577 + 320 (757) 466-3448
Fax: (866) 516-3513
E-Mail: info@geeksoncall.com
Web Site: www.geeksoncallfranchise.com
Ms. Deneen Wiley, Exec. Asst. of Franchise Devel.

On-site computer support includes troubleshooting, virus/spyware removal, repairs, upgrades, wired/wireless networking, one-on-one training and custom-built PCs. Franchisee needs only business experience, however, only certified technicians may perform computer services. Mobile business concept. Low overhead, coupled with central dispatching, advertising, marketing campaigns and proven support make GEEKS ON CALL the logical choice. Single and multi-units available. Highly ranked in Entrepreneur Magazine

BACKGROUND:	IFA MEMBER
Established: 1999;	1st Franchised: 2001
Franchised Units:	345
Company-Owned Units	0
Total Units:	345
Dist.:	US-345; CAN-0; O'seas-0
North America:	NR
Density:	69 in VA/DC, 33 in TX, 26 CA

Projected New Units (12 Months): 175
Qualifications: 4, 4, 1, 4, 4, 5
Registered: All Except AB

FINANCIAL/TERMS:

Cash Investment:	$20K Min.
Total Investment:	$55.9-87.2K
Minimum Net Worth:	$50K
Fees: Franchise —	$25K
Royalty — 11%;	Ad. — $275/Wk.
Earnings Claim Statement:	Yes
Term of Contract (Years):	10/10
Avg. # Of Employees:	1 FT
Passive Ownership:	Not Allowed
Encourage Conversions:	NA
Area Develop. Agreements:	Yes/10
Sub-Franchising Contracts:	No
Expand In Territory:	No
Space Needs: NA SF; HB	

SUPPORT & TRAINING PROVIDED:

Financial Assistance Provided:	Yes(I)
Site Selection Assistance:	NA
Lease Negotiation Assistance:	NA
Co-Operative Advertising:	NA
Franchisee Assoc./Member:	No
Size Of Corporate Staff:	78
On-Going Support:	C,D,G,H,I

Training: 4 Days Norfolk, VA; 1-3 Days in Franchise Territory.

SPECIFIC EXPANSION PLANS:

US:	All United States
Canada:	No
Overseas:	No

Geeks on Call provides on-site computer solutions for small businesses that cannot afford to keep technicians on-staff and ordinary households whose computers have crashed. Warranties and manufacturer support do not always provide the help a client may need. Often, problems have more to do with usability issues rather than a need to replace hardware, so

Geeks on Call steps in with a solution that traditional manufacturer support does not offer.

Among the services provided are computer repair, custom-built computers, network solutions and upgrades, as well as one-on-one training for people who don't know where to begin when using computer equipment. Powered by a demand for tech support in a market where hardware lasts longer but problems like viruses and corrupted files have multiplied, Geeks on Call has thrived in the fastest growing sector of the computer industry.

Operating Units	8/31/2003	8/31/2004	8/31/2005
Franchised	82	158	281
% Change	--	92.7%	77.8%
Company-Owned	0	0	0
% Change	--	0.0%	0.0%
Total	82	158	281
% Change	--	92.7%	77.8%
Franchised as % of Total	100.00%	100.00%	100.00%

Investment Required
The fee for an initial Geeks on Call franchise is $25,000.

Geeks on Call provides the following range of investments required to open your initial franchise. The range assumes that all items are paid for in cash. To the extent that you choose to finance any of these expense items, your front-end investment could be substantially reduced.

Item	Established Low Range	Established High Range
Franchise Fee	$25,000	$25,000
Advertising	$15,000	$15,000
Vehicle	$1,250	$18,750

Equipment, Supplies & Inventory	$3,000	$5,000
Insurance, Deposits, Permits	$1,500	$2,000
Real Property/Office Furnishings	$0	$4,900
Training Expenses	$100	$1,500
Additional Funds (for 3 months)	$10,000	$15,000
Total Investment	$55,850	$87,150

On-Going Expenses
The franchisee pays an ongoing royalty fee equal to 11% of all gross receipts and an advertising fee of $275 a week.

What You Get—Training and Support
Franchisees are given secure territories, with possibilities of additional work in other territories when another franchisee is unable to serve a particular customer. Franchisees determine their level of income by deciding how many jobs to accept, and the Geeks on Call support system takes care of advertising, business start-up training and answering service requests through their call center.

Franchisees themselves do not need to be computer experts, but all field technicians are certified with networking experience and must pass an oral exam.

Territory
Geeks on Call does not grant exclusive territories.

Glass Doctor

We fix your panes!

1020 N. University Parks Dr.
Waco, TX 76707
Tel: (800) 280-9858 (254) 759-5850
Fax: (800) 209-7621
E-Mail: glassdoctorfranchise@dwyergroup.com
Web Site: www.glassdoctor.com
Ms. Pat Humburg, Lead Development Manager

For over 40 years, GLASS DOCTOR has been helping entrepreneurs and existing glass professionals build strong and successful glass businesses. GLASS DOCTOR guarantees quick response to glass replacement needs of insurance companies, apartment communities, auto dealers, etc. We are the nation's largest glass replacement providers. We provide a set of proven, result-producing methods for running and promoting business. Professionally prepared advertising, marketing/promotional programs and materials, etc.

BACKGROUND: IFA MEMBER
Established: 1962;   1st Franchised: 1974
Franchised Units: 143
Company-Owned Units   0
Total Units: 143
Dist.:   US-142; CAN-1; O'seas-0
  North America: 44 States, 1 Province
  Density: 16 in CA, 12 in FL, 9 in OH

Projected New Units (12 Months):   55
Qualifications: 4, 4, 2, 2, 3, 5
Registered: All States

FINANCIAL/TERMS:
Cash Investment: $50-100K
Total Investment: $107.6-259.6K
Minimum Net Worth: $Varies
Fees: Franchise — $22K
  Royalty — 4-7%;   Ad. — 2%
Earnings Claim Statement: Yes
Term of Contract (Years):   10/10
Avg. # Of Employees: 4 FT
Passive Ownership: Discouraged
Encourage Conversions: Yes
Area Develop. Agreements: No
Sub-Franchising Contracts: No
Expand In Territory: Yes
Space Needs: 1,500 SF; FS, SF

SUPPORT & TRAINING PROVIDED:
Financial Assistance Provided: Yes
Site Selection Assistance: No
Lease Negotiation Assistance: No
Co-Operative Advertising: No
Franchisee Assoc./Member: Yes/No
Size Of Corporate Staff: 18
On-Going Support: A,B,C,D,E,F,G,H,I
Training: 5 Days in Waco, TX (offered Every Month except October).

SPECIFIC EXPANSION PLANS:
US: All United States
Canada: All Canada
Overseas: No

Since 1962, Glass Doctor has been replacing glass worldwide. The majority of its business is replacing automobile windshields and tempered glass, while the rest is divided between replacing residential glass and mirrors and commercial plate glass. Glass Doctor is a business on wheels, with a complete inventory and all necessary supplies transported in customized Glass Doctor service vehicles.

Glass Doctor has no comparable national competition, and thus enjoys an untapped market with almost unlimited potential. Glass Doctor franchisees provide customers with optimal results and the best value for their dollar, and reap the rewards with repeat business and referrals.

Glass Doctor is part of the Dwyer Group, an established organization that provides a "world of specialty services" via franchising.

Operating Units	12/31/2002	12/31/2003	12/31/2004
Franchised	99	111	132
% Change	--	12.1%	18.9%
Company-Owned	0	0	0
% Change	--	0.0%	0.0%
Total	99	111	132
% Change	--	12.1%	18.9%
Franchised as % of Total	100.00%	100.00%	100.00%

Investment Required
The fee for a Glass Doctor franchise is $22,000.

Glass Doctor provides the following range of investments required to open your initial franchise. The range assumes that all items are paid for in cash. To the extent that you choose to finance any of these expense items, your front-end investment could be substantially reduced.

Item	Established Low Range	Established High Range
Franchise Fee	$22,000	$22,000
Advertising & Promotional	$2,000	$4,000
Desposits, Permits & Licenses	$2,000	$5,000

Equipment, Supplies, Inventory	$38,681	$95,681
Insurance	$2,000	$6,000
Real Estate	$4,500	$15,000
Training Expenses	$1,000	$4,000
Vehicle	$2,500	$60,000
Additional Funds (for 3 months)	$35,000	$50,000
Total Investment	$109,681	$261,681

On-Going Expenses

Glass Doctor franchisees pay a franchise service fee equal to 4-7% of gross sales (minimum of $100-$1400, depending on territory size), and a national advertising fee equal to 2% of gross sales. Other ongoing fees include costs of Z-ware proprietary software, training and maintenance fees; annual convention registration fees; and training fees for extra employees (Three people are given training free of charge).

What You Get—Training and Support

Franchisees have access to a range of resources and training, including the following: professional marketing and sales support materials; methods to attract and retain the best employees; extensive training and support by the home staff; sales and marketing training to increase market share; opportunities to interact and exchange ideas with other franchisees; corporate management expertise that generates new ideas and insights within the industry; and financial management tools and guidance to achieve profit goals. Glass Doctor franchisees also benefit from national advertising that increases brand awareness, purchasing power available through Glass Doctor's pre-negotiated pricing, alliances with national organizations that generate additional revenue and supplier responsiveness from national purchasing programs.

Territory

Glass Doctor grants exclusive territories.

Great Clips

Great Clips for hair.

7700 France Ave. S., # 425
Minneapolis, MN 55433
Tel: (800) 999-5959 (952) 893-9088
Fax: (952) 844-3443
E-Mail: franchise@greatclips.com
Web Site: www.greatclipsfranchise.com
Mr. Steve Gemlo, Director of Development

High-volume haircutting salon, specializing in hair-cuts for the entire family. Unique, attractive decor, with quality, comprehensive advertising programs. Strong, local support to franchisees, excellent training programs. Tremendous growth opportunities.

BACKGROUND: IFA MEMBER
Established: 1982; 1st Franchised: 1983
Franchised Units: 2,500
Company-Owned Units 0
Total Units: 2,500
Dist.: US-2,400; CAN-100; O'seas-0
North America: 43 States, 2 Provinces
Density: 190 in CA, 176 in OH, 164 IL
Projected New Units (12 Months): 200
Qualifications: 5, 4, 1, 3, 3, 5
Registered: CA,FL,IL,IN,MD,MI,MN,NY,ND,OR,SD,VA,WA,WI,DC,AB

FINANCIAL/TERMS:
Cash Investment: $150-250K
Total Investment: $98.8-184.4K
Minimum Net Worth: $250K
Fees: Franchise — $25K
Royalty — 6%; Ad. — 5%
Earnings Claim Statement: Yes
Term of Contract (Years): 10/5/5
Avg. # Of Employees: 3 FT, 5 PT
Passive Ownership: Allowed
Encourage Conversions: No
Area Develop. Agreements: Yes
Sub-Franchising Contracts: No
Expand In Territory: Yes
Space Needs: 1,000-1,200 SF; SF, SC

SUPPORT & TRAINING PROVIDED:
Financial Assistance Provided: Yes(I)
Site Selection Assistance: Yes
Lease Negotiation Assistance: Yes
Co-Operative Advertising: Yes
Franchisee Assoc./Member: Yes/Yes
Size Of Corporate Staff: 200
On-Going Support: A,B,C,D,E,f,G,H,I
Training: 5 Days Minneapolis, MN; 2.5 Weeks Local Market.

SPECIFIC EXPANSION PLANS:
US: All United States
Canada: Western Canada
Overseas: No

Great Clips provides value-priced haircuts and perms for the entire family, without appointments – providing a necessary service to consumers who want quality, value, service and convenience from a trusted brand name. Great Clips has over 2,500 salons in 120 markets throughout North America, and with an extensive support system, is positioned for further growth. The higher density of stores operating in a particular market means greater brand awareness, convenience for the customer and increased revenue per salon.

Great Clips satisfies a built-in demand that is stable and immune to recessions. Serious franchisees are allowed to purchase multiple units to increase their market penetration. Great Clips is efficiently run as a cash business with no receivables and little inventory. Salons can be operated by managers and franchisees can maintain their corporate positions while opening multiple units.

Operating Units	12/31/2001	12/31/2002	12/31/2003
Franchised	1,604	1,819	2,052
% Change	--	13.4%	12.8%
Company-Owned	0	0	0
% Change	--	0.0%	0.0%
Total	1,604	1,819	2,052
% Change	--	13.4%	12.8%
Franchised as % of Total	100.00%	100.00%	100.00%

Investment Required
The fee for a Great Clips franchise is between $98,750 and $184,350.

Great Clips provides the following range of investments required to open your initial franchise. The range assumes that all items are paid for in cash. To the extent that you choose to finance any of these expense items, your front-end investment could be substantially reduced.

Item	Established Low Range	Established High Range
Franchise Fee	$20,000	$20,000
Advertising	$15,000	$15,000
Training Expenses	$1,500	$2,500
Leasehold Improvements/ Fees	$15,150	$44,650
Rent/Security Deposits	$1,000	$8,000
Fixtures, Signage and Furnishings, Computer	$25,000	$36,500

Freight	$1,200	$2,200
Opening Inventory and Supplies	$4,700	$6,400
Insurance	$1,000	$1,800
Additional Funds (for 6-12 months)	$12,000	$45,000
Total Investment	$96,550	$182,050

On-Going Expenses

Great Clips franchisees pay a continuing franchise fee equal to 6% of gross sales and a continuing advertising fee equal to 5% of gross sales.

What You Get—Training and Support

Great Clips provides comprehensive training to the franchisee, salon manager and stylists. Franchisees begin with New Franchisee Orientation and Training, and then receive marketing training and ongoing support at area training centers. Professional Stylist Training and employee training are also given at area training centers, reducing costs. Great Clips focuses on recruitment and provides a range of custom recruiting tools to gain quality staff.

In addition to constantly updated operating manuals, forms, brochures, tools and handbooks that assist in everyday operations, Great Clips provides an informative newsletter for franchisees, management staff and stylists. Annual meetings, conventions and leadership conferences take place to provide further educational opportunities and exchange news and ideas.

Great Clips promotes the Great Clips brand in print, radio and television. Great Clips devotes itself to consumers' needs, and assists franchisees in maintaining local public relations, community relations and marketing and advertising efforts.

Territory

Great Clips grants exclusive territories.

Gymboree Play & Music

GYMBOREE PLaYe MUSiC

500 Howard St.
San Francisco, CA 94105
Tel: (800) 520-7529 (415) 278-7000
Fax: (415) 278-7452
E-Mail: cms_gymboree@ifxonline.com
Web Site: www.gymboree.com
Mrs. Eva Crosland, Manager Franchise Development

GYMBOREE PLAY & MUSIC has been providing childhood development programs for young children and their parents for 30 years. GYMBOREE's core belief is that children should develop at their own pace via physical, mental and creative activities in a fun environment-with parents by their side. There are more than 500 GYMBOREE locations in 24 countries. Franchisees have access to a wide selection of branded consumer products for resale, and gain a competitive advantage with children's clothing stores.

BACKGROUND: IFA MEMBER
Established: 1976; 1st Franchised: 1978
Franchised Units: 539
Company-Owned Units 4
Total Units: 543
Dist.: US-299; CAN-20; O'seas-224
  North America: 42 States, 4 Provinces
  Density: 39 in CA, 31 in NY, 24 in NJ
Projected New Units (12 Months): 15

Qualifications: 4, 4, 3, 3, 2, 4
Registered: CA,FL,HI,IL,IN,MD,MI,MN,NY,OR,RI ,SD,VA,WA,WI,DC,AB

FINANCIAL/TERMS:

Cash Investment:	$70K
Total Investment:	$141-287K
Minimum Net Worth:	$250K
Fees: Franchise —	$45K
Royalty — 6%;	Ad. — 2.25%
Earnings Claim Statement:	No
Term of Contract (Years):	10/10
Avg. # Of Employees:	1 FT, 3 PT
Passive Ownership:	Not Allowed
Encourage Conversions:	No
Area Develop. Agreements:	No
Sub-Franchising Contracts:	No
Expand In Territory:	Yes
Space Needs: 2,400 SF; SF, SC, RM	

SUPPORT & TRAINING PROVIDED:

Financial Assistance Provided:	No
Site Selection Assistance:	Yes
Lease Negotiation Assistance:	Yes
Co-Operative Advertising:	Yes
Franchisee Assoc./Member:	Yes
Size Of Corporate Staff:	19
On-Going Support:	B,D,G,h,I
Training: 8 Days Headquarters.	

SPECIFIC EXPANSION PLANS:

US:	All United States
Canada:	All Canada
Overseas:	India, Europe

Gymboree Play & Music has been providing childhood development programs for young children and their parents for 30 years. Gymboree's core belief is that children should develop at their own pace via physical, mental and creative activities in a fun environment—with their parents by their side. Parents and children participate at a level that is appropriate for their age and development. Gymboree now offers innovative programs like Mommy and Baby Yoga, Baby Signs, yoga for toddlers and big kids, music and art from around the world and a drop-off class for older chil-

265

dren. There are more than 500 Gymboree locations in 27 countries.

Gymboree franchisees have access to a wide selection of branded consumer products for resale, and gain a competitive advantage in synergy opportunities with Gymboree children's clothing stores.

Operating Units	1/31/2004	1/29/2005	1/30/2006
Franchised	504	519	541
% Change	--	3.0%	4.2%
Company-Owned	15	7	4
% Change	--	-53.3%	-42.9%
Total	519	526	543
% Change	--	1.3%	3.2%
Franchised as % of Total	97.11%	98.67%	99.6%

Investment Required
The fee for a Gymboree franchise is $45,000. For franchisees who open more than one unit, the fee for additional units is discounted.

Gymboree provides the following range of investments required to open your initial franchise. The range assumes that all items are paid for in cash. To the extent that you choose to finance any of these expense items, your front-end investment could be substantially reduced.

Item	Established Low Range	Established High Range
Franchise Fee	$45,000	$45,000
Real Estate/Construction Fees	$3,000	$92,000
Furniture, Fixtures, Equipment, Signage	$37,100	$58,900
Opening Inventory	$6,800	$11,800
Training Expenses	$250	$4,000

Office Equipment and Supplies	$1,600	$6,715
Other Costs and Additional Funds (for 3 months)	$47,650	$68,350
Total Investment	$141,400	$286,765

On-Going Expenses
Gymboree franchisees pay a royalty fee equal to 6% of gross receipts, a marketing and public relations program fee that may equal up to 5% of gross receipts and a PlayWeb License Fee equal to $95 every month per website.

What You Get—Training and Support
All Gymboree franchisees go through initial, comprehensive training. Franchisees may later build upon that training through optional business instruction, regional training and annual meetings. Franchisees also have access to the latest news in child development theory and updates in business systems, while the corporate staff is on hand for additional assistance with programs, operations, marketing, resale products, teacher training and personnel.

Franchisees also receive professionally designed marketing and advertising materials, and benefit from ongoing research and development.

Territory
Gymboree grants exclusive territories.

Hilton

Hilton

9336 Civic Center Dr.
Beverly Hills, CA 90210
Tel: (800) 286-0645 (310) 278-4321
Fax: (310) 205-7655
E-Mail: bill_fortier@hilton.com
Web Site: www.hiltonfranchise.com

Mr. Bill Fortier, SVP Franchise Development

The modern concept of lodging hospitality was created by Conrad Hilton over 85 years ago. HILTON's hotels celebrate individuality, diversity and localization, creating local market relevance within an environment of luxurious comfort and consistently impeccable service. A smaller HILTON full-service prototype has been designed to deliver upscale services in smaller, growing urban and resort markets and uses a compact design footprint. Development also continues with larger-scale, full-service hotels.

BACKGROUND: IFA MEMBER
Established: 1919; 1st Franchised: 1967
Franchised Units: 169
Company-Owned Units: 67
Total Units: 236
Dist.: US-221; CAN-10; O'seas-5
  North America: 39 States, 4 Provinces
  Density: 37 in CA, 25 in FL, 22 in TX
Projected New Units (12 Months): NR
Qualifications: 5, 5, 5, 3, 1, 3
Registered: All States

FINANCIAL/TERMS:
Cash Investment: $Varies
Total Investment: $33-57MM
Minimum Net Worth: $60K/Rm.

Fees: Franchise — $85K Min.
  Royalty — 5% Gross Rm. Rev; Ad. — 4% GrRm-Rev
Earnings Claim Statement: No
Term of Contract (Years): 22/10-20
Avg. # Of Employees: 150 FT
Passive Ownership: Allowed
Encourage Conversions: Yes
Area Develop. Agreements: No
Sub-Franchising Contracts: No
Expand In Territory: Yes
Space Needs: 135,000 SF; FS

SUPPORT & TRAINING PROVIDED:
Financial Assistance Provided: Yes(I)
Site Selection Assistance: NA
Lease Negotiation Assistance: No
Co-Operative Advertising: Yes
Franchisee Assoc./Member: No
Size Of Corporate Staff: 2,332
On-Going Support: b,C,D,E,G,H,I
Training: 4 Days Dallas, TX; 3 Days Beverly Hills, CA; 3 Days Regional Office.

SPECIFIC EXPANSION PLANS:
US: All United States
Canada: All Canada
Overseas: Mexico, Latin America

Hilton is a name that is synonymous with first-class hospitality. For more than 90 years, the Hilton Family has been offering the business and leisure traveler worldwide the very finest in accommodations, service, amenities and value. At Hilton, we believe travel is more than just A to B. Travel should transform you. It's about enjoying the journey and allowing travel to awaken your mind, spirit and senses. At Hilton, we know that you look at things differently when you travel. It's in these amplified moments of renewal, excitement and inspiration that you discover the one thing that is most different is you. Hilton hotels celebrate individuality, diversity and localization, creating local market relevance within an environment of luxurious comfort and consistently impeccable service. A stay at Hilton offers guests an experience that is warmly welcoming, comforting, empowering and even inspiring, as we strive to help each guest along their own personal journey.

Portfolio

Number of operating properties	236
Number of rooms	92,608
% franchised	73.3%

Investment Required
The fee for a Hilton franchise is a minimum of $85,000 for the first 275 rooms, plus an added fee of $300 per each additional room.

On-Going Expenses
Hilton franchisees pay a monthly royalty fee equal to 5% of gross room revenue and a monthly program fee equal to 4% of gross room revenue. Other ongoing fees include charges related to the Frequent Traveler/Guest Reward program and OnQ™ software and hardware system fees.

For complete information on franchise fees and requirements, please refer to the current Uniform Franchise Offering Circular for Hilton. This can be viewed by visiting www.hiltonfranchise.com.

Powerful Brand Name. Powerful Brand Support.
You are backed with support long before you break ground. We feel that you should be just as comfortable and relaxed owning one of our hotels as you would be staying in one. That's why we provide you with a superior level of service and support — prior to, during and after opening. Advantages like our friendly and dedicated corporate staff, management and franchising expertise and competitive fees make this a hotel company you'll want to stay with for a long time.

- Hilton HHonors® — The Hilton HHonors guest reward program is the only program to let members Double Dip® to earn both hotel points for free nights and airline miles for free flights — for the same stay at more than 2,700 hotels worldwide.
- Cross-selling — With a wide array of brands from which to choose in the Hilton Family of Hotels, a guest should never be left without a room. Your property could benefit from referrals from other Hilton Family hotels in the area.

- Marketing and Sales Support — This includes national sales and marketing efforts, meeting referrals through Hilton Direct®, national and regional advertising, public relations, special marketing programs and access to a range of support materials, such as camera-ready ad slicks, logos, rack brochures and more.
- Quality Assurance — To help you protect your asset, and the value of the brand in which you've invested, specialists evaluate each hotel twice annually with the focus of maintaining brand integrity. Consultation on your capital replacement program is also provided by this team to help your property maintain a positive perception in the eyes of our guests.
- Design and Construction — Includes site review, design consulting, referrals to architects and contractors and monitoring construction progress.
- Hotel Performance Support — A unique consultative field team offers tools and support so your hotel can have the opportunity to leverage the most from Hilton worldwide support programs.
- Communication — Open communication is promoted through advisory council meetings with leaders from representative hotels and annual/regional conferences.
- Commitment to Technology — OnQ™ is the Hilton Family of Hotels' proprietary technology platform that integrates multiple capabilities onto one system to support hotel reservations and sales, guest service, operations and business intelligence-gathering activities. OnQ provides guest information to team members on demand – prompting them to act "on cue" to guest preferences and service recovery alerts – delighting customers and helping create a bond of loyalty to the Hilton Family of Hotels. It is a suite of technology components that "cue" hotel operators to respond decisively to current market conditions and make informed business decisions with historical trends and competitive data at hand. It's all you need, and it's included in one system – OnQ. That's amazing enough, but getting this turnkey solution is also easy to acquire and maintain.

Given both the importance of technology and the rapid pace of technological change, Hilton Hotels Corporation has taken a leading stand in providing technology to hotels that is continually refreshed with the hardware platform necessary to support this leading-edge solution. We believe by providing your hotel with the right technology tools and an easy way to obtain it, we can help your property become more efficient and effective to help you drive more profit to your bottom line. The considerable buying power of the Hilton Family of Hotels keeps technology costs economical while delivering a huge upside benefit. Each brand has a financial assistance program available to help minimize the need for a capital budget to get started and keep hardware refreshed.

Expansion
In addition to conversions, which are an important part of our growth, new Hilton construction continues. A smaller Hilton full-service prototype has been designed to deliver upscale services in smaller, growing urban and resort markets and uses a compact design footprint allowing for lower construction costs and shorter building times. Development also continues with traditional, larger-scale, full-service hotels.

Territory
Hilton does not grant exclusive territories.

House Doctors
Handyman Service

575 Chamber Dr.
Milford, OH 45150

Tel: (800) 319-3359 (513) 831-0100
Fax: (513) 831-6010
E-Mail: info@housedoctors.com
Web Site: www.housedoctors.com
Mr. Steve M. Cohen, President

There's big money in house calls. Millions of dollars are being spent every day on those odd jobs around the house that people don't have the time or skill to do. You don't need a screwdriver or hammer to own

this franchise. Financing and training provided.		Avg. # Of Employees:	3 FT, 2 PT
		Passive Ownership:	Discouraged
BACKGROUND:	IFA MEMBER	Encourage Conversions:	Yes
Established: 1994;	1st Franchised: 1995	Area Develop. Agreements:	Yes/10
Franchised Units:	235	Sub-Franchising Contracts:	No
Company-Owned Units	0	Expand In Territory:	No
Total Units:	235	Space Needs: NA SF; NA	
Dist.:	US-234; CAN-0; O'seas-1		
North America:	42 States	**SUPPORT & TRAINING PROVIDED:**	
Density:	10 in OH, 9 in IN, 9 in IL	Financial Assistance Provided:	Yes(D)
Projected New Units (12 Months):	30	Site Selection Assistance:	NA
Qualifications: 2, 3, 2, 2, 4, 5		Lease Negotiation Assistance:	NA
Registered: CA,FL,IL,IN,MD,MI,MN,NY,ND,OR,R		Co-Operative Advertising:	NA
I,VA,WA,WI		Franchisee Assoc./Member:	No
		Size Of Corporate Staff:	12
FINANCIAL/TERMS:		On-Going Support:	A,B,C,D,E,G,H,I
Cash Investment:	$14-28K	Training: 1 Week Cincinnati, OH.	
Total Investment:	$26-54K		
Minimum Net Worth:	$26K	**SPECIFIC EXPANSION PLANS:**	
Fees: Franchise —	$12-30K	US:	All United States
Royalty — 6%;	Ad. — 3%	Canada:	All Canada
Earnings Claim Statement:	No	Overseas:	All Countries
Term of Contract (Years):	10/10/10		

House Doctors takes care of the odd jobs and repairs that homeowners lack the time or skill to complete themselves. Franchisees are not required to perform repair work; they need only to manage employees and do not need prior construction experience. House Doctors' house calls cover it all – carpentry, painting, tile repair, flooring, wallpapering, window treatment and more – and free homeowners from the need to consult and contract multiple craftsmen to maintain their homes.

House Doctors is a turnkey operation, and franchisees are taught everything they need to know to run their unit successfully. House Doctors is a cash business and clients are expected to pay immediately after a job's completion, so billing and account receivables are not necessary. Franchisees can also operate their businesses from the comfort of their own home, and without inventory or equipment expenditures, only the required investment is relatively low.

Operating Units	12/31/2002	12/31/2003	12/31/2004
Franchised	7	11	10

% Change	--	57.1%	-9.1%
Company-Owned	0	0	0
% Change	--	0.0%	0.0%
Total	7	11	10
% Change	--	57.1%	-9.1%
Franchised as % of Total	100.00%	100.00%	100.00%

Investment Required

The fee for a House Doctors franchise ranges from $15,900 to $29,900, depending on the population of the desired territory.

House Doctors provides the following range of investments required to open your initial franchise. The range assumes that all items are paid for in cash. To the extent that you choose to finance any of these expense items, your front-end investment could be substantially reduced.

Item	Established Low Range	Established High Range
Franchise Fee	$15,900	$35,900
Furniture, Equipment, Computer System	$2,000	$3,500
Initial Rent, Telephone, Bank and Other Deposits	$350	$650
Insurance	$1,000	$3,000
Monthly Office Rental Payment	$200	$500
Pre-Opening Promotion	$1,000	$3,000
Training Expenses	$1,000	$2,000
Additional Funds (for 3 months)	$10,000	$12,000
Total Investment	$31,450	$60,550

On-Going Expenses

House Doctors franchisees pay a royalty fee equal to 6% of gross revenue and an advertising fee equal to 3% of gross revenue. Other ongoing fees include a local advertising fee of $1,500 per month for the first 2 years (at which time it changes to 4% of gross revenue) and a variable cooperative advertising fee.

What You Get—Training and Support

The initial House Doctors training program instructs franchisees in the following: hiring and managing quality craftsmen; bidding on projects; computer-based business operations; accounting software; budgeting and time-management techniques; understanding the target market; marketing and building a recognizable name in the local community.

Franchisees receive a "Humorous Home Remedies" newsletter to distribute to and build relationships with customers. House Doctors also provides assistance including field visits, telephone support, corporate newsletters and technical assistance. A detailed year-round marketing program features a complete advertising package full of pre-approved artwork for direct mail, newspaper ads, magazine ad slicks, color brochures, gift certificates, coupons and site signs. Other ongoing support services come in the forms of pre-opening and grand opening assistance, an accounting system and control forms, and financing.

Territory

House Doctors grants exclusive territories.

HouseMaster Home Inspections

	421 W. Union Ave.
	Bound Brook, NJ 08805-1220
	Tel: (800) 526-3939 (732) 469-6565
	Fax: (732) 469-7405
	E-Mail: bill.preston@housemaster.com

Web Site: www.housemaster.com	Fees: Franchise — $18-30K
Mr. Bill Preston, VP Marketing/Development	Royalty — 6.75%; Ad. — 2.5%

HOUSEMASTER is the oldest and most experienced home inspection franchise. HOUSEMASTER is the recognized authority on home inspections and has been featured as such on CNN, CNBC, Our Home Show and many more! You will be impressed with the level of expertise and the unsurpassed level of support that HOUSEMASTER franchise operators enjoy.

Fees: Franchise —	$18-30K
Royalty — 6.75%;	Ad. — 2.5%
Earnings Claim Statement:	No
Term of Contract (Years):	5/5
Avg. # Of Employees:	Varies
Passive Ownership:	Allowed
Encourage Conversions:	NA
Area Develop. Agreements:	No
Sub-Franchising Contracts:	No
Expand In Territory:	Yes
Space Needs: NA SF; HB	

BACKGROUND: IFA MEMBER
Established: 1979;	1st Franchised: 1979
Franchised Units:	365
Company-Owned Units	0
Total Units:	365
Dist.:	US-332; CAN-33; O'seas-0
North America:	48 States,10 Provinces
Density:	23 in NJ, 20 in NY, 18 in FL
Projected New Units (12 Months):	40
Qualifications: 4, 3, 2, 2, 5, 5	
Registered: All States	

SUPPORT & TRAINING PROVIDED:
Financial Assistance Provided:	Yes(D)
Site Selection Assistance:	NA
Lease Negotiation Assistance:	NA
Co-Operative Advertising:	NA
Franchisee Assoc./Member:	Yes/Yes
Size Of Corporate Staff:	22
On-Going Support:	D,G,H,I
Training: 2-3 Weeks Bound Brook, NJ.	

FINANCIAL/TERMS:
Cash Investment:	$18-40K
Total Investment:	$20-55K
Minimum Net Worth:	$75K

SPECIFIC EXPANSION PLANS:
US:	All United States
Canada:	All Canada
Overseas: Most Countries, Australia, United Kingdom	

HouseMaster is the oldest and most experienced name in home inspections. Since 1979, HouseMaster has completed almost 2 million home inspections in North America. One of the special services HouseMaster offers is a written guarantee that gives partial reimbursement for certain repairs to inspected elements whose condition was reported as satisfactory. HouseMaster also offers added value services through companies that offer complementary services, such as alarm inspections with Brinks Home Security.

As more and more astute home buyers and sellers recognize the practical and financial benefits of a professional home inspection, the home-inspection market continues to grow.

Operating Units	12/31/2002	12/31/2003	12/31/2004

Franchised	342	346	333
% Change	--	1.2%	-3.8%
Company-Owned	0	0	0
% Change	--	0.0%	0.0%
Total	342	346	333
% Change	--	1.2%	-3.8%
Franchised as % of Total	100.00%	100.00%	100.00%

Totals exclude units in Canada.

Investment Required

The fee for a HouseMaster franchise ranges from $18,000 to $30,000 depending on the population of the desired territory.

HouseMaster provides the following range of investments required to open your initial franchise. The range assumes that all items are paid for in cash. To the extent that you choose to finance any of these expense items, your front-end investment could be substantially reduced.

Item	Established Low Range	Established High Range
Franchise Fee	$18,000	$30,000
Conference Travel Expenses	$1,000	$3,000
HouseMaster Manual Deposit	$250	$250
Insurance	$3,000	$4,250
Legal Services	$1,000	$2,500
Prepaid Expenses	$250	$2,500
Rent	$0	$750
Supplies, Office Equipment, Furniture, Computer	$2,000	$11,700
Training Expenses	$500	$2,000

Additional Funds (for 3 months)	$5,000	$10,000
Total Investment	$31,000	$66,950

On-Going Expenses

HouseMaster franchisees pay a royalty fee that ranges from 5% to 7.5% of gross sales and an advertising fee that ranges from 2% to 2.5% of gross sales.

What You Get—Training and Support

The National Institute of Building Inspectors (NIBI ®) was established by the HouseMaster Technical Staff in 1986 to provide the technical training and annual re-certification testing for inspectors. NIBI classroom training is provided at no charge to HouseMaster franchisees and their staffs for the life of the franchise. NIBI is a state-approved educational training provider. NIBI training consists of a week of classroom training as well as additional field practicum. Marketing and Operations topics are covered in a separate week of training. Training topics include the HouseMaster Marketing Strategy, Advertising and Public Relations, Telephone Marketing, Insurance, Hiring Inspectors and Budgeting.

The HouseMaster Support Team is one of the most dedicated support staffs in franchising, focused on supporting their franchisees and growing the HouseMaster Brand. Just about everything the business needs is available through the company's franchise intranet. Franchisees can order marketing materials, apparel or schedule a trade show display for use in a local event – at no charge. Successful media exposure in leading publications and national television programs, such as Reader's Digest and CNN, as well as national ad campaigns to targeted audiences on HGTV and HGTV Canada continues to support local marketing efforts and build on the HouseMaster reputation for quality service.

Territory

HouseMaster grants exclusive and protected territories. Territory sizes are among the largest in the home inspection franchise industry.

Huntington Learning Center

496 Kinderkamack Rd.
Oradell, NJ 07649-1512
Tel: (800) 653-8400 (201) 261-8400
Fax: (800) 361-9728
E-Mail: franchise@huntingtonlearning.com
Web Site: www.huntingtonfranchise.com
Mr. Russ W. Miller, VP Business Development

Offers tutoring to 5-19 year-olds, and occasionally to adults, in reading, writing, language development study skills and mathematics, as well as programs to prepare for the SAT and ACTexams. Instruction is offered in a tutorial setting and is predominately remedial in nature.

BACKGROUND: IFA MEMBER
Established: 1977; 1st Franchised: 1985
Franchised Units: 267
Company-Owned Units 33
Total Units: 300
Dist.: US-300; CAN-0; O'seas-0
  North America: 34 States
  Density: 29 in FL, 27 in CA, 26 in NY
Projected New Units (12 Months): 50
Qualifications: 5, 3, 1, 3, 1, 5
Registered: All Except HI, ND, SD

FINANCIAL/TERMS:
Cash Investment: $60K
Total Investment: $158.3-273.4K
Minimum Net Worth: $250K
Fees: Franchise — $40K
  Royalty — 8%/$1.5K Min.; Ad. — 2%/$500 Min
Earnings Claim Statement: Yes
Term of Contract (Years): 10/10
Avg. # Of Employees: 2-4 FT, 12-20 PT
Passive Ownership: Not 1st Yr.
Encourage Conversions: No
Area Develop. Agreements: Yes
Sub-Franchising Contracts: No
Expand In Territory: Yes
Space Needs: 2,000-2,500 SF; SF, SC, RM

SUPPORT & TRAINING PROVIDED:
Financial Assistance Provided: Yes(D)
Site Selection Assistance: Yes
Lease Negotiation Assistance: No
Co-Operative Advertising: Yes
Franchisee Assoc./Member: Yes/Yes
Size Of Corporate Staff: 90+
On-Going Support: B,C,D,E,F,G,h,I
Training: 4 Weeks at Oradell, NJ (Corporate Headquarters). On-Going Regional.

SPECIFIC EXPANSION PLANS:
US: Contiguous US
Canada: No
Overseas: No

Founded in 1977, Huntington Learning Center is a pioneer and leader in the franchise learning center industry. Each year, quality instruction is provided to tens of thousands of students in kindergarten through 12th grade through a national network of franchise and company-owned Huntington Learning Centers. Parents trust Huntington, because they understand that Huntington's mission is to give every child the best education possible, and that Huntington does this by building the basic skills they need to succeed in school.

There are more students today than ever before and more parents who want to have them tutored. According to the U.S. Department of Education, enrollment in elementary and secondary schools rose 20% between 1985 and 2003 to more than 54 million students. The pool of school-age children is constantly being refreshed and is expected to grow by an additional 2 million over the next 10 years. One of the most important factors is that parents are increasingly looking for a branded tutoring program because parents now, more than ever, are consumers of education.

Operating Units	12/31/2003	12/31/2004	10/20/2005
Franchised	184	209	261
% Change	--	13.6%	24.9%
Company-Owned	33	33	33
% Change	--	0.0%	0.0%
Total	217	242	294
% Change	--	11.5%	21.5%
Franchised as % of Total	84.79%	86.36%	88.78%

Investment Required

The fee for a Huntington Learning Center franchise is $40,000

Huntington Learning Center provides the following range of investments required to open your initial franchise. The range assumes that all items are paid for in cash. To the extent that you choose to finance any of these expense items, your front-end investment could be substantially reduced.

Item	Established Low Range	Established High Range
Franchise Fee	$40,000	$40,000
Architect Design	$3,500	$8,000
Center Graphics	$3,800	$5,000
Equipment/Signs	$20,000	$40,000
Insurance (for 3 months)	$1,300	$2,500

Opening Advertising	$6,000	$6,000
Opening Inventory	$30,000	$32,000
Professional Fees	$900	$3,500
Real Estate/Improvements	$10,000	$70,000
Security and Utility Deposits; license fees	$2,000	$8,000
Training Expenses	$300	$4,500
Other Costs and Additional Funds (for 3 months)	$40,470	$53,900
Total Investment	$158,270	$273,400

On-Going Expenses

Huntington Learning Center franchisees pay a royalty fee equal to 8% of gross revenue and an advertising fee equal to 2% of gross revenue. Other expenses include local advertising costs, annual maintenance fees, software fees, phone-number license agreement fees, call-center license agreement fees, conference-service license agreement fees, school service royalties and fees and accreditation fees.

What You Get—Training and Support

Franchisees receive assistance with the following: site selection, hiring and training personnel, center layout and design, pre-packaging of equipment and learning materials and marketing and advertising materials. All franchisees go through formal training and are given supplemental support through Huntington's Success Series – a series of operational manuals that detail the business and education system. On-site consultation and a management information system are also provided. Marketing materials are aimed at demonstrating Huntington's effectiveness in tutoring children, and the package includes ad slicks, radio commercials, television commercials, direct mail and brochures.

Territory

Huntington Learning Center offers exclusive areas.

InterContinental Hotels Group

3 Ravinia Dr., # 100
Atlanta, GA 30346-2118
Tel: (770) 604-2000 + 2910
Fax: (770) 604-2107
E-Mail: brown.kessler@ichotelsgroup.com
Web Site: www.ichotelsgroup.com
Mr. Brown Kessler, VP Franchise Sales/Dev.

INTERCONTINENTAL HOTELS GROUP is the world's global hotel company. Operates or franchises more than 3,500 hotels and 535,000 guest rooms in more than 100 countries. Franchisor of INTER-CONTINENTAL HOTELS, CROWNE PLAZA HOTELS, HOLIDAY INN, HOLIDAY INN EXPRESS AND STAYBRIDGE SUITES HOTELS, CANDLEWOOD SUITES and HOTEL INDIGO.

BACKGROUND: IFA MEMBER
Established: 1952; 1st Franchised: 1952
Franchised Units: 3,529
Company-Owned Units 68
Total Units: 3,597
Dist.: US-3,597; CAN-0; O'seas-0
North America: 50 States
Density: NR
Projected New Units (12 Months): NR
Qualifications: 5, 4, 4, , ,

Registered: All States and AB

FINANCIAL/TERMS:
Cash Investment: $1-20MM
Total Investment: $Varies
Minimum Net Worth: $Varies
Fees: Franchise — $50K Min.
  Royalty — 5-6%; Ad. — 2.5-3%
Earnings Claim Statement: Yes
Term of Contract (Years): 10/10
Avg. # Of Employees: Varies
Passive Ownership: Allowed
Encourage Conversions: Yes
Area Develop. Agreements: No
Sub-Franchising Contracts: No
Expand In Territory: Yes
Space Needs: Hotel Site, F SF; FS

SUPPORT & TRAINING PROVIDED:
Financial Assistance Provided: Yes(I)
Site Selection Assistance: Yes
Lease Negotiation Assistance: No
Co-Operative Advertising: Yes
Franchisee Assoc./Member: Yes
Size Of Corporate Staff: 1,000
On-Going Support: C,D,E,H,I
Training: 4 - 5 Days Atlanta, GA. 4 - 5 Regional.

SPECIFIC EXPANSION PLANS:
US: All United States
Canada: All Canada
Overseas: All Countries

InterContinental Hotels Group specializes in providing great hotel brands in just the right places at just the right prices. Addressing the needs of every guest and every budget by having the right brand for every opportunity, IHG franchises such recognizable brands as Holiday Inn, Holiday Inn Express, Crowne Plaza, Staybridge Suites, Candlewood Suites, InterContinental Hotels and Hotel Indigo.

Each brand has its own marketing strategy tailored to specific market opportunities, and these are enhanced through brand alliances with partners such as American Express and Delta Airlines.

With over 50 years of hotel experience, IHG has proven its commitment to service and quality by enabling operators to maximize their profits while ensuring a superior guest experience. More than 90% of all US travelers stay in IHG brand hotels, and IHG expects that the standards they've maintained will keep them ahead of their competition into the future.

Operating Units	12/31/2003	12/31/2004	9/30/2005
Franchised	2,345	2,307	3,000
% Change	--	-1.6%	30.0%
Company-Owned	203	188	572
% Change	--	-7.4%	204.3%
Total	2,548	2,495	3,572
% Change	--	-2.1%	43.2%
Franchised as % of Total	92.03%	92.46%	83.99%

Investment Required
The fee for an InterContinental Hotels Holiday Inn franchise is $500 per room with a $50,000 minimum. The minimum varies depending on the InterContinental brand franchised.

InterContinental Hotels provides the following range of investments required to open your initial franchise. The range assumes that all items are paid for in cash. To the extent that you choose to finance any of these expense items, your front-end investment could be substantially reduced. The following figures refer to a 100-room, two-story Holiday Inn hotel.

Item	Established Low Range	Established High Range
Franchise Fee	$50,000	$50,000

Real Estate	Not determinable	Not determinable
Building	$4,012,000	$6,300,000
Furniture, Fixtures, Equipment, Signs	$835,000	$1,700,000
Insurance	$75,000	$100,000
License/Permits	$2,500	$15,000
Opening Inventory	$100,000	$200,000
Professional Fees	$75,000	$150,000
Security Deposits	$2,500	$15,000
Other Costs and Additional Funds (for 3 months)	$214,870	$361,454
Total Investment	$5,366,870	$8,891,454

On-Going Expenses
IHG Holiday Inn franchisees pay a royalty fee equal to 5% of gross room revenue and service fees equal to 2.5% of the preceding month's gross room revenue. For other IHG hotel brands, the royalty fee is equal to 6% of gross room revenue and service fees equal 3% of gross room revenue. Other ongoing fees include special marketing contributions for the frequency program, capital reserve charges and a monthly technology fee of $10.80 per room.

What You Get—Training and Support
Around-the-clock support is provided first through a field services representative, who functions as an on-site consultant on guest service, product quality and revenue management. The representative also hosts regional workshops that offer further networking opportunities with other hotel franchisees, along with opportunities to fulfill additional training certification requirements. Each hotel also has a dedicated service manager, the liaison between the franchisee and corporate headquarters, who answers questions on policy, procedures, systems and new initiatives.

Among many advanced technological tools, the HIRO Revenue Management System maximizes and optimizes reservations by developing strategies to deal with changes in occupancy-demand conditions, forecasting future business and tracking room inventory levels. IHG was also the first to offer real-time bookings online, a service who use continues to grow dramatically every year. The IHG Central Reservation system processes 13 million room nights a year through its connection to more than 430,000 terminals worldwide, making it convenient for travelers and agents to book with an IHG brand hotel.

IHG maintains a global sales team of 100 professionals. Sales and marketing is coordinated on local, regional and global levels so that every hotel benefits from the brand's increasing around-the-world recognition.

Territory
InterContinental Hotels does not grant exclusive territories.

Interiors by Decorating Den

INTERIORS
by Decorating Den™

8659 Commerce Dr.
Easton, MD 21601-7425
Tel: (877) 918-1500
Fax: (410) 820-5131
E-Mail: reginab@decoratingden.com
Web Site: www.decoratingden.com
Mr. Kevin V. Atkinson, VP Program Development

Celebrating our 36th successful year, INTERIORS BY DECORATING DEN is the oldest international, shop-at-home interior decorating franchise in the world. Our company-trained interior decorators bring thousands of samples including window coverings, wall coverings, floor coverings, furniture and accessories to their customers' homes in our uniquely equipped COLORVAN ©. Special business features include: home-based, marketing systems, business systems, training, support and complete sampling.

BACKGROUND:	IFA MEMBER
Established: 1969;	1st Franchised: 1970
Franchised Units:	468
Company-Owned Units	0
Total Units:	468
Dist.:	US-403; CAN-50; O'seas-15
North America:	NR
Density:	33 in FL, 28 in NC, 27 in TX
Projected New Units (12 Months):	50
Qualifications: 5, 5, 3, 3, 5, 5	
Registered: All States	

FINANCIAL/TERMS:	
Cash Investment:	$15K
Total Investment:	$40-70K
Minimum Net Worth:	$40K
Fees: Franchise —	$24.9K
Royalty — 7-9%;	Ad. — 4%/$100 Min
Earnings Claim Statement:	No

Term of Contract (Years):	10/10	Lease Negotiation Assistance:	NA
Avg. # Of Employees:	1 FT	Co-Operative Advertising:	Yes
Passive Ownership:	Not Allowed	Franchisee Assoc./Member:	Yes/Yes
Encourage Conversions:	Yes	Size Of Corporate Staff:	40
Area Develop. Agreements:	Yes/10	On-Going Support:	C,D,E,G,H,I
Sub-Franchising Contracts:	Yes	Training: 10.5 Days in Easton, MD; Continuous.	
Expand In Territory:	No		
Space Needs: NA SF; HB		**SPECIFIC EXPANSION PLANS:**	
		US:	All United States
SUPPORT & TRAINING PROVIDED:		Canada:	All Canada
Financial Assistance Provided:	Yes(D)	Overseas:	No
Site Selection Assistance:	NA		

Interiors by Decorating Den has been the world's premier interior-decorating franchisor since 1969. Franchisees enjoy using their imaginations to transform rooms, and they have the skills and flexibility to incorporate clients' original furniture, style preferences and budget into their tasks. Designers work with windows, trims, floor coverings, wall hangings and more to create the homeowner's dream room—or dream house. Clients often begin by wanting to transform one room, and positive results encourage them to rework with the rest of their homes. Designers can also provide custom upholstery, bedding, lighting and other accessories to complete a client's vision.

Interiors by Decorating Den has a conveniently mobile showroom—the ColorVan—that brings a large selection of home furnishings and materials right to a customer's home. Increasing numbers of people are looking for a way to transform their house into a sanctuary, and Interiors looks to fulfill all of their house decorating, supplying and consulting needs.

Operating Units	12/31/2003	12/31/2004	12/31/2005
Franchised	389	408	467
% Change	--	4.9%	14.5%
Company-Owned	0	0	0
% Change	--	0.0%	0.0%
Total	389	408	467
% Change	--	4.9%	14.5%

Franchised as % of Total	100.00%	100.00%	100.00%

Investment Required

The fee for an Interiors by Decorating Den franchise is $29,900.

Interiors by Decorating Den provides the following range of investments required to open your initial franchise. The range assumes that all items are paid for in cash. To the extent that you choose to finance any of these expense items, your front-end investment could be substantially reduced.

Item	Established Low Range	Established High Range
Franchise Fee	$29,900	$29,900
Furniture, Fixtures and Equipment	$2,039	$3,012
Opening Inventory	$500	$750
Advertising and Grand Opening Event	$3,500	$5,000
Insurance	$780	$1,634
Additional Funds (for 3 months)	$3,400	$6,000
Total Investment	$40,119	$46,296

On-Going Expenses

Interiors by Decorating Den franchisees pay a service fee equal to 7% to 9% of gross sales and a national marketing fund fee equal to 4% of gross sales or a minimum of $100 per month.

What You Get—Training and Support

Franchisees begin with a 45-day home-study preparation program that instructs them in the basics of interior-design principles, home furnishings, sales and marketing strategies and business management skills. This is followed by the Professional Decorating and Sales School, two weeks of classroom training at corporate headquarters' Lifestyle University. Following the two weeks of school, there are twelve modules of training called "Directions." Each module focuses on a different aspect of the business (marketing, window treatments, furniture, etc.). Ongoing training includes updates on new products and trends, follow-up sessions, regional meetings and annual conferences. Additional classes on sketching, in-home sales, lifestyle design and furniture are also offered. Franchisees also receive access to an exclusive franchisee intranet, a variety of business management software and product guarantees.

Local advertising materials are updated monthly and are available online, and a national advertising program works with publications such as *Better Homes and Gardens* and *Good Housekeeping*. Partnerships with many major home furnishings manufacturers give franchisees abundant resources and a broad product selection to offer clients, as well as supplies not typically available to independent decorators.

Territory
Interiors by Decorating Den grants exclusive territories.

Jani-King International

16885 Dallas Pkwy.
Addison, TX 75001-5215
Tel: (800) 552-5264 (972) 991-0900
Fax: (972) 239-7706
E-Mail: gdick@janiking.com
Web Site: www.janiking.com
Mr. Gary Dick, VP Franchising

JANI-KING INTERNATIONAL is the world's largest commercial cleaning franchisor, with locations in 19 countries and over 110 regions in the U. S. and abroad. Our franchise opportunity includes initial customer contracts, training, continuous local support , administrative and accounting assistance, an equipment leasing program and national advertising. If you are searching for a flexible business opportunity, look no further.

BACKGROUND:	IFA MEMBER
Established: 1969;	1st Franchised: 1974
Franchised Units:	11,000
Company-Owned Units	<u>27</u>
Total Units:	11,027
Dist.:	US-10,148; CAN-351; O'seas-528
North America:	39 States, 7 Provinces
Density:	880 in TX, 737 in CA, 307 FL
Projected New Units (12 Months):	1,500

Qualifications: 2, 2, 1, 2, 2, 3
Registered: CA,FL,HI,IL,IN,MI,MN,NY,OR,SD,VA ,WA,WI,DC

FINANCIAL/TERMS:		SUPPORT & TRAINING PROVIDED:	
Cash Investment:	$2.9-33K	Financial Assistance Provided:	No
Total Investment:	$2.9-40K	Site Selection Assistance:	NA
Minimum Net Worth:	$2.9-33K	Lease Negotiation Assistance:	NA
Fees: Franchise —	$8-33K	Co-Operative Advertising:	NA
Royalty — 10%;	Ad. — 0%	Franchisee Assoc./Member:	Yes/Yes
Earnings Claim Statement:	Yes	Size Of Corporate Staff:	65
Term of Contract (Years):	20/20	On-Going Support:	A,B,C,D,G,H,I
Avg. # Of Employees:	NR	Training: 2 Weeks Local Regional Office.	
Passive Ownership:	Allowed		
Encourage Conversions:	NA	SPECIFIC EXPANSION PLANS:	
Area Develop. Agreements:	Yes/20	US:	All United States
Sub-Franchising Contracts:	Yes	Canada:	All Canada
Expand In Territory:	Yes	Overseas:	All Countries
Space Needs: NR SF; HB			

Jani-King is the largest commercial cleaning franchise worldwide, with thousands of franchisees and over 110 regional support offices. All regional support offices, located in major metropolitan areas, give franchisees business advice, administrative support and sales and account assistance. Franchisees can even maintain their current jobs as they open a Jani-King business. Jani-King franchisees also benefit from a low total investment, a well-structured business plan and being part of a stable commercial cleaning industry resistant to recession. Jani-King offers people the opportunity to be in business for themselves, but not by themselves.

The overall commercial cleaning and maintenance market is a $94 billion industry, and the demand for custodians is expected to increase by as much as 20% between 2002 and 2012. Clients benefit from contracting Jani-King because they lower their own costs and gain the services of a respected industry leader. Jani-King serves a variety of facilities, including offices, manufacturing, retail, restaurants, hotels and educational institutions. Since opening its doors in 1969, Jani-King has enjoyed consistent growth in the commercial cleaning industry.

Operating Units	12/31/2002	12/31/2003	12/31/2004
Franchised	9,442	10,046	10,715
% Change	--	6.4%	6.7%
Company-Owned	0	0	0

% Change	--	0.0%	0.0%
Total	9,442	10,046	10,715
% Change	--	6.4%	6.7%
Franchised as % of Total	100.00%	100.00%	100.00%

Investment Required

The fee for a Jani-King franchise ranges from $8,600 to $16,250, depending on the plan selected – plus a fee of $2,750 for each level above the standard plan. For the franchise fee, Jani-King offers several payment plans without interest.

Jani-King provides the following range of investments required to open your initial franchise. The range assumes that all items are paid for in cash. To the extent that you choose to finance any of these expense items, your front-end investment could be substantially reduced.

Item	Established Low Range	Established High Range
Franchise Fee	$8,600	$16,250
Real Estate	$0	$5,000
Supplies	$500	$800
Equipment	$1,300	$2,500
Security Deposits, etc.	$100	$1,000
Additional Funds (for 3 months)	$800	$8,500
Total Investment	$11,300	$34,050

On-Going Expenses

Jani-King franchisees pay a service fee equal to 10% of monthly gross revenue and an accounting fee equal to 3% of monthly gross revenue. Other ongoing fees include varying finder's fees and advertising fees equal to 1% of monthly gross revenue.

What You Get—Training and Support

Jani-King provides franchisees with the following: initial and ongoing training, on-site direction, business protection, cash flow assistance, administrative assistance (including invoicing and collecting) and a range of marketing and support tools. Initial training is supplemented by classroom lectures and discussions, demonstrations both in person and on video and hands-on training. Regional offices also provide additional training seminars and refresher courses. Franchisees need no previous experience in the industry, as training involves teaching the most advanced and efficient cleaning techniques, personnel management, client relations, bid and proposal preparation, administrative procedures, sales and other business-related issues.

Franchisees also have access to customized manuals covering aspects such as customer relations, operations, accounting, business management and marketing.

Territory

Jani-King does not grant exclusive territories.

Kampgrounds of America

**Great people.
Great camping.™**

550 N. 31st St., FL. 4
Billings, MT 59101
Tel: (800) 548-7239 (406) 248-7444
Fax: (406) 254-7440
E-Mail: cpreble@koa.net
Web Site: www.koa.com

Mr. Pat Hittmeier, VP Franchise Development

KAMPGROUNDS OF AMERICA is North America's largest franchise system of open-to-the public campgrounds; no membership fees or annual dues are required. All KOA campgrounds offer RV and tent sites; 90% also offer Kamping Kabins. Nearly 2 million copies of the KOA directory are printed and distributed to campers. KOA campgrounds are located in 45 of the contiguous United States, 8 Canadian Provinces, Mexico and Japan.

BACKGROUND:

Established: 1961;	1st Franchised: 1962
Franchised Units:	409
Company-Owned Units	21

Total Units:	430	Area Develop. Agreements:	No
Dist.:	US-390; CAN-33; O'seas-7	Sub-Franchising Contracts:	No
North America:	44 States, 8 Provinces	Expand In Territory:	Yes
Density:	25 in CA, 24 in FL, 21 in CO	Space Needs: 10+ acres SF; NR	
Projected New Units (12 Months):	8		
Qualifications: 5, 3, 2, 3, 4, 4		**SUPPORT & TRAINING PROVIDED:**	
Registered: All States		Financial Assistance Provided:	No
		Site Selection Assistance:	Yes
FINANCIAL/TERMS:		Lease Negotiation Assistance:	No
Cash Investment:	$150-500K	Co-Operative Advertising:	Yes
Total Investment:	$200K-4MM	Franchisee Assoc./Member:	Yes/Yes
Minimum Net Worth:	$300K	Size Of Corporate Staff:	65
Fees: Franchise —	$30/22.5/7.5K	On-Going Support:	A,B,C,D,E,F,G,h,I
Royalty — 8%;	Ad. — 2%	Training: 5 Days at Billings, MT.	
Earnings Claim Statement:	Yes		
Term of Contract (Years):	5	**SPECIFIC EXPANSION PLANS:**	
Avg. # Of Employees:	5 PT (Varies)	US:	All United States
Passive Ownership:	Discouraged	Canada:	All Canada
Encourage Conversions:	Yes	Overseas:	No

Kampgrounds of America (KOA) has made camping convenient, fun and affordable—with the comforts of home. KOA locations can be found throughout the states, offering travelers options ranging from a basic cabin to a roomy lodge. Every cabin or lodge has beds, interior lighting and lockable doors, so visitors can always be safe and comfortable while enjoying the great outdoors.

KOA distinguishes itself from the competition by providing all the amenities that guests will need. Weary travelers on a road trip or vacationing families will appreciate the coin laundries, playgrounds and immaculate bathrooms with individual showers and dressing areas. Many campgrounds have swimming pools, and some have hot tubs, bike rentals, miniature golf, camper kitchens and nightly entertainment. The KOA Kampground Store takes care of any other needs.

KOA allows franchisees to purchase an existing KOA campground, convert an ordinary campground into a KOA or build a new KOA.

Operating Units	12/31/2002	12/31/2003	12/31/2004
Franchised	417	404	391

% Change	--	-3.1%	-3.2%
Company-Owned	13	14	17
% Change	--	7.7%	21.4%
Total	430	418	408
% Change	--	-2.8%	-2.4%
Franchised as % of Total	96.98%	96.65%	95.83%

Investment Required

The fee for a new Kampgrounds of America franchise is $30,000, the fee for a conversion is $22,500, and the fee for buying an existing KOA franchise is either $5,000 or $7,500.

Kampgrounds of America provides the following range of investments required to open your initial franchise. The range assumes that all items are paid for in cash. To the extent that you choose to finance any of these expense items, your front-end investment could be substantially reduced. The following figures refer to the building of a new KOA campground.

Item	Established Low Range	Established High Range
Franchise Fee	$30,000	$30,000
Training Expenses	$1,500	$1,500
Real Estate	$36,000	$600,000
Main Building and Residence	$270,000	$475,000
Site Costs/Other Buildings	$532,745	$635,543
Optional Facilities	$12,000	$130,000
Equipment	$21,700	$26,700
Opening Inventory	$10,000	$30,000
Advertising Costs and Fees	$7,800	$21,500
Computer Equipment	$1,800	$10,000

Other Costs and Additional Funds (for 3 months)	$63,200	$160,400
Total Investment	$986,745	$2,070,643

On-Going Expenses

Kampgrounds of America franchisees pay a royalty fee equal to 8% of total registration receipts and an advertising fee equal to 2% of total registration receipts. Other costs include 50% of proceeds from Value Kard Sales and an annual administrative fee of $500.

What You Get—Training and Support

KOA has over 40 years of experience in owning, operating and supporting the largest chain of campgrounds in North America. Franchisees benefit from national and international marketing programs, access to management experts, proprietary camper and campground computer support systems, an in-depth franchisee magazine and design and development.

KOA's campground management training center instructs franchisees, while a frequently updated video-training library offers supplementary help. KOA also holds an annual convention to provide franchisees with the opportunity to network and attend workshops focused on improving operational aspects.

Territory

Kampgrounds of America grants exclusive territories.

Kinderdance International

EducationThroughDance

INTERNATIONAL

1333 Gateway Dr., # 1003
Melbourne, FL 32901
Tel: (800) 554-2334 (321) 984-4448
Fax: (321) 984-4490
E-Mail: kindercorp@kinderdance.com
Web Site: www.kinderdance.com
Mr. Bernard Friedman, Executive Vice President

KINDERDANCE® franchisees are trained to teach 4 developmentally unique "Education Through Dance and Motor Development" programs: KINDERDANCE®, KINDERGYM®, KINDERTOTS® and KINDERCOMBO (TM), which are designed for boys and girls ages 2-8. Children learn the basics of ballet, tap, gymnastics and creative dance, as well as learning numbers, colors, shapes and songs. No studio or dance experience required. Franchisees teach at child care centers and other viable locations.

BACKGROUND: IFA MEMBER
Established: 1979; 1st Franchised: 1985
Franchised Units: 112
Company-Owned Units: 1
Total Units: 113
Dist.: US-110; CAN-1; O'seas-2
  North America: 38 States, 3 Provinces
  Density: 14 in FL, 12 in CA, 11 in TX
Projected New Units (12 Months): 20

Qualifications: 2, 2, 1, 2, 2, 5
Registered: CA,FL,HI,IL,MD,MI,MN,NY,OR,VA,WA,DC,AB

FINANCIAL/TERMS:
Cash Investment: $7-28K
Total Investment: $14.9-34.1K
Minimum Net Worth: $NA
Fees: Franchise — $12-28K
  Royalty — 6-15%; Ad. — 3%
Earnings Claim Statement: Yes
Term of Contract (Years): 10/10
Avg. # Of Employees: 1-2 PT+
Passive Ownership: Discouraged
Encourage Conversions: Yes
Area Develop. Agreements: Yes
Sub-Franchising Contracts: No
Expand In Territory: Yes
Space Needs: NR SF; NR

SUPPORT & TRAINING PROVIDED:
Financial Assistance Provided: Yes(D)
Site Selection Assistance: NA
Lease Negotiation Assistance: NA
Co-Operative Advertising: Yes
Franchisee Assoc./Member: Yes/Yes
Size Of Corporate Staff: 8
On-Going Support: A,B,C,D,E,F,G,H,I
Training: 6 Days in Melbourne, FL and On-Site.

SPECIFIC EXPANSION PLANS:
US: All United States
Canada: All Canada
Overseas: Europe, Asia, New Zealand, Australia, S. America, Mexico and China.

Kinderdance blends dance, gymnastics, physical education and academics into an innovative learning program for children between the ages of 2 and 8. The combination of these disciplines means that parents no longer need to enroll their children in multiple activities. Through Kinderdance programs, children learn creative movement, ballet, tap, gymnastics and modern dance skills, in addition to colors, numbers, shapes, words and songs.

They develop physical, verbal and social skills and imagination – an early foundation for higher education. Kinderdance teaches children to love learning by associating it with movement, music, dance and fun.

Along with the standard Kinderdance program for pre-schoolers, the following specialized programs are offered: Kindertots for two-year olds; Kindergym, which emphasizes gymnastics, and Kindercombo, which introduces children between the ages of 6 and 8 to beginning dance techniques.

Franchisees can teach all of the Kinderdance programs themselves or complete training to manage a team of instructors. Franchisees work out of their own home and take their services straight to the day-care centers, preschools, YMCAs, churches and community centers where Kinderdance programs are most in demand.

Operating Units	12/31/2003	12/31/2004	12/31/2005
Franchised	100	111	116
% Change	--	11.0%	4.5%
Company-Owned	1	1	1
% Change	--	0.0%	0.0%
Total	101	112	117
% Change	--	10.9%	4.5%
Franchised as % of Total	99.01%	99.11%	99.15%

Investment Required

The fee for a Kinderdance franchise varies depending on the type of territory desired. The fee for a Bronze franchise is $12,000 for up to 10 locations in a non-exclusive area; the fee for a Silver franchise is $18,000 for up to 20 locations in a non-exclusive area; and the fee for a Gold franchise is $28,000 for an unlimited number of locations in an exclusive territory.

Kinderdance provides the following range of investments required to open your initial franchise. The range assumes that all items are paid for in cash.

To the extent that you choose to finance any of these expense items, your front-end investment could be substantially reduced.

Item	Established Low Range	Established High Range
Franchise Fee	$12,000	$28,000
Training Expenses	$450	$1,000
Insurance	$400	$600
Additional Funds	$2,100	$4,500
Total Investment	$14,950	$34,100

On-Going Expenses
Kinderdance franchisees pay variable royalty fees depending on the level of their franchise. Bronze franchisees pay the greater of 15% of monthly gross sales or $200; Silver franchisees pay the greater of 7-10% of monthly gross sales or $300; and Gold franchisees pay the greater of 6-7% of monthly gross sales or $500. All franchisees pay an advertising contribution fee equal to 3% of monthly gross sales and an initial inventory fee ranging from $100 to $500.

What You Get—Training and Support
Kinderdance franchisees receive six days of training at corporate headquarters, which includes classroom sessions, video instruction, individual meetings and on-site participation with children. Instruction covers all necessary aspects of running a Kinderdance franchise, as well as how to teach all of the Kinderdance programs. Each program has its own written curriculum and video instructional tapes.

Franchisees are not required to invest in real estate, meaning that the total investment is minimal and they can open up their businesses within a few weeks of completing initial training. Franchisees receive continuing support from annual education conferences, quarterly informational newsletters, an operations manual, a toll-free hotline, discounted insurance rates and more. Kinderdance also provides an initial supply of brochures, posters, promotional letters and other forms of advertising support, as well as sales agreements, order forms, a bookkeeping and accounting system and a billing system.

Territory
Kinderdance only grants exclusive territories to Gold franchisees.

Kitchen Solvers

401 Jay St.
La Crosse, WI 54601-4064
Tel: (800) 845-6779 (608) 791-5516 + 515
Fax: (608) 784-2917
E-Mail: rick@kitchensolvers.com
Web Site: www.kitchensolvers.com
Mr. Rick McGarry, VP Business Development

Specialize or diversify... It's your option. Two different models to choose from. Six different profit centers. We are the most experienced kitchen and bath remodeling franchise in the US. Home-based business with no inventory required. Complete start-up and on-going support. Personalized marketing strategies. Experienced technical training and support.

BACKGROUND:	IFA MEMBER
Established: 1982;	1st Franchised: 1984
Franchised Units:	132
Company-Owned Units	0
Total Units:	132
Dist.:	US-128; CAN-4; O'seas-0
North America:	32 States, 4 Provinces
Density:	17 in IL, 15 in WI, 12 in IA
Projected New Units (12 Months):	20
Qualifications: 2, 2, 2, 2, , 5	

Registered: CA,FL,IL,IN,MD,MI,MN,ND,NY,OR,SD,VA,WA,WI,AB

FINANCIAL/TERMS:	
Cash Investment:	$40-60.2K
Total Investment:	$48-82K
Minimum Net Worth:	$250K
Fees: Franchise —	$27.5-32.0K
Royalty — 6%;	Ad. — 1%
Earnings Claim Statement:	Yes
Term of Contract (Years):	10/10
Avg. # Of Employees:	1 FT
Passive Ownership:	Not Allowed
Encourage Conversions:	Yes
Area Develop. Agreements:	No
Sub-Franchising Contracts:	No
Expand In Territory:	Yes
Space Needs: NA SF; HB	

SUPPORT & TRAINING PROVIDED:	
Financial Assistance Provided:	Yes(D)
Site Selection Assistance:	NA
Lease Negotiation Assistance:	NA
Co-Operative Advertising:	NA
Franchisee Assoc./Member:	Yes/Yes
Size Of Corporate Staff:	10
On-Going Support:	a,B,C,D,G,h,I
Training: 2 Weeks LaCrosse, WI Corporate Headquarters.	

SPECIFIC EXPANSION PLANS:	
US:	All United States
Canada:	All Canada
Overseas:	No

Kitchen Solvers provides cabinet refacing as a convenient and efficient alternative to traditional cabinet replacement. By installing new fronts on

297

existing cabinetry, Kitchen Solvers presents homeowners with a beautiful new kitchen without the time and expense of overall replacement. Studies have shown that remodeling kitchens and bathrooms provides the best return on homeowners' money, and homeowners have and will continue to remodel these areas at a faster pace than ever before.

Since being founded in 1982, Kitchen Solvers has expanded to offer pre-built and custom cabinetry, solid surface countertop replacement, acrylic bathtub liners, glueless laminate flooring and closet organizing systems.

Franchisees have the option of being a hands-on owner-operator or an owner-executive who manages a staff. Due to strategic alliances that supply necessary products on an as-needed basis, franchisees do not have to invest capital in fabricating tools, nor do they need a warehouse to hold excess inventory.

Operating Units	12/31/2002	12/31/2003	12/31/2004
Franchised	127	134	131
% Change	--	5.5%	-2.2%
Company-Owned	0	0	0
% Change	--	0.0%	0.0%
Total	127	134	131
% Change	--	5.5%	-2.2%
Franchised as % of Total	100.00%	100.00%	100.00%

Investment Required

The owner-operator fee for a Kitchen Solvers franchise is $27,500, plus an additional fee of $150 per every 1,000 households over 50,000 in the territory. The owner-executive fee for a Kitchen Solvers franchise is $31,995, plus an additional fee of $150 per every 1,000 households over 100,000 of the territory.

Kitchen Solvers provides the following range of investments required to open your initial franchise. The range assumes that all items are paid for in cash. To the extent that you choose to finance any of these expense items, your front-end investment could be substantially reduced. The following figures refer to an owner-operator franchise.

Item	Established Low Range	Established High Range
Franchise Fee	$27,500	$27,500
Training Expenses	$425	$925
Supplies	$12,500	$12,500
Installer's Tools	$700	$2,300
Initial Advertising and Literature (3 months)	$6,000	$6,000
Other Costs and Additional Funds (for 3 months)	$2,325	$15,745
Total Investment	$49,450	$64,970

On-Going Expenses

Kitchen Solvers franchisees pay a royalty fee that ranges from 4% to 8% of gross sales, a local marketing fee equal to the greater of 5% of gross sales or $7,500, and a marketing fee equal to 1% of gross sales.

What You Get—Training and Support

Owner-operators receive five days of training at corporate headquarters. Training covers effective techniques for marketing, professional selling, product installation, competitive pricing and efficient business operations. Franchisees go through the actual process of refacing a kitchen by experimenting with an actual model, and also receive installation videos, an accompanying manual and other resources for kitchen and bath remodeling.

Owner-executives attend two separate training sessions. The first covers advanced marketing and selling techniques, personnel management, risk management, good business practices and efficient business operations. The second covers solid-surface, bath-lines and wall-surround installation techniques, as well as the Planet Millennium software, which is designed to provide virtual remodeling for customer presentations. Owner-executives also learn how to train employees.

All franchisees receive support from a toll-free phone number, a Director of Installation who is knowledgeable with all Kitchen Solvers products, an online franchisee network, annual conventions and more. Marketing campaigns will be tailored to individual franchisee needs, factoring in personalized demographics, cost-effectiveness and market analyses. Other marketing support includes turnkey marketing materials, print and radio advertising, direct mail campaigns and a database of region-specific newspapers and publications.

Territory
Kitchen Solvers grants exclusive territories.

Kumon North America

MATH. READING. SUCCESS.

300 Frank W. Burr Blvd., Fl. 5
Teaneck, NJ 07666-6703
Tel: (866) 633-0740 (201) 928-0444 + 338
Fax: (201) 928-0044
E-Mail: dklein@kumon.com
Web Site: www.kumon.com
Mr. Deven Klein, Vice President Franchising

KUMON NORTH AMERICA is the premier supplemental education franchise, where you'll find success, one child at a time.

BACKGROUND:

Established: 1958;	1st Franchised: 1980
Franchised Units:	1,543
Company-Owned Units	31
Total Units:	1,574
Dist.:	US-1,574; CAN-325; O'seas-24,300
North America:	50 States, 9 Provinces

Density: 252 in CA, 93 in NY, 87 NJ
Projected New Units (12 Months): 125
Qualifications: 4, 3, 3, 4, 4, 4
Registered: All States

FINANCIAL/TERMS:

Cash Investment:	$NR
Total Investment:	$10-30.5K
Minimum Net Worth:	$50K
Fees: Franchise —	$1K
Royalty — $30-33K;	Ad. — NA
Earnings Claim Statement:	No
Term of Contract (Years):	2/5
Avg. # Of Employees:	1 FT, 1-3 PT
Passive Ownership:	Not Allowed
Encourage Conversions:	NA
Area Develop. Agreements:	No
Sub-Franchising Contracts:	No
Expand In Territory:	No
Space Needs: Varies SF; FS, SF, SC, RM	

SUPPORT & TRAINING PROVIDED:

Financial Assistance Provided:	NA
Site Selection Assistance:	Yes

Lease Negotiation Assistance:	Yes	race, IL.
Co-Operative Advertising:	NA	
Franchisee Assoc./Member:	Yes	**SPECIFIC EXPANSION PLANS:**
Size Of Corporate Staff:	300	US: All United States
On-Going Support:	B,C,D,E,G,H,I	Canada: All Canada
Training: 9 Days Total Training in 4-5-Day Periods; National Training Department in Oakbrook Ter-		Overseas: All Countries

Kumon is an after-school program that inspires children to be more self-confident and disciplined by improving their academic skills in math and reading. It is the largest and most established program of its kind in the world. Whether students are struggling or seeking enrichment, Kumon helps children of any age reach their full potential by letting on the individual needs and abilities of each child to dictate their progress in the program. Different from tutoring, Kumon facilitates self-acquisition of not only skills, but also the study habits needed to improve academic performance.

Kumon offers innovative programs that motivate students and offer recognition for their accomplishments, such as the Advanced Student Honor Roll for students who work beyond their grade level; the Kumon Cosmic Club, which allows younger students to collect points that may be redeemed for prizes; and the Kumon Math Challenge, an annual event that allows students in grades one through 10 to compete for scholarships.

With franchisees in 43 countries, Kumon has helped more students succeed than any other after-school program.

Operating Units	12/31/2002	12/31/2003	12/31/2004
Franchised	1,057	1,097	1,158
% Change	--	3.8%	5.6%
Company-Owned	23	16	12
% Change	--	-30.4%	-25.0%
Total	1,080	1,113	1,170
% Change	--	3.1%	5.1%

Franchised as % of Total	97.87%	98.56%	98.97%

Investment Required

The fee for a Kumon franchise is $1,000.

Kumon provides the following range of investments required to open your initial franchise. The range assumes that all items are paid for in cash. To the extent that you choose to finance any of these expense items, your front-end investment could be substantially reduced.

Item	Established Low Range	Established High Range
Franchise Fee	$1,000	$1,000
Training Expenses	$1,900	$3,000
Follow-up Training	$700	$1,000
Rent	$750	$3,500
Furniture, Signs, Personal, Equipment & Supplies	$2,000	$10,000
Other Costs and Additional Funds (for 3 months)	$3,688	$11,853
Total Investment	$10,038	$30,353

On-Going Expenses

Kumon franchisees pay various royalty fees depending on the number of students enrolled. The initial enrollment fee for each new student is $15; the monthly royalty fee is $33.75 for each full-paying student and $16.88 for each partially exempt and/or prorated student. These fees are reduced to $30 and $15 respectively after the temporary license period has ended.

What You Get—Training and Support

Kumon has a National Training Team that conducts all start-up training for franchisees, including 7 days in Chicago on methods, site selection, student assessment and enrollment, instruction and learning materials, Center Management Software, marketing, in-center training, parent communication and business plan presentations.

After opening a Kumon franchise, franchisees benefit from follow-up training, access to monthly instructor meetings in the region, ongoing support and consultation from the regional office and an annual national instructor conference.

Territory
Kumon does not grant exclusive territories.

Liberty Tax Service

1716 Corporate Landing Pkwy.
Virginia Beach, VA 23454
Tel: (800) 790-3863 (757) 493-8855
Fax: (757) 301-8080
E-Mail: sales@libtax.com
Web Site: www.libertytaxfranchise.com
Mr. Scott Arbuckle, Dir. Franchise Development

We're #1! LIBERTY TAX SERVICE is the fastest-growing international tax service ever! In 9 years, LIBERTY TAX SERVICE has grown to a size it other national tax franchises 15 years to realize. LIBERTY has surged to the forefront of a constantly evolving and technological tax industry. LIBERTY's growth id fueled by a proven operating system that has been fine-tuned by the leadership and field support staff's 500 total years of experience. John Hewitt was the IFA's Entrepreneur of the Year.

BACKGROUND:	IFA MEMBER
Established: 1996;	1st Franchised: 1997

Franchised Units:	2,000
Company-Owned Units:	<u>22</u>
Total Units:	2,022
Dist.:	US-1,722; CAN-300; O'seas-0
North America:	50 States
Density:	NR
Projected New Units (12 Months):	300-400
Qualifications: , , , , ,	
Registered: All States and AB	

FINANCIAL/TERMS:	
Cash Investment:	$30K
Total Investment:	$41.8-52.4K
Minimum Net Worth:	$28K
Fees: Franchise —	$30K
Royalty — Varies;	Ad. — 5%
Earnings Claim Statement:	No
Term of Contract (Years):	5/5
Avg. # Of Employees:	4-6 FT, 2 PT
Passive Ownership:	Discouraged
Encourage Conversions:	NR
Area Develop. Agreements:	Yes/10
Sub-Franchising Contracts:	No
Expand In Territory:	Yes
Space Needs: 400+ SF; FS, SF, SC, RM	

SUPPORT & TRAINING PROVIDED:	
Financial Assistance Provided:	Yes
Site Selection Assistance:	Yes
Lease Negotiation Assistance:	Yes

Co-Operative Advertising:	No	SPECIFIC EXPANSION PLANS:	
Franchisee Assoc./Member:	No	US:	All United States
Size Of Corporate Staff:	250+	Canada:	All Canada
On-Going Support:	C,D,G,H,I	Overseas:	No
Training: 5 Days in Virginia Beach, VA.			

Liberty Tax Service was founded by John Hewitt in 1997. Hewitt began his career in the retail income-tax preparation industry 37 years ago at H&R Block; he then founded Jackson Hewitt Tax Service and sold it in 1996 for $483 million. He used this entrepreneurial experience and tax industry knowledge to found Liberty Tax Service, which has become the fastest-growing retail tax preparation service in history. Liberty Tax Service has set the standard for the number of both offices opened and tax returns prepared (more than 1 million in the 2005 fiscal year).

Operating Units	4/30/2003	4/30/2004	4/30/2005
Franchised	691	1,122	1,417
% Change	--	62.4%	26.3%
Company-Owned	14	17	25
% Change	--	21.4%	47.1%
Total	705	1,139	1,442
% Change	--	61.6%	26.6%
Franchised as % of Total	98.01%	98.51%	98.27%

Investment Required
The fee for a Liberty Tax Service franchise is $30,000.

Liberty Tax Service provides the following range of investments required to open your initial franchise. The range assumes that all items are paid for in cash. To the extent that you choose to finance any of these expense items, your front-end investment could be substantially reduced.

Item	Established Low Range	Established High Range

Franchise Fee	$30,000	$30,000
Initial Advertising	$2,000	$3,000
Training Expenses	$100	$2,000
Equipment and Furniture	$2,000	$3,000
Signs	$500	$1,000
Rent	$3,000	$6,000
Payroll	$3,000	$5,000
Insurance	$200	$400
Additional Funds (for 3 months)	$3,000	$4,500
Total Investment	$43,800	$54,900

On-Going Expenses

Liberty Tax Service franchisees pay a royalty fee equal to 14% of gross receipts (minimum of $5,000 for the first year, $8,000 for the second year and $11,000 for the third year and beyond) and an advertising fee equal to 5% of gross receipts.

What You Get—Training and Support

Training is divided into three phases. Effective Operations Training takes five and a half days to instruct new franchisees in the basics of operating an income tax office. Other subjects include accounting, marketing, hiring and staffing, budgeting and office procedures. This is followed by a five-day Intermediate Operations Training session that details tax return preparation procedures and the computer applications needed to process returns and maintain accurate accounting records. Two of these five days focus on marketing to help the franchisee develop an effective local marketing plan. The last phase is Advanced Operations Training, which covers tax-related topics, advanced management training issues and in-depth marketing methods in three days. Franchisees also benefit from a support system of employees who have a combined total of 400 years of industry experience.

Every year, a two-day training session is conducted across the country to update franchisees on new tax laws, software and marketing programs.

Liberty Tax Service has a unique form of marketing: People dressed as the Statue of Liberty or Uncle Sam draw customers to stores. More traditional local marketing and grand opening plans are also provided, and promotional events at the national level create media awareness and exposure.

Territory
Liberty Tax Service grants exclusive territories in which typically 7,000 to 8,500 paid federal tax returns are prepared.

The Little Gym

8970 E. Raintree Dr., # 200
Scottsdale, AZ 85260-7300
Tel: (888) 228-2878 (480) 948-2878
Fax: (480) 948-2765
E-Mail: erandle@thelittlegym.com
Web Site: www.thelittlegym.com
Mr. J. Ruk Adams, SVP Franchise Development

THE LITTLE GYM child development centers are for children 4 months to 12 years, and offer a unique, integrated approach to child development. THE LITTLE GYM'S highly motivational and individualized programs are curriculum-based and provide physical, social and intellectual development. Classes develop basic motor skills, build self-esteem and encourage risk-taking through gymnastics, karate and sports skills development.

BACKGROUND: IFA MEMBER
Established: 1992; 1st Franchised: 1992
Franchised Units: 230
Company-Owned Units: 0
Total Units: 230
Dist.: US-160; CAN-15; O'seas-55
  North America: 35 States, DC
  Density: 28 in TX, 26 in CA, 19 in NY
Projected New Units (12 Months): 65
Qualifications: 4, 4, 2, 3, 4, 5

Registered: CA,FL,IL,IN,MD,MI,MN,NY,OR,WA

FINANCIAL/TERMS:
Cash Investment: $50K
Total Investment: $145.7-228K
Minimum Net Worth: $200K
Fees: Franchise — $57.5K
  Royalty — 8%; Ad. — 1%
Earnings Claim Statement: Yes
Term of Contract (Years): 10/10/10
Avg. # Of Employees: 2 FT, 2-3 PT
Passive Ownership: Discouraged
Encourage Conversions: Yes
Area Develop. Agreements: Yes/10
Sub-Franchising Contracts: No
Expand In Territory: Yes
Space Needs: 3,500-4,000 SF; SC, Destination

SUPPORT & TRAINING PROVIDED:
Financial Assistance Provided: Yes(I)
Site Selection Assistance: Yes
Lease Negotiation Assistance: Yes
Co-Operative Advertising: No
Franchisee Assoc./Member: No
Size Of Corporate Staff: 30+
On-Going Support: C,D,E,G,H,I
Training: 2 Weeks Scottsdale, AZ; 1 Week Internship
  at Site To Be Determined.

SPECIFIC EXPANSION PLANS:
US: All United States
Canada: All Canada
Overseas: Asia, Australia, Europe, Mexico

The Little Gym "builds confidence in kids that leads to a lifetime of success." Programs help children between the ages of 4 months and 12 years build motor skills using fun and entertaining methods, resulting in enhanced emotional, intellectual and social abilities. Activities involve movement, music, gymnastics, sports, exercise, games, listening and cooperation. Children receive individual attention, each program is tailored to ensure that children learn at an age- and need-appropriate pace and parents always receive feedback on their children's progress.

The 30-year-old Little Gym business is the world leader in children's motor skills development, with more than 90,000 children visiting a Little Gym every week.

Operating Units	12/31/2002	12/31/2003	12/31/2004
Franchised	94	130	155
% Change	--	38.3%	19.2%
Company-Owned	5	2	0
% Change	--	-60.0%	-100.0%
Total	99	132	155
% Change	--	33.3%	17.4%
Franchised as % of Total	94.95%	98.48%	100.00%

Investment Required
The fee for a Little Gym franchise is $64,500.

The Little Gym provides the following range of investments required to open your initial franchise. The range assumes that all items are paid for in cash. To the extent that you choose to finance any of these expense items, your front-end investment could be substantially reduced.

Item	Established Low Range	Established High Range
Franchise Fee	$64,500	$64,500

Equipment and Inventory	$41,000	$47,000
Signs, Fixtures, Other Fixed Assets	$7,000	$11,000
Furnishings & Other Supplies	$5,200	$8,000
Initial Sales Promotion	$7,500	$12,500
Security Deposits	$500	$2,000
Training Expenses	$5,000	$10,000
Miscellaneous Expenses	$5,000	$13,000
Additional Funds	$20,000	$70,000
Total Investment	$155,700	$238,000

On-Going Expenses
The Little Gym franchisees pay a royalty fee equal to 8% of gross monthly revenue, a marketing fund fee equal to 1% of gross monthly revenue and a requirement of local advertising equal to 4% of gross monthly revenue ($1,250 minimum annually).

What You Get—Training and Support
Intense training occurs prior to the launch of a gym as well as after it opens, and additional training programs are offered on all topics on an ongoing basis. Franchisees receive frequently updated materials and manuals that cover business and curriculum practices, including information on front desk operation, customer service, financial training, staffing and parent-child gymnastics.

A New Business Consultant assists franchisees with gym openings, and an adviser assists in post-opening development. All specialists and advisers have successfully managed or owned The Little Gym in the past, ensuring that their advice is backed by personal knowledge and experience.

Professionally prepared promotional programs provide franchisees with a detailed marketing methodology and the materials necessary to follow through with those techniques. The package includes print advertising, television ads, direct mail and point-of-sale materials to guarantee exposure and establish a competitive edge in the marketplace.

Territory
The Little Gym grants exclusive territories.

Martinizing Dry Cleaning

422 Wards Corner Rd.
Loveland, OH 45140-6950
Tel: (800) 827-0207 + 365 (513) 351-6211
Fax: (513) 731-0818
E-Mail: cleanup@martinizing.com
Web Site: www.martinizing.com
Mr. Jerald E. Laesser, Vice President

MARTINIZING is the most recognized brand name in dry cleaning. The # 1 Dry Cleaning Franchise: MARTINIZING has been ranked the # 1 dry cleaning franchise 20 out of the last 23 years by Entrepreneur Magazine.

BACKGROUND: IFA MEMBER
Established: 1949; 1st Franchised: 1949
Franchised Units: 625
Company-Owned Units 0
Total Units: 625
Dist.: US-378; CAN-17; O'seas-230
North America: 38 States, 3 Provinces
Density: 82 in MI, 59 in CA, 34 in WI
Projected New Units (12 Months): 25
Qualifications: 5, 4, 1, 3, 1, 5
Registered: All States

FINANCIAL/TERMS:
Cash Investment: $110K
Total Investment: $252.5-411K
Minimum Net Worth: $225K
Fees: Franchise — $35K
  Royalty — 4%; Ad. — 0.5%
Earnings Claim Statement: Yes
Term of Contract (Years): 20
Avg. # Of Employees: 2 FT, 4 PT
Passive Ownership: Discouraged
Encourage Conversions: Yes
Area Develop. Agreements: Yes/3-20
Sub-Franchising Contracts: Yes
Expand In Territory: Yes
Space Needs: 1,500-2,000 SF; FS, SC

SUPPORT & TRAINING PROVIDED:
Financial Assistance Provided: Yes(I)
Site Selection Assistance: Yes
Lease Negotiation Assistance: Yes
Co-Operative Advertising: Yes
Franchisee Assoc./Member: Yes/Yes
Size Of Corporate Staff: 16
On-Going Support: C,D,E,G,H,I
Training: 1 Week Classroom; 2 Weeks In-Store.

SPECIFIC EXPANSION PLANS:
US: All United States
Canada: All CAN Except AB,ON
Overseas: Europe and Far East

Martinizing Dry Cleaning is America's largest dry cleaning franchise with more than 600 locations around the world. It offers a compelling alternative to the average consumer, who think of dry cleaning stores as dark, small shops. Martinizing stores are crisp, clean and efficient, with a proven name, system and track record.

The demand for dry cleaning is relatively stable: Regardless of the economy, it remains a necessary service. Competition is slim with only independently owned dry cleaning stores as the standard in most markets. Franchisees have the edge with the recognized name of Martinizing, and more than 20% of existing franchisees have taken advantage of the promising growth in the industry by expanding to multiple stores.

Operating Units	12/31/2002	12/31/2003	12/31/2004
Franchised	474	407	383
% Change	--	-14.1%	-5.9%
Company-Owned	0	0	0
% Change	--	0.0%	0.0%
Total	474	407	383
% Change	--	-14.1%	-5.9%
Franchised as % of Total	100.00%	100.00%	100.00%

Investment Required
The fee for a Martinizing Dry Cleaning franchise is $35,000.

Martinizing Dry Cleaning provides the following range of investments required to open your initial franchise. The range assumes that all items are paid for in cash. To the extent that you choose to finance any of these expense items, your front-end investment could be substantially reduced.

Item	Established Low Range	Established High Range
Franchise Fee	$35,000	$35,000
Training Expenses	$500	$3,000
Equipment, Store Furnishings, Signage and Initial Inventory	$130,000	$210,000
Equipment Installation	$22,000	$35,000
Leasehold Improvements	$35,000	$60,000

Security/Utility Deposits	$1,000	$5,000
Grand Opening/Initial Marketing	$10,000	$10,000
Legal, Accounting, Other Fees	$1,500	$5,000
Rent and Additional Funds (for 3 months)	$17,500	$48,000
Total Investment	$252,500	$411,000

On-Going Expenses

Martinizing Dry Cleaning franchisees pay a royalty fee of 4% of total gross sales per month and an advertising fee equal to 0.5% of total gross sales.

What You Get—Training and Support

Franchisees and their managers go through the Martinizing Training Program, which covers the fundamentals of managing a Martinizing operation and consists of both classroom and hands-on training. One week is spent at corporate headquarters in Ohio, and another 80 hours is spent at the franchisee's Martinizing store prior to opening. Franchisees receive analyses and market evaluations to assess a location's promise. Martinizing provides a work flow pattern that increases a store's productivity and growth potential by ensuring that staff can complete their jobs efficiently at any given work station.

The type and amount of equipment for the store is customized to suit the needs of the surrounding market, and Martinizing staff will provide support before and after the equipment is installed. This equipment includes a computer program that manages orders, cash flow and inventory, and enables the franchisees to monitor long-term trends and develop a database of marketing information.

The marketing package includes a grand opening promotion with step-by-step guidelines; high-quality marketing support materials for local use in television, radio and direct mail promotions; in-store point of purchase posters and specialty promotional items. Training also helps franchisees learn how to create an effective marketing plan and improve upon initial results. Franchisees will also be alerted to issues and events in the dry cleaning industry through a quarterly newsletter, and can exchange valuable assistance through the Martinizing Advisory Council.

Territory
Martinizing Dry Cleaning grants exclusive territories.

Meineke Car Care Centers

128 S. Tryon St., # 900
Charlotte, NC 28202-5001
Tel: (800) 275-5200 (704) 377-8855
Fax: (704) 372-4826
E-Mail: franchise.info@meineke.com
Web Site: www.ownameineke.com
Ms. Sammy DiBenedetto, Franchise Devel. Coordinator

MEINEKE has been offering superior automotive repair services at discount prices for over 30 years. We are a nationally-recognized brand with a proven system. Brand recognition, comprehensive training and on-going technical and operational support are some of the benefits enjoyed by MEINEKE franchisees.

BACKGROUND:	IFA MEMBER
Established: 1972;	1st Franchised: 1973
Franchised Units:	873
Company-Owned Units	2
Total Units:	875
Dist.:	US-839; CAN-18; O'seas-18
North America:	49 States, 5 Provinces
Density:	69 in NY, 57 in PA, 56 in TX
Projected New Units (12 Months):	69
Qualifications: 4, 3, 3, 2, 2, 5	

Registered: All States

FINANCIAL/TERMS:

Cash Investment:	$60K
Total Investment:	$190-352K
Minimum Net Worth:	$150K
Fees: Franchise —	$30K
Royalty — 3-7%;	Ad. — 8%
Earnings Claim Statement:	Yes
Term of Contract (Years):	15/15
Avg. # Of Employees:	4 FT
Passive Ownership:	Not Allowed
Encourage Conversions:	Yes
Area Develop. Agreements:	Yes/Varies
Sub-Franchising Contracts:	No
Expand In Territory:	Yes
Space Needs: 2,880-3,880 SF; FS	

SUPPORT & TRAINING PROVIDED:

Financial Assistance Provided:	Yes(I)
Site Selection Assistance:	Yes
Lease Negotiation Assistance:	No
Co-Operative Advertising:	Yes
Franchisee Assoc./Member:	Yes/Yes
Size Of Corporate Staff:	110
On-Going Support:	A,B,C,D,G,h,I
Training: 4 Weeks Charlotte, NC.	

SPECIFIC EXPANSION PLANS:

US:	All United States
Canada:	All Canada
Overseas:	All Countries

In 1972, Sam Meineke had with one store, a single product line and the simple concept of providing quality products and workmanship at a fair price –fixing cars the first time. Over the years, while the concept has stayed the same, the number of stores and services offered has increased, but Meineke has expanded its services to become a comprehensive center for car maintenance, working with exhaust systems, brake systems, steering and suspension systems, radiators, motor and transmission mounts, batteries and more.

Currently a vehicle's average age continues to increase as people keep their cars around longer, increasing the need and opportunity for professional repair and maintenance services. Meineke is positioned for strong growth with its strong name recognition and new tagline, "Right Service, Right Price." With nearly 900 franchisees, Meineke is one of the largest automotive franchises and has serviced more than 50 million vehicles.

Operating Units	6/30/2003	6/30/2004	6/30/2005
Franchised	873	879	873
% Change	--	0.7%	-0.7%
Company-Owned	23	1	2
% Change	--	-95.7%	100.0%
Total	896	880	875
% Change	--	-1.8%	-0.6%
Franchised as % of Total	97.43%	99.89%	99.77%

Investment Required
The fee for a Meineke franchise is $30,000.

Meineke provides the following range of investments required to open your initial franchise. The range assumes that all items are paid for in cash. To the extent that you choose to finance any of these expense items, your front-end investment could be substantially reduced. The following figures refer to a six-bay location.

Item	Established Low Range	Established High Range
Franchise Fee	$30,000	$30,000
Training Expenses	$1,500	$2,400
Real Estate	$6,005	$28,438
Opening Inventory	$13,295.23	$13,723.93
Equipment, Signs, Equipment, Installation	$93,004.14	$132,972.76
Computer System	$7,302.33	$8,583.32
Shop Supplies	$11,098.55	$11,098.55
Insurance	$1,230.75	$5,743.44
Legal and Accounting Expenses	$200	$4,000
Pre-Paid Expenses	$12,126.54	$25,537.00
Freight	$2,000.00	$3,000.00
Initial Marketing	$5,000.00	$7,000.00
Additional Funds (for 3 months)	$30,000	$80,000
Total Investment	$212,762.54	$352,497.00

On-Going Expenses
Meineke franchisees pay a royalty fee that ranges from 3 to 7% of gross revenue, varying according to the types of services or products provided, and an advertising fund fee equal to 1.5% of gross revenue generated from tire sales and 8% of all other gross revenue.

What You Get—Training and Support
Franchisees attend four weeks of exhaustive training that address both managerial and technical issues, from marketing and financial workshops to Shop Bay Safety and hands-on repairs. Franchisees use a unique "Point of Sale" computer system to manage business needs. Ongoing training and consulting are provided by the operations and training departments, and an online franchisee website provides additional training resources and a communication network.

Meineke has a detailed advertising program that includes exposure on television, on the Internet and in Yellow Pages, as well as creative materials and local marketing programs. Franchisees also benefit from Meineke's supply-purchasing power with vendors and relationships with financial institutions that help secure competitive loan terms.

Territory
Meineke grants exclusive territories.

Merry Maids

merry maids®

3839 Forest Hill-Irene Rd.
Memphis, TN 38125
Tel: (800) 798-8000 (901) 597-8100
Fax: (901) 597-8140
E-Mail: franchisesales@mmhomeoffice.com
Web Site: www.merrymaids.com
Ms. Vickie Alexander, Franchise Sales Specialist

MERRY MAIDS is the largest and most recognized company in the home cleaning industry. The company's commitment to training and on-going support is unmatched. MERRY MAIDS is highly ranked as an established and fast growing franchise opportunity according to leading national publications. We offer low investment, cross-selling promotions with our partner companies, research and development and excellent marketing support.

BACKGROUND:	
Established: 1979;	IFA MEMBER 1st Franchised: 1980
Franchised Units:	1,287
Company-Owned Units	160
Total Units:	1,447
Dist.:	US-941; CAN-72; O'seas-434
North America:	49 States, 7 Provinces
Density:	123 in CA, 51 in TX, 42 IL
Projected New Units (12 Months):	32
Qualifications: 5, 3, 1, 3, 4, 5	

Registered: All States

FINANCIAL/TERMS:	
Cash Investment:	$24-27K
Total Investment:	$44-52K
Minimum Net Worth:	$Varies
Fees: Franchise —	$19-27K
Royalty — 5-7%;	Ad. — 0.25-1%
Earnings Claim Statement:	No
Term of Contract (Years):	5/5
Avg. # Of Employees:	2 FT, 12 PT
Passive Ownership:	Discouraged
Encourage Conversions:	Yes
Area Develop. Agreements:	No
Sub-Franchising Contracts:	No
Expand In Territory:	Yes
Space Needs: 800 Minimum SF; FS	

SUPPORT & TRAINING PROVIDED:	
Financial Assistance Provided:	Yes(D)
Site Selection Assistance:	No
Lease Negotiation Assistance:	No
Co-Operative Advertising:	NA
Franchisee Assoc./Member:	No
Size Of Corporate Staff:	65
On-Going Support:	C,D,G,H,I
Training: 8 Days Headquarters, Memphis, TN.	

SPECIFIC EXPANSION PLANS:	
US:	All United States
Canada:	All Canada
Overseas:	All Countries

Merry Maids provides dependable cleaning services with a satisfaction guarantee—if the customer is unhappy, Merry Maids will return to clean the area at no extra charge. Merry Maids employees are carefully screened to ensure that they are qualified and trustworthy, and each member is trained according to the specific techniques and quality standards of Merry Maids. Efficient two-person cleaning teams are armed with all the necessary tools and supplies to clean homes effectively and safely.

As the number of working women, as well as the desire for more leisure time, continues to increase, the maid industry and its time-saving services has enjoyed impressive growth. Merry Maids maintains a systematic approach to training, cleaning and office management to encourage the growth for each franchisee. The company has more than 20 years of experience in the maid-service industry and has more franchisees in the United States than its next three competitors combined.

Operating Units	12/31/2002	12/31/2003	12/31/2004
Franchised	754	759	773
% Change	--	0.7%	1.8%
Company-Owned	130	139	145
% Change	--	6.9%	4.3%
Total	884	898	918
% Change	--	1.6%	2.2%
Franchised as % of Total	85.29%	84.52%	84.20%

Investment Required

The fee for a Merry Maids franchise varies according to market size. The fee is $27,000 in a full-sized market, $23,000 in a mid-sized market and $19,000 in a small market.

Merry Maids provides the following range of investments required to open your initial franchise. The range assumes that all items are paid for in cash. To the extent that you choose to finance any of these expense items, your front-end investment could be substantially reduced.

Item	Established Low Range	Established High Range
Franchise Fee	$3,800	$27,000
Training Expenses	$600	$1,000
Real Estate and Improvements	$2,000	$4,000
Equipment	$3,950	$4,950
Advertising (3 months)	$4,000	$5,000
Seminar Attendance Fee	$1,000	$1,000
Direct Mail Fund	$2,000	$2,000
Additional Funds (for 3 months)	$6,000	$9,500
Total Investment	$23,350	$54,450

On-Going Expenses

Merry Maids franchisees pay a royalty fee equal to 7% of gross sales (5% if sales are above $500,000) and a software lease fee equal to $14.40 a week if weekly gross sales are $3,000 or below.

What You Get—Training and Support

Franchisees begin with eight days of home-office training, which is followed by meetings with the Merry Maids franchise development team and support from an existing franchise owner. Throughout these phases, franchisees will be instructed in the necessary preparation, procedures and systems for developing, managing and operating a Merry Maids franchise. Topics include hiring, training, marketing, selling, scheduling and cleaning; methods include training manuals, videotape presentations, CD-ROMs, on-the-job and in-the-field experience and computer instruction. Additional resources and learning opportunities include newsletters, quarterly regional meetings, invitational conferences, specialized field seminars, advanced performance training seminars and an annual convention.

The franchisee fee conveniently includes the equipment, supplies and Merry Maids proprietary cleaning products to equip two cleaning teams.

More than 300 home cleaning-related products can be ordered through the Merry Maids Resource Center, which can be accessed online or by phone. Tools and materials for selecting, training, developing and compensating cleaning team members are also provided, such as training videos, hiring and safety presentations, recognition and reward programs and a quarterly newsletter.

Merry Maids has multiple marketing, advertising and public relations programs in place to achieve the maximum return on franchisees' investments and expand their customer bases. TV campaigns generate thousands of customer calls to Merry Maids franchisees around the country, and Merry Maids customizes websites for franchisees to make it easy for customers to locate the nearest Merry Maids in their area.

Territory
Merry Maids grants exclusive territories; full-sized markets have a minimum of 10,000 qualified households, mid-sized markets have a minimum of 5,000 and a small-sized market has a maximum of 5,000.

Midas

1300 Arlington Heights Rd.
Itasca, IL 60143-3174
Tel: (800) 621-0144 (630) 438-3000
Fax: (630) 438-3700
E-Mail: bkorus@midas.com
Web Site: www.midasfran.com
Ms. Barbara Korus, Franchise Recruitment Coord.

MIDAS is one of the world's largest providers of automotive service, offering exhaust, brake, steering and suspension services, as well as batteries, climate control and maintenance services at 2,700 franchised, company-owned and licensed MIDAS shops in 19 countries, including nearly 2,000 in the United States and Canada.

BACKGROUND: IFA MEMBER
Established: 1956; 1st Franchised: 1956
Franchised Units: 2,600
Company-Owned Units: 73
Total Units: 2,673
Dist.: US-1,657; CAN-220; O'seas-796
North America: NR
Density: NR
Projected New Units (12 Months): 40
Qualifications: 4, 4, 2, 2, 3, 5
Registered: All States

FINANCIAL/TERMS:
Cash Investment: $100-150K
Total Investment: $360-487K
Minimum Net Worth: $300K
Fees: Franchise — $20K

Royalty — 10%;	Ad. — Incl. Roy.
Earnings Claim Statement:	No
Term of Contract (Years):	20/20
Avg. # Of Employees:	6 FT, 4 PT
Passive Ownership:	Discouraged
Encourage Conversions:	Yes
Area Develop. Agreements:	Varies
Sub-Franchising Contracts:	No
Expand In Territory:	Yes
Space Needs: 4,000-5,000 SF; FS	

SUPPORT & TRAINING PROVIDED:
Financial Assistance Provided: Yes(I)

Site Selection Assistance:	Yes
Lease Negotiation Assistance:	Yes
Co-Operative Advertising:	Yes
Franchisee Assoc./Member:	Yes/Yes
Size Of Corporate Staff:	NR
On-Going Support:	B,C,D,e,f,G,H,I

Training: 1-2 Weeks of Self Study; 1-2 Weeks In-Shop Assignment; 3 Weeks in Palatine, IL.

SPECIFIC EXPANSION PLANS:
US: All United States
Canada: All Canada
Overseas: Select Countries

Since 1956, Midas has been providing auto repair and maintenance services for brakes, tires, exhaust and more. Midas maintains its reputation for service, quality and reliability by offering customers a depth of knowledge and a variety of services. As North America's brake service leader, Midas completes more brake jobs than any of its competitors, and each Midas brake pad and shoe has a lifetime guarantee. Midas has also expanded its services to include preventive vehicle maintenance, exhaust and suspension services, climate control, oil changes, tires, alignments and auto tune-ups.

Operating Units	12/31/2002	12/31/2003	12/31/2004
Franchised	1,586	1,552	1,518
% Change	--	-2.1%	-2.2%
Company-Owned	111	73	73
% Change	--	-34.2%	0.0%
Total	1,697	1,625	1,591
% Change	--	-4.2%	-2.1%
Franchised as % of Total	93.46%	95.51%	95.41%

Investment Required
The fee for a Midas franchise is $20,000.

Midas provides the following range of investments required to open your

initial franchise. The range assumes that all items are paid for in cash.
To the extent that you choose to finance any of these expense items, your
front-end investment could be substantially reduced.

Item	Established Low Range	Established High Range
Franchise Fee	$15,000	$20,000
Site Selection/ Construction Fees	$1,000	$2,500
Training Expenses	$3,000	$4,000
Rent/Real Estate Taxes (for 3 months)	$9,000	$27,000
Computer/Phone System, Furniture, Fixtures, Equipment	$132,300	$150,200
Signage, Opening Inventory and Supplies	$37,000	$44,000
Opening Costs & Advertising	$4,350	$12,500
Insurance	$1,500	$4,500
Additional Funds (for 3 months)	$40,000	$65,000
Total Investment	$243,150	$329,700

On-Going Expenses
Midas franchisees pay a royalty fee equal to a maximum of 10% of net
revenue. If Midas owns the property that the franchisee is renting, then the
franchisee will pay rent equal to the greater of $3,000-$9,000 per month or
7% of gross sales, plus real estate taxes and insurance.

What You Get—Training and Support
Franchisees are required to complete an extensive training program that
will last approximately five to seven weeks. The first half consists of two
to four weeks of self-study and in-shop experience as a foundation for
further training; franchisees are taught to analyze competition and observe

customer service operations. The second half takes place over three weeks in an interactive shop and classroom at the Midas Institute of Technology.

Franchisees receive site-selection assistance, including essential information on traffic counts, population growth, zoning and retail shopping patterns, and financing assistance through a list of lenders. Midas also spends half of all royalties on advertising. Typically, $50 million is spent on television, radio and billboard promotions, local newspaper announcements and special events. Franchisees also receive support to develop revenue-increasing plans involving local media, direct mail, Yellow Pages and grand opening promotional materials.

Territory
Midas does not grant exclusive territories.

Motel 6

4001 International Pkwy.
Carrollton, TX 75007
Tel: (888) 842-2942 (972) 360-2547
Fax: (972) 360-5567
E-Mail: franchisesales@accor-na.com
Web Site: www.motel6.com
Ms. Cynthia Gartman, Sr. Dir., Franchise Support
   Serv.

With 4,000 hotels worldwide, Accor is the industry leader. Of Accor's 1,200+ N. American properties, today 280 are franchised. An integral part of our strategy will include franchise relationships with a diverse mix of entrepreneurs that share the Accor spirit of quality, fairness and respect. We received the AAFD Fair Franchising Seal of Approval. MOTEL 6 has a quality product, proven operational results and is easy to operate. Many open markets are available.

MOTEL 6 is a well-established brand.

BACKGROUND:	IFA MEMBER
Established: 1962;	1st Franchised: 1996
Franchised Units:	159
Company-Owned Units	684
Total Units:	843
Dist.:	US-839; CAN-4; O'seas-0
North America:	48 States
Density:	171 in CA, 120 in TX, 47 AZ
Projected New Units (12 Months):	23
Qualifications: 4, 4, 1, 1, 1, 3	
Registered: All States	

FINANCIAL/TERMS:	
Cash Investment:	$100-500K
Total Investment:	$1.9-2.3MM
Minimum Net Worth:	$1.5MM
Fees: Franchise —	$25K
Royalty — 4%;	Ad. — 3.5%
Earnings Claim Statement:	Yes
Term of Contract (Years):	15/20
Avg. # Of Employees:	2-4 FT, 4-10 PT
Passive Ownership:	Allowed
Encourage Conversions:	Yes
Area Develop. Agreements:	No

Sub-Franchising Contracts:	No	Size Of Corporate Staff:	550
Expand In Territory:	No	On-Going Support:	A,b,C,d,e,h,I
Space Needs: 1.5 Acres SF; FS		Training: 2 Days Dallas, TX for Owner's Orientation; 1 Week Manager Training Dallas, TX.	

SUPPORT & TRAINING PROVIDED:

Financial Assistance Provided:	Yes(I)	**SPECIFIC EXPANSION PLANS:**	
Site Selection Assistance:	NA	US:	All United States
Lease Negotiation Assistance:	No	Canada:	All Canada
Co-Operative Advertising:	Yes	Overseas:	No
Franchisee Assoc./Member:	Yes/Yes		

Motel 6 is a true American icon, offering clean and comfortable rooms for an excellent value. It enjoys stronger brand awareness than any other budget-lodging brand as well as high guest loyalty. Motel 6 first set up shop in 1962, and since then its motels have set themselves apart from the competition by being budget-priced, yet functional and modern.

Motel 6 accommodates value-conscious travelers, and also caters to seniors, families with young children, students, military personnel, international travelers and even pets. Motel 6 was acquired by Accor in 1990, and now has its name on more than 845 properties and 87,000 rooms. Motel 6 is now the largest company-owned and company-operated budget-lodging chain in the United States.

Operating Units	12/31/2002	12/31/2003	12/31/2004
Franchised	137	153	167
% Change	--	11.7%	9.2%
Company-Owned	682	683	679
% Change	--	0.1%	-0.6%
Total	819	836	846
% Change	--	2.1%	1.2%
Franchised as % of Total	16.73%	18.30%	19.74%

Investment Required

The fee for a Motel 6 franchise is $25,000.

Motel 6 provides the following range of investments required to open your initial franchise. The range assumes that all items are paid for in cash. To the extent that you choose to finance any of these expense items, your front-end investment could be substantially reduced.

Item	Established Low Range	Established High Range
Franchise Fee	$25,000	$25,000
Construction	$1,510,000	$1,801,500
Furniture, Fixtures and Equipment	$170,000	$185,000
Systems	$50,000	$60,000
Signage	$45,000	$75,000
Opening Inventory	$22,000	$24,000
Insurance	$12,600	$15,750
Utility Deposits	$5,000	$20,000
Training Expenses	$1,400	$5,400
Software License Fee, Installation and Training	$5,500	$8,000
Additional Funds (for 3 months)	$55,000	$65,000
Total Investment (not including real estate)	$1,901,500	$2,284,650

On-Going Expenses
Motel 6 franchisees pay a royalty fee equal to 4% of gross room revenue and a marketing and reservation contribution fee equal to 3.5% of gross room revenue.

What You Get—Training and Support
Franchisees and managers receive initial and ongoing training at the Accor Academie campus in Carrollton, Texas, and through Element K computer classes. Curriculums available include classes for the first-time operator or the experienced hotelier. Accor also offers the Ambassador Program, part of Accor's commitment to diversity, which offers potential

hotel operators of diverse backgrounds industry assistance. Through the Ambassador program, franchisees learn the lodging trade from a proven operator and receive support in construction, architecture, marketing and hotel operations.

Motel 6 manages smart marketing programs like the "Click 6" Internet promotion, as well as strategic partnerships with Visa and American Express. As part of Accor, Motel 6 franchisees yield the purchasing power – and pocket the subsequent savings – of a family of 4,000 hotels.

Territory
Motel 6 grants exclusive territories.

Mr. Electric Corp.

1020 N. University Parks Dr., P.O. Box 3146
Waco, TX 76707
Tel: (800) 805-0575 (254) 759-5850
Fax: (800) 209-7621
E-Mail: leadgeneration@dwyergroup.com
Web Site: www.mrelectric.com
Ms. Pat Humburg, Lead Development Manager

Serving the electrical repair needs of residential and light commercial establishments, in addition to offering other electrical products to the 'same user,' including such items as surcharge protectors, communication and data cabling, ceiling fans, decorative light fixtures, security and landscape lighting, etc.

BACKGROUND:	
Established: 1994;	1st Franchised: 1994
Franchised Units:	183
Company-Owned Units	0
Total Units:	183
Dist.:	US-130; CAN-2; O'seas-51
North America:	42 States, 2 Provinces

IFA MEMBER

Density:	18 in TX, 13 in FL, 7 in OH
Projected New Units (12 Months):	36
Qualifications: 4, 4, 2, 2, 3, 5	
Registered: All States	

FINANCIAL/TERMS:

Cash Investment:	$30.2-68K
Total Investment:	$64-155K
Minimum Net Worth:	$Varies
Fees: Franchise —	$22K/100KPop
Royalty — 3-6%;	Ad. — 2%
Earnings Claim Statement:	No
Term of Contract (Years):	10
Avg. # Of Employees:	4 FT, 1 PT
Passive Ownership:	Discouraged
Encourage Conversions:	Yes
Area Develop. Agreements:	No
Sub-Franchising Contracts:	No
Expand In Territory:	Yes
Space Needs: 500-1,000 SF; FS, HB	

SUPPORT & TRAINING PROVIDED:

Financial Assistance Provided:	Yes(B)
Site Selection Assistance:	NA
Lease Negotiation Assistance:	NA
Co-Operative Advertising:	No
Franchisee Assoc./Member:	No
Size Of Corporate Staff:	14
On-Going Support:	A,B,C,D,E,F,G,H,I

Training: 5 Business Days at Corporate Offices; 3 Business Days On-Site in Business; On-Going.	SPECIFIC EXPANSION PLANS:	
	US:	All United States
	Canada:	All Canada
	Overseas:	No

Mr. Electric provides electrical repairs and services to residential, commercial and moderately sized industrial customers. Mr. Electric has formed national alliances with electrical manufacturers and trains franchisees to work with, among other things, outlets and circuits, breakers and fuses, service panel upgrades, inside/outside lighting, ceiling fan installation, surge protection, exhaust fans and smoke detectors. Customers appreciate Mr. Electric's prompt service, professionalism, skill, round-the-clock availability and dedication to honesty, security and safety. Instead of costs based on time and materials, Mr. Electric uses a unique menu pricing system, which allows customers to see the prices of services ahead of time.

Operating Units	12/31/2002	12/31/2003	12/31/2004
Franchised	107	105	115
% Change	--	-1.9%	9.5%
Company-Owned	0	0	0
% Change	--	0.0%	0.0%
Total	107	105	115
% Change	--	-1.9%	9.5%
Franchised as % of Total	100.00%	100.00%	100.00%

Investment Required
The fee for a Mr. Electric franchise is $19,500 for a territory with population of 100,000. Additional territory may be purchased at a cost of $195 per additional 1,000 people.

Mr. Electric provides the following range of investments required to open your initial franchise. The range assumes that all items are paid for in cash. To the extent that you choose to finance any of these expense items, your front-end investment could be substantially reduced.

Item	Established Low Range	Established High Range
Franchise Fee	$19,500	$19,500
Vehicle	$850	$26,000
Equipment, Supplies & Inventory	$11,000	$17,000
Insurance	$1,200	$2,500
Advertising/Promotion	$5,000	$35,000
Training Expenses	$2,000	$6,000
Deposits/Permits/Licenses	$1,000	$2,500
Additional Funds (for 3 months)	$25,000	$50,000
Total Investment (not including Real Estate)	$65,550	$158,500

On-Going Expenses
Mr. Electric franchisees pay royalties equal to 3% to 6% of gross sales and national advertising fees equal to 2% of gross sales. Ongoing costs also include an cooperative advertising fee that may equal up to 2% of gross sales and maintenance and support fees for computer equipment and proprietary software.

What You Get—Training and Support
Franchisees receive comprehensive business, marketing and management training, and ongoing training on new industry developments is available to keep technicians up to date. After operations begin, franchisees may simply contact a Franchise System Manager for help and consultation. Additional benefits, like employee health care, health plans and life insurance are offered through a third party vendor.

Mr. Electric's support also includes a series of integrated systems – detailed business practices for subjects such as operations, marketing and advertising, human resources, finance and business. Mr. Electric also offers a full line of training materials (manuals, audio, video), an annual convention, regional meetings, site visits, Z-Ware management software and sales and product training. Franchisees have access to a variety of Mr. Electric supplies, forms and documents, which make business processes more efficient to manage, as well as professionally designed promotional items such as custom-decaled service vans and marketing materials are also provided.

Territory
Mr. Electric grants exclusive territories with an approximate minimum population of 100,000 and an approximate maximum population of 1.5 million people.

Mr. Rooter Corp.

1020 N. University Parks Dr.
Waco, TX 76707
Tel: (800) 298-6855 (254) 759-5850
Fax: (800) 209-7621
E-Mail: leadgeneration@dwyergroup.com
Web Site: www.mrrooter.com
Ms. Pat Humburg, Lead Development Manager

Full-service plumbing and sewer/drain cleaning. Franchise specializing in conversion of existing trades people to our method of doing business.

BACKGROUND:

	IFA MEMBER
Established: 1968;	1st Franchised: 1972
Franchised Units:	300
Company-Owned Units	0
Total Units:	300
Dist.:	US-279; CAN-15; O'seas-6
North America	41 States, 4 Provinces
Density:	35 in CA, 18 in ON, 17 in TX
Projected New Units (12 Months):	40
Qualifications: 3, 3, 5, 2, 3, 4	
Registered: All States	

FINANCIAL/TERMS:

Cash Investment:	$35-75K
Total Investment:	$46.8-120.5K
Minimum Net Worth:	$Varies
Fees: Franchise —	$22.5K/100KPop
Royalty — 4-7%;	Ad. — 2%
Earnings Claim Statement:	No
Term of Contract (Years):	10/5
Avg. # Of Employees:	Depends on Sales
Passive Ownership:	Not Allowed
Encourage Conversions:	Yes
Area Develop. Agreements:	Yes/10
Sub-Franchising Contracts:	No
Expand In Territory:	Yes
Space Needs: NR SF; HB	

SUPPORT & TRAINING PROVIDED:

Financial Assistance Provided:	Yes(I)
Site Selection Assistance:	NA
Lease Negotiation Assistance:	NA
Co-Operative Advertising:	No
Franchisee Assoc./Member:	No
Size Of Corporate Staff:	17
On-Going Support:	A,B,C,D,E,F,G,H,I
Training: 1 Week Waco, TX; On-Going.	

SPECIFIC EXPANSION PLANS:

US:	Uncovered Areas

Canada:	All Canada	Overseas:	All Countries

Mr. Rooter is the perfect franchise for contractors and technicians looking for ways to build a stronger and more successful plumbing repair business. Mr. Rooter is committed to giving customers superior service in plumbing and drain cleaning as well as supporting franchisees who are uncomfortable with the business—but not technical—aspects of plumbing.

Mr. Rooter is part of The Dwyer Group, an international corporation that also includes franchises offering services in electrical work, carpet care and restoration and appliance repair. The Dwyer Group has more than 1,200 locations in 24 countries, and their continual goal is: "To teach our franchisees the principles of personal and business success so they, and all people they touch, will live happier and more successful lives."

Operating Units	12/31/2002	12/31/2003	12/31/2004
Franchised	183	181	173
% Change	--	-1.1%	-4.4%
Company-Owned	0	0	0
% Change	--	0.0%	0.0%
Total	183	181	173
% Change	--	-1.1%	-4.4%
Franchised as % of Total	100.00%	100.00%	100.00%

Investment Required

The fee for a Mr. Rooter franchise is $22,500 for a territory with population of 100,000. Additional territory may be purchased at a cost of $225 per additional 1,000 people.

Mr. Rooter provides the following range of investments required to open your initial franchise. The range assumes that all items are paid for in cash. To the extent that you choose to finance any of these expense items, your front-end investment could be substantially reduced.

Item	Established Low Range	Established High Range
Franchise Fee	$22,500	$22,500
Vehicle	$550	$27,000
Equipment, Supplies & Inventory	$9,500	$30,000
Insurance	$1,200	$2,500
Advertising/Promotion	$6,000	$25,000
Training Expenses	$1,200	$4,000
Deposits/Permits/Licenses	$0	$1,000
Additional Funds (for 3 months)	$10,000	$30,000
Total Investment (not including Real Estate)	$50,950	$142,000

On-Going Expenses

Mr. Rooter franchisees pay royalties equal to 4% to 7% of gross sales and national advertising fees equal to 2% of gross sales. Ongoing costs also include an advertising cooperative fee that may equal up to 2% of gross sales and maintenance and support fees for computer equipment and proprietary software.

What You Get—Training and Support

Franchisees begin with a proprietary training course taught by a team of Mr. Rooter instructors. This covers the essential knowledge necessary to run the. Subjects taught include: identifying and attracting new customers, controlling overhead costs, recruiting and retaining plumbing technicians and accounting and marketing systems.

Franchisees also have access to additional, long-term resources, such as national conferences, one-on-one visits and a variety of marketing materials. Ongoing support is provided by the Mr. Rooter world headquarters staff, which also investigates new products and services, researches equipment, refines current business systems and negotiates greater buying power on behalf of franchisees.

Territory

Mr. Rooter grants exclusive territories with an approximate minimum population of 100,000 and an approximate maximum population of 1.5 million people.

Navis Pack & Ship Centers

5675 DTC Blvd., # 280
Greenwood Village, CO 80111
Tel: (866) 738-6820 (303) 741-6626
Fax: (303) 531-6530
E-Mail: franchising@gonavis.com
Web Site: www.navispackandship.com
Mr. Roy D. Billesbach, Director of Franchise Licensing

NAVIS PACK & SHIP CENTERS, established in 2001, specialize in packaging, shipping and fulfillment of items that are fragile, large, awkward and valuable. NAVIS PACK & SHIP CENTERS is a B2B marketing-oriented concept that primarily services commercial clients with handling business equipment, computers, office furniture, art and antiques. Locations are in light industrial or warehouse areas. NAVIS has been franchising since 1984 with Handle With Care Packaging Store, a retail entity.

BACKGROUND:	IFA MEMBER
Established: 1980;	1st Franchised: 1984
Franchised Units:	66
Company-Owned Units	0
Total Units:	66
Dist.:	US-65; CAN-1; O'seas-0
North America:	21 States, 1 Province
Density:	5 in CO, 5 in TX, 4 in IL
Projected New Units (12 Months):	32
Qualifications: 5, 5, 2, 4, 5, 5	

Registered: CA,FL,IL,IN,MD,MI,MN,NY,OR,RI,SD,VA,WA,WI,DC

FINANCIAL/TERMS:

Cash Investment:	$75-95K
Total Investment:	$100-175K
Minimum Net Worth:	$175K
Fees: Franchise —	$32.5K
Royalty — 5%;	Ad. — 3%
Earnings Claim Statement:	Yes
Term of Contract (Years):	10/5/5
Avg. # Of Employees:	3-5 FT
Passive Ownership:	Not Allowed
Encourage Conversions:	Yes
Area Develop. Agreements:	No
Sub-Franchising Contracts:	No
Expand In Territory:	Yes
Space Needs: 3,000 SF; Light Industrial	

SUPPORT & TRAINING PROVIDED:

Financial Assistance Provided:	Yes(I)
Site Selection Assistance:	Yes
Lease Negotiation Assistance:	Yes
Co-Operative Advertising:	Yes
Franchisee Assoc./Member:	Yes/Yes
Size Of Corporate Staff:	30
On-Going Support:	A,B,C,D,E,F,G,h,I
Training: 9 Wks Online Training; 2 Wks Denver, CO; 1 Wk. Certified Training Facility; 2-3 day Certif. visit by Support Staff.	

SPECIFIC EXPANSION PLANS:

US:	All United States
Canada:	All Canada
Overseas:	All Countries

Navis Pack & Ship Centers provide "simple solutions for difficult ship-ments." Navis specializes in handling packaging and shipping for items that need extra care, or – as the company describes them – FLAV, mean-ing Fragile, Large, Awkward and Valuable. With a focus on transporting items that weigh between 100 and 2,000 pounds and services such as door-to-door delivery and insurance coverage, Navis fills a niche in the over-whelmed mail and parcel industry by giving this "non-conforming freight" the care it requires.

Navis caters mainly to businesses and occupies a relatively uncrowded market that is expected to experience continued growth. However, custom-ers making small residential and commercial moves also turn to Navis to transport anything from equipment to antiques efficiently.

A nationally recognized brand with 20 years of experience in the FLAV industry, Navis is positioning itself to become the brand leader in its market, and is committed to using technology to enhance relationships with key vendors and customers and continue to succeed in the future.

Operating Units	12/31/2003	12/31/2004	12/31/2005
Franchised	31	43	62
% Change	--	38.7%	44%
Company-Owned	0	0	0
% Change	--	0.0%	0.0%
Total	31	43	62
% Change	--	38.7%	44%
Franchised as % of Total	100.00%	100.00%	100.00%

Investment Required
The fee for a Navis Pack & Ship Center franchise is $34,500.

Navis Pack & Ship Centers provides the following range of investments required to open your initial franchise. The range assumes that all items are paid for in cash. To the extent that you choose to finance any of these expense items, your front-end investment could be substantially reduced.

Item	Established Low Range	Established High Range
Franchise Fee	$34,500	$34,500
Initial Marketing Fund Contribution	$6,000	$6,000
Training Expenses	$2,000	$3,000
Real Estate and Improvements	$2,500	$26,000
Fixtures, Equipment, Computer Hardware and Software	$20,000	$39,000
Signs	$500	$3,700
Training	$9,500	$11,500
Opening Inventory	$2,000	$6,000
Insurance	$500	$1,500
Facilities Costs/Fees	$6,750	$11,750
Other Costs and Additional Funds (for 3 months)	$9,500	$37,500
Total Investment	$93,750	$180,450

On-Going Expenses
Navis franchisees pay a royalty fee equal to 5% of gross volume, a marketing fund contribution fee equal to 3% of gross volume, a cooperative advertising fee equal to 1% of gross volume and an ongoing licensing fee of $75 per week.

What You Get—Training and Support
The intensive Navis training program gears up with three weeks of start-up training in operations and sales for both franchisees and managers, and continues with ongoing field support provided, in part, through a packaging and insurance hotline, marketing materials, sales training and the Life

Line intranet system. Navis maximizes its Internet presence to attract and serve customers, and franchisees are given free websites that can be customized to promote their location-specific services.

Franchisees receive the exclusive benefits of a proprietary insurance program that covers shipped items at their full value and point-of-sale software designed for managing FLAV transactions. In addition, franchisees receive quality referrals as a result of Navis' strategic relationships and national accounts with carriers. With its system-wide buying power, Navis has also negotiated freight rates that bestow its franchisees with instant discounts.

Territory
Navis Pack & Ship Centers grants exclusive territories.

New Horizons Computer Learning Center

1900 S. State College Blvd., # 200
Anaheim, CA 92806
Tel: (714) 940-8000
Fax: (714) 940-8230
E-Mail: na.franchising@newhorizons.com
Web Site: www.newhorizons.com
Mr. Tom Bresnan, President/CEO

NEW HORIZONS COMPUTER LEARNING CEN-
TERS, Inc. is the world's largest independent IT training company, meeting the needs of more than 2.4 million students each year. NEW HORIZONS offers a variety of flexible training choices: instructor-led classes, Web-based training, computer-based training, computer labs, certification exam preparation tools and 24-hour, 7-day-a-week help-desk support.

BACKGROUND:

	IFA MEMBER
Established: 1982;	1st Franchised: 1992
Franchised Units:	269
Company-Owned Units	29
Total Units:	298
Dist.:	US-181; CAN-1; O'seas-116
North America:	42 States, 1 Province
Density:	14 in CA, 9 in FL, 6 in NY
Projected New Units (12 Months):	10
Qualifications: 5, 5, 2, 3, 3, 5	
Registered: All States	

FINANCIAL/TERMS:

Cash Investment:	$150-200K
Total Investment:	$400-500K
Minimum Net Worth:	$500K
Fees: Franchise —	$25-75K
Royalty — 6%;	Ad. — 1%
Earnings Claim Statement:	No
Term of Contract (Years):	10/5
Avg. # Of Employees:	15 FT
Passive Ownership:	Discouraged
Encourage Conversions:	Yes
Area Develop. Agreements:	Yes/10

Sub-Franchising Contracts:	Yes	Franchisee Assoc./Member:	Yes/Yes
Expand In Territory:	Yes	Size Of Corporate Staff:	200+
Space Needs: 4,000-5,000 SF; FS, OB, IP, Business Park		On-Going Support:	B,C,D,E,G,H
		Training: 2 Weeks Headquarters; 1 Week Franchise Location; 2 Days Regional.	
SUPPORT & TRAINING PROVIDED:			
Financial Assistance Provided:	Yes(D)	**SPECIFIC EXPANSION PLANS:**	
Site Selection Assistance:	Yes	US:	All United States
Lease Negotiation Assistance:	Yes	Canada:	All Canada
Co-Operative Advertising:	Yes	Overseas:	All Countries

As technology constantly advances, companies must also upgrade their systems – and their employees. That's where New Horizons comes in, presenting quality information-technology training in an ever-changing industry.

The world's largest network of vendor-authorized training centers with thousands of classrooms and more than 2,700 instructors, New Horizons classes include technical training and certification packages from vendors such as Microsoft and CompTIA. Instruction is also offered for the newest and most popular computer applications, and classes are tailored to train individuals learn to complete real-world business tasks and projects. The programs can be customized to each client's needs and features like open enrollment, private classes and club memberships provide businesses with even more flexibility.

New Horizons utilizes a unique approach with its eLearning environment, which involves using Web-based training to enhance the classroom experience. Through eLearning, content is delivered more efficiently and additional information and services such as skill assessments and a 24-hour help desk are also available – and fit any schedule or budget.

Operating Units	12/31/2002	12/31/2003	12/31/2004
Franchised	190	185	177
% Change	--	-2.6%	-4.3%
Company-Owned	15	15	15
% Change	--	0.0%	0.0%

Total	205	200	192
% Change	--	-2.4%	-4.0%
Franchised as % of Total	92.68%	92.50%	92.19%

Investment Required

The fee for a New Horizons franchise depends on the number of personal computers in the franchisee's territory: For a territory encompassing 500,000 computers or more, the start-up fee is $75,000; for a territory with 250,000 to 499,999, the fee is $60,000; for a territory with 100,000 to 249,999, $40,000; and a territory with less than 100,000 computers, $20,000.

New Horizons provides the following range of investments required to open your initial franchise. The range assumes that all items are paid for in cash. To the extent that you choose to finance any of these expense items, your front-end investment could be substantially reduced.

Item	Established Low Range	Established High Range
Franchise Fee	$20,000	$75,000
Training Expenses	$2,000	$5,000
Computer Hardware/ Software	$85,000	$130,000
Content Management System Fees	$4,431	$10,425
Software Vendor Fees	$0	$10,000
Furniture/Furnishings	$30,000	$52,000
Inventory and Supplies	$1,500	$3,000
Leasehold Improvements	$3,000	$13,000
Exterior Signs	$2,000	$5,000
Rent/Deposits/Insurance	$6,000	$44,000
Additional Funds (for 3 months)	$200,000	$200,000

Total Investment	$354,931	$547,925

On-Going Expenses

New Horizons franchisees pay a royalty fee equal to the greater of 6% of monthly gross revenue or a minimum of between $1,000 and $1,500 depending of the size of the franchisee's territory, and a marketing and advertising fee equal to 1% of gross revenue. Other ongoing costs include a fee for providing online classes.

What You Get—Training and Support

The New Horizons business model, programs, products and services are designed to minimize cost and maximize revenue. The New Horizons library of printed and e-learning courseware includes more than 1,000 titles from a many prominent vendors, much of which is available free or at deep discounts. Other technology resources include the Integrated Learning Manager, a Web-based portal for building management techniques, and other software.

Training is provided for franchisees and their employees at the New Horizons University. New owners and managers cut their teeth in an intensive two-week training program, but New Horizons also provides ongoing training events at corporate headquarters as well as around the world. All staffing levels also have access to additional training at regional conferences and an annual international conference, and through live e-learning events and self-paced e-learning resources. Regional managers, corporate sales managers, product managers, marketing professionals and technical support personnel are also available for on-site and regional assistance.

Territory

New Horizons grants exclusive territories.

PostNet

1819 Wazee St.
Denver, CO 80202
Tel: (800) 841-7171 (303) 771-7100
Fax: (303) 771-7133
E-Mail: info@postnet.com
Web Site: www.postnet.com
Mr. Brian Spindel, Executive Vice President

POSTNET's franchise opportunity offers a proven method of marketing products and services, which consumers and businesses need on a daily basis. The opportunity to get in on the ground floor of a rapidly expanding business is a rarity -- POSTNET's domestic and international franchisees have the opportunity to tap into the world market, offering personal and business services including UPS, DHL, FedEx, Shipping, B/W and color copy services, private mail boxes, fax, printing and much more.

BACKGROUND: IFA MEMBER
Established: 1992;   1st Franchised: 1993
Franchised Units: 900
Company-Owned Units   0
Total Units: 900
Dist.:   US-542; CAN-8; O'seas-350
  North America: 39 States, 2 Provinces
  Density: 89 in CA, 54 in TX, 31 in FL
Projected New Units (12 Months):   100
Qualifications: 5, 3, 1, 3, 4, 5

Registered: All States

FINANCIAL/TERMS:

Cash Investment:	$50K
Total Investment:	$174.3-195.8K
Minimum Net Worth:	$300K
Fees: Franchise —	$29.9K
Royalty — 5%;	Ad. — 2%
Earnings Claim Statement:	No
Term of Contract (Years):	15/15
Avg. # Of Employees:	2 FT, 1 PT
Passive Ownership:	Not Allowed
Encourage Conversions:	Yes
Area Develop. Agreements:	Yes/Varies
Sub-Franchising Contracts:	No
Expand In Territory:	Yes
Space Needs: 1,200 SF; SC	

SUPPORT & TRAINING PROVIDED:

Financial Assistance Provided:	Yes(I)
Site Selection Assistance:	Yes
Lease Negotiation Assistance:	Yes
Co-Operative Advertising:	No
Franchisee Assoc./Member:	No
Size Of Corporate Staff:	30
On-Going Support:	C,D,E,F,G,H,I

Training: 2 Weeks in Denver, CO; 1 Week at Store Opening; 2-3 Days Follow-Up.

SPECIFIC EXPANSION PLANS:

US:	All United States
Canada:	All Canada

Overseas: All Countries Not Currently Represented

"More than a mail store," PostNet offers an array of products and services that fulfill the needs of small businesses and home offices as well as general consumers conveniently. From copying and printing to packing and shipping, PostNet's services help customers get everything they need to do done all in one place, including ordering signs and banners, picking out a greeting card or some much-needed office supplies, getting a passport photo or having a document notarized. Customers can even rent computers, use the Internet, scan and print digital images. PostNet installs Adobe and Microsoft Office programs on all of its computers so customers can easily bring files to the centers for simple output to the printers. PostNet's complete packaging services allow customers to choose from the services provided by FedEx, UPS and the U.S. Postal Service. Some stores allow 24-hour access to private and secure mailboxes.

Operating Units	12/31/2002	12/31/2003	12/31/2004
Franchised	794	796	819
% Change	--	0.3%	2.9%
Company-Owned	0	0	0
% Change	--	0.0%	0.0%
Total	794	796	819
% Change	--	0.3%	2.9%
Franchised as % of Total	100.00%	100.00%	100.00%

Investment Required
The fee for a PostNet franchise is $29,900.

PostNet provides the following range of investments required to open your initial franchise. The range assumes that all items are paid for in cash. To the extent that you choose to finance any of these expense items, your front-end investment could be substantially reduced.

Item	Established Low Range	Established High Range
Franchise Fee	$29,900	$29,900
Center Development Fee	$97,900	$97,900
Real Property	$1,375	$6,000
Equipment Lease Payments	$700	$700
Security Deposit Fees	$3,000	$8,000
Insurance	$900	$2,000
Classroom Training	$500	$1,000
First Year Deposit	$7,500	$7,500

Business License	$50	$300
Other Costs and Additional Funds (for 3 months)	$32,500	$42,500
Total Investment	$174,325	$195,800

On-Going Expenses

PostNet franchisees pay a royalty fee equal to 4% of gross sales and a national advertising fund fee equal to 2% of gross sales.

What You Get—Training and Support

Franchisees work with PostNet's commercial real estate department to identify the best location in reference to more than 20 factors, including demographics, traffic patterns and counts, physical attributes and competition. PostNet offers franchisees a complete development package that includes construction management, modular store fixtures, interior partitions, painting and carpeting, interior and exterior signage, initial inventory and supplies, an equipment package and a store-management system – a fully integrated point-of-sale system that manages sales, credit card transactions, inventory and mailboxes and processes domestic and international shipments. To assist in marketing, it also includes a customer database.

PostNet training takes place in a multi-tiered classroom, as well as through on-site learning opportunities. Additional training is offered through online programs and workshops at the annual convention and regional meetings. A PostNet trainer provides immediate support to franchisees prior to and during their grand openings.

After the opening, PostNet's support department – accessible by phone – can can answer questions, provide advice and monitor the achievement of financial goals. Field support is not only provided during the initial set-up phase, but also as necessary as the business matures. In addition, PostNet maintains an online franchisee network.

Territory
PostNet grants exclusive territories.

RE/MAX International

The Real Estate Leaders

P. O. Box 3907
Englewood, CO 80155-3907
Tel: (800) 525-7452 (303) 770-5531
Fax: (303) 796-3599
E-Mail: petergilmour@remax.net
Web Site: www.remax.com
Mr. Peter Gilmour, VP Intl. Franchising/Brokerage

The RE/MAX real estate franchise network, now in its 33rd year of consecutive growth, is a global system of more than 6,100 offices worldwide, engaging more than 117,000 members. RE/MAX sales associates lead the industry in professional designations, experience and production while providing real estate services in residential, commercial, referral, relocation and asset management. For more information visit www.remax.com.

BACKGROUND:	IFA MEMBER
Established: 1973;	1st Franchised: 1975
Franchised Units:	6,122
Company-Owned Units	28
Total Units:	6,150
Dist.:	US-3,985; CAN-609; O'seas-1,556
North America:	50 States,12 Provinces
Density:	426 in CA, 255 in ON, 248 TX
Projected New Units (12 Months):	550

Qualifications: 3, 4, 5, 1, 4, 4
Registered: All States

FINANCIAL/TERMS:

Cash Investment:	$20-200K
Total Investment:	$20-150K
Minimum Net Worth:	$Varies
Fees: Franchise —	$10-25K
Royalty — Varies;	Ad. — Varies
Earnings Claim Statement:	No
Term of Contract (Years):	5/5
Avg. # Of Employees:	2-4 FT, 1 PT
Passive Ownership:	Discouraged
Encourage Conversions:	Yes
Area Develop. Agreements:	No
Sub-Franchising Contracts:	Yes
Expand In Territory:	Varies
Space Needs: Varies SF; FS, SF, SC, RM	

SUPPORT & TRAINING PROVIDED:

Financial Assistance Provided:	Yes(D)
Site Selection Assistance:	Yes
Lease Negotiation Assistance:	Yes
Co-Operative Advertising:	NA
Franchisee Assoc./Member:	No
Size Of Corporate Staff:	400
On-Going Support:	C,D,G,h,I

Training: 40+ Hours at Headquarters in Englewood, CO.

SPECIFIC EXPANSION PLANS:

US:	All United States
Canada:	All Canada

Overseas: All Free World Countries. Already in 60 countries. Yet to open in Japan.

RE/MAX is a real estate network that was founded in 1973 by Dave and Gail Liniger that began with a group of just 21 agents. Throughout more than 3 decades of consecutive growth, RE/MAX became an industry leader in transaction sides, productivity and education. It is present in more than 60 countries and territories, and RE/MAX was the first in the industry to achieve 1 million transaction sides. This incredible growth is complemented by a professional and productive sales force, technologically advanced resources that provide support on the Internet and through satellite TV and an extensive television advertising campaign that generates 5 billion impressions in North America. RE/MAX is a giant within the industry, and though it has more than 100,000 Associates already, it plans to continue its impressive growth streak in the years ahead.

Operating Units	12/31/2002	12/31/2003	12/31/2004
Franchised	3,070	3,256	3,549
% Change	--	6.1%	9.0%
Company-Owned	21	28	28
% Change	--	33.3%	0.0%
Total	3,091	3,284	3,577
% Change	--	6.2%	8.9%
Franchised as % of Total	99.32%	99.15%	99.22%

Investment Required

The fee for a RE/MAX franchise is $25,000 in areas with a general population of more than 40,000 people. The fee is reduced to $17,500 for areas with a general population of 10,000 to 40,000, and it is $12,500 for areas with a population of less than 10,000 people.

RE/MAX provides the following range of investments required to open your initial franchise. The range assumes that all items are paid for in cash. To the extent that you choose to finance any of these expense items, your front-end investment could be substantially reduced.

Item	Established Low Range	Established High Range
Franchise fee	$12,500	$25,000
Office Set-up/Improvements	$1,000	$30,000

Exterior Office Signage	$500	$4,000
Furniture, Fixtures and Equipment	$1,500	$25,000
Inventory and Supplies	$500	$3,000
Training Fees and Expenses	$500	$2,000
Miscellaneous Opening Costs	$1,000	$10,000
Additional funds (3 months)	$5,000	$30,000
Total Investment	$22,500	$129,000

On-Going Expenses

RE/MAX franchisees pay monthly on-going fees that have two components: the first equals the greater of $120 per month for each sales associate or 1/5 of the monthly management fee that the franchisee charges each of them; the other component equals the greater of 20% of all broker service fees charged to sales associates or 1% of commissions received by the office. Other fees include annual dues of $390 for each sales associate and a regional advertising fund fee of $75 per month for each sales associate.

What You Get—Training and Support

RE/MAX maintains its own satellite television network for training, which allows agents and recruits to earn credits towards continuing education and more advanced designations in the convenience of their own home or office. Every month, 60 hours of programming are aired, which includes coaching programs with leading coaches of the industry. Subjects cover mastery of recent Internet strategies and computer programs, which are relevant to the work of all real estate professionals.

Another advantage of RE/MAX is the network of RE/MAX Affiliates, which is extensive and offers unlimited opportunities for making partners, who in turn can generate referrals. One valuable resource is RE/MAX's quarterly 48-page newsletter, which allows franchisees to advertise for referral partners. Affiliates refer customers to more than 90,000 Sales

Associates at more than 5,000 offices around the world.

RE/MAX maintains a national television advertising campaign to maintain its status as one of the best-known names in the world. Support is provided from a franchise development consultant, and the Approved Supplier program connects franchisees with the suppliers who can provide quality products and services. An exclusive members-only website offers resources such as presentations, marketing materials and more networking opportunities.

Territory
RE/MAX does not grant exclusive territories.

Red Roof Inn

ACCOR hotels

4001 International Pkwy.
Carrollton, TX 75007
Tel: (888) 842-2942 (972) 360-2547
Fax: (972) 360-5567
E-Mail: franchisesales@accor-na.com
Web Site: www.redroof.com
Ms. Cynthia Gartman, Sr. Dir., Franchise Support Serv.

With 4,000 hotels worldwide, Accor is the industry leader. Of Accor's 1,200+ N. American properties, today 280 are franchised. An integral part of our strategy will include franchise relationships with a diverse mix of entrepreneurs that share the Accor spirit of quality, fairness and respect. We received the AAFD Fair Franchising Seal of Approval. RED ROOF INNS, a well-established brand, has a quality product, proven operational results and is easy to operate. Many open markets are available.

BACKGROUND:	IFA MEMBER
Established: 1972;	1st Franchised: 1996
Franchised Units:	100
Company-Owned Units	246
Total Units:	346
Dist.:	US-346; CAN-0; O'seas-0
North America:	39 States
Density:	32 in OH, 25 in TX, 22 in GA
Projected New Units (12 Months):	15
Qualifications: 4, 4, 1, 1, 1, 3	
Registered: All States	

FINANCIAL/TERMS:	
Cash Investment:	$100-500K
Total Investment:	$2.6-3.9MM
Minimum Net Worth:	$1.5MM
Fees: Franchise —	$30K
Royalty — 4.5%;	Ad. — 4%
Earnings Claim Statement:	Yes
Term of Contract (Years):	15/20
Avg. # Of Employees:	2-4 FT, 4-10 PT
Passive Ownership:	Allowed
Encourage Conversions:	Yes
Area Develop. Agreements:	No
Sub-Franchising Contracts:	No
Expand In Territory:	No
Space Needs: 2.5 Acres SF; FS	

SUPPORT & TRAINING PROVIDED:		Training: 2 Days Dallas, TX for Owner's Orientation; 2 Weeks Dallas, TX for Manager Orientation..
Financial Assistance Provided:	Yes(I)	
Site Selection Assistance:	No	
Lease Negotiation Assistance:	No	**SPECIFIC EXPANSION PLANS:**
Co-Operative Advertising:	Yes	US: All United States
Franchisee Assoc./Member:	Yes/Yes	Canada: All Canada
Size Of Corporate Staff:	550	Overseas: No
On-Going Support:	A,b,C,d,e,h,I	

Red Roof Inn has offered business travelers consistency and value at an economy price for the past 30 years. Emphasizing a "smart by design" lay-out, the Red Roof Inn concept is flexible, leading to innovative and modern designs. The company's customer base is loyal to the Red Roof brand, as evidenced by the 750,000-plus members of the RediCard Frequency Program. A recent national Red Roof renovation has given guest rooms a European-inspired, contemporary look, featuring residential accents like granite countertops and pewter-finished light fixtures.

Red Roof Inn has 350 locations who serve millions of guests each year as part of the Accor family, which is one of the largest owner-operators in the lodging industry with nine major hotel brands and over 150,000 associates in 140 countries. Accor has over 4,000 hotels around the world and maintains higher-than-average profit margins. Every day 14 million people in 34 countries use Accor's services. With a diverse and balanced portfolio ranging from one-star to five-star hotels, Accor brands are accessible in both gateway cities and suburban locations.

Operating Units	12/31/2002	12/31/2003	12/31/2004
Franchised	95	98	100
% Change	--	3.2%	2.0%
Company-Owned	259	251	247
% Change	--	-3.1%	-1.6%
Total	354	349	347
% Change	--	-1.4%	-0.6%
Franchised as % of Total	26.84%	28.08%	28.82%

Investment Required

The fee for a Red Roof Inn franchise is $30,000.

Red Roof Inn provides the following range of investments required to open your initial franchise. The range assumes that all items are paid for in cash. To the extent that you choose to finance any of these expense items, your front-end investment could be substantially reduced.

Item	Established Low Range	Established High Range
Franchise Fee	$30,000	$30,000
Construction	$2,058,000	$2,283,200
Furniture, Fixtures and Equipment	$285,000	$295,000
Systems	$64,000	$78,000
Signage	$45,000	$75,000
Opening Inventory	$25,500	$30,700
Insurance	$13,800	$17,250
Utility Deposits	$10,000	$30,000
Training Expenses	$7,800	$11,300
Software License Fee, Installation and Training	$7,000	$10,000
Additional Funds (for 3 months)	$90,000	$125,000
Total Investment (not including real estate)	$2,636,100	$2,985,450

On-Going Expenses

Red Roof Inn franchisees pay a royalty fee equal to 4.5% of gross room revenue with the opportunity of a 0.5% Quality Rebate, and a marketing and reservation contribution fee equal to 4% of gross room revenue. Other ongoing costs include a fee equal to 3-5% of the gross room revenue collected from RediCard Preferred Members, in addition to various booking fees and commissions.

What You Get—Training and Support

The Accor Academie provides all training for Red Roof Inn franchisees and managers. In addition, Red Roof Inn maintains multiple innovative marketing and advertising programs, including the RediCard Preferred Member program, Red Hot Deals online promotions and a strategic partnership with T-Mobile Hotspot. Red Roof Inn franchisees also receive benefits given to all members of the Accor family, such as the purchasing power and savings of a family of worldwide hotels 4,000 strong, lowering costs for insurance, furnishings and supplies. Typical 99-room Red Roof Inn properties enjoy an average occupancy of 63%.

Territory

Red Roof Inn grants exclusive territories.

Renaissance Executive Forums

7855 Ivanhoe Ave., # 300
La Jolla, CA 92037-4500
Tel: (858) 551-6600
Fax: (858) 551-8777
E-Mail: shawna@executiveforums.com
Web Site: www.executiveforums.com
Ms. Shawna Nolan, Director Franchise Development

RENAISSANCE EXECUTIVE FORUMS bring together top executives from similarly sized, non-competing companies into an advisory board process in which thousands of chief executives throughout the world participate. These CEOs, presidents and owners meet once a month in small groups of approximately eight to fourteen individuals. The meetings provide an environment designed to address the opportunities and challenges they face as individuals and leaders of their respective organizations.

BACKGROUND: IFA MEMBER
Established: 1994;	1st Franchised: 1994
Franchised Units:	44
Company-Owned Units	0
Total Units:	44
Dist.:	US-35; CAN-1; O'seas-8
North America:	19 States
Density:	6 in CA, 3 in FL
Projected New Units (12 Months):	10
Qualifications: 4, 5, 4, 4, 4, 5	
Registered: All States	

FINANCIAL/TERMS:
Cash Investment:	$39.5-76K
Total Investment:	$70-110K
Minimum Net Worth:	$500K
Fees: Franchise —	$39.5K
Royalty — 20%;	Ad. — 0%
Earnings Claim Statement:	No
Term of Contract (Years):	10/10
Avg. # Of Employees:	1 FT

Passive Ownership:	Not Allowed	Lease Negotiation Assistance:	No
Encourage Conversions:	NA	Co-Operative Advertising:	No
Area Develop. Agreements:	Yes/10	Franchisee Assoc./Member:	Yes/Yes
Sub-Franchising Contracts:	No	Size Of Corporate Staff:	15
Expand In Territory:	Yes	On-Going Support:	A,a,B,b,C,c,D,G,H,h
Space Needs: NA SF; Executive Suite		Training: 7 Days La Jolla, CA.	

SUPPORT & TRAINING PROVIDED:

Financial Assistance Provided: No

Site Selection Assistance: No

SPECIFIC EXPANSION PLANS:

US: All United States

Canada: All Canada

Overseas: All Countries

A Renaissance Executives Forums franchise provides consulting and coaching services to client businesses using a turnkey format and a proven business model.

Franchisees work with CEOs, presidents and owners to improve their businesses' performances and thus to enhance their quality of life. Members pay an annual fee and meet every month to take part in a peer advisory board process. This Monthly Forum Meeting connects 8-14 executives from similarly sized, non-competing companies, allowing them to discuss the opportunities and challenges facing them and exchange experiences and expertise. These monthly meetings are divided into three components: education, a focused executive review and a roundtable peer review. Specialized annual and quarterly sessions take place to generate feedback, evaluate progress and develop strategies.

Operating Units	12/31/2002	12/31/2003	12/31/2004
Franchised	39	34	30
% Change	--	-12.8%	-11.8%
Company-Owned	0	0	0
% Change	--	0.0%	0.0%
Total	39	34	30
% Change	--	-12.8%	-11.8%
Franchised as % of Total	100.00%	100.00%	100.00%

Investment Required

The fee for a Renaissance Executive Forums franchise is $24,500.

Renaissance Executive Forums provides the following range of investments required to open your initial franchise. The range assumes that all items are paid for in cash. To the extent that you choose to finance any of these expense items, your front-end investment could be substantially reduced.

Item	Established Low Range	Established High Range
Franchise Fee	$24,500	$24,500
Training/Support Materials Fee	$15,000	$15,000
Training Expenses	$185	$2,499
Rent	$800	$4,400
Deposits	$300	$1,300
Equipment/Fixtures	$0	$800
Initial Inventory and Supplies	$200	$500
Insurance	$200	$300
Marketing Investment	$12,000	$12,000
Other Costs and Additional Funds (for 3 months)	$2,160	$12,067
Total Investment	$55,345	$73,264

On-Going Expenses

Renaissance Executive Forums franchisees pay a royalty fee equal to equal to 20% of total gross received revenue, which includes all dues, fees, charges and other income received from members.

What You Get—Training and Support

Support provided by Renaissance Executive Forums is divided into three phases: training, certification and ongoing maintenance. Step one, the certification program, takes place at corporate headquarters in La Jolla, California, and there, franchisee learn about marketing, presentation techniques and scripts, meeting facilitation skills and coaching, as well as building a personal business plan.

Other valuable resources and support services include: a database of prospects within the franchisee's protected territory; GoldMine software and training for managing the database and contacts; a comprehensive set of training operations manuals; a complete printing start-up kit; an initial supply of marketing materials and field support from experienced marketing personnel; access to a franchisee intranet with a library of materials and templates and a discussion forum; access to a monthly Teleforum for new franchisees; the opportunity to participate in spring and fall business meetings for ongoing training; and access to an exclusive internal telemarketing group for appointment scheduling.

Territory
Renaissance Executive Forums grants exclusive territories.

ServiceMaster Clean

3839 Forest Hill-Irene Rd
Memphis, TN 38125
Tel: (800) 786-9687 (901) 597-7500
Fax: (901) 597-7580
E-Mail: dmessenger@smclean.com
Web Site: www.ownafranchise.com
Mr. David Messenger, Vice President

SERVICEMASTER CLEAN is a division of The ServiceMaster Company. With over 52 years of franchising experience and over 4,000 franchises, SERVICEMASTER CLEAN continues to grow each year and offers 5 different franchise licenses: 1) a residential services license costs $16,900; 2) commercial services $18,900; 3) disaster restoration services $43,000; 4) janitorial services $ 29,000; and 5) small market services $25,000. Financial assistance is offered.

BACKGROUND:	IFA MEMBER
Established: 1947;	1st Franchised: 1952
Franchised Units:	4,488
Company-Owned Units	0
Total Units:	4,488
Dist.:	US-2,914; CAN-176; O'seas-1,398
North America:	50 States,10 Provinces
Density:	200 in IL, 155 in CA, 139 OH
Projected New Units (12 Months):	150
Qualifications: 5, 3, 2, 2, 3, 5	
Registered: All States and AB	

FINANCIAL/TERMS:	
Cash Investment:	$12K
Total Investment:	$18.8-100K

Minimum Net Worth:	$50K	Financial Assistance Provided:	Yes(D)
Fees: Franchise —	$16.9-43K	Site Selection Assistance:	No
Royalty — 4-10%;	Ad. — 0.5-1%	Lease Negotiation Assistance:	No
Earnings Claim Statement:	No	Co-Operative Advertising:	Yes
Term of Contract (Years):	5/5	Franchisee Assoc./Member:	Yes/Yes
Avg. # Of Employees:	3 FT, 2 PT	Size Of Corporate Staff:	200
Passive Ownership:	Discouraged	On-Going Support:	A,B,C,D,F,G,H,I
Encourage Conversions:	Yes	Training: 2 Weeks Memphis, TN; 1 Week on Loca-	
Area Develop. Agreements:	No Sub-Franchising	tion.	
Contracts:	Yes		
Expand In Territory:	Yes	**SPECIFIC EXPANSION PLANS:**	
Space Needs: NA SF; NA		US:	All United States
		Canada:	All Canada
SUPPORT & TRAINING PROVIDED:		Overseas:	All Countries

ServiceMaster Clean provides cleaning services that cater to an extensive customer base, including disaster restoration, commercial cleaning, residential cleaning and janitorial cleaning. This extraordinary range of services also encompasses mold remediation and fire restoration for damaged homes to carpet and upholstery maintenance required by homes and offices.

ServiceMaster Clean has more than 50 years of franchising experience and 4,500 franchises around the world. It strives to remain on the cutting edge, and most recently has pursued a "healthy building maintenance" initiative that uses cleaning products that exceed current environmental standards.

Operating Units	12/31/2002	12/31/2003	12/31/2004
Franchised	2,645	2,739	2,942
% Change	--	3.6%	7.4%
Company-Owned	0	0	0
% Change	--	0.0%	0.0%
Total	2,645	2,739	2,942
% Change	--	3.6%	7.4%
Franchised as % of Total	100.00%	100.00%	100.00%

Investment Required

The fee for a ServiceMaster Clean franchise depends on the type of franchise license selected. The costs of different licenses are as follows: for residential services, $16,900; commercial services, $18,900; disaster restoration services, $45,000; janitorial services, $29,000; small market services, $25,000. Financial assistance is offered.

ServiceMaster Clean provides the following range of investments required to open your initial franchise. The range assumes that all items are paid for in cash. To the extent that you choose to finance any of these expense items, your front-end investment could be substantially reduced. The following figures apply to the opening of a residential cleaning services franchise.

Item	Established Low Range	Established High Range
Franchise Fee	$16,900	$16,900
Advertising	$3,000	$7,500
Vehicle	$3,000	$4,000
Computer Equipment	$2,500	$3,500
Insurance	$2,200	$2,200
Internet	$60	$150
Misc. Opening Costs	$1,000	$4,200
Opening Package	$4,243	$21,215
Additional Funds (3 months)	$12,000	$30,000
Total Investment (does not include real estate)	$44,903	$89,665

On-Going Expenses

The franchisee pays an on-going royalty fee equal to the greater of $250.00 or 10% of gross monthly service sales, and a national advertising fund fee equal to the greater of $20.00 or 1% of gross monthly service sales billed.

What You Get—Training and Support

The ServiceMaster Acceptance Company offers financing programs with a range of options that are convenient and affordable, as well as suited to the needs of the franchisee. A two-week program includes extensive training in the classroom and hands-on experience. ServiceMaster Clean provides year-round support, national advertising and marketing, business counseling, a franchise orientation guide and start-up materials.

Territory

ServiceMaster Clean does not grant exclusive territories.

Sign-A-Rama

SIGN★A★RAMA
WHERE THE WORLD GOES FOR SIGNS

2121 Vista Pkwy.
West Palm Beach, FL 33411
Tel: (800) 286-8671 (561) 640-5570
Fax: (561) 478-4340
E-Mail: signinfo@signarama.com
Web Site: www.signarama.com
Franchise Development Team,

World's largest full-service sign franchise. Almost 800 locations in 45 countries. Ranked #1 in industry. No experience needed. Full training, local back-up and support. Financing available.

BACKGROUND: IFA MEMBER
Established: 1986;   1st Franchised: 1987
Franchised Units: 758
Company-Owned Units 0
Total Units: 758
Dist.: US-536; CAN-25; O'seas-197
North America: 44 States
Density: 67 in CA, 51 in FL, 30 in NJ
Projected New Units (12 Months): 100
Qualifications: 5, 4, 1, 1, 4, 5
Registered: All States and AB

FINANCIAL/TERMS:

Cash Investment:	$40-50K
Total Investment:	$135-140K
Minimum Net Worth:	$60K
Fees: Franchise —	$39.5K
Royalty — 6%;	Ad. — 0%
Earnings Claim Statement:	No
Term of Contract (Years):	35/35
Avg. # Of Employees:	3 FT
Passive Ownership:	Discouraged
Encourage Conversions:	Yes
Area Develop. Agreements:	No Domestic
Sub-Franchising Contracts:	Yes
Expand In Territory:	Yes
Space Needs: 1,200 SF; SC	

SUPPORT & TRAINING PROVIDED:

Financial Assistance Provided:	Yes(I)
Site Selection Assistance:	Yes
Lease Negotiation Assistance:	Yes
Co-Operative Advertising:	Yes
Franchisee Assoc./Member:	Yes/Yes
Size Of Corporate Staff:	150
On-Going Support:	A,B,C,D,E,F,G,H,I
Training: 2 Weeks West Palm Beach, FL; 2 Weeks On-Site; 1 Week On-The-Job.	

SPECIFIC EXPANSION PLANS:

US:	All United States
Canada:	All Canada
Overseas:	All Countries

The world's largest sign-production franchise, Sign-A-Rama is at the helm of a $12 billion industry where repeat business accounts for 70% of transactions. The company acts as a one-stop source for businesses' signage needs, fulfilling requests for menu boards, screen printing, banners, lighted signs, vehicle lettering, real estate signs and window graphics – product offerings so diverse that almost every business has a need for at least one of them.

Sign-A-Rama franchises pride themselves on being full-service resources for their customers, while Sign-A-Rama the franchisor prides itself on providing its franchisees with a turnkey business concept based on nearly two decades of experience culled from hundreds of stores across the world. Franchisees enjoy low-inventory requirements and easy-to-use computer programs, as well a franchise system with connections the world over, linking franchisees with fellow franchisees and international customers.

Operating Units	12/31/2002	12/31/2003	12/31/2004
Franchised	602	662	697
% Change	--	10.0%	5.3%
Company-Owned	0	0	0
% Change	--	0.0%	0.0%
Total	602	662	697
% Change	--	10.0%	5.3%
Franchised as % of Total	100.00%	100.00%	100.00%

Investment Required
The fee for a Sign-A-Rama franchise is $39,500. Existing owners pay $19,500 to open an additional location. Financing is available for up to 65% of a franchisee's total investment. The fee includes site renovation costs.

Sign-A-Rama provides the following range of investments required to open your initial franchise. The range assumes that all items are paid for in cash. To the extent that you choose to finance any of these expense items,

353

your front-end investment could be substantially reduced. Those who qualify can get financing for Sign-A-Rama's entire equipment package.

Item	Established Low Range	Established High Range
Franchise fee	$19,500	$39,500
Travel and living expenses while training	$210	$490
Real estate	Varies	Varies
Equipment package deposit (if leased)	$4,500	$4,500
Equipment package	$98,869	$98,869
Yellow page advertisement (for 6 months)	$300	$1,200
Insurance	$750	$2,000
Security deposit, utility deposits and licenses	$0	$3,000
Additional funds (for 6 months)	$25,000	$55,000
Total	$149,129	$204,559

On-Going Expenses
Sign-A-Rama franchisees pay a royalty fee equal to 6% of total gross sales and a monthly marketing fund fee of $150.

What You Get—Training and Support
Before a franchise is awarded, Sign-A-Rama reviews proposed locations, leases and marketing areas, as well as traffic studies, business counts and area growth.

Sign-A-Rama franchisees don't need prior experience in the sign business and they won't be responsible for making the signs they sell themselves (they hire someone to do that for them). However, the company believes it's important that they understand every aspect of the process. And at five weeks in length, Sign-A-Rama training is long but thorough, beginning with an all-inclusive two weeks of instruction in sign production, computer graphics, bookkeeping, management principles and sales and marketing. After those initial lessons, franchisees spend one week in hands-on training at an up-and-running store and finish up with marketing and technical training at their own store for two weeks, after which a marketing representative will continue to work with them personally. Franchisees also have the option of contributing to a national advertising fund that is run by an advisory board made up of corporate staff and franchise owners.

Sign-A-Rama franchisees join a support network that is nearly 700 stores strong and spreads across 30 countries – bestowing franchisees with mass purchasing power, an efficient supply system and a global peer base that comes together at regional meetings and a world expo.

Sign-A-Rama also boasts 20 regional offices staffed with both business and marketing personnel, in addition to software that helps with the hiring and training process, an 800 number and an online support infrastructure that is available at any time of the day, every day.

Territory
Sign-A-Rama does not grant exclusive territories.

Spherion

2050 Spectrum Blvd.
Ft. Lauderdale, FL 33309
Tel: (800) 903-0082 (678) 867-3702
Fax: (954) 308-7770
E-Mail: robertamarcantonio@spherion.com
Web Site: www.spherion.com
Ms. Roberta Marcantonio, VP Market Expansion

SPHERION franchise/license opportunities provide individuals a chance to join an exciting and rewarding industry: temporary staffing. We placed millions of workers in flexible and full-time jobs during our nearly 60 years in business. Continuous innovation and decades of growth have helped SPHERION become an industry leader. Entrepreneur Magazine ranked SPHERION Best Staffing Service for five straight years. Our franchisees contribute their talent, commitment and passion to building our brand.

BACKGROUND:	IFA MEMBER
Established: 1946;	1st Franchised: 1956
Franchised Units:	245
Company-Owned Units	350
Total Units:	595

355

Dist.:	US-563; CAN-32; O'seas-0	Sub-Franchising Contracts:	No
North America:	46 States, 8 Provinces	Expand In Territory:	Yes
Density:	29 in CA, 29 in FL, 27 in OH	Space Needs: 1,500 SF; SF, RM	
Projected New Units (12 Months):	10		
Qualifications: 5, 5, 2, 3, 4, 5		**SUPPORT & TRAINING PROVIDED:**	
Registered: All States		Financial Assistance Provided:	No
		Site Selection Assistance:	Yes
FINANCIAL/TERMS:		Lease Negotiation Assistance:	Yes
Cash Investment:	$Varies	Co-Operative Advertising:	Yes
Total Investment:	$68.3-391.7K	Franchisee Assoc./Member:	No
Minimum Net Worth:	$Varies	Size Of Corporate Staff:	4,000
Fees: Franchise —	$10-15K	On-Going Support:	a,B,C,D,E,G,H,I
Royalty — 3-6%/25%;	Ad. — 0.25%	Training: Extensive Training - Over 112 Hours In-	
Earnings Claim Statement:	No	Office Instruction; Addl. Self-Paced Instruction.	
Term of Contract (Years):	10/5		
Avg. # Of Employees:	5 FT	**SPECIFIC EXPANSION PLANS:**	
Passive Ownership:	Not Allowed	US:	Targeted Cities in US.
Encourage Conversions:	Yes	Canada:	No
Area Develop. Agreements:	No	Overseas:	No

At the end of a year's work, Spherion can ring in the new year knowing that it has brought together hundreds of thousands of workers and their employers through a full range of direct hiring, temp-to-hire and flexible staffing services for both office and industrial positions. Spherion also provides professional services in limited markets. With 60 years of experience, nearly 700 offices cater to more than 7,000 employer clients, 85% of whom are Fortune 100 companies.

Spherion's role involves more than just acting as an employment match-maker. As a resource provider for companies looking to improve their bottom lines, Spherion provides workforce solutions as well as insight into processes and technologies to optimize performance. Spherion provides flexible employees and candidates with tools such as online training and assessments to advance their careers. Spherion is also a recognized leader in providing business intelligence through its various reports and studies it releases throughout the year.

Operating Units	12/26/2003	12/31/2004	12/31/2005
Franchised	89	80	80

% Change	--	-10.1%	0.0%
Company-Owned	310	296	285
% Change	--	-4.5%	-3.7%
Total	399	376	365
% Change	--	-5.8%	-2.9%
Franchised as % of Total	22.3%	21.3%	21.92%

Investment Required

The fee for a Spherion franchise is $10,000.

Spherion provides the following range of investments required to open your initial license. The range assumes that all items are paid for in cash. To the extent that you choose to finance any of these expense items, your front-end investment could be substantially reduced.

Item	Established Low Range	Established High Range
License	$10,000	$10,000
Real property	$1,000	$3,200
Leasehold improvements, furniture and fixtures	$7,200	$15,000
Computer systems or services	$3,500	$5,500
Equipment	$10,000	$20,000
Opening advertising	$1,000	$5,000
Training expenses	$1,000	$3,000
Start-up supplies	$500	$1,000
Insurance	$2,000	$5,000
Utility deposits	$150	$1,000
Professional fees	$300	$2,500
Business license	$150	$1,000
Additional funds (for 12 months)	$20,000	$60,000

Total		$57,500	$133,200

On-Going Expenses

Spherion franchisees pay a monthly commission split equal to 25% of gross profit dollars (the rate declines as sales grow), and a national advertising fee equal to 0.25% of sales.

What You Get—Training and Support

Connections are the key to thriving business and Spherion franchisees have plenty. Through the franchisor, franchisees benefit from alliances with well-known companies, many of which are Fortune 100. In addition, franchisees join a system with a history of innovation. Spherion claims to be the first to use television as a recruiting tool, develop on-site workforce management and employ voice-response technology to prescreen job candidates. Additionally, candidate and client portals provide 24/7 access to Spherion which means on-line applications and job ordering to all the stakeholders of our services. Spherion's KnowledgeSphere is the industry's only fully integrated software package, and covers everything from skills assessment to job matching.

As a Spherion franchisee, you are invited to take advantage of regional meetings and mentoring opportunities. Sales and marketing materials along with individual marketing plans are tailored to each licensee market.

Territory

Spherion grants protected territories.

Spring-Green Lawn Care

11909 Spaulding School Dr.
Plainfield, IL 60585
Tel: (800) 435-4051 (815) 436-8777
Fax: (815) 436-9056

E-Mail: cleiner@spring-green.com
Web Site: www.spring-green.com
Mr. James Young, VP Franchise Development

SPRING-GREEN delivers lawn and tree care services nationwide. Our service is centered on the beautification of middle class and affluent neighborhoods and communities. Our customers include both and commercial establishments. SPRING-GREEN has been beautifing the environment for 27+ years, in now more than 20 states. SPRING-GREEN's success has continued through slow economic times. Program includes lead generation. No heavy investing in equipment and personnel. Loyal and profitable customers.

BACKGROUND: IFA MEMBER

Established: 1977;	1st Franchised: 1977
Franchised Units:	100
Company-Owned Units	21
Total Units:	121
Dist.:	US-121; CAN-0; O'seas-0
North America:	20 States
Density:	26 in IL, 13 in WI, 7 in VA
Projected New Units (12 Months):	15
Qualifications: 4, 3, 1, 3, 2, 4	
Registered: IL,IN,MD,MI,MN,OR,VA,WA,WI	

FINANCIAL/TERMS:

Cash Investment:	$54K
Total Investment:	$112-155K
Minimum Net Worth:	$125K
Fees: Franchise —	$21.9K
Royalty — 9-6%;	Ad. — 2%

Earnings Claim Statement:	Yes
Term of Contract (Years):	10/10
Avg. # Of Employees:	3 FT, 1 PT
Passive Ownership:	Not Allowed
Encourage Conversions:	Yes
Area Develop. Agreements:	No
Sub-Franchising Contracts:	No
Expand In Territory:	No
Space Needs: NA SF; HB	

SUPPORT & TRAINING PROVIDED:

Financial Assistance Provided:	Yes(D)
Site Selection Assistance:	NA
Lease Negotiation Assistance:	NA
Co-Operative Advertising:	NA
Franchisee Assoc./Member:	Yes/Yes
Size Of Corporate Staff:	15
On-Going Support:	A,B,C,D,E,F,G,H,I
Training: On-Line Pre-Training; 1 Week Training at Corp. HQ; 3 On-Site Visits (Min. 2 Days Each).	

SPECIFIC EXPANSION PLANS:

US:	All Exc. AK,AZ,CA,FL,NY,NV,ND,SD,HI
Canada:	No
Overseas:	No

The business of keeping lawns and trees green and healthy may be a more evergreen endeavor than you realize. The average Spring-Green franchisee provides active lawn, tree and landscape care to customers for eight to 11 months of every year, all the while enjoying a flexible schedule and the fresh air and open spaces that come with a job that transcends office walls.

Spring-Green's industry and the business itself boast impressive credentials. According to a Gallup poll, more than 20 million households in the United States sign up for professional landscape services and more than 80% of Spring-Green clients renew their services. Low product and labor costs contribute to higher gross-profit margins, expansion opportunities are available for a minimal cost and, after more than 20 years in the business, the Spring-Green system is experienced in handling greenery quirks and demands in a variety of climates.

Spring-Green does not require franchisees to have any previous experience in the landscape-care industry. Services offered by Spring-Green include lawn fertilization and weed control, disease and insect control and root feeding.

Operating Units	12/31/2003	12/31/2004	12/31/2005
Franchised	95	101	109
% Change	--	6.3%	7.9%
Company-Owned	21	21	21
% Change	--	0.0%	0.0%
Total	116	122	130
% Change	--	5.2%	6.5%
Franchised as % of Total	81.9%	82.79%	83.85%

Investment Required

The fee for a Spring-Green franchise ranges from $25,000 (for an area containing 40,000 single-family homes) to $36,000 (for an area containing a maximum of 60,000 single-family homes).

Spring-Green provides the following range of investments required to open your initial franchise. The range assumes that all items are paid for in cash. To the extent that you choose to finance any of these expense items, your front-end investment could be substantially reduced.

Item	Established Low Range	Established High Range
Franchise fee	$30,000	$36,000
Vehicles, equipment and fixtures	$5,841	$9,977
Opening inventory and supplies	$3,595	$3,595
Initial marketing campaign	$25,000	$25,000
Training expenses	$950	$1,525
Real estate	Varies	Varies

Miscellaneous opening costs	$1,525	$2,300
Additional funds (for 12 months)	$30,000	$40,000
Total	$96,911	$118,397

On-Going Expenses
The royalty fee paid by Spring-Green franchisees is 9% for the first $50,000 in gross sales every year, after which the fee declines by 0.5% for each additional $50,000 in gross sales until it reaches a yearly minimum of 6%. Other costs include an advertising fund contribution equal to 2% of gross sales, a software support fee of $95 to $125 per month, an online learning center fee of $132 a year and a franchise advisory council assessment fee of $20 per month from April to November.

What You Get—Training and Support
Online pre-training following by one week in the classroom at Spring-Green's corporate headquarters acquaints franchisees with the following: marketing and operating systems, business development, the technical aspects of lawn and tree care, equipment operation and maintenance. After initial training, field support representatives meet with franchisees in their own territories to go over sales and lawn and tree treatments. Regional meetings, national events, development seminars, publications, an intranet system and an on-line learning center round out Spring-Green's support resources.

On the technical side, franchisees benefit from computer-software automation that efficiently manages marketing, customer service, production management and office operations. Spring-Green also develops marketing supplies for franchisees that include items such as direct mailings, brochures, newspaper ads, special customer promotions, seasonal campaigns and door hangers.

Territory
Spring-Green grants territories in which franchisees have the exclusive

right to serve residential customers. The definition of the area could be based on factors including population density, market statistics and competition.

Supercuts

SUPERCUTS®

7201 Metro Blvd.
Minneapolis, MN 55439-2103
Tel: (888) 888-7008 (952) 947-7394
Fax: (952) 995-3406
E-Mail: franchise.mail@regiscorp.com
Web Site: www.regisfranchise.com
Ms. Stephanie Theis, Franchise Coordinator

Our strategy is simple: give men and busy families what they want. That's why SUPERCUTS salons offer a contemporary and comfortable atmosphere that appeals to those in search of current hairstyles at affordable prices.

BACKGROUND: IFA MEMBER
Established: 1987;   1st Franchised: 1988
Franchised Units: 971
Company-Owned Units   1,032
Total Units: 2,003
Dist.:   US-1,937; CAN-48; O'seas-18
 North America: 48 States
 Density: 387 in CA, 177 in FL, 164 TX
Projected New Units (12 Months):   100
Qualifications: 5, 5, 1, 3, 4, 5
Registered: All States

FINANCIAL/TERMS:
Cash Investment: $30-35K
Total Investment: $106.9-197.9K
Minimum Net Worth: $300K
Fees: Franchise — $25K
 Royalty — 4-6%;   Ad. — 4%
Earnings Claim Statement: No
Term of Contract (Years):   Evergreen
Avg. # Of Employees: 5 FT, 4 PT
Passive Ownership: Allowed
Encourage Conversions: Yes
Area Develop. Agreements: Yes/3
Sub-Franchising Contracts: No
Expand In Territory: Yes
Space Needs: 1,000 SF; SC

SUPPORT & TRAINING PROVIDED:
Financial Assistance Provided: Yes(I)
Site Selection Assistance: Yes
Lease Negotiation Assistance: Yes
Co-Operative Advertising: Yes
Franchisee Assoc./Member: Yes
Size Of Corporate Staff: 900
On-Going Support: C,D,E,G,H
Training: 4-5 Days Minneapolis, MN.

SPECIFIC EXPANSION PLANS:
US: All United States
Canada: All Canada
Overseas: No

Supercuts broke new ground more than 25 years ago with its establishment as an affordable haircutting salon. With salons located in convenient, high-traffic areas such as strip centers, Supercuts welcome walk-in business and can give both men and busy families what they want in 20 minutes or less. With almost 2,000 locations around the world, Supercuts salons enjoy name brand recognition of more than 90%.

Supercuts is part of the Regis Corporation – the salon leader that also includes brands such as Cost Cutters, Pro-Cuts, City Looks, First Choice Haircutters and Magicuts – making Supercuts franchisees part an industry family with depth of experience and resources. Regis has been in the salon business for more than 80 years and has generated $3 billion in system-wide sales from its nearly 10,000 salons around the world.

Operating Units	6/30/2002	6/30/2003	6/30/2004
Franchised	952	950	959
% Change	--	-0.2%	0.9%
Company-Owned	667	752	845
% Change	--	12.7%	12.4%
Total	1,619	1,702	1,804
% Change	--	5.1%	6.0%
Franchised as % of Total	58.80%	55.82%	53.16%

Investment Required
The fee for a Supercuts franchise is $22,500.

Supercuts provides the following range of investments required to open your initial franchise. The range assumes that all items are paid for in cash. To the extent that you choose to finance any of these expense items, your front-end investment could be substantially reduced.

Item	Established Low Range	Established High Range
Franchise Fee	$22,500	$22,500
Leasehold Improvements	$35,000	$60,000
Furniture, Equipment & Supplies	$18,000	$25,000
Opening Inventory	$5,000	$8,000
Training Expenses	$2,050	$3,500
Grand Opening Expenses	$5,000	$5,000

Signs	$2,000	$5,000
Other Costs and Additional Funds (for 3 months)	$17,310	$41,080
Total Investment	$106,860	$170,080

On-Going Expenses

Supercuts franchisees pay a royalty fee equal to 4% of combined net service revenue and net merchandise revenue during the first year of operations, after which the fee increases to 6%. Franchisees also pay an advertising fee equal to 5% of net monthly service revenue.

What You Get—Training and Support

Supercuts offers several different levels of training to cater to the many aspects of operating a salon. Franchisees start their training at a detailed orientation, which is followed by instruction that covers topics including sales tracking, financial systems, retail marketing, sales and merchandising methods, pricing systems and customer service. Further learning opportunities are available through national and regional meetings, seminars and work sessions.

Ongoing training programs are held for store managers to improve management skills and encourage a positive working environment. In-salon training workshops bring a team of artistic directors and vendor experts to the franchisee's location to demonstrate the latest styling techniques to keep stylists on the cutting edge of hair design. All Supercuts stylists also attend a five-day training session in proprietary techniques at the Supercuts Hairstylist Academy.

Throughout the entire start-up process, franchisees receive assistance with everything from leasing a site to opening a newly constructed store, as well as with employment recruitment and retention programs. Ongoing support is offered through more than 200 field representatives who respond to franchisee's operational needs. All Supercuts branding and promotion are developed by marketing and advertising professionals, who formulate campaigns for television, radio, print, Internet and in-store promotions.

Supercuts salons also generate additional revenue from the sales of professional haircare and styling products. With $400 million generated systemwide annually, valuable vendor relationships are created and volume buying power is increased for each individual franchisee.

Territory
Supercuts does not grant exclusive territories.

Sylvan Learning Centers

1001 Fleet St.
Baltimore, MD 21202-4382
Tel: (800) 284-8214 (410) 843-8880
Fax: (410) 843-6265
E-Mail: pete.lorenzo@educate.com
Web Site: www.sylvanfranchise.com
Mr. Pete Lorenzo, Director Franchise Development

SYLVAN is the leading provider of educational services to families, schools and industry. SYLVAN services kindergarten through adult-levels from more than 1,000 SYLVAN LEARNING CENTERS worldwide.

BACKGROUND: IFA MEMBER
Established: 1979;   1st Franchised: 1980
Franchised Units: 900
Company-Owned Units   150
Total Units: 1,050
Dist.:   US-971; CAN-75; O'seas-4
  North America: 50 States
  Density: CA, TX, NY
Projected New Units (12 Months):   50
Qualifications: 4, 4, 2, 3, 2, 5
Registered: All States

FINANCIAL/TERMS:
Cash Investment:	$101.1-171.3K
Total Investment:	$121.1-219.3K
Minimum Net Worth:	$250K
Fees: Franchise —	$38-46K
Royalty — 8-9%;	Ad. — 5-13%
Earnings Claim Statement:	Yes
Term of Contract (Years):	10/10
Avg. # Of Employees:	2 FT, 5 PT
Passive Ownership:	Not Allowed
Encourage Conversions:	No
Area Develop. Agreements:	Yes/Varies
Sub-Franchising Contracts:	No
Expand In Territory:	Yes
Space Needs: 1,600-2,500 SF; FS, SF, SC	

SUPPORT & TRAINING PROVIDED:
Financial Assistance Provided:	Yes(B)
Site Selection Assistance:	Yes
Lease Negotiation Assistance:	No
Co-Operative Advertising:	Yes
Franchisee Assoc./Member:	Yes
Size Of Corporate Staff:	500
On-Going Support:	B,C,D,E,G,H,I
Training: 6 Days Baltimore, MD; 5 Days in Various Other Locations.	

SPECIFIC EXPANSION PLANS:
US:	All United States
Canada:	All Canada
Overseas:	Asia, Europe, South America

Operating a Sylvan Learning Centers franchise is your opportunity to make a difference. As public school enrollment rises and public schools' budgets dwindle, it has become clear that many students must look elsewhere for extra educational guidance. That's where Sylvan comes in. Providing students with individualized diagnostic and prescriptive education services, Sylvan franchisees not only generate satisfaction for their clients, but also for themselves.

Sylvan serves students of all ages, including remedial students and students looking to keep up their proficiency in particular skills.

The company has been featured on "Nightline," the "Today Show" and CNN.

Operating Units	12/31/2003	12/31/2004	12/31/2005
Franchised	776	896	876
% Change	--	15.5%	-2.2%
Company-Owned	135	163	245
% Change	--	20.7%	50.3%
Total	911	1059	1121
% Change	--	16.2%	5.9%
Franchised as % of Total	85.18%	84.61%	78.14%

Investment Required
The fee for a Sylvan Learning Center franchise is $77,550 for a Type A territory (containing approximately 18,000 to 30,000 school-age children ages 5 to 19) and $69,550 for a Type B territory containing approximately 8,000 to 18,000 school-age children. The fees include educational materials and equipment.

Sylvan Learning Centers provides the following range of investments required to open your initial franchise. The range assumes that all items are paid for in cash. To the extent that you choose to finance any of these expense items, your front-end investment could be substantially reduced.

Item	Established Low Range	Established High Range
Franchise fee	$40,000	$48,000
Travel and living expenses while training	$2,815	$4,100
Initial six months rent and security deposit	$14,583	$43,750
Real estate improvements and site preparation	$10,000	$55,000
Initial inventory of learning materials	$29,550	$29,550
Specialized furnishings	$12,000	$14,000
Other furniture and miscellaneous supplies	$10,000	$12,000
Signage	$4,000	$8,000
Computers, copier, printers, facsimile, telephone, Internet access and software	$25,000	$35,000
Additional funds (for 6 months)	$48,000	$48,000
Total	$195,948	$249,400

On-Going Expenses

New franchisees with a Type A territory pay a royalty fee equal to 8% of monthly gross revenue. Those with a Type B territory pay a royalty fee equal to 9% of monthly gross revenue. Other fees include a national advertising fee equal to 1.5% to 5% of monthly gross revenue, varying local advertising and co-op costs, an online maintenance fee of $350 a year, a software maintenance fee of $1,250 a year and an educational program and software support maintenance fee of $249 a year.

What You Get—Training and Support

Sylvan franchisees receive site-selection assistance as well as training in administering educational programs and managing and growing their business operations. As a center grows, a group of regional business and education consultants are also available for additional guidance.

Sylvan also maintains strategic partnerships to encourage synergistic opportunities and acquire national advertising supplies including ad slicks, brochures, television and radio commercials and direct mailings.

Territory
Sylvan grants exclusive territories.

The UPS Store

The UPS Store™

6060 Cornerstone Ct. W.
San Diego, CA 92121-3762
Tel: (877) 623-7253
Fax: (858) 546-7493
E-Mail: fransale@mbe.com
Web Site: www.theupsstore.com/franchise/fraopp.html
Mr. Don Wells, Sales Department

In April 2001, Mail Boxes Etc., Inc., the world's largest franchisor of retail shipping, postal and business service centers, became a subsidiary of UPS, the world's largest express carrier and package delivery company. In 2003, the company introduced The UPS STORE franchise opportunity to offer franchisees and customers the best of both businesses. With over 5,500 The UPS Store and Mail Boxes Etc., Inc. locations in more than 40 countries and territories, the network is the global leader in its market.

BACKGROUND: IFA MEMBER
Established: 1980;   1st Franchised: 1980
Franchised Units: 5,554
Company-Owned Units   0
Total Units: 5,554
Dist.:   US-4,317; CAN-276; O'seas-961
  North America: 50 States,10 Provinces

Density: 556 in CA, 346 in FL, 215 TX
Projected New Units (12 Months):   500
Qualifications: 5, 4, 3, 3, 3, 5
Registered: All States

FINANCIAL/TERMS:
Cash Investment: $7.5K
Total Investment: $138.7-245.5K
Minimum Net Worth: $50K (Varies)
Fees: Franchise — $29.9K
  Royalty — 5%;   Ad. — 3.5%
Earnings Claim Statement: No
Term of Contract (Years):   10/10
Avg. # Of Employees: 2 FT, 2+ PT
Passive Ownership: Discouraged
Encourage Conversions: Yes
Area Develop. Agreements: Yes/10
Sub-Franchising Contracts: No
Expand In Territory: No
Space Needs: 1,400 SF; SF, SC, RM, Non-Tradit.

SUPPORT & TRAINING PROVIDED:
Financial Assistance Provided: Yes
Site Selection Assistance: Yes
Lease Negotiation Assistance: Yes
Co-Operative Advertising: Yes
Franchisee Assoc./Member: Yes/Yes
Size Of Corporate Staff: 300
On-Going Support: A,B,C,e,G,h,I
Training: 10 Days San Diego, CA; Ongoing.

SPECIFIC EXPANSION PLANS:	Canada:	All Canada
US: All United States	Overseas:	All Countries

In 2001, Mail Boxes Etc. – the world's largest franchisor of retail shipping, postal and business services – joined the UPS family – the world's largest express carrier and package delivery company. In 2003, The UPS Store franchise opportunity was introduced, offering franchisees and customers the convenient combination of the services of both Mail Boxes Etc. and UPS. The UPS Store offers a wide variety of services that fulfill a number of related needs, such as shipping, packaging, mailbox and postal services, copying, finishing, printing and moving supplies.

Qualified franchisees have the opportunity to own multiple franchises and may also specialize in rural or other niche markets. The UPS network is a global leader, a pioneer who has led the industry for more than 25 years, contributing to a global brand presence built over the years out 5,000 locations in more than 40 countries and territories.

Operating Units	12/31/2002	12/31/2003	12/31/2004
Franchised	3,389	3,612	4,067
% Change	--	6.6%	12.6%
Company-Owned	7	5	0
% Change	--	-28.6%	-100.0%
Total	3,396	3,617	4,067
% Change	--	6.5%	12.4%
Franchised as % of Total	99.79%	99.86%	100.00%

Investment Required
The fee for a franchise of The UPS Store is $29,950.

The UPS Store provides the following range of investments required to open your initial franchise. The range assumes that all items are paid for in cash. To the extent that you choose to finance any of these expense items, your front-end investment could be substantially reduced.

Item	Established Low Range	Established High Range
Franchise Fee	$19,950	$29,950
Initial Marketing Plan Fee	$7,500	$7,500
Design Fee	$950	$950
Center Development Fee	$5,000	$5,000
Training Fees/Expenses	$9,500	$10,000
Site Rent/Deposit	$4,000	$16,000
Leasehold Improvements, Construction, Signage, Furniture	$38,945	$95,700
Computer Equipment/ Support Fee	$18,142	$19,983
Other Costs and Additional Funds (for 3 months)	$41,544	$60,411
Total Investment	$145,531	$245,494

On-Going Expenses

The UPS Store franchisees pay a royalty fee equal to 5% of gross sales and commissions, a marketing fee equal to 1% of gross sales and commissions and a national advertising equal to 2.5% of gross sales and commissions. Other ongoing fees include varying advertising co-op dues and an annual technology development and support fee of $595.

What You Get—Training and Support

While an experienced staff at UPS corporate headquarters provides franchisees with general support, UPS Store operators also receive local support from regional field representatives. Other benefits bestowed on franchisees include buying power and the opportunity to work with pre-established corporate customers in addition to assistance with financing, real estate development, store design and construction, training and technology development and support.

Territory
The UPS Store grants exclusive territories.

Window Genie

We Do Windows and a Whole Lot More!

10830 Milllington Court
Cincinnati, OH 45242
Tel: (800) 700-0022 (513) 793-4364
Fax: (513) 984-2757
E-Mail: rik@windowgenie.com
Web Site: www.windowgenie.com
Mr. Richard (Rik) Nonelle, President

Residential window cleaning, window tint and pressure washing business.

BACKGROUND: IFA MEMBER
Established: 1994;   1st Franchised: 1998
Franchised Units: 39
Company-Owned Units   0
Total Units: 39
Dist.:   US-39; CAN-0; O'seas-0
  North America: 12 States
  Density: 6 in OH, 4 in CO, 3 in KY
Projected New Units (12 Months):   19
Qualifications: 4, 4, 1, 3, 3, 5
Registered: CA,FL,IL,IN,MD,MI,NY,VA,WA

FINANCIAL/TERMS:
Cash Investment: $40-50K
Total Investment: $40-50K
Minimum Net Worth: $Varies
Fees: Franchise — $19.5K
  Royalty — 6%;   Ad. — 1%
Earnings Claim Statement: No
Term of Contract (Years):   10/5
Avg. # Of Employees: 2 FT, 2 PT
Passive Ownership: Discouraged
Encourage Conversions: Yes
Area Develop. Agreements: No
Sub-Franchising Contracts: No
Expand In Territory: Yes
Space Needs: NA SF; NA

SUPPORT & TRAINING PROVIDED:
Financial Assistance Provided: No
Site Selection Assistance: NA
Lease Negotiation Assistance: NA
Co-Operative Advertising: NA
Franchisee Assoc./Member: No
Size Of Corporate Staff: 3
On-Going Support: B,C,D,E,F,G,H,I
Training: 5 Days Corporate, Cincinnati, OH; 5 Days
  On-Site.

SPECIFIC EXPANSION PLANS:
US: All United States
Canada: No
Overseas: No

As more and more homes become two-income households, the demand for home services multiplies. The U.S. Bureau of Labor Statistics estimated that the industry would be the second-largest source of new jobs through 2005, and Window Genie is an ideal franchise vehicle to tap into the market growth of an industry in which a national leader has yet to emerge.

But Window Genie does more than windows. In addition to window cleaning, the company also performs window tinting (which helps homeowners boost security and shrink energy costs) and pressure washing for exterior surfaces such as decks. Still, no matter how high the caliber of a Window Genie franchise's work, the cycle of nature guarantees that windows and decks will always get dirty again, ensuring an ongoing need for repeat services.

Window Genie provides services that maids frequently do not, and though they cater to both commercial and residential customers (current homeowners as well as those showcasing their homes for sale), Window Genie franchises usually stick to a weekday schedule, leaving weekends open for leisure and family time. Managers can work from home and the business requires little inventory to serve a broad market.

Operating Units	12/31/2002	12/31/2003	12/31/2004
Franchised	33	38	32
% Change	--	15.2%	-15.8%
Company-Owned	0	0	0
% Change	--	0.0%	0.0%
Total	33	38	32
% Change	--	15.2%	-15.8%
Franchised as % of Total	100.00%	100.00%	100.00%

Investment Required

The fee for a Window Genie franchise varies according to the size of the marketing territory assigned. For a territory with a population of approximately 100,000, the fee is $19,500; for a territory with a population of approximately 175,000, the fee is $29,500; and for a territory of approximately 250,000, the fee is $39,500.

Window Genie provides the following range of investments required to open your initial franchise. The range assumes that all items are paid for in cash. To the extent that you choose to finance any of these expense items, your front-end investment could be substantially reduced. The following figures refer to the opening of a franchise in a territory with a population of approximately 175,000.

Item	Established Low Range	Established High Range
Franchise fee	$29,500	$29,500
Equipment and supply package	$4,500	$5,500
Office package	$2,200	$3,200
Window Genie logo wear	$500	$700
Initial training	$600	$1,300
Advertising/promotional package	$1,200	$1,500
Opening advertising	$12,000	$12,000
Additional start-up costs	$1,200	$2,200
Vehicle	$0	$2,000
Real estate	$0	$500
Additional working capital (for 3 months)	$10,000	$15,000
Total	$61,700	$73,400

On-Going Expenses

Window Genie franchisees pay a local advertising fee that varies by the size of their marketing territory. For a territory with a population of approximately 100,000, the fee ranges from $17,750 to $25,000; the fee for a territory with a population of approximately 175,000 ranges from $25,000 to $35,000; and the fee for a territory of approximately 250,000 ranges from $31,250 to $45,000.

Window Genie franchisees also pay a royalty fee equal to 6% of gross revenue and a regional and national advertising fee equal to 1% of gross revenue.

What You Get—Training and Support

Each Window Genie market is evaluated according to its demographics, population, housing values and forecasted growth. Then Window Genie franchisees undergo five days of training at the franchisor's corporate office to familiarize themselves with business operations, marketing, sales and administration, and practice service procedures at the "window wall" training center. That training is supplemented by five days with a trainer in the franchisee's own territory, a visit that is scheduled to coincide with the franchisee's grand opening.

As a member of the Window Genie system, franchisees have access to national plans for health and business insurance, advertising, equipment purchasing, products, supplies and promotional materials, including business cards, stationery, brochures, postcards, door hangers, uniforms, vehicle and office signage and radio scripts.

Assistance is later available with employee hiring, software applications, services procedures and sales through phone calls, operations manuals and training videos. Additional resources include proprietary software for billing, scheduling and record-keeping, newsletters, monthly teleconferences, an online bulletin board and an annual winter meeting with fellow franchisees.

Territory
Window Genie grants protected marketing territories, meaning that franchisees can work with but not market their services to customers outside their designated territories.

Alphabetical Listing of Franchisors

Categorical Listing of Franchisors

Food Service Franchises

Retail Franchises

Tips & Traps When Buying A Franchise
2nd Edition (Completely revised in 1999)

By Mary Tomzack, President of FranchiseHelp, Inc., an international information and research company servicing the franchising industry.

Key Features:

- Completely updated version of the 1994 reader-ac claimed classic on franchising, with the same practical advice, non-textbook approach. Provides an insight ful crash course on selecting, negotiating and financing the right franchise, and turning it into a lucrative, satisfying business.
- How to select the best franchise for your personal finances and lifestyle; navigate the legal maze; and finance your investment.
- Reveals the hottest franchise opportunities for the 21st Century and discusses co-branding. Provides advice on building a business empire through franchising.
- "This book is the bible for anyone who is considering a franchise investment."

Yes, I want to order ____ copy(ies) of *Tips & Traps When Buying a Franchise* (2nd Edition) at US$19.95 each, plus US$7.00 for shipping & handling (international shipments at actual cost).

Name _____ Title _____

Company _____ Telephone No. (_____) _____

Address _____

City _____ State/Prov. _____ Zip _____

☐ Check Enclosed or

Charge my: ☐ American Express ☐ MasterCard ☐ Visa

Card #: _____ Expiration Date: _____

Signature: _____

Please return to: **Source Book Publications,** 1814 Franklin St., Suite 815, Oakland, CA 94612 or call (800) 841-0873 or (510) 839-5471 or fax (510) 839-2104

* Note: All books shipped by USPS Priority Mail.
Satisfaction Guaranteed. If not fully satisfied, return for a prompt, 100% refund.